IMMORTAL

IMMORTAL

A Military History
of Iran and Its
Armed Forces

STEVEN R. WARD

In cooperation with
The Center for Peace and Security Studies,
Edmund A. Walsh School of Foreign Service,
Georgetown University

GEORGETOWN UNIVERSITY PRESS
Washington, DC

Georgetown University Press, Washington, D.C.
www.press.georgetown.edu
© 2009 by Steven R. Ward. All rights reserved. No part of this
book may be reproduced or utilized in any form or by any means,
electronic or mechanical, including photocopying and recording,
or by any information storage and retrieval system, without
permission in writing from the publisher.

Library of Congress Cataloging-in-Publication Data

Ward, Steven R.
    Immortal : a military history of Iran and its armed forces /
by Steven R. Ward.
        p.   cm.
    Includes bibliographical references and index.
    ISBN-13: 978-1-58901-258-5 (hardcover : alk. paper)
    ISBN-10: 1-58901-258-5 (hardcover : alk. paper)
    1. Iran—History, Military. 2. Iran—Armed
Forces—History. I. Title.
    DS273.3.W37   2008
    355.00955—dc22

                                        2008031770

⊗ This book is printed on acid-free paper meeting the requirements
of the American National Standard for Permanence in Paper for
Printed Library Materials.

16 15 14 13 12 11 10 09   9 8 7 6 5 4 3 2
First printing

Printed in the United States of America

For Martha Ann,
my one and only

Contents

Figures

Preface and Acknowledgments

THIS HISTORY OF IRAN'S ARMED FORCES attempts to illustrate some important truths that can be helpful in understanding the Iranian military's potential role in the world in the coming century. Iran has not done well during the past two centuries in the box-score shorthand of wars that include the number of battles lost, men killed and wounded, and equipment destroyed. Nonetheless, this book will show that Iranian men-at-arms, despite a modern history dominated by poor leadership, maltreatment, and a poverty of means, have demonstrated qualities that bear careful consideration by potential opponents. It would be a serious mistake to overlook the bravery and perseverance of Iranian soldiers or the costs they have imposed on their enemies by hard fighting, clever tactics, and the exploitation of Iran's imposing geography. While final victory has often eluded them, Iran's armed forces have enjoyed surprising tactical successes at home and abroad against their foes. This history also tries to provide background on the nationalist, tribal, and religious heritages that motivate Iranian military personnel at all ranks and that are necessary for comprehending Iran's armed forces today and in the future.

I have tried to make this narrative as easy to read as possible by being consistent in spelling and in the transliteration of Persian (or Farsi), Arabic, and other foreign language terms. I have stayed with the more common and recognizable versions of names. For example, I use "Cyrus" rather than "Kurash" for the name of the founder of the first Persian Empire and use "Muhammad" rather than "Muhammed," "Mohammad," or other spellings of this name. Elsewhere, I have followed the current practices of major U.S. news media to simplify spelling, using, for example, "Shia" rather than "Shi'i" or "Shiite" for the branch of Islam predominant in Iran and "Koran" for "Qur'an." One major exception in consistency is that the terms "Persia" and "Persian" are used in their historical context to refer to a geopolitical entity and its multiethnic people before "Iran" and "Iranian" take their proper place.

In conducting my research for this book I am indebted to many works on pre-Islamic Persia and on Iran between the seventh and twentieth centuries, and these are presented in the bibliography. Beyond these published works, I was able to mine very useful information about Iran's armed forces during the U.S. military advisory effort between 1942 and 1979 from the National Archives at College Park, Maryland, and the Army Military History Institute in Carlisle, Pennsylvania. In addition, I was fortunate to find several books and three doctoral dissertations in English that drew on Iranian archives and publications and helped provide a greater Iranian perspective on the development of the modern Iranian military. I also benefited from having access to translated Iranian media produced by the U.S. government's Open Source Center, previously known as the Foreign Broadcast Information Service. The *Middle East Journal* graciously allowed me to draw from my article "The Continuing Evolution of Iran's Military Doctrine" for portions of chapter 10.

As I have tried to highlight important aspects of Iran's military history, I have had to refrain from more detailed analysis of the Iranian armed forces today. As a U.S. government intelligence analyst actively working Middle Eastern subjects, I have a responsibility to maintain the confidence of consumers of intelligence in the objectivity and policy neutrality of my agency's work product. So, with regard to more recent developments, I have tried to present facts and assessments as they are generally presented by nongovernment regional experts and leave it to the readers to draw their own conclusions about some issues. Readers should understand that all statements of fact, opinion, or analysis expressed are those of the author and do not reflect the official positions or views of the Central Intelligence Agency (CIA) or any other U.S. government agency. Nothing in the contents should be construed as asserting or implying U.S. government authentication of information or CIA endorsement of the author's views. Also, this material has been reviewed by the CIA to prevent the disclosure of classified information. I want to thank the CIA Publication Review Board and all those agency officers involved for their time and effort in helping me move my manuscript through the clearance process for publication. In addition, I am very grateful to David Gordon, the former Vice-Chairman of the National Intelligence Council; Alan Pino, the National Intelligence Officer for the Near East; and Timothy Buch, the former director of the CIA's Office of Near Eastern and South Asian Analysis. All three were very supportive in allowing me to take an unpaid leave of absence to write this book.

I have often read acknowledgments in books but did not know until writing my own how heartfelt they were. This book would not have been possible without the encouragement, advice, and assistance of a number of good friends and colleagues. I owe a huge debt of gratitude to Daniel Byman, the director of the Center for Peace and National Security Studies at Georgetown University, who helped me think through many of the issues in the book and provided numerous suggestions for improving the substance and presentation. Dan's cheerful and generous support throughout the process was indispensable. Kenneth Pollack, the director of research at the Saban Center for Middle East Policy of the Brookings Institution, provided invaluable assistance in virtually every aspect of the effort. From conception through research, outlining, and drafting, I benefited greatly from Ken's ideas, his knowledge of military history, and his understanding of Iran. I also want to thank Richard Mobley, a first-class military analyst who reviewed portions of the draft and helped ensure that the chapters on Iran's postrevolution history are as accurate as possible. Job Dittberner, an associate from the National Intelligence Council, was more than generous with his time in reviewing my manuscript and providing sage and practical advice on improving its style, grammar, and clarity. Michael Podolny, an outstanding cartographer, not only created this volume's maps but also patiently advised me on the best means to present this information. And, last but not least, Don Jacobs, my editor at Georgetown University Press, and his associates were all tremendously helpful in guiding me through the publishing process. Of course, even with the assistance of such great people, a few mistakes may have slipped into the text, and I am solely responsible for such errors.

Finally, I could not have written this book without the loving support of my wonderful wife, Martha Ann. She made it possible for me to devote all the time that I needed to the book and was very tolerant of my long disappearances into the basement study with my constant writing companion, our beloved Welsh Terrier, Bailey.

I.1 Nest of the Phoenix

Introduction

The Iranian Phoenix

IN 1978 IRAN AND ITS ARMED FORCES seemed to stand at the peak of their power and prestige in the modern era. Bountiful oil revenues and a strategic position overlooking the vital Persian Gulf oil export routes boosted Iran's standing in the world. Cold War competition made Iran a recipient of Western and Soviet arms and attention. Iran had just passed Egypt, a far more populous country, in having the largest armed forces in the Middle East. In fact, the Iranian military was outpacing some large European countries in the quantity and sophistication of its equipment. Iran was the only country other than the United States to possess the state-of-the-art F-14 Tomcat fighter. Iran's military also was funding the development of the advanced British Challenger tank with its then revolutionary Chobham composite armor. These programs represented only the middle stages of an extravagant rearmament process, with numerous sophisticated ground, air, and naval systems on order. In addition, the Iranian armed forces, the Artesh, had polished their reputation by gaining combat experience battling rebels in neighboring Oman and by participating in a UN peacekeeping mission in Lebanon.[1]

The shah of Iran, Muhammad Reza Shah Pahlavi, took special pride in reestablishing Iran's military might after more than a century of Iranian humiliation as a victim of Russian and British imperialism. The shah constantly conjured up images of the majesty of ancient Persia, which, 2,500 years earlier, had become the world's first superpower. This heritage was used to help legitimize Pahlavi rule but also supported Iran's claim to a position among the prevailing great powers. During one of his regular military parades in Tehran in October 1978, the shah hosted a delegation of American military officials that included U.S. Army colonel Colin Powell. As the colonel sat in the reviewing stand, an elite troop named the "Immortals" in conscious imitation of fabled Persian warriors of antiquity marched by. Powell, a future chairman of the Joint Chiefs of Staff and secretary of state, noted favorably their tailored uniforms and martial élan.[2] American support to its Iranian ally seemed to be paying off with the creation of a strong and well-armed defender of the strategic and vulnerable region of southwest Asia.

Less than three months later, American hopes for Iran had crumbled. Amid widespread popular opposition to his rule, the shah abandoned the Immortals, the rest of his military, and his country in January 1979. The Iranian armed forces virtually collapsed, unwilling to support their undependable monarch and loath to confront the Iranian people. The military's passivity and partial dissolution cleared the way for religious extremists, led by Grand Ayatollah Ruhollah Khomeini, to hijack the revolution and initiate the militantly anti-Western Islamic Republic of Iran. Powell later commented, not quite correctly, that the elite units had "cracked like a crystal goblet." For Americans it seemed that the investment in building up the shah as a regional bulwark for the West had come to naught.[3]

Within another two years, the shattered Iranian military and newly formed revolutionary forces responded bravely and effectively to stop the Iraqi invasion of September 1980. Despite the loss of tens of thousands of U.S. technicians needed to support Iran's advanced equipment and a vigorous international arms embargo, the Iranians fought on for eight years. The regular military and revolutionary forces nearly prevailed by putting so much pressure on Iraq that Baghdad repeatedly offered to end the conflict on terms favorable to Tehran. Only the incompetent statecraft of their theocratic leadership denied Iran's fighting men a triumph. Ultimately the Islamic Republic overreached its objectives, wore down its own forces in pointless offensives, and compelled the Iraqis—by giving them no option but victory—to create the improved military forces used to win the war in 1988. The Iranians view what they call the "Imposed War" as a victory, and, in some respects, the Iranian military deserves no shame for losing the conflict, which ended with a return to the prewar status quo. While virtually isolated and relying almost totally on its own resources, Iran held out for nearly a decade against a regional military power backed by generous Arab allies and both Cold War superpowers. Still, Iran was left militarily exhausted and was stripped of much of the military power the shah had developed.

Over the subsequent two decades Iran has risen from the ashes to become once again a major regional military power. Iran's more than seventy million people make it the third largest country in the Middle East, behind Egypt and Turkey, and the eighteenth largest in the world. More important, Iran possesses the second largest known oil reserves after Saudi Arabia and is a major producer of natural gas. Its substantial oil and gas revenues provide the regime the wherewithal to add to its military strength and have made Iran an attractive market for China, Russia, and other dealers of sophisticated arms. Iran's conventional armed forces, however, have made only slow and fitful progress in recovering from their 1988 defeat and remain primarily a defensive force. Instead, it has been the buildup of missile, naval, and unconventional capabilities under the control of the Islamic Revolutionary Guard Corps, the religiously radical counterpart to the regular armed forces, that has given Iran the ability to project limited power throughout the region and beyond. Iran's security posture was greatly improved after the U.S. military removed Tehran's two closest rivals with the rapid defeat of the Taliban in Afghanistan in 2001 and Saddam Hussein's Iraq in 2003. Indeed, Iran in the near term may prove capable of "punching above its weight" on the strength of its strategic location, its control of oil and gas resources, and its unconventional and missile deterrent capabilities.[4]

The rise, fall, and recovery of Iran and its armed forces over the past generation are not new features of this ancient country's history. Instead it is the latest in a series of ascents and declines demonstrating the Iranians' remarkable perseverance. Although not literally "immortal," Iran's various armed forces have repeatedly given the appearance of indestructibility. In the ancient, medieval, and early modern periods, the repeated resurrection of the Iranian military dramatically affected the course of world history. Parthian and Sassanian armies often bested the ancient Western powers of Rome and Byzantium, setting the frontier between East and West. The Safavids' use of the sword to establish an Islamic state following the Shia creed to offset the power of the Sunni Ottomans in the sixteenth century had important implications for the entire Middle East and Christendom. Nader Shah's later victories over Mughal armies eased the British conquest of India. Even Iran's prolonging of the Imposed War after 1983 had far-reaching consequences as the war spurred Iraq's pursuit of weapons of mass destruction and set the stage for the 1991 Gulf War, the repercussions of which played out amid the American invasion and occupation of Iraq in 2003.

The Persian empires of the Achaemenids, Parthians, and Sassanians ruled much of western Asia from the Mediterranean to the Hindu Kush, a source of pride for Iranians today. Iranians rightly believe that the high civilization of medieval Islam flowed largely from Persia's influence. Even the 1978–79 Islamic Revolution's humiliation of the United States and the unflinching battle with Saddam's Iraq stir national pride. By the same token, the insecurity and distrust that mark Iran's dealings with the outside world stem from a history in which each Iranian empire and nearly all subsequent Iranian polities succumbed to foreign invaders or internal decay. Following Iran's conquest by the Arabs and conversion to Islam in the seventh and eighth centuries, the Iranians have constantly struggled to secure their independence from foreign political, military, economic, and cultural domination. And throughout the centuries, despite invasions by Greeks, Arabs, Turks, and Mongols, Iran's strong culture survived. Still, the resulting nationalist sentiments and xenophobia have driven Iran's national security goals and have been used by monarch and mullah alike in the complex interplay of politics, religion, and military power in Iran.

The force structure and administration of Iran's various militaries have been greatly influenced by the competition for power between the central government and other Iranian elites, especially the clergy. A major result has been that for most of Iran's history since the rise of the Safavid Empire the country has had dual and sometimes dueling militaries and the attendant problems with control, coordination, and reliability. The primary armed forces have been supported by and loyal to central authority. The offsetting forces of tribal levies, local militias, and other organizations have given their allegiance to khans, feudal landlords, the clergy, or, at the start of the twentieth century, antimonarchical and other political groups. Because all sides were suspicious of strong militaries and their ability to threaten the throne or enforce central authority, enthusiasm for modernizing reforms and military professionalism has often been limited and unsustained. In addition, in the modern era the clerics have been wary of Western influences on the rank and file's observance of the mosque's guidance. To protect their interests, the Muslim clerics or mullahs repeatedly undermined reforms, discipline, and the power of the military in enforcing central authority, except, of course, since 1979 when the clerics became the central authority. Throughout the modern era, the military also was often beset by debilitating corruption and politicization that impeded Iran's fighting forces from reaching their potential.

In turn, the previously mentioned factors generated dynamics that sometimes ensured Iranian success but in the modern era mostly have inhibited military effectiveness. Iranian fighting forces regularly have been hampered by their leaders' uneven appreciation for technology. From the Safavids' early refusal to incorporate firearms through the Pahlavi shahs' procurement of sophisticated yet unsustainable systems to the Pasdaran's disregard for combined arms operations in favor of zealous ill-trained volunteers, Iran's soldiers have paid the price of flawed approaches to warfare. Similarly, poor leadership by politicized and selfish officers and stingy support and outright maltreatment have regularly undercut the perseverance, resourcefulness, and patriotism of Iranian fighting men.

Nest of the Phoenix: Iran's Geostrategic Position and Military Geography

Two constants in Iran's military history and enduring security interests are the country's strategic location and geography. Situated at the crossroads of Europe and Asia, Iran has benefited from dominating major trade routes and from the mix of diverse peoples and the transfer of knowledge and skills that being a bridge between East and West has provided. For much of two millennia, Persia held the commanding heights of the world economy by straddling the Silk Road, the key land trade route between the Mediterranean and China. At the beginning of the twenty-first century, Iran's position astride the Persian Gulf,

Caspian, and Central Asian export routes for the region's large oil and gas reserves once again places it at the center of global attention and, possibly, global rivalries.

Conversely, poised between the great Eurasian steppe to the north and the rich lands of Mesopotamia and the Indian subcontinent to the west and east, Iran has been vulnerable to constant invasions. In particular, the great Mongol warriors Genghis Khan (Chingis Khan) in 1220 and Tamerlane in 1405 devastated Iran with murderous campaigns of conquest. During much of the past three centuries, Iran's potential as an avenue to the warm waters of the Indian Ocean or as an invasion route into Russia made it a special target of czarist and Soviet rulers. In turn, this put Iran in the crossfire of Russian and British imperialism as London sought to protect its Indian "Jewel in the Crown." The Ottomans, the British, and later Iraq desired hegemony over Iran's oil-rich and Arab-dominated southwestern region.

Iran is not only a surface crossroads but sits atop the subterranean intersection of the giant Arabian, Eurasian, and Indian plates, which have formed and still influence the region by their uplifting and folding effect on the earth's crust. The pressure between these gigantic plates created the major mountain ranges that virtually surround the country and make Iran a major earthquake zone. The high mountains, in turn, affect weather patterns by blocking moist air's passage into the interior, making Iran a country of extremes in precipitation, temperatures, and topography. If Iran were superimposed over a map of North America, it would extend north to south from Reno, Nevada, to Monterey, Mexico, and west to east from San Diego, California, to Amarillo, Texas. In fact, the terrain, climate, and latitude of Iran bear considerable resemblance to corresponding features of the American southwest and northwestern Mexico. Iran, however, is much more arid with more extremely hot and barren areas, especially in its central and eastern deserts. The country also is marked by large swamps and marshlands in the southwest, dense subtropical forests in the Caspian region, and nearly two thousand miles of mostly rugged coastline. Iran has only one partially navigable river, the Karun, which flows into the confluence of the Tigris and Euphrates rivers to form the Shatt al-Arab waterway (called the *Arvand Rud* by the Iranians), which divides southwestern Iran and Iraq. The country's one major interior body of water, Lake Urmia in northwestern Iran, is larger and saltier than Utah's Great Salt Lake.

The most noticeable impact of geography on Iran's military history has been the limited role of sea power, despite long coasts on the Caspian Sea, Persian Gulf, and Indian Ocean. Nearly all of Iran's Persian Gulf coast is cut off by mountains from the plateau's high plains, and the Iranians for most of their history seemed uninterested in developing naval skills. In addition, the Karun River is navigable only by shallow craft and then only until rapids north of Ahvaz. The main problem during the age of wooden ships was that much of the Iranian Plateau lacked suitable timber for shipbuilding. In the early nineteenth century, a British Indian Army captain collected all the available geographical intelligence on Iran and reported that the northern shores of the Persian Gulf provided neither timber nor naval stores. Although forests of oak abounded in southwestern Iran, he wrote, the trees were too small for shipbuilding and would have to be transported a considerable distance to the shores over "stupendous rocks and frightful precipices." As a result, wood for ships had to be brought over long distances from India and other faraway locales.[5]

Because the people of the Iranian Plateau had limited experience with larger watercraft, Iran has lacked reliable naval crewmen and commanders throughout the centuries. Cyrus the Great, the founder of the Achaemenid Empire, relied on Phoenicians to battle Greek and Egyptian fleets during the sixth century BC, and only much later did Persians serve on ships and become commanders and admirals. Another Achaemenid emperor, Darius the Great, resorted to moving seafaring people from the Mediterranean to the head of the Persian Gulf to improve his maritime capabilities. During the mid-sixth century, the Sassanian emperor Chosroes I needed a navy to prevent the development of alternative trade routes to the Silk Road that would undercut his ability to collect tolls and duties. He briefly created maritime forces that relied on ethnic Arab or mixed-blood people living along the coast to conduct a series of naval operations to conquer Sarandib (modern Sri Lanka) and Yemen. After the Arab conquest, the empires and other kingdoms in Iran faced no neighbors with significant naval forces. As a result, few rulers exhibited interest in developing sea power, but focused instead on the more imminent threats from Mongol, Ottoman, Afghan, and Russian armies. Iran continued to rely on various foreigners, including Arabs and later Europeans, to provide its sailors and fleets through the early twentieth century. The Islamic Republic has had more success in developing indigenous naval forces, as shown by the creative tactics used by revolutionary naval units during the Tanker War with the United States in the 1980s.[6]

Iran's geography and the limited military wherewithal the heartland provided to protect the nascent Persian state possibly created the impetus for its initial territorial expansion. Around 559 BC Cyrus II, later called Cyrus the Great, took the throne of the petty kingdom of Anshan, in the southwest of modern Iran. His initial holdings, however, did not provide many resources for a would-be conqueror. Although the Persians later were known as great horsemen, Cyrus's forces were not initially mounted. The dry plains of Anshan and neighboring Parsa to the east made poor horse country, and the locals relied on donkeys. With his early conquests Cyrus gained the abundant high summer pastures of the Zagros Mountains, which provided good breeding grounds for the famous Median chargers that became the foundation of Persian cavalry. At the same time, Persian infantry and cavalry became masters of the composite bow because the heartland lacked the ferrous metals with which to fashion good swords. In the hands of Cyrus's men, the composite bow could shoot effectively over several hundred yards and gave the Persians a significant advantage over many of their opponents. It was only with the early expansion of the Persian Empire that Cyrus gained the mineral wealth, especially in iron, to make his army so formidable.[7]

To provide extra protection against invading armies and to support offensive operations, the Persians developed engineering skills to enhance the land's natural obstacles. During the Sassanian Empire between 226 and 641, the Persians constructed massive walls to help fortify the frontiers. One major bulwark was six to ten meters wide and extended from the eastern coast of the Caspian Sea northwest for nearly one hundred miles. It was the largest defensive wall in the world after the Great Wall of China, and its remnants are known by their Turkic name, the *Qizil Yilan,* or "red snake." A second wall near Sari in north central Iran was built in the mid-sixth century to hold off Turkic raiders and probably included a large moat on its eastern side. Another Sassanian defensive fortification included a wall that extended several miles into the Caucasus Mountains from the great citadel at Derbend—or Derbent, now the southernmost city in Russia—on the western coast of the Caspian Sea. Persian engineers also became skilled in handling problems involving waterways as their imperial ambitions led them to the great rivers of the ancient world. Darius the Great had a canal wide enough to accommodate two war galleys dug between the Nile and the Red Sea. During his massive invasion of the Greek city-states in 480 BC, Xerxes had a lengthy canal dug across a peninsula between Thrace and Macedonia to allow his six-hundred-ship navy to avoid a stormy coast where an earlier Persian flotilla had been lost in a gale. Centuries later, at the start of the Iran-Iraq War, Iranian engineers took advantage of the swamps and canals in southwestern Iran to induce flooding to create massive water barriers that helped stop the Iraqi invasion.

Fortress Iran

It is not much of an exaggeration to describe Iran as a fortress because of its extensive natural defenses. In general, the terrain around Iran's periphery favors the defender and is ill-suited to maneuver warfare, whether conducted by ancient armies or modern armored and mechanized ground forces. Iran's extensive mountain ranges virtually encircle the country and parallel the coast and land boundaries. Snow-covered during the winter and spring, most of Iran's mountains are steep and bleak with minimal tree cover and vegetation. Their narrow, winding mountain passes are the only means to access the high basin areas of

Iran's interior. Supply lines are constrained by a still limited road network that is vulnerable to sabotage and ambush. The loss of bridges and blockages of the mountain passes would be a significant impediment to troop movements. Major built-up areas along the main avenues of approach into Iran also form effective artificial obstacles to invading forces. Tehran, the Iranian capital since the late eighteenth century, had more than fourteen million residents in 2007, and the uncontrolled urban sprawl surrounding the city would make an opposed entry into it a daunting prospect for foreign military forces. To the north, the Caspian region is Iran's wettest, and rain and fog hinder visibility and movement there. Along the northern slope of the Alborz Mountains, small trees, bushes, and vines make the woods nearly impenetrable. The woodlands in the southern part of the Gilan region also consist of dense foliage and swampy ground that limit off-road movement. The heavily forested areas of the region have served for centuries as a haven for rebels and revolutionaries.[8]

In the modern era the mountains surrounding Iran have not been an obstacle to airpower, but even here Iran's vulnerability has some limits. Iraqi air and missile attacks against Iranian cities during the Iran-Iraq War showed that it is still difficult to harm Iran decisively from the air. Many of Iran's major strategic facilities and Tehran are positioned well within its interior at distances that can be challenging to pilots operating from bases outside the country. Air operations do benefit from Iran's normally cloudless skies. At the same time, Iran's dryness contributes to blowing dust and suspended dust particles that create a haze affecting visibility. The condition, called desert "brownout," causes the blending of the ground's grayish-brown color with overcast skies and can seriously impede low-level air operations, especially by helicopters. Such a dust storm was instrumental in the U.S. military's failed attempt in April 1980 to rescue fifty-two American hostages held by Iran.

Where Iran's borders are not marked by mountains, they are covered by major water obstacles and rugged coastlines. Behind the mountains and along the western border, precipitation and snowmelt can render ground virtually impassable to military vehicles in areas prone to natural flooding, in the mountain valleys, and along intermittently dry stream beds. Even when water levels are low, the steep riverbanks are difficult to traverse by infantry and wheeled and tracked vehicles conducting fording operations. Mobility also is hindered by irrigation canals and ditches in these regions. The Persian Gulf coast of Iran, meanwhile, is generally unfavorable to amphibious operations because of adverse surf conditions and the small number of suitable inland exits from the beaches. In addition, behind the southern beaches the land is low and swampy and is ill-suited for anything but infantry or amphibious combat. The conduct of operations in the Persian Gulf requires passage through the choke point of the narrow Strait of Hormuz, which Iran dominates from its mainland and from numerous nearby islands. The eastern frontier is mostly arid, but the point where the Iran-Afghanistan-Pakistan borders meet is a sunken, low-lying alluvial basin with swampy lagoons. The water in these marshy areas is replenished each year by the Helmand River's spring flow from the Hindu Kush snowmelt.

At the other extreme, desert covers about one-fifth of Iran. The Dasht-e Kavir in the north and the Dasht-e Lut in the south are the desiccated remains of ancient lakebeds. The northern desert is noteworthy for areas, called *kavirs,* where a brittle saline crust covers a layer of viscous mud. Iran also suffers from excessive summer heat conditions throughout most of the country, desert or not. Stress from the high heat and humidity can make hard physical labor almost impossible, even when troops are young, fit, and fully acclimatized. Summer heat, for example, is over 120 degrees Fahrenheit in southwestern Iran and can cause temperatures in closed vehicles without air conditioning to exceed 140 degrees. Such conditions complicate water needs and supply problems and intensify the wear and tear on all types of equipment. The shamal, a persistent northwesterly wind lasting for one to five days from May through September, blows down the Tigris and Euphrates river valleys of Iraq into Iran bringing extremely dry air, dust storms, and dust haze that affect operations and foul weapons and other types of machinery. Nighttime cooling is limited, even along the southern Iranian coastal plain, so military forces engaged in combat in Iran get little relief from the heat.[9]

The geography of "Fortress Iran" along with its stark climatic conditions combine with the country's heritage to contribute to an Iranian sense of uniqueness and insularity that today is seen in its strongly nationalistic posture when dealing with the outside world. Most of Iran's neighbors are Arab or Turkic peoples who have at some point invaded the Iranian homeland and even today compete with Iran for influence in the region. In this sense, Iran stands alone with few natural allies. Since the sixteenth century, Iran has been the largest and most significant Islamic state following the Shia creed, and the Iranians' rejection of many Sunni beliefs isolates them from much of the wider Islamic community. In the coming century, this uniqueness and the historical memory of the greatness of past Persian empires could feed the Islamic Republic's ambitions for regional preeminence and a more strategically significant revival of Iran's armed forces.

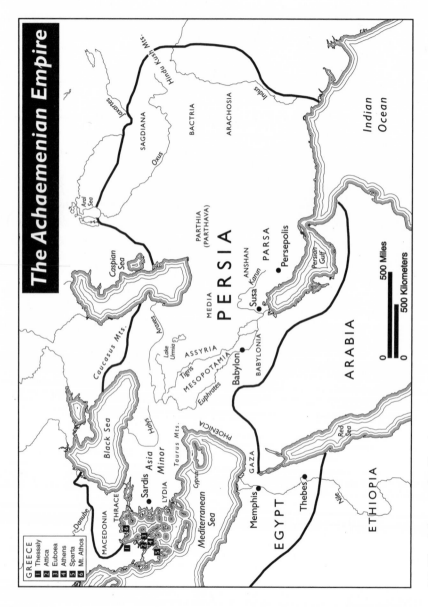

1.1 The Achaemenian Empire.

1

Heritage of Greatness, Legacy of Loss

THE FIRST GREAT PERSIAN DYNASTY, the Achaemenids, was a diverse but powerful empire that lasted for just over two centuries and provided inspiration for subsequent Iranian polities down through the ages. In the late ancient and medieval eras, southwest Asia witnessed the rise of the Parthian and Sassanian dynasties, whose constant competition with the leading Western empires is viewed in modern Iran as a source of cultural pride. These centuries also included some of the darkest pages of Iran's past, including the fall of the empires and the destruction caused by the later Mongol invasions. Iranian perseverance, resourcefulness, and adaptability—qualities present in subsequent centuries—served as critical elements of the empires' military might and effectiveness. When these characteristics were absent or weakened by poor leadership and strategic mismanagement, however, the overthrow of the Persian and Persian-influenced political orders was never far behind.

The Achaemenid Superpower

Cyrus the Great (r. 550–530 BC) has been called the first great captain of recorded history because of his extensive conquests but also by virtue of his political and administrative genius.[1] Cyrus inherited the core of his empire and his military system. But in less than thirty years he created a more professional and effective army, and his conquests followed one another "with a rapidity scarcely equaled except by Alexander and by the Arabs in the first generation after the death of Muhammad."[2] The first Persian emperor set the military standard that successor dynasties so often tried but failed to emulate. Cyrus demonstrated the importance of having a strong core of well-trained and professional forces loyal to the state, developed the means to integrate military levies while maintaining central authority, adapted new technology and methods when he found them, and ensured that his army was well led and sustained. The result was a robust military system that under subsequent Achaemenid kings could withstand occasional defeats until its leadership faltered and the last Achaemenid emperor was outgeneraled and overthrown.

The original Persian state that started its rise to become the first world superpower was founded by tribes that migrated from the Central Asian steppes, probably pushed south by exhausted pasturelands, overpopulation, or more aggressive neighbors. They established themselves in Parsa, a land between the Zagros Mountains to the west and deserts to the east, called Persis by the ancient Greeks. Cyrus's forebears sprang from these tribes and from the Medes, another Indo-European tribe of nomadic horsemen who had migrated into the Iranian Plateau. Among the most notable was Hakhamanish, a seventh century BC king, who was known as Achaemenes to the Greeks and whose name has been used to denote the first Persian dynasty. These Aryans, or Iranians in their native language, created fortified settlements and relied on cavalry raids in their warfare. Repeated incursions by the bellicose Assyrian Empire encouraged the tribal chiefs to unite, and more formal Median and Persian states began to emerge as vassals of the Assyrians. The Medes, possessing more fertile and productive land, expanded quickly and under King Cyaxares (r. 625–585 BC) developed perhaps the first Middle Eastern army divided into units with distinct bodies of spearmen, archers, and cavalry rather than groups of infantry and mounted warriors led by tribal chiefs. The Medes allied with the Babylonians to overthrow the Assyrians and then expanded Cyaxares' domains to the Mediterranean coast and extended military operations, if not control, almost as far as the Indus River in the east.

Cyaxares' great-grandson, Cyrus II, later called the Great, began his rise as conqueror from the Persian kingdom of Anshan, which he inherited from his father in 559 BC. After overthrowing his grandfather and establishing himself as the new ruler of combined Persian and Median kingdoms, Cyrus spent much of the first decade of his reign consolidating control over the Medes' former dominions as the new Persian Empire. To do this, the new king built a standing army loyal to him with ten thousand Persian infantry armed primarily with bow, spear, and a wood-and-wicker shield; ten thousand Persian cavalrymen bearing bows, javelins, and short swords; and perhaps a similar force of Medes. For a campaign, Cyrus expanded his imperial army by incorporating warriors from his subject peoples and adding more Medes, who had second position in the empire and provided many of the imperial generals.

Cyrus increased the emphasis on training and discipline in his standing army. He also used his early battles to refine the Median way of war, which helped to make his force more responsive and maneuverable on the battlefield. His first major challenger was the famously wealthy King Croesus of Lydia in western Asia Minor. After some initial indecisive battles, Cyrus's smaller army met the Lydian forces, who were backed by Egyptian, Spartan, and Babylonian allies, near Croesus's capital of Sardis on the plain of Thymbra in early 546 BC. The battle was notable because Cyrus organized his army in depth in a great square formation in the first recorded deviation from the normal practice of forming a line parallel to the enemy front. He deployed his best infantry, cavalry, and chariots to protect his flanks while placing his archers within the large square of infantrymen. On the advice of Hypargus, the Median general commanding his army, Cyrus created an improvised camel corps from his baggage train and placed the animals in the front of his formation. The unaccustomed smell and sight of the camels was reported to have thrown the Lydian cavalry into disarray. As he planned, Cyrus's army further disrupted the Lydian advance with barrages of arrows. It then exploited gaps in the Lydian lines as they overextended themselves assailing the Persian flanks. After pushing through to the Lydian rear, the Persian cavalry put Croesus's army to flight. The Lydian king and the remnants of his army retreated behind the walls of Sardis, which fell after a two-week siege.

Cyrus's experiment with tactical formations created several advantages for the Persian army. First, the new tactics depended less on coordination within the formation because, unlike advancing infantrymen in a shield wall, the archers could use their weapons without depending on others, firing as fast as each man's skill and circumstances allowed. Second, arrayed in several ranks and capable of rapid and accurate barrages, the archers could stop their enemies at a distance. Finally, the use of overhead fire involved more soldiers than line formations in which the rear ranks of spearmen provided only replacements for the fallen and some moral support. Cyrus's exposure to other fighting styles also helped improve his military. Impressed by their foes, the Persians adopted many of the cavalry tactics of the formidable Lydian horsemen. The Spartan infantrymen fighting for Lydia similarly made an impression, and Cyrus initiated the practice of including Greek mercenaries in the Persian army. During the next six years he established his rule in the east over a region stretching from the Caspian Sea to the Oxus and Jaxartes rivers (now called the Amu Darya and Syr Darya) in the north to the Hindu Kush in the east. While the nearly continuous warfare helped to perfect the Persian war machine, Cyrus also was a master of political warfare. He used a mix of military demonstrations and sedition to annex the Chaldeans' empire, which radiated from Babylon into northern Mesopotamia, across modern Syria to the Mediterranean, and into the Nejd-Hejaz borderlands of the Arabian Peninsula.

Like many great conquerors, Cyrus was not satisfied with his domains. Starting in 537 BC he launched expeditions to capture the areas west of the Indus River in what is modern Pakistan and to expand the empire to the region just below the Aral Sea and Jaxartes River. In the latter region Cyrus tried to use a line of forts to halt raiders of the Massagetae tribe but resorted to war to stop this warrior people's depredation. Accounts of Cyrus's final battles with and death at the hands of the Massagetae and their queen, Tomyris, in 530 BC vary, but after a savage and lengthy campaign, the Massagetae gained the upper hand in the final battle, killed Cyrus, and then destroyed the larger part of his army. The Greek historian Herodotus, who presents Cyrus as the aggressor, concludes his account by having Tomyris cut off Cyrus's head and plunge it into a barrel of blood in a mocking effort to satisfy the great king's supposed insatiable appetite for blood and conquest.

The elder of Cyrus's sons, Cambyses II (r. 529–522 BC), became emperor and fulfilled his father's ambition to conquer Egypt in 526 BC, proving himself a capable warrior and commander. His thorough preparations to provide the campaign's sea transport and adequate water supplies for the desert crossing of Gaza were essential to his victory. Cambyses' military operations also expanded the empire as far west as the Greek colony of Cyrene in modern Libya and up the Nile River valley to Thebes. While conducting an expedition against Nubia and Ethiopia during the fourth year of his western expedition, Cambyses was informed that an imposter claiming to be his brother, Bardiya, had seized the throne. As Cambyses was returning to Persia to remove the usurper, he was accidentally injured and died. Amid various intrigues, Cambyses' cousin, Darius, gained the throne and took the empire to its greatest heights.

The Persian Wars with the Greeks

Darius I (r. 521–486 BC) was a product of the Persian military system and, despite many challenges, enhanced the armed forces and empire he inherited. His overthrow of Bardiya was met by numerous revolts as various provincial governors made their own bid for Cambyses' throne or sought independence from the Persians. In 521 BC, Darius launched a swift and often brutal campaign, fighting nineteen battles and capturing nine petty kings in a year. After restoring his empire Darius then expanded it into the Indus valley, the Caucasus Mountains, and southeastern Europe.

Under Darius the basis for the army's success remained its skill with cavalry and archery, its resourcefulness, and its spirit. It also retained its versatility and adapted to various extreme conditions in the mountains of Armenia, the deserts of the eastern Iranian Plateau and Pakistan, and the Indus River valley where Darius conducted his early military campaigns. The Persian tactical system continued to rely on a combination of cavalry and bowmen to disorganize the opposing forces and make them vulnerable to close-quarters combat. In practice, the Persian cavalry attacked the flank of an enemy's infantry formation, which, as it stopped to defend against the horsemen wielding bows, javelins, and spears, would be hit by a hail of arrows from the distant archers. Unable to withstand the barrage, enemy formations usually broke, at which point the lightly armored and fleet-footed Persian infantrymen moved in for the kill. These tactics emerged from wartime experience and not faint-heartedness over closing with their enemies; Herodotus noted that "for in boldness and warlike spirit the Persians were not a whit inferior to the Greeks."[3] The Persians, however, were either unaware or unconcerned that the mountainous Greek mainland made their long-range arms and fluid tactical maneuver less practical against the superior armor, weapons, and discipline of the Greek phalanx.

Darius also tried to improve Persia's maritime prowess by moving seafaring Greeks from the Mediterranean to the head of the Persian Gulf. Cyrus had relied on Phoenicians to battle the Greek and Egyptian fleets, and Cambyses had added the Egyptian navy to the empire's forces. For many decades, however, the most Persian thing about the fleet was its flag. The Persians took great pains to reconcile the foreign naval commanders to their service, but over time, especially after Darius became emperor, more Persians served on ships and rose in the ranks to become commanders and admirals. Eventually, the entire fleet was in the hands of Persian admirals and included contingents of Persian, Mede, and Scythian marines while the Phoenicians and Egyptians continued to provide ships and sailors.

War with the Greek city-states only gradually became part of Darius's plans. The Persians and Greeks had been in contact with each other throughout the period, and at one point the Athenians had sought an alliance with the Persians against rival Greek states. In return, the Athenian envoys were required to recognize Persian suzerainty over Athens. When the Athenians eventually disowned the agreement, the Persians may well have regarded them as rebellious subjects. The proximate cause of the series of Greco-Persian wars that raged for roughly a half-century, however, was the revolt in 499 BC of the Ionian Greeks in Asia Minor. After nearly six years of bloody ground combat, Darius assembled a fleet that defeated the Ionian navy off the coast of Asia Minor in 494 BC, isolating and sealing the fate of the remaining rebellious cities.

Legend has it that Darius was furious at the Athenians for their role in the revolt and instructed one of his servants to say to him three times before each day's dinner, "Master, remember the Athenians."[4] In 492 BC the Persian army marched into Europe and moved west along the Athos Peninsula between Macedonia and Thrace, where it was joined by a Persian fleet for the push toward Athens. A sudden gale caught the fleet in an unprotected position off the coast from Mount Athos, and three hundred ships with all hands were lost. This initial invasion was abandoned, but, undeterred, Darius issued orders to create a larger amphibious force that would advance directly across the Aegean Sea and land close to Athens. In late summer of 491 BC the Persians assaulted the island of Euboea and captured, plundered, and burned Eretria, one of the city-states that had supported the Ionian revolt. By early 490 BC, the Persian commander had positioned his forces on the open beach at Marathon to try to exact Darius's retribution on the Athenians.

The goal of the imperial forces' landing at Marathon was to draw the Athenian military out of the city while half the Persians sailed around Attica, where it was hoped an antidemocratic faction plotting to reclaim power in Athens with Persian support would surrender the city to them. After a standoff of several days, the Greeks attacked the Persian expeditionary force when most of the Persian cavalry left the field, either to embark on transports for the dash by sea to Athens or simply to get the horses watered. The Greek phalanx, which had been strengthened on the wings and thinned in the center, faced a Persian line in which the best troops, reinforced by picked tribal warriors from the eastern frontier, were in the center while less reliable units were stationed on the flanks. Without cavalry to disrupt the Greek attack, the Persian lines were in a much weaker position to stop the spear- and sword-bearing hoplites in the advancing Greek phalanxes. In the face of the onrushing bronze-clad Greek soldiers, the Persian archers were able to unleash only a few arrows before retreating behind their spearmen. In the center, the Persians were successful in throwing back the Greeks. However, they were not able to exploit the Greek center's failure before the heavier Greek flanks wheeled inward to hit the less-well-protected Persian soldiers from the side and rear. Having pushed forward in the center, the Persians now found themselves the victims of a double envelopment as the Greek flanks came crashing in. Facing the prospect of being surrounded and annihilated, the Persian soldiers broke and fled toward the transports drawn up on the beach, ending the battle in the Greeks' favor. Taking advantage of their interior lines, the Greek commanders rapidly marched their warriors back to Athens before the Persian navy arrived. Chastened, the Persian force returned to Asia. Darius, however, saw Marathon as only a temporary check on his ambitions and immediately began preparations for a new invasion. For a great empire with extensive resources, the worst casualty of the campaign was the army's reputation as an irresistible force.

Darius died in 486 BC, and his son and successor, Xerxes I (r. 485–465 BC), after a brief distraction by a major revolt in Egypt, undertook the greatest expedition recorded in ancient times to fulfill his father's ambitions. With an empire that covered nearly three million square miles and contained as many as twenty million people, Xerxes mobilized a multinational army and made excellent logistic preparations. The emperor and his generals, however, apparently did not understand all of the earlier expeditions' failings and made no significant adaptations to the Persian military system or its tactics. During the delay, Athens discovered a rich new vein in its silver mines and, after much internal debate, used its newfound wealth to start a crash shipbuilding program. The city's naval strength was tripled, providing the foundation for a stronger Greek alliance against the Persians. As a result, Xerxes found the Greeks an even tougher enemy when the Persian army returned to Europe.

As they embarked on their invasion, the Persians had a large and disciplined military organization and were well provisioned for expeditionary warfare. Studies of historical records regarding topography, logistics, and official orders of battle suggest that the number of Persian forces probably ranged from as low as 70,000 infantry and 9,000 horsemen to the higher and more likely figure of roughly 360,000 in the Persian camp. It was probably during Xerxes' time that one corps of the army became known as the Immortals. This unit served as the Imperial Guard, and the emperor mandated that the corps' strength never rise or fall from 10,000, which meant that casualties were immediately replaced, giving the appearance that no loss had been suffered.[5] Modern scholars put the Persian fleet between 600 and 800 warships at the time of the war's first major naval battle at Artemisium and, after losses to weather and combat, perhaps 450 to 600 triremes at the subsequent fight at Salamis. Ship for ship the Persians and Greeks probably were evenly matched, but the Persian ships tended to be top-heavy, were less manageable in rough seas, and were less sturdy in battle than the Greek ships. The multinational character of the fleet, which had numerous languages in use, probably complicated communication and coordination.[6]

During more than four years of preparations, the Persians demonstrated their prowess in logistics and engineering. Agents sent out by Xerxes ensured that the lands on the route of march would have sufficient stocks of food and provender for the army. To avoid a recurrence of the disaster that befell Darius's first invasion fleet, Xerxes had his engineers dig a canal across the isthmus behind Mount Athos. The canal was wide enough for two triremes to pass abreast while rowing. To ensure that Persian lines of communication were adequate for the mission, Xerxes' engineers improved many of the roads in Asia Minor and constructed a road in Thrace that was regarded with wonderment a generation later. The Persians repaired many of the bridges built during earlier expeditions and famously constructed two solid boat bridges linked by strong flax and papyrus cables across the Hellespont. One was for the fighting men and the other for the baggage train, and each reportedly was built with sections that opened to allow ships to pass up the strait. The Persians easily could have ferried their forces across the waterway, but the bridges were a strong statement of will and capability.

In the spring of 480 BC, Xerxes put his great plan in motion. The Persian army crossed the Hellespont and, with the Persian fleet following just offshore, marched unopposed along the northern coast of the Aegean Sea through Thrace and Macedonia before turning south into Thessaly. The Persians sought to bring the Greeks to battle, destroy their armies, and end the war quickly. The

1.2 Ancient battlefields.

large and slow-moving Persian host, however, did not run into the first Greek
defensive line until reaching the narrow pass of Thermopylae in central Greece.
There a picked force of three hundred men under Spartan king Leonidas, joined
by six thousand additional hoplites from other Greek cities and supported by
the Greek fleet offshore, defended the pass. The Spartan defensive position and
shield wall represented an intimidating obstacle.

The clash of arms began badly for the Persians. Xerxes' navy, unable to
find a harbor large enough for the entire fleet, lost hundreds of ships and in-
numerable crewmen in a three-day gale just before the battle. Over the course
of three days off the coast of the town of Artemisium on Euboea, the Persians
were stymied in a series of small naval battles with the Greeks and were prevented from making an amphibious landing behind the Spartan position. Unable to find a way around the Spartans, Xerxes launched several costly and unsuccessful frontal assaults on Leonidas's position. No match for the Greeks in
man-to-man combat, the Medes and then the Immortals broke like waves on the
Spartan shield wall and were badly mauled. The Persian cavalry, Xerxes' main
offensive arm, lacked the room to deploy and stood by idly watching the contest.
After two days of fighting, Xerxes received information from a local Thessalian

about a route through the mountains around Thermopylae. Xerxes quickly ordered a picked force of the remaining Immortals on a rare night march to surprise the Greek detachment guarding this path. The Immortals easily defeated the detachment and other Greek troops sent to stop them and then joined in a general Persian attack on the Spartans, who fought courageously until all were killed. The Spartans' final stand cemented the battle's reputation as a heroic struggle against hopeless odds. The usual disparagement of the Persians in the telling of this story, however, is unfair because most depictions rely heavily on Herodotus's far from unbiased account. The Persians fought bravely in the battle against a better-armed and disciplined foe in a strong defensive position.

Xerxes' army resumed its march south and by early September had captured Athens. The decisive battle, however, came not on land but at sea. After the Athenians abandoned their exposed city and fled to the nearby island of Salamis for safety, the Greek naval forces concentrated in the constricted waters between Athens and Salamis. Before he could attack the remaining Greek forces, which had fallen back south of the Isthmus of Corinth, Xerxes needed to neutralize the Greek fleet to protect his sea lines of communications and his ability to resupply his ground forces. In the ancient accounts of Salamis there is "a wealth of incident but no clear picture of the formations of the fleets or their situation in relation to the coasts."[7] Although there is a scholarly debate about its methods, the Persian fleet moved into position to cut off the Greeks in the channel during the night before the battle. Xerxes' fleet was roughly twice as large as the Greek naval forces, but the Persians could not fully develop their combat power and found their numbers a hindrance. The Salamis Strait was not much more than a mile wide at the time, and during the battle close to one thousand triremes may have been squeezed into about a square mile of ocean.[8] The Greeks exploited the Persians' difficulty operating in the crowded waterway, and the battle became a series of engagements in which the Greek triremes darted among the Persian ships, harrying them and driving them against each other. When the Persians finally retreated, the pursuing Greeks attacked and sank the stragglers, resulting, at battle's end, with two hundred or more Persian warships being sunk or captured.

The defeat at Salamis signaled the end of the invasion. Xerxes returned to Asia, leaving behind the remaining Persian expeditionary force of possibly one hundred thousand men. In the spring of 479 BC, the Persians marched south and again captured Athens, enacting Darius's revenge and destroying the city. After withdrawing north and establishing a defensive line on the Asopus River near Plataea, the Persians engaged in a final battle with the Greeks where, after their commander was killed, the Persian infantry lost heart and retreated with heavy losses. Following the battle, the Persian army began the long retreat to Asia. After Salamis and Plataea, the myth of Persian invincibility was shattered.

The war continued for another thirty years, during which the Athenians, except for a serious defeat in Egypt, stripped provinces from a declining Persian Empire before agreeing to the Peace of Callias in 448 BC.

The Fall of the Persian Empire

Persia continued to be the predominant power in the world for another century and a half after Xerxes' failure, but it also was a troubled empire and suffered through a series of revolts and internal upheavals. The most noteworthy was the rebellion in 401–400 BC by Cyrus, the satrap of Lydia, against his older brother, the Emperor Artaxerxes II (r. 404–358 BC). Cyrus enlisted Greek mercenaries for his war but was killed during the Battle of Cunaxa. A young Greek officer, Xenophon, was among the mercenaries and related in his history of the war, *Anabasis* (Upcountry March), how the Greeks won the battle but had to fight their way back to Greece in the famous "March of the 10,000." Based on his experience in the East, Xenophon made the assessment that Persia belonged to the man who had the courage to attack it.[9] In 334 BC, the armed forces of the last Achaemenian king, Darius III (r. 336–330 BC), met that man when Alexander the Great arrived to fight for the rule of Asia.

Although Darius had apparently been brave in his early military career, he did not demonstrate any real capacity for kingship or leadership of Persia's armed forces during his brief reign. The Persian military system had changed little in terms of arms and armament, but heavy infantry provided by Greek mercenaries had supplanted the traditional light infantry formations of Persian archers and spearmen, with the exception of the Immortals. When the Persians faced Alexander III, later called the Great, they did not recognize how his father, Phillip II of Macedonia, had adjusted the Greek tactical system while uniting Greece under his control. The Macedonians were organized to allow coordinated tactical action by infantry and cavalry with larger and more powerful phalanxes and several categories of light infantrymen who gave the formations more agility and better protection for the flanks and rear areas. Heavy cavalry, the system's decisive arm, served as the hammer that crushed the enemy against the anvil formed by Phillip's phalanxes. The still formidable Persians also depended on cavalry attacks to decide battles. However, wearing only mail shirts and relying more on bows and javelins than on swords or lances, the Persian horsemen were not prepared for Alexander's heavy cavalry, especially the force called the Companions that the young Macedonian king personally led. Darius's army also was outmatched in its resolve as the mixture of nationalities that made up the ancient Persian military no longer fought with as much determination when faced by Alexander's better disciplined, trained, and equipped forces.[10]

The Persians still commanded the sea as Alexander prepared to wage war against them, but their naval forces had many limitations. Just as in Xerxes' time, Persian ships could only remain at sea for short periods because they were designed to minimize weight and bulk to maximize speed. Unable to carry many provisions, the fleet had to stay close to the coast for frequent replenishment, making it vulnerable to any land army capable of patrolling the shores and preventing a landing to restore the fleet's water supplies. Alexander lacked an adequate fleet to challenge the Persians and was unwilling to risk a naval battle out of concern over the political consequences of defeat. The Persian naval threat to his ambitions was substantial because, even though Alexander sought to conduct a land war in Asia, his main line of communications back to Macedonia crossed the Hellespont and would be open to interdiction by the Persian navy. In addition, the Persians had successfully used their navy to help provoke and support Greek revolts against Macedonian power in the recent past and could repeat this threat unless Alexander was able to neutralize it. As a result, the Persian navy determined the initial stages of the war as Alexander chose to attack the mostly Greek maritime cities of the eastern Mediterranean to deny Darius's fleets the ability to enter ports to resupply and recruit sailors.

The history of how the Persians lost their empire in a series of three major engagements separated by Alexander's conquest of the eastern Mediterranean coast and Egypt is well known and requires no detailed retelling here. The Persians demonstrated their usual bravery, adapted as best they could to Alexander's military, and improved their military performance. Alexander's generalship was greater, however, and Darius's faintheartedness and the mistakes and misfortunes common to all wars undid the Persians. The Persian emperor was not at the first battle near the Granicus River, where a Persian force of about 10,000 cavalry and 4,000 to 5,000 mercenary Greek infantrymen faced Alexander's army of 12,000 heavy infantry, 1,000 light infantry, and 5,100 cavalry. Rejecting advice from Greek mercenaries to adopt a scorched-earth strategy and deprive the Macedonians of the provisions needed to stay on campaign, Darius's commanders set up a strong defensive position along the river. Their intent was to compel Alexander to attack, minimize his advantage in infantry, and optimize the Persian advantage in cavalry. For reasons that remain unclear, however, the Persians had their cavalry form up in front of the mercenary Greek infantrymen, which sacrificed the cavalry's mobility while leaving the infantry in a useless rear position. Historians have speculated that the Persian commanders did not intend to defeat the larger Macedonian force with their deployments. Instead, they may have been trying to position their cavalry to use their superior number of horsemen to kill Alexander in the early phases of the battle and perhaps end the invasion before it truly started. In this they nearly succeeded, as Alexander was almost killed during the course of the very intense early fighting. Ultimately, the weakness of the Persian dispositions invited a devastating defeat when the deaths of the senior Persian commanders in a melee with Alexander caused their soldiers to lose heart and allowed the center to collapse.[11]

The immediate result of the battle was that no Persian forces remained in western Asia Minor to stop Alexander from neutralizing the Persian fleet, which set the stage for the next major battle. The Macedonian commander moved quickly to liberate the mostly undefended Greek cities on the Ionian coast and then conducted a brief campaign to capture Persian strongholds in central Asia Minor and Syria. Darius took to the field and moved his army into the Macedonian rear, setting up his forces in a strong defensive position behind the Pinarus River on the Syrian coastal plain near the town of Issus. This relatively narrow area forced the estimated one hundred thousand Persian soldiers to deploy in formations in greater depth than usual. Most of the Persian horsemen were posted on the far left on terrain suited for a cavalry engagement and where Alexander was expected to lead the Companions' attack. The rest were placed on the far right, next to the ocean, to conduct the decisive attack into Alexander's rear. Darius positioned himself behind the center of his lines with his bodyguard and waited for Alexander's twenty-five thousand infantry and five thousand cavalry to come to him. The Macedonian leader extended his line to make it more difficult for the Persians to outflank him and then ordered his infantry to advance gradually to give his cavalry the time to crush the Persian left. The furious attacks and counterattacks along the lines witnessed strong Persian stands, gaps in the Macedonian line, and the steady retreat of Greek troops in front of Darius's cavalry along the ocean. Alexander, however, had the time he needed to defeat the Persian left flank and start an envelopment there. Darius apparently lost his nerve and fled the field, joined, in short order, by the rest of the Persian army, a signal that the end of the empire was indeed near.[12]

Darius had almost two years to prepare for his next battle with Alexander as the Macedonians consolidated their control over the eastern Mediterranean and Egypt before turning to the Persian heartland. For the third and final battle with Alexander near Arbela (modern Arbil [Irbil] in northern Iraq), Darius assembled a large, heterogeneous army of between one hundred thousand and two hundred thousand men from his remaining empire. Unable to obtain new Greek mercenaries, Darius was forced to rely more heavily on his mounted soldiers. The cavalry, which numbered from forty thousand to fifty thousand, was reequipped with longer spears to match the Macedonian pikes. Darius also revived the long forgotten scythed chariot, training a regiment to compensate for the lack of heavy infantry to throw against Alexander's phalanxes. Against Darius's host, the Macedonian army probably fielded approximately eight thousand cavalry and forty thousand infantry.

Anticipating Alexander's likely line of march for invading Mesopotamia, Darius established his forces on the wide plain at Gaugamela. Darius stayed on the defensive to set up a double envelopment. His strategy apparently was to defeat Alexander's mounted forces with his numerically superior cavalry and, if successful, outflank the powerful advancing Macedonian phalanxes and destroy them. The plan's weakness was its dependence on inadequate infantry forces holding back the Macedonians long enough for the cavalry battle to be decided. Still, after two major engagements with the Macedonians, the Persians had a good tactical grasp of Alexander's weaknesses and preferences in battle and were able to craft a reasonable combat plan to defeat the invader using their size and mobility. With their greater numbers, the Persians lengthened their battle lines to deny Alexander his usual flank attack while increasing opportunities to surround the Macedonian infantry should their advance create a pocket in the center of the line. The terrain at Gaugamela was well suited for the cavalry fight Darius envisioned, and to further improve his forces' mobility, Darius had his engineers clear obstacles and level the ground. In some places the engineers cleared runways for the chariots. In other places, the Persians set out traps and spikes to injure the Greek horses, but much engineering work was incomplete, especially in front of the Persian left wing, when Alexander arrived.

In early October 331 BC, with mounted forces in the fore and the weaker infantry behind, the Persians stood fast as Alexander maneuvered his army, as expected, to the right across Darius's front. The Great King, holding his post in the center of the line with his few Greek infantry and the remaining Immortals, ordered his left wing cavalry into action to halt Alexander's march. Darius, however, fell victim to a feint that caused him to commit his forces to the planned double envelopment too early. The subsequent fighting caused the Persian line to thin, and the battle became a race between both sides' cavalry to penetrate their opponents' lines. Anticipating this development, Alexander watched for a gap to open and then drove a wedge into it for a direct assault on the Great King. A frightened Darius once again abandoned his army and left the field. As his flight became known, the Persians began a retreat that quickly turned into a rout.

Alexander pursued Darius across the Zagros Mountains and captured the Achaemenid capital of Persepolis. After burning the city in delayed retribution for Xerxes' destruction of Athens, Alexander chased Darius east through the Alborz Mountains into the Caspian region. As his empire crumbled beneath him, Darius grew apathetic and reluctant to continue his retreat. Persian nobles took the Great King prisoner to keep him out of Alexander's hands and then killed him at Damghan in the summer of 330 BC. Bessus, Darius's cousin, proclaimed himself emperor, but Alexander prevented the eastern satraps from raising new forces and eventually captured and executed Bessus.[13]

The Persian failure against Alexander was a result of bad strategy in defending against the initial invasion. In the later stages of the war, the greatest problem was Darius's failure as a battlefield commander rather than any shortcomings as a strategist and tactician. The Persians clearly would have been better off if they had used a logistics strategy from the start and heeded the advice to avoid direct conflict with the superior Macedonian infantry and use scorched-earth tactics. Had the Persians destroyed fodder and burned crops, strengthened garrisons, and used their navy more aggressively to prevent supplies from being moved from Greece across the Aegean Sea, Alexander's invasion would have been virtually unsupportable, and he likely would have expended his army in lengthy sieges to secure his base. The Persians had the advantage of greater numbers and benefited from shorter supply lines, a combination that probably added to their morale and willingness to fight at the beginning of the war. These attributes, however, increased the severe psychological impact of Alexander's victories. The decisiveness of Alexander's first two victories caused many of the western satrapies of the Persian Empire to submit without strong resistance and allowed Alexander to keep his field army large because he needed only small garrisons to hold the submissive municipalities.[14]

Once Darius determined to confront Alexander directly, his strategies for the battles of Issus and Gaugamela were reasonable but were undermined by their poor execution. The Persians had little choice except to rely heavily on their cavalry, yet they failed to develop the coordination between mounted forces and infantry units necessary to maintain a stable front. Such measures, which earlier Persian armies had understood, might have prevented the repeated instances of Darius's line becoming detached from his wings and allowing gaps to open. Darius's commanders also failed to come up with tactical plans to counter Alexander's clever use of light infantry archers and javelin throwers interspersed among the Companion cavalry to offset the Persian superiority in horsemen. In addition, given that Alexander was leading an expeditionary force at the end of a lengthy and potentially tenuous line of supply, Darius's failure to use the large number of light cavalry he had at hand to harass the Macedonians is unfathomable. The Persians also failed throughout the campaign to try to hold several mountain passes that Alexander had to cross to slow and wear down the Macedonians. In short, although Darius had the means, he still failed to match them to the ends of his strategy to defeat the Macedonians. Achaemenian rule had given most of the empire nearly two hundred years of stability, but Alexander brought an end to this, especially after his death in 323 BC led to forty years of conflict as his generals fought for control and then division of his empire. It would be left to new Persian dynasties and fighting men to reassert their heritage of military excellence.

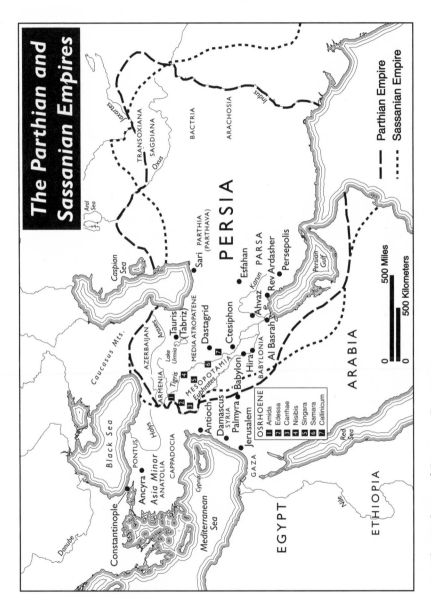

1.3. The Parthian and Sassanian Empires.

The Parthian Empire

The Parthians were a tribe of nomadic Aryans from Central Asia who became a bridge between Alexander's Hellenism in southwest Asia and a resurgent Persia. The Parthians took their name from the former Achaemenid province of Parthava, which corresponded roughly with modern northeastern Iran. In size, the Parthian Empire was smaller than Achaemenid realms, but Parthian ambitions brought them into conflict with the newly risen Roman Empire. Parthia also faced constant challenges from Turkic tribes from the eastern Central Asian steppes and the Caucasus and from the Kushans of Bactria. These nomadic invasions and the prospect of fighting wars on two fronts strongly influenced the Parthian military system.

Starting from a base between the Caspian and the Aral seas, Mithridates I (r. 171–138 BC) is credited with founding the Arsacid dynasty. He did this roughly a century after the Parthians first claimed independence from the Seleucids, whose dynasty was founded by one of Alexander's successors and ruled most of southwest Asia and Asia Minor from 323–200 BC. Once established, the new dynasty annexed nearly all of the Iranian Plateau and surrounding mountains, Babylonia, and Armenia. The Parthians then reoccupied the eastern provinces of the old Persian Empire under Mithridates II (r. 138–83 BC), called the Great. To give formal expression to his increased power, Mithridates assumed the Achaemenid title of "shahanshah," or "King of Kings."

Despite its imperial successes, Parthia was a feudal and decentralized conglomeration of eighteen separate and semiautonomous vassal states under Arsacid suzerainty. Maintaining internal unity and stability was the primary concern of every emperor, and the Parthian military system was not fully capable of mobilizing the considerable military resources of the Iranian Plateau and adjacent lands. As a result, after Mithridates the Great, the Parthians generally were not an expansionist power and remained on the strategic defensive except when contesting control over border provinces key to the empire's security. Despite the Parthians' accomplishments in the service of a Persian national identity, over the centuries the Iranians have dismissed their fellow Aryans, who were less closely related to the Persians than the Medes, referring to them as "Kings of the Tribes."[15] Still, the Parthians claimed lineage from the Achaemenids, and their armies were manned by many of the same peoples who fought for Cyrus, Darius, and Xerxes.

The Parthian military won renown as an outstanding cavalry-based force capable of meeting multiple threats. Emulating the Achaemenids' high level of training, the Parthian forces, mounted on a new breed of larger horses with more stamina, mastered the difficult art of fighting as heavy cavalry in the age before the invention of the stirrup. By combining the two tactical elements of missile power and shock, the Parthians created a system that caught their foes off guard and unbalanced them. After upsetting enemy formations with barrages of arrows, the Parthian horsemen attacked gaps and exposed flanks with bow-shots capable of piercing armor and lances effective against shields. The Parthians never developed a siege train and were so unfamiliar with the technology that they failed to make use of the significant amounts of equipment captured from the Romans. The Parthians also had no major naval capabilities despite the extension of the empire to the Persian Gulf and the Indian Ocean.

The Parthian heavy cavalryman was one of the most able and feared fighters of antiquity. Called a "cataphract," the Parthian mounted warriors were equipped much like medieval European knights. The cataphract wore a steel helmet and a coat of mail that reached to the knees and was made of rawhide covered with scales of iron or steel that enabled it to resist strong blows. His charger also was covered from head to knees by scale armor of either steel or bronze. The cataphract was armed with a lance long and thick enough to give it the weight and power to unseat, if not kill, an opponent. He also carried a large and powerful compound bow that outranged Roman and others' weapons and was capable of propelling arrows strongly enough to penetrate the armor of Roman legionaries. Fielding an armored horseman was so expensive that the number of Parthian cataphracts was limited. At the Parthians' first major battle with the Romans, there probably was only one cataphract for every ten light cavalrymen, although this ratio improved over time. The light cavalry, armed with a bow and arrows and probably a sword, was not suitable for sustained close combat with infantry but was perfect for skirmishes, hit-and-run tactics, and flank attacks. Most of the tribal levies were light cavalry, and these riders were trained from boyhood in the arts of horsemanship and archery and could shoot at full gallop while swarming the enemy or withdrawing from the battlefield.[16]

The primary Parthian tactic was a classic combination of firepower and shock effect. The light cavalry used hit-and-run attacks to harass the enemy and disorganize his forces while the heavy cavalry forced the enemy to remain in closed ranks by the threat of a charge. As a result, the enemy infantry could not come to grips with the bowmen, whose arrows took an increasing toll, nor could it march away to shelter. If gaps were created in the enemy's lines, the heavy cavalry moved in as a shock force to try to roll up the exposed flank, although the cataphracts still avoided hand-to-hand combat in favor of the bow and lance. The overall goal was to wear down the enemy's strength and morale, surround them with more mobile cavalry forces, and then compel a surrender or destroy him with volleys of arrows and other missiles. These Parthian tactics were highly effective in defeating disciplined infantry forces. When facing an opponent in a strong defensive position or behind walls, however, the Parthians lacked the tactics and means to overcome the enemy's lines or conduct protracted sieges.

The Wars with Rome

The contest for supremacy in southwest Asia started during the initial contacts between Parthia and Rome during the late Roman Republic and continued through the early Roman Empire. By the time of the First Triumvirate of Julius Caesar, Pompey, and Crassus in 60 BC, the reported riches of Asia tempted the Romans. Crassus, the proconsul of Syria and jealous of Caesar's and Pompey's military fame, planned the first war on Parthia after the Roman-backed contestant for the Parthian throne was defeated by his brother, Orodes I (r. 57–38 BC). The proconsul was overconfident about his heavy infantry's chances against the more mobile Parthians, ignoring reports that "by flight it is impossible to escape (them) . . . and as impossible to overtake them when they flee."[17] Orodes' first countermove was to advance into Armenia to deny local reinforcements to the Romans and block the best avenues of approach into the empire. To the south, Orodes left operations in the hands of his main army's general, Rustam Suren-Pahlav, known in the west as Surena.[18] Crassus ignored advice to march northeast through Armenia, which had ample supplies and more secure terrain for his offensive. He instead advanced southeast along a more direct but difficult desert route into Mesopotamia. The Roman legions were exhausted and in complete disorder when they reached the town of Carrhae (modern Harran, Turkey), and Crassus's scouts reported that the Parthians were massing nearby.

Surena's highly mobile army was composed of a thousand armored cataphracts, nine thousand horse archers in the main body, and a baggage train of a thousand camels with extra stocks of arrows. When Crassus's larger army stumbled into the Parthians near Carrhae, Surena gave the Romans time to deploy but kept most of his heavy cavalry hidden. Choosing his moment, Surena ordered the cataphracts to reveal themselves and join with the other Parthian fighters in yelling and beating drums to demoralize the Romans, who recognized that they were surrounded in a semidesert plain. Surena had his light cavalry spread out and shoot arrows into the massed Roman square, and, thanks to the ample supplies of arrows brought forward by the camels, the archers were able to maintain their fire to wear down their enemy. The Romans suffered great losses, not just from the arrows, but from the sun and thirst. Crassus tried to retreat, only to be brought to bay by the Parthians. The exhausted and frightened legionaries demanded that Crassus negotiate, and before the first parlay ended the Parthians seized and executed Crassus, causing the Romans to fall into further disarray. Crassus's defeat was nearly total: fewer than five thousand Romans returned to Syria from the campaign while the Parthians, with few losses to their forces, killed nearly twenty thousand Romans, enslaved ten thousand more, and seized seven Roman "eagles," the standards carried by the legions.

Carrhae possibly was the first time an army depended entirely on long-range weapons to win a battle, and it had two major impacts on the future East-West conflict. First, by illustrating the tremendous advantage of a highly mobile force with missile weapons over an army lacking these elements, the Parthian victory forced Rome to increase the role of cavalry in its legions, presaging the eventual eclipse of infantry by cavalry in the following centuries. Second, it excited a Roman desire for revenge and concern about the security of the eastern frontier. These Roman views were matched by the Parthians' undying anger over Rome's breach of the peace, and both combined to fuel subsequent wars. On the Parthian side, the battle may have sown the seeds of the dynasty's final collapse. Surena's success caused Orodes to become jealous of his general, and soon after Carrhae the emperor devised a pretext to have Surena executed. This murder embittered Surena's family and divided it from the Parthians. More than two centuries later, the Suren-Pahlavs threw their support behind the Persian Sassanians to overthrow the Arsacid dynasty.

The Parthians were confronted by Rome again during the Second Triumvirate, when Caesar's former lieutenant, Mark Antony, marched his army through Armenia into Media Atropatene (respectively, modern Armenia plus eastern Turkey and northwestern Iran) in 36 BC. Details are sparse, but the battle apparently was similar to Carrhae. The Parthians inflicted such severe casualties that the Romans were forced to retreat after losing their siege train and as many as thirty thousand men. A treaty was negotiated in 20 BC by which, in return for a peace along the frontier, the Parthians gave Rome suzerainty over Armenia and Osrhoene (upper Mesopotamia) along with the eagles taken from Crassus and Antony. The two empires might have maintained a guarded coexistence, but the long border and rich prizes on either side tempted leaders and fed ambitions that, once the peace was broken, led to repeated wars over the subsequent two centuries.

The initial solution to preventing conflict had been to keep Armenia and Osrhoene as neutral buffer states. Keeping them neutral probably was more important for Rome because of the challenges it faced in maintaining its vast empire against various barbarian threats. From the perspective of defending the Parthian realm, northern Mesopotamia was the most important because it was the quickest route for Roman armies into the prosperous region of ancient cities and rich agriculture controlled by the Arsacids. Conversely, if Parthia were free to station armies in Armenia, then Rome would need to create, man, and support two frontier armies in Cappadocia and Pontus capable of containing Parthian attacks until the arrival of strategic reinforcements from Syria and the west. Without an advanced base, Parthian forces advancing toward Pontus and Cappadocia by way of Armenia could move no faster than the legions of

Syria advancing to intercept them on the Euphrates and would have much more trouble gaining strategic surprise.[19] Despite being chronically weakened by internal struggles, the Parthians regularly succumbed to efforts by Rome's client rulers in Armenia and Mesopotamia to involve them in political battles with the caesars.

Between AD 113 and 216, the Parthians and Romans repeatedly fought over these provinces. When the Parthians replaced the king of Armenia with their own candidate, the Roman emperor Trajan responded with a four-year war from 113 to 117. In the course of this conflict the Parthians lost Armenia and all of Mesopotamia as Trajan marched to the Persian Gulf in the farthest advance of any Roman commander in the east. Only Parthian raids on Trajan's extended lines of communication coupled with a revolt in Judea compelled the emperor and his successor Hadrian to pull out of Parthian territory and the buffer states. Later, the Parthian emperor Vologases III (r. 105–47) seized the frontier provinces for several decades until Marcus Aurelius sent an army under Lucius Verus in 162 to recapture it. Wars with the Roman emperor Septimius Severus and his successor Caracalla between 195 and 216 weakened Parthia's hold on its feudal dependencies, especially over Parsa, the home province of the Sassanian family. There, a young noble, Prince Ardeshir, began his rise to supplant the Arsacids, creating a new and more serious challenge to Roman dominance in western Asia.

The Sassanians

The Sassanian dynasty built an empire that at its height stretched west to east between the Nile and Indus rivers and from Yemen in the south to the Caucasus in the north. Ardeshir I (r. 224–41) steadily stripped the Parthians of valuable territory, completely defeating them at the Battle of Hormuz in 226. The Sassanians were obsessed with asserting their control over their new empire to avoid the Parthians' problems. Ardeshir and his successors sought to create a strongly centralized state, which they called *Iranshahr,* or Iran. Setting a precedent followed repeatedly in Iran's history, the government tied itself closely to religion. Sir Percy Sykes suggested that lines from Iran's epic poem, the *Shahnameh,* or Book of Kings, best described Ardeshir's political testament: "Consider the altar and the throne as inseparable; they must always sustain one another."[20] To achieve this, the Sassanians resuscitated Zoroastrianism as the state religion. This faith, derived from the teachings of the sixth century BC Persian prophet Zoroaster, worshiped a single supreme being in the context of a universal struggle between good and evil and included beliefs in devils, angels, heaven, hell, redemption, and a final judgment that influenced Judaism, Christianity, and Islam.

The Sassanian military, like its surrounding culture, was neither simple nor static. Ardeshir had been a military commander when younger and apparently was knowledgeable of the military art and history, as shown in his restoration of Achaemenid military organizations, retention of the Parthian cavalry, and employment of new-style armor and siege engines. The backbone of the army remained the heavy cavalry, which, in addition to being formed by nobles and other men of rank, was made more professional by hard discipline and constant training maneuvers. This Sassanian heavy cavalry force, supported by light cavalry, archers, and a very proficient cadre of combat engineers, was capable of fighting the Romans and later the Byzantines on equal terms, even in direct combat. An elite corps of the cavalry was called "the Immortals," evidently numbering, like their Achaemenid namesakes, ten thousand men and serving tactically as a hard-hitting reserve. The Sassanians also resurrected the infantry, placing them at the front and center of battle formations and relying on them to set the conditions for the decisive cavalry engagement. Although at various times during the dynasty the Sassanian infantry was reported to have been no more than a levy of peasants with little tactical value, for most of this period they appear to have been a disciplined and skilled force. During sieges, the infantry supported the engineers by digging mines and participating in attacks on the walls. Up through the fourth century, according to claims made by Roman writers, Sassanian armies also included substantial numbers of women, who were conscripted as sutlers to gather and sell provisions to the soldiers but who also were found among the fallen and prisoners dressed and armed like men.

The Sassanians developed other war-making capabilities that the Parthians generally lacked. Most important was the establishment of an efficient siege train for reducing enemy forts and walled towns. Adapting Roman methods, Sassanid siege technology advanced greatly between the first and sixth centuries. The Sassanians employed offensive siege weapons such as scorpions, ballistae, battering rams, and moving towers. The latter were used to good effect during a siege in 337 of the great fortified garrison of Nisibis (modern Nusaybin in southeastern Turkey), where archers in siege towers poured devastating fire on the Roman-held walls. The Persian engineers also became skilled at building fortifications and walls that included embellishments for local defense such as murder-holes for pouring boiling liquid or dropping stones and firebrands on attackers. To protect the borders, the engineers constructed frontier watchtowers and forts to survey the extended walls and limes, some of which included large moats. In addition to the great walls in the Caspian region near Sari and Derbend, limes along the edge of the Arabian Desert and a large moat between Al Basrah and the Persian Gulf were constructed in southern Mesopotamia against the Arab tribes. The Sassanians also used war elephants in their army, despite the enormous logistic requirements. The Sassanian elephants usually were accompanied by large infantry contingents and provided support as a reserve from the rear of the foot formations. The pachyderms sometimes were used in conjunction with the cavalry, usually to spook the enemy's horses with their size, noise, and smell.[21]

The Sassanid tactical system rested on an improved combination of heavy and light cavalry, although the character of warfare was essentially one of raids, cavalry skirmishing, and occasional cavalry engagements followed by siege operations. The standard deployment for large Sassanian armies was in five parts: a main battle line, a reinforcing line, a small reserve formed by the Immortals, and two cavalry wings. Another formation involved cavalry forming a front line while the army advanced, only to retire to the wings and allow the following infantry to surprise an enemy expecting to face mounted troops. The Sassanians tried to establish the center of their line on high ground so that the main lines of cavalry and infantry could resist enemy charges more efficiently. The emperor or the army commander in chief was stationed in the center of the forces, sitting on an elevated throne to gain a wide view of the battlefield and controlling his forces with various types of signals. In combat with Roman or similarly organized enemy forces, the Sassanians made their left wing stronger but kept it on the defensive. This was a countermeasure to infantrymen, whose practice of carrying their shield on the left created the tendency to attack to the right, with the opposing lines each trying to outflank their enemy in that direction. Battles were usually decided by the shock cavalry of the front line charging the opposite ranks with heavy lances while archers gave support by discharging storms of arrows.[22]

The empire's one major shortcoming was its failure to develop a naval force capable of supporting its ambitions and worthy of its control, at various times, of shores on the Persian Gulf, northern Indian Ocean, and the eastern Mediterranean, Caspian, and Red Seas. The Sassanians encouraged native seafaring for trade purposes and founded numerous port cities, including Ahvaz, Al Basrah (now in Iraq), and Rev Ardasher near the contemporary port of Bushehr. Using Arab vassals, the Sassanians successfully captured and settled colonists on the island of Bahrain in the Persian Gulf, annexing it to the empire in 326. Despite a lack of naval power, the Sassanians still gained control of the sea trade in the Persian Gulf and, after conquering Yemen, in the Red Sea.

The Sassanian Wars with Rome

Once established, the Sassanians almost immediately challenged the Romans and in 230 initiated a conflict that resulted in ten major wars over the course of four centuries. Ardeshir, however, was repeatedly stymied by the Romans. His son, Shapur I (r. 241–72), adopted the provocative title of shahanshah of Iran and *aneran*, a slightly pejorative term for non-Iranians or barbarians. In 260, at the Battle of Edessa (modern Urfa in southeastern Turkey), Shapur's army surrounded the Roman emperor Valerian and more than seventy thousand legionaries. Like Crassus, Valerian agreed to negotiations only to be seized by the Persians. Unlike Crassus, he was not killed but was sent along with his soldiers as a captive to Persia, where he eventually died. Despite this decisive victory and his pretensions to ruling non-Iranians, Shapur failed to extend his domains beyond the established frontiers into Syria. The Sassanians continued to fight intermittently for control of Armenia until 296. Then, in the Peace of Nisibis, the Sassanians recognized Roman claims to northern Mesopotamia, Armenia, and five provinces northeast of the Tigris River and acknowledged Roman suzerainty over the Caucasus region.

During the years of general peace with Rome, Shapur II became emperor in 310, perhaps the only monarch in history to have been crowned in utero. He remained on the throne for nearly seventy years until 379. Early in his reign, the Sassanians became aware of the Roman Empire's final split when Emperor Constantine adopted Christianity and moved the capital from Rome to Constantinople on the site of the city of Byzantium. Shapur, who later was called the Great, wasted little time in taking advantage of the Romans' problems and invaded Roman Mesopotamia in 337. Over more than a dozen years at least nine major battles and three sieges were fought before a truce was arranged in 350 between Shapur and Constantine's son and successor, Constantius.

The conflict with Byzantium resumed in 358 and Sassanian pressure caused Constantius to make the fateful decision to order his cousin Julian, the top commander in Gaul, to send his legions east. Julian's soldiers were unwilling to leave their commander and rebelled, proclaiming Julian the new emperor and touching off a civil war that was settled when Constantius died from fever as he returned west to fight his cousin. Julian decided to continue the Persian war and, with the largest expeditionary force the Romans had ever assembled in the East, attacked the Sassanians in 363. Shapur's forces relied on raids and surprise attacks to harass enemy columns, cut off outlying detachments and foraging parties, and burn the countryside to deny Julian's legions the opportunity to live off the land. Shapur drew up his army for battle only after Julian's columns were seriously overextended.

Shapur was defeated by Julian in their first battle near Ctesiphon (south of Baghdad in modern Iraq) and withdrew farther east. In the flush of victory, Julian cut his links to his Tigris River supply line. He then set off in pursuit of the Persian army. Supply shortages, murderous heat, flooded rivers, and Mesopotamia's infamous flies—so thick they blotted out the sun, according to contemporary accounts—sapped Roman morale and eventually forced Julian to withdraw to northern Mesopotamia. Choosing his moment, Shapur attacked near Samarra and, although the Persians lost the battle, Julian was mortally wounded and was succeeded by another general, Jovian, whom the soldiers proclaimed emperor. Desirous of peace, Jovian accepted Shapur's harsh terms for the return of provinces previously ceded to Rome. Shapur also got the de facto renunciation of Roman claims to Armenia, which was turned into a satellite of the Persian Empire. An interesting footnote to this victory was that the Persians may have helped to ensure the continued spread of Christianity by killing Julian, who was known as "the Apostate" because of his conversion to the worship of Zeus and the Roman pagan gods. During his short reign as the Byzantine emperor, Julian had tried to roll back Christian influence, but Jovian reversed Julian's policies and restored Christianity as the empire's religion.

For most of the subsequent two centuries the Sassanians held their own against depredations by nomadic raiders from Central Asia and withstood the negative effects of sporadic civil wars and conflicts with Byzantium. The Sassanian emperor Kavadh I (r. 488–531) tried to push the empire's boundaries west, but the Byzantine emperor Justinian and his famous Thracian general Belisarius defeated these attempts and forced Kavadh's successor, Chosroes I, to conclude an "eternal peace" with the Byzantines in 532. Instead, sporadic hostilities over Armenia and eastern Anatolia marked most of the next sixty years. By the end of the sixth century, Sassanian Persia tottered near collapse from internal rebellions when Chosroes II (r. 591–628) claimed his crown with the help of Byzantine emperor Maurice and temporarily stabilized Sassanian rule.

In 602 Chosroes received word that a Byzantine centurion named Phocas had led a rebellious army to Constantinople and forced Maurice to abdicate before killing him. The emperor immediately declared war on the murderer of his benefactor and, with the Byzantines in disarray, the Persian army swept west in 603 and captured Mesopotamia, Syria, and Armenia. As Byzantine resistance collapsed, the Persians overran Cappadocia as well as the Black Sea coast of north central Anatolia and the region around modern Ankara. By 608, Chosroes's army had reached the vicinity of Constantinople. Lacking the ships to cross the Bosporus, the Persians were halted by this narrow strait between the Black Sea and the Sea of Marmara and the campaign stalled. Phocas stupidly picked this time to start an all-out campaign to convert Byzantium's Jews to Christianity, and those who did not revolt fled to Persian-held territory to ally with the Sassanians. Phocas's unhappy reign was ended in 610 when Heraclius overthrew him and was crowned emperor. Heraclius continued the war but concentrated on restoring his army before conducting any major counteroffensives, effectively allowing the Persians to run free in western Asia and northern Africa for the next twelve years.

Although unable to deliver a decisive defeat to Constantinople, Chosroes's other successes possibly awakened the dream of fully restoring the Achaemenid Empire and reducing, if not eliminating, Persia's Byzantine rival's power and influence. The Sassanian emperor kept his army on the road to conquest in Asia

Minor and the Levant. In short order, Antioch, Damascus, and then Jerusalem fell to the Persians. The Church of the Holy Sepulcher was burnt to ashes, and its True Cross and other relics were seized and carried away to Ctesiphon, allegedly for the pleasure of Chosroes's Christian wife. The Persians captured Egypt, the chief source of Byzantium's grain, and the resulting famine further weakened the Greek Empire. During this campaign led by Chosroes, the Persians marched across the Libyan Desert to Cyrene, a Greek city in northeastern Libya. At the same time, the Sassanians captured Chalcedon, roughly a mile from the walls of Constantinople, where they remained for the next decade. The Sassanians then captured Ancyra (modern Ankara) and the remaining Byzantine fortresses in Armenia, cutting off a principal recruiting ground for Constantinople's soldiers.

Despite the Sassanian successes, by 622 the Byzantine military had recovered sufficiently to take to the field. With the significant advantage of command of the sea, Heraclius moved the Greek army south by ship, landing near Issus, where Alexander had routed the Persians nearly a millennia earlier. The Byzantines moved north to confront the main Persian army under the general Shahr-Baraz. After months of indecisive fighting, skirmishes, maneuvers, and countermarches, the two armies drew up along the upper Halys River. An attempt by Shahr-Baraz to envelop the Byzantines failed, and Heraclius's counterattack caused the remaining Persian forces to flee. The following year, Chosroes declined to fight Heraclius as the Byzantines moved through Armenia into Media and captured Tauris (modern Tabriz). Heraclius invaded the Sassanian heartland between 624 and 625, advancing as far as Esfahan and forcing Chosroes to recall some of his army from Chalcedon. The Persians continued to get the worst of this war of maneuver, steadily losing territory in Asia Minor and Mesopotamia. To salvage his situation, Chosroes made an alliance with the Avars, a nomadic people who had migrated from Asia into eastern Europe in the preceding century, and put in motion plans for an all-out effort to capture Constantinople.

The Persians and their Avar allies were ready to attack the Byzantine capital by the summer of 626. The siege began with the Avars attacking the city walls from the European side, but the Sassanian allies' catapults were unable to create a breach. Most of the Persian force, now under Shahr-Baraz, attempted to cross the Bosporus on rafts, but this makeshift flotilla was surrounded by Byzantine ships and destroyed. Repeatedly repulsed and short of supplies, the Avars withdrew. The Sassanians, who never made a landing in Europe, also abandoned the siege. During the next two years, the Byzantines repeatedly defeated Persian armies in Mesopotamia under the command of the Sassanian general Shahin. After falling into a depressed state of mind over his defeats, Shahin died. An angry and frustrated Chosroes scourged his dead general's body, an act that stirred concern at court about the aging monarch's sanity. Meanwhile, Shahr-Baraz had become isolated at Chalcedon. Hearing that Chosroes planned to have him executed, the Persian general surrendered to the Greeks. With the two most experienced Persian generals gone, Heraclius began a march against the palace of the Great King at Dastagird.

The Persian army, now under the command of Razates, avoided combat, probably hoping the Greek move across Anatolia would wear down the soldiers and overextend their lines. An impatient Chosroes, however, ordered his general to fight. In December 627, Razates inauspiciously attacked smaller Greek forces under Heraclius near Gaugamela. The bloody daylong battle between the armies was a draw that ended when Razates challenged Heraclius to single combat, which the Byzantine emperor won. Without their general, the Persian army evaporated. The Byzantines continued their march and burned the palace at Dastagird. Lacking an adequate siege train, Heraclius decided not to assault Ctesiphon and instead offered terms to end the war. After Chosroes rejected the Greek offer, his court flung him into prison. His son and successor Kavadh II killed Chosroes there in 628. The new emperor, who reigned for only a year, signed a peace treaty that surrendered all of the conquered territories and returned the True Cross and other relics to the Byzantines. Worn out by war, decades of misrule, and dynastic competition for the throne that resulted in four rulers in as many years, the Sassanian Empire was exhausted and exceedingly vulnerable to the Islamic armies then erupting from the south.

The Arab Conquest of Persia

For centuries the Persians had not feared anything more than raids from the relatively primitive and sparsely populated desert vastness of Arabia. At the time of the first Muslim invasion, the Sassanians were dealing with rebellious provinces and recovering from the debilitating wars with Byzantium. Although the Persian army still had substantial forces, it was not prepared for the Arab tribes' new unity under Islam. It may have regarded the initial Muslim advance in 633 as another large Bedouin raid because, after occupying Hira, the Arabs left, marching to Palestine to aid the Muslim armies battling the Byzantines there. The Persians then inflicted a minor defeat on a mounted Muslim force at the Battle of the Bridge near Hira in late 634. Yazdegird III (r. 632–51), the grandson of Chosroes II, assembled an imperial army of fifty thousand to sixty thousand men that in 637 met a returning army of roughly thirty thousand Muslim warriors at the Battle of al-Qadisiya.

After the Sassanians failed to draw the Arabs across the Euphrates for battle on favorable ground, Yazdegird ordered his army to cross the river to attack the Muslim forces assembled on the open plain of Qadisiya to the west of Hira. Despite using war elephants to intimidate the Arab horsemen, the Persians failed to break the Muslim line. Inconclusive fighting raged for two more days until, as night fell on the third day amid a sudden sandstorm, a Muslim assault breached the center of the Persian line and killed the Sassanian commander. Some Persian units escaped intact, but most of Yazdegird's soldiers scattered through the night or drowned while trying to swim the Euphrates. Yazdegird was too young and inexperienced to salvage the situation and left the field with his soldiers. The last Sassanian King of Kings then fled into the Iranian heartland for the final, anti-climactic battles of his reign.

The armies of the Muslim conquest steadily improved during this period, possibly from an influx of Persian commanders and troops. Allegedly, after Qadisiya many Persian soldiers, including some four thousand troops of the Imperial Guard, joined the Muslim army. A large group of cavalry abandoned the Sassanian army, became Muslims, settled in Al Basrah, and became clients of an Arab tribe there. All these soldiers probably had converted to Islam primarily to be on the winning side or to escape paying the head tax imposed on non-Muslims. In time, the former Sassanian commanders and fighters came to dominate the Muslim army of conquest and contributed to the "Persianization" of Central Asia as they spread their language and culture under the banner of Islam. The first Arab Muslim dynasty, the Umayyads in Damascus, were overthrown in 750 by the Abbasid dynasty, which was based in Mesopotamia but drew most of its military strength from the Khorasan region in eastern Persia. After years of intermarriage the Arab Abbasids were barely distinguishable from indigenous Persians and were initially led by a Persian general called Abu Muslim. In all, the Persians proved to be the Arabs' most difficult adversary during the Muslim Conquests, and they eventually carved out a separate Islamic identity for themselves and a variety of dynastic principalities that were politically and culturally autonomous.

The Tragedies of Medieval Persia

Starting in the ninth century, the Persians broke away from the Arabs and re-established their independence in a series of national and regional governments. The main dynasty, the Tahirids, started as Abbasid governors but broke away and came to control most of Persia and parts of Transoxiana (the area around Bukhara, Uzbekistan, to the west of Samarkand). Over time various regions rebelled and created overlapping local dynasties, many of which relied on Turkish slaves as troops for their military forces. By the late tenth century, most of these governments had fallen under the dominion of encroaching Turkic dynasties, but were heavily Persianized. It was during the tenth century that Ferdowsi, Iran's most famous poet, wrote the *Shahnameh*, which has been an important font of Iranian culture and pride over the centuries. The poem covers Iran's history from the genesis of the Iranians and their first mythic kings through the

Achaemenids to the Sassanians' defeat at the hands of the Arab Muslims. According to Sandra Mackey, the poem helped to resurrect the Iranian identity within the world of Islam by celebrating the history and mythology of Persian kingship. As a long hymn to honor, valor, wisdom, and patriotism, it holds a range of images—heroism, justice, national glory, and tragic defeat—that Iranians continue to hold essential to their culture and identity.[23]

The Seljuk Turks were the next group to control Iran, expanding their control over the Abbasid caliphate to the Iranian Plateau in the eleventh century. The Turks' mastery of the military art during this period overshadowed any contributions made by their Persian subjects. During this time, however, a small offshoot of the Ismaili creed of Shia Islam opposed Seljuk rule with a campaign of political warfare that involved the murder of Seljuk officials and other political opponents. Based in Dailam, in the Alborz Mountains between the modern cities of Rasht and Tehran, these Persian zealots became known by their Arabic name, *Hashashiyyun*, which referred to the belief that the group smoked hashish before committing their crimes. This name was later borrowed by Europeans, which in usage became "Assassins." The Dailam sect spread its influence into other parts of the Middle East, which it retained for centuries. By the beginning of the thirteenth century, another group of Turks from Khwarezm, the region along the Amu Darya in modern Turkmenistan, captured central Persia and Mesopotamia, briefly reestablishing a powerful but ill-fated Persian-influenced empire that extended from Baghdad to India.[24]

The thirteenth and fourteenth centuries were catastrophic for Persia as a series of Mongol invasions devastated and depopulated the Iranian Plateau. The Khwarezm ruler Muhammad Shah (r. 1206–21) invited his destruction by mistreating Mongol merchants and diplomats and intentionally insulting Genghis Khan, who had established a new Mongol kingdom at the turn of the thirteenth century. To answer these indignities, Genghis declared war and dispatched four armies with a total strength of two hundred thousand warriors against Muhammad in 1219. The opponents were both bow-armed cavalry forces and used similar tactics, but the Mongols' discipline and coordination were superior. In addition, Genghis had thousands of Chinese siege engineers, who enabled his armies to build and use battering rams, catapults, and other war machines.[25]

The Mongols proved unstoppable, spreading devastation wherever they went. In 1220, the Mongols plundered Bukhara and then sacked Samarkand and brutally massacred its citizens. The Mongols pursued Muhammad Shah through the Persian heartland to Qazvin and Hamadan and back through Tabriz to the Caspian coast, where the Khwarezm king died in 1222. The Persians occasionally resisted the Mongol conquerors, but the outcomes were usually horrific. At Nishapur (modern Neyshabur), the citizens revolted and killed one of Genghis's sons-in-law. The Mongols sacked Nishapur and, to terrorize other Persian cities, they allegedly killed every living person and animal there, stacking the skulls of men, women, and children into three separate pyramids. Esfahan, which was surrounded by extensive fortifications and had organized military units, resisted the Mongols for more than a decade before finally succumbing in 1236. During the war, the Mongols destroyed the centuries-old *qanat* underground tunnel irrigation system that had helped Persian agriculture prosper. The result was that the Mongols left behind expanding deserts and numerous isolated oasis cities. Overall, the Mongol violence and depredations killed up to three-fourths of the population of the Iranian Plateau, possibly ten to fifteen million people. Some historians have estimated that Iran's population did not again reach its pre-Mongol levels until the mid-twentieth century.[26]

Genghis's grandson, Hulagu, invaded Persia in midcentury, destroying the power of the Assassins in Dailam and then sacking Baghdad in 1258. After failing to conquer Egypt, Hulagu returned to Persia to live and rule. Like previous conquerors, he was soon captured by Persian culture and adopted Islam. Persia's agony from Mongol invaders was not over, however, as the great conqueror Tamerlane swept south from Central Asia in 1381 and overran the country. Although his initial campaigns were ruthless, and he massacred the Persians indiscriminately, Tamerlane was at his worst when punishing rebellious regions. He leveled Shiraz after a revolt and is alleged to have razed Esfahan and killed more than seventy thousand people, stacking their skulls into a pyramid, to suppress a rebellion there. The steppe warrior king saw the value of the remaining vestiges of the earlier Persian empires, and Tamerlane integrated Persians into administrative roles to help him govern his new empire. Following Tamerlane's death in 1405, his empire crumbled, and several Mongol and Turkish tribes laid claim to various parts of the region until a new dynasty revived Persia's fortunes.

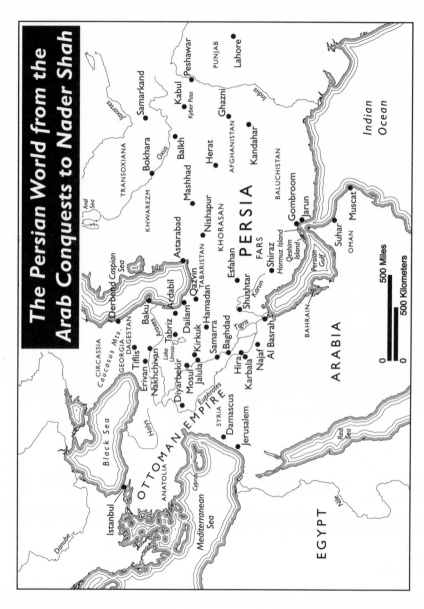

2.1 The Persian World from the Arab Conquests to Nader Shah.

2

Powerful Predecessors

The Safavids and Nader Shah

IN THE PERIOD BETWEEN TAMERLANE and the late eighteenth century, Iran was home to one more great empire and to the last great Asian conqueror. The Safavid dynasty (1501–1760), which made Persia once again a center of high civilization and wealth, joined Persian culture to the creed of Shia Islam, which has ever since defined and inspired Iran as a nation. The Safavids built the first Persian army to incorporate gunpowder weapons and set the stage for increased interaction with the West and the Persian military's conquests under Nader Shah. The wars of the Safavids and Nader Shah demonstrated again how Iran's military fortunes and traditions have been shaped by the interplay of politics and religion. In addition, the repeated problems with adopting and adapting to new means of warfare hindered the Safavids, but were eventually overcome by Nader Shah. The armed forces developed during this period were strongly shaped by the ongoing dilemma over building effective forces that were loyal to the crown, but not so strong that praetorianism or military coups threatened the monarchs' power.

Islam and Iran

A brief review of Islam's development is necessary to understand Iran's military history since the sixteenth century. The split between Sunni and Shia Islam began as a dispute within the early Muslim community over who should succeed the Prophet Muhammad as temporal and spiritual leader following his death in 632. Those Muslims who would later be called Sunnis believed that the Prophet did not designate a successor, or caliph, and that it was up to the community of believers to select their leader based on his integrity, honesty, and righteousness. Other Muslims, however, believed that the Prophet wanted his successors to come from his household's bloodline. This group favored Ali, Muhammad's son-in-law and cousin, as the rightful heir and leader. They became know as partisans of Ali, *Shi'at Ali* in Arabic or, more simply, Shia. The Shia believe that the succession process was thwarted when the first three caliphs were chosen ahead of Ali. Then, shortly after becoming the fourth caliph in 661, Ali was murdered. Hussein, Ali's surviving son by Fatima, the daughter of the Prophet, made no immediate claim to the position, but when the fifth caliph, Mu'awiyah, died in 680, Hussein asserted his right to lead the Muslims. In one of the key events in Shia history, Yazid, Mu'awiyah's son and the founder of the Umayyid dynasty, attacked Hussein and a small band of followers near Karbala in southern Iraq. Hussein and perhaps two hundred men and women followers were overwhelmed by Yazid's army of four thousand fighters, and Hussein was killed and decapitated. His martyrdom and the mythology of fighting in doomed causes became central to Shia theology.[1]

Most Persians today are Twelver Shia, the mainstream Shia denomination that follows the line of five imams descended from Musa, the son of the sixth imam, Jafar. (Some Shia, called Fivers, do not accept Jafar and his line, while others, called Ismailis, follow the line of Jafar's other son, Ismail.) In 874, the eleventh imam, Hasan, died and was buried in Samarra in northern Iraq without having a clear successor. A few years later, the Shia who would become Twelvers faced a potential collapse of their sect because of its uncertain leadership. Their solution was to announce that Hasan had a son, Muhammad, who had succeeded his father but had gone into occultation, or supernatural hiding, to avoid being murdered by the Sunni caliph. This Twelfth, or Hidden, Imam, like the other eleven imams, is considered infallible and is believed to influence the affairs of the world from his concealed location. His promised return and prophesied role in the ultimate victory of good over evil is a central tenet of the Twelver Shia faith. The occultation of Muhammad led to the evolution of the practice among the Twelver Shia of relying on the leadership of learned men to serve as sources of emulation, interpreters of the Koran, and, in some cases, as the representatives of the Hidden Imam on earth. Twelver beliefs grew most strongly among the pastoral nomadic peoples of eastern Anatolia, Syria, and northwestern Iran. In the latter region, the Sunni Sufi (or mystic) order of the Turkman Safavids grew strong in reaction to the Mongol depredation of Muslim lands and, over time, adopted Twelver Shia beliefs to take advantage of the creed's appeal to the oppressed masses. This merger of beliefs, along with the admixture of Persian blood from intermarriage, helped the Safavids gain a large number of dedicated adherents in the region. By the late fifteenth century, the Safavids were ready to advance their faith by military means under their new leader, Ismail, who claimed to be the Hidden Imam's representative.

The Safavid Dynasty

The Safavids established the first independent Persian state in nearly nine centuries. Although based on Turkman tribes, the Safavids attracted Persian,

Syrian, Turkish, and other adherents during the fifteenth century and, after the dynasty was established, adopted Persian culture to become increasingly Persian in nature. As Shia, the Safavids rejected the authority of the caliphate, which was then in the hands of the Sunni Ottomans, and the two groups would be in nearly constant conflict for more than two centuries because of their religious differences and imperial ambitions. Toward the end of the fifteenth century as they were becoming a significant power, the Safavids began to wear distinctive scarlet headgear. The Ottomans derisively called them *qizilbash* or redheads, a name the Safavids adopted as a mark of pride for the disciples of their tribal leader.

The march to empire began in earnest in 1500 when Ismail, who had become the Safavid leader in 1494, set out to conquer territories and establish a divine Shia kingdom on earth. By early 1501, Ismail had defeated the army of the ruler of Azerbaijan, seized Tabriz, and made the city his capital. In short order, the Safavids conquered the rest of Azerbaijan and then Armenia. Declared shah in 1502, Ismail I (r. 1502–24) became the monarch of a theocratic state that harnessed the dynamic theology of its Twelver Shiism official religion. The new shah would take most of the next decade to consolidate his control over Iran, where most of the Persian population was still Sunni. His army spread out first to the central regions in 1504. He then pacified the western frontier and captured Baghdad and southwestern Iran between 1505 and 1508 before finally conquering the Khorasan region and the city of Herat in 1510. Ismail made Shia Islam mandatory for the whole nation and forced the conversion of the local populations while Sunni clerics were either killed or exiled.[2]

The army Ismail commanded at the start of his campaign of conquest was the prototype for later Safavid military forces. A tribal confederation in which subordinate units were composed of warriors from Turkman, Kurdish, and other tribes, its cavalrymen were armed with sabers, lances, and bows and manned the main battalions. The Safavids had only a few firearms, and none were fully adopted into the army as an organized force because the Qizilbash chiefs considered their use unmanly and cowardly. Although the Ottomans had used cannon and harquebuses for decades in attacks on the Safavids, the zealous Qizilbash may have seen little value in these unwieldy weapons. Cannon of the day were simply iron tubes so heavy that they were suitable only for siege operations or to defend fortifications. A harquebus, meanwhile, was merely a "hand cannon" with a wooden butt end held by the soldier, who needed a forked stick or some other object on which to rest the heavy barrel before firing. A "professional" corps of units loyal solely to Ismail was recruited from the Qizilbash tribes. During Ismail's conquest of the lands that make up modern Iran, other diverse elements, such as Persians, Azeris, and Kurds from the conquered territories, joined the Safavid army. The Safavids lacked a navy and had no choice but to accept the initial European intrusion into their territory in 1507 when the

Portuguese captured Hormuz Island in the southern Persian Gulf and turned it into a naval base and trading outpost.[3]

The early Safavid state had a predominantly military character. Ismail's Qizilbash commanders were given provinces to rule and demanded and obtained the highest offices in the state, including the two top military posts, the *amir al-umara*, or commander in chief of the army, and the *qurchibashi*, or commander of the Qizilbash tribal regiments. In addition to setting the tone for governance and establishing themselves as a military elite, the Turkman Qizilbash created a major division within Shah Ismail's new state. The Qizilbash disdained Persian traditions and did not mix freely with the Persians. They were "men of the sword" and found it dishonorable to be commanded by Persians. The Turkman chiefs derisively and short-sightedly viewed the Persians as being fit only to fill the ranks of the bureaucracy, which the Persians promptly did to their overall advantage. As early as 1507 Ismail became apprehensive about the power of his Qizilbash chiefs, and he soon appointed a Persian to the office of vakil, the highest administrative post in the state.

The Sunni Ottomans saw the establishment of a new state with a militantly Shia ideology on its eastern frontier as a grave challenge. The Ottoman sultan, Bayezid II, initially congratulated Shah Ismail on his victories but advised the young monarch to stop destroying the graves and mosques of Sunni Muslims. Ismail, who was convinced of the righteousness of his cause and was strongly anti-Sunni, ignored the sultan's warning and continued to spread the Shia faith by the sword. In turn, the Ottomans became greatly concerned about subversion among the Shia Turkman tribes inside Ottoman domains. When Bayezid's son, Selim, seized the Ottoman throne in 1513 after four years of civil war against his father and brothers, the new sultan took out his wrath over Safavid support of his siblings on the Turkman tribes in the Ottomans' eastern domains. Selim was a devout Sunni who hated the Shia as much as Ismail despised the Sunni. He saw the Shia Turkman of Anatolia as a potential "fifth column" and deported them to Ottoman lands in Europe in 1514, killing up to forty thousand in the process of securing what would become the rear area of his invasion of Safavid Iran.[4]

In late summer of 1514, Safavid forces in Azerbaijan were confronted by a large Ottoman army gathered by Selim. Using scorched-earth tactics to complicate the enemy's advance, Ismail withdrew his forces to the Plain of Chaldiran (near modern Khoy). Ignoring advice to conduct an immediate attack, Ismail waited while the Ottomans formed a defensive barrier with gun carriages linked together by chains behind which janissaries armed with muskets took up fighting positions. Ismail's initial cavalry attack breached the enemy's left flank, but the Safavid horsemen could not roll up Selim's center. As the Ottoman janissaries, backed by cannon and mortars, held fast, the Ottoman right swung around onto the Safavid flank. Ismail's army broke and began a retreat to Tabriz, resorting again to scorched-earth tactics to slow the Ottomans. Although failing to stop Selim from capturing the Safavid capital, Ismail had salvaged his situation by increasing the strain on Selim's supply lines. Ottoman troops soon mutinied over the prospect of wintering in Tabriz when the surrounding countryside had been stripped of the resources they needed to survive, and Selim withdrew.

The Safavid defeat at Chaldiran was almost exclusively a result of their inability to counter Ottoman firepower. Ismail appears to have learned his lesson and began to add artillery and harquebuses to his army by 1516. The loss to the Ottomans, however, undermined Ismail's reputation as being divine and hurt his relations with the Qizilbash chiefs, who began to behave more like feudal barons than loyal lieutenants. Chastened by the defeat, Ismail became inattentive to the nonmilitary affairs of state and acceded to his Persian vakils' handling of day-to-day administration in ways that deepened divisions among the empire's Turkic and Persian elite. In 1523, the Qizilbash assassinated one overreaching vakil, and, when Ismail died the following year, an era of sporadic civil war and wars against opportunistic neighbors began.

Ismail's heir, Tahmasp (r. 1524–76), came to the throne as a ten-year-old under a regency, and fortunately for the dynasty, he grew to be a good and brave leader. He continued to face problems from disaffected Qizilbash chiefs, but held the state together with the army's assistance against the neighboring Ozbegs or Uzbeks in the east and the Ottomans encroaching from the west. Tahmasp's army was mostly unchanged from his father's time, but the number of handguns, muskets, and harquebuses among the forces was increasing. Cannons were slowly added to the army despite their relative immobility. In 1569, the shah received an envoy sent by Ivan the Terrible of Russia to seek an alliance against the Ottomans. The envoy brought thirty cannons and four thousand muskets along with five hundred musketeers to instruct and drill Safavid soldiers in marksmanship. Tahmasp continued the practice of using scorched-earth tactics in front of invading Turkish forces. The new Safavid shah also relied on allied Kurdish and other frontier tribal forces to harass Ottoman lines of communication and rear areas.

The shah made another important adaptation to deal with the Qizilbash's continued restiveness by introducing Georgian, Circassian, and other slaves into the army. Military slavery in the Islamic world was fairly common at the time as a means to contain the decentralizing tendencies of tribal forces and to consolidate royal authority. The process began with the enslavement of non-Muslims, their conversion to Islam, and then their emancipation, although they remained in the service of their master. In Safavid Iran, the newly converted slaves were trained and appointed to occupy key military and administrative posts to supplant the Qizilbash elite and increase the professionalization of these functions.[5]

Under Tahmasp, the Safavids held off three major Ottoman invasions ordered by Selim's son, Suleiman the Magnificent. During the first of Suleiman's invasions, the Safavids initially were successful in holding the northwestern highlands and blocking the Turkish advance from Armenia. Tahmasp eventually had to withdraw in the face of superior Ottoman forces, and Suleiman captured Tabriz, Hamadan, and Baghdad, although Persian and Kurdish tribal forces inflicted heavy losses on the Ottomans. Sporadic fighting continued through 1538 as Suleiman pursued Tahmasp in a vain effort to bring him to battle. Suleiman's subsequent invasions in 1548 and 1552 differed only in the involvement of dissident Safavid forces under the shah's brother, Alqas Mirza, during the second incursion. When the Ottomans withdrew as before, Suleiman detached the disloyal brother and his rebel fighters to draw away Qizilbash troops that were harrying his retreat. Alqas Mirza marched into central Iran but was soon captured after failing to win support for his rebellion. The third war was as costly and ultimately indecisive as the first two, and, when a Safavid patrol captured one of the Sultan's intimate companions, the Ottoman leader was ready to enter into serious peace negotiations.

The Treaty of Amasia, signed in 1555, promised thirty years of peace between these Sunni and Shia rivals but did not end tensions. Because Tabriz was so vulnerable, the Safavid shah moved his capital to Qazvin in central Iran and devoted the remaining years of his reign to consolidating the empire and his authority. Tahmasp failed spectacularly, however, in preparing for succession. For more than a decade after his death in 1576, Iran was roiled by internal problems and factional fighting among the Qizilbash elite. Throughout this period of unrest the Ottomans and Uzbeks inflicted repeated defeats on Safavid military forces along the frontiers. The Ottomans occupied Tabriz in 1585, and after the Uzbeks invaded Khorasan in 1587, the Qizilbash factions finally settled on a consensus candidate for shah, Tahmasp's grandson Abbas.

Abbas the Great

Shah Abbas I (r. 1587–1629) began his reign at age six, staying on the throne for more than forty years. His need to assert authority against the Qizilbash chiefs caused him to make concessions to the Ottomans to buy the peace and time he needed to break with the Safavids' tribal and messianic past. To avoid the problems that had crippled the empire in the preceding decades, Abbas worked to neutralize the decentralizing tendencies of tribal loyalties and ambitions and built an army loyal to the crown by fully institutionalizing military and domestic slavery. In time, Abbas would eliminate the Uzbek threat from the east, expel the Ottomans, and reclaim the boundaries of Sassanian Persia. Abbas restored Persian military prestige so much that, according to an Ottoman officer, "Those conceited heroes who in the coffee-houses have mocked at the qizilbash for their cowardice, now when they behold the most insignificant of them three miles away on the road, compare him with Rustam, the son of Zal."[6] (Rustam, the hero of the *Shahnameh*, is the Persian equivalent of the West's Achilles or Hercules.) Abbas reformed the economy while exploiting Iran's position on continental trading routes to generate the national wealth needed to support a royal army and his ambitions.[7]

Abbas's primary solution to the latent threat of insurrection was to expand and rely on the institution of slavery, where master and slave had a moral obligation to be loyal to and trust each other. Despite their title of *ghulam* (slave or crown servant), these Georgians, Armenians, and Circassians were freed and converted Muslims. Under Abbas, many of the *ghulams* entered the royal household as adopted brothers and sons and were educated and groomed for positions within the army and the bureaucracy. Abbas relied on them heavily, and, by the mid-seventeenth century, the *ghulams* held all key positions in the military and financial structure of the empire. Because the *ghulams* were more trusted, they were given control of the newly acquired firearms as the shah's musketeers, non-tribal cavalry, and artillery. Abbas even gave command of his armed forces during one period to a Georgian *ghulam* who liberated Khorasan from the Uzbeks and Bahrain from the Portuguese.[8]

Two English adventurers, Sir Anthony and Robert Sherley, assisted Abbas's reorganization of the Persian army. The two Englishmen were part of a mission sent to Iran in 1598 to get Abbas to ally with the Christian nations of Europe against the Ottomans. Robert Sherley helped to organize the expanded artillery force and created the first standing musket-armed infantry units. These Safavid formations were established along European lines, a model the Ottomans had already adopted, and were given European-style training. The Sherley brothers had been accompanied by a party of cannon founders, who helped transfer European artillery production skills to the Safavids. Other gunpowder weapons for the army had to be imported, however, because the Persians lacked the ability to mass produce muskets and firearms. At roughly the same time, the English East India Company arrived to provide Abbas new trade routes to Europe that avoided Ottoman interference and duties. In addition to improving Abbas's economic position, the English naval presence in the Persian Gulf provided a potential ally against Persia's enemies in that area.

Abbas's military career began auspiciously with victories against the Uzbeks in 1598 in a campaign that preceded the reorganization and modernization of the Safavid army. The Uzbek army relied on tribal cavalry best suited to raiding and, once confronted, retreated into their steppe homelands in Afghanistan and Central Asia to wait until the Safavids were forced to retire by the cost of keeping an army in the field. After chasing the main Uzbek force into the well-fortified city of Herat, Abbas pretended to withdraw to lure them out from behind the city's walls. The trap worked, and at a key moment in the fight Abbas led a charge that wounded the Uzbek commander and caused a general Uzbek retreat. The Safavid pursuit destroyed nearly a third of the Uzbek force, and the victory resulted in the capture of Herat. Abbas then stabilized his eastern frontier with alliances with the local Uzbek chiefs, enabling him to switch his attention to his western and Persian Gulf borders.

The shah recognized that the Ottomans were vulnerable to a military challenge because military revolts, internal unrest, and the sultan's weakening authority distracted the Ottomans. Starting in 1603, Abbas easily defeated local Ottoman units occupying the region around Tabriz and then advanced north into the Caucasus, pushing Ottoman forces back to well-stocked fortifications at Erivan (or Yerevan, the capital of modern Armenia) and throughout eastern Anatolia. Abbas besieged the frontier area through early 1604, but none of the forts in the region capitulated. It took the Ottomans until 1606 to marshal the forces to try to win back the territory taken by Abbas. At the Battle of Sis, near Lake Urmia, Abbas and an estimated sixty-two thousand troops drew up defensive lines to stop as many as one hundred thousand Ottomans under Sultan Ahmed. During the initial skirmishes, the Ottomans apparently mistook a cavalry raid as the main Persian attack and tried to reorient their forces toward this foray. Seeing his opportunity, Abbas struck the Ottoman line hard with his disciplined infantry, cavalry, and artillery and routed the disorganized combatants. After a vigorous counteroffensive, Abbas by 1607 had expelled the last Ottoman soldier from Persian territory as defined by the 1555 Treaty of Amasia. Although a new treaty was negotiated, continuing border incidents frustrated efforts to conclude a peace. A series of invasions and counteroffensives followed between 1616 and 1626, resulting in steady Safavid expansion as Georgia, Baghdad, and parts of Iraq were captured. After surrendering territory to the Ottomans at the beginning of his reign, Abbas convinced them to look no longer for easy conquests in Safavid dominions.

Abbas removed a third enemy from Persian lands during his reign, although he relied on the help of Arabs and Europeans to eject these occupiers. Before going after the Ottomans in 1603, Abbas decided to recapture the island of Bahrain from the Portuguese. When the Portuguese became a major naval power and began their voyages of exploration to Asia, they soon arrived off the island of Hormuz in the Persian Gulf and saw its strategic importance to their trading interests in India. In 1507, a Portuguese fleet captured Hormuz and temporarily made its twelve-year-old potentate a vassal of Lisbon. After a brief departure, the Portuguese returned in 1515 and again occupied the island. Shah Ismail, lacking a navy and bogged down in constant warfare with the Ottomans, had no choice but to accept the occupation. The Portuguese settled in and soon thereafter captured Bahrain, keeping it for the next eighty years. They also occupied and fortified a coastal strip of the Persian mainland opposite Hormuz, including the port of Jarun, near the site of modern Iran's largest port, Bandar Abbas.

Recovering Bahrain was a daunting task because in 1602 the Safavids still had not developed a navy. The Safavid solution was to recruit Arab vassals in southern Iran to provide experienced sailors and ships from their small fleets of fishing boats and merchant vessels. Details are sparse, but musketeers and cavalrymen embarked on the ships and landed on the island, dislodging the Portuguese troops there. Over the course of several years Shah Abbas sought to improve his position against the Portuguese, and by 1614 the Safavid army had recaptured the port of Jarun and had landed troops on Qeshm Island, just to the west of Hormuz, which cut off the Portuguese outpost's main source of fresh water. The Safavids then gained the cooperation of English naval units in the Gulf. Over the subsequent eight years, Abbas, with English help, continued to weaken the Portuguese with a series of naval and land battles. In 1622 an English flotilla supported the landing of Safavid troops on Hormuz. Once ashore, the Safavid forces dug trenches and pushed forward breastworks to begin mining operations to destroy the walls of the Portuguese fort. Isolated and facing inevitable defeat, the Portuguese surrendered to the English, although the Safavids controlled the island and captured several large cannon and siege guns.

The Safavid Decline

When Shah Abbas died in 1629, the Safavid state started to decay. Recent scholarship suggests that earlier attributions of Safavid decline to the rise of European maritime trade, less commercial activity along the Silk Road and other trade routes in Persia, and an outflow of wealth were overdrawn. Instead, with no serious external enemies, the Safavid rulers paid less attention to governance, and the resultant neglect left the dynasty less able to deal with problems from drought, lower agricultural productivity, disease, internal dissent, and nomadic raiders. The succession of bad leaders began with Abbas's successor, Safi I (r. 1629–42), who killed potential rivals to his throne as well as most of the generals, officers, and councilors he inherited from his father. In the wake of this cruelty, court politics became even more intense and selfish as the Qizilbash actively tried to regain their power and influence. Nearly all of the later Safavid shahs had numerous shortcomings, including a disruptive religious zeal by one and addictions to drink, drugs, and general profligacy among the others. As each year passed, Persia's tribes and neighbors challenged the Safavids, and the prestige and authority of the central state weakened with each setback.[9]

Through the end of the seventeenth century the Uzbeks and the Mughals from India encroached on and captured Safavid territory and cities in the east.

In 1664 the Russian czar Alexis sent Cossacks on a raid deep into Iran, where they caused considerable damage before withdrawing. The Afghans began to push into the empire in the early eighteenth century, meeting little resistance from Safavid forces, which were undermined by dissension between the Turkman and Persian levies. Sensing the Safavids' weakness, the Afghans occupied Khorasan in 1717. When Shah Sultan Hussein (r. 1694–1722) tried to convert his Afghan subjects in eastern Iran from Sunni to Shia Islam, one Afghan chief rebelled and pushed the Safavid army out of Kandahar and most of Afghanistan. In 1722, the chief's son, Mahmud, went to war with the Safavids, marching west to besiege and capture Esfahan, the Safavid capital since 1598.

The Safavids made a stand outside the city with an army made up of royal guard troops, Persian cavalry, and tribal cavalry provided by Lurs and Arabs of the southwest. The army's overall capabilities were mixed, but it had a battalion of twenty-four cannon whose commander was assisted by a French mercenary. With his major commanders divided over tactics, Sultan Hussein decided to attack the advancing Afghan army near the town of Golnabad. After the two armies formed up on the battlefield, the impatient Safavid royal guard and Arab cavalry on the right flank launched an attack that briefly threatened to get behind the Afghan line. The commander of the Safavid center, however, held his troops fast, unwilling to engage the enemy. This inaction might not have been fatal if the Arabs had continued to push into the Afghan rear, but the tribal horsemen left the fight to loot their adversary's camp. When the Lur tribal cavalry on the left moved forward, it was drawn into a crossfire volley of one hundred small Afghan cannon called *zanburak*, or "Little Wasp," which were carried by camels and fired from the kneeling animal's back. The Afghans then charged the Lurs and swept them from the battlefield, continuing on to overrun the Safavid artillery. With the Safavid center still immobile, Mahmud had the rest of his army move to the Afghan left to surround and destroy the royal guard. As the surviving guardsmen tried to escape, the rest of the army began its retreat to Esfahan. During the subsequent six-month siege of the city, nearly one hundred thousand citizens died of starvation and illness before Esfahan finally fell. Mahmud ravaged the capital and killed many of the remaining Persian nobility, after which he claimed the title of shah.[10]

During the same year, the Russians returned as Peter the Great sent one hundred thousand men along the Caspian coast into the Gilan region. The Safavids offered no opposition, but the Russians were forced to retire because of supply shortages, losses to the extreme heat, and concern about the hostility shown by the Ottoman government to the incursion. Two years later, the Ottomans and Russians agreed to partition Iran's northwest provinces in the 1724 Treaty of Constantinople, and Russian military units soon repeated their march into the Caspian region. Safavid power continued to decline as the Ottomans and

Afghans conducted further encroachments. The dynasty's institutions and its prestige were so strong that they lingered on in growing states of decrepitude. From the ruins, however, a new monarch ascended to lead the Persians, Turkmans, and their fellow warriors from the region on new wars of conquest.

Nader Shah, the Persian Napoleon

Nader Shah, a former *ghulam*, seized effective control of the empire under the last Safavid shah before claiming the throne for himself in 1736. The future conqueror started out as Nader Khan, an able leader from the Turkman Afshar tribe in northern Khorasan. He had initially fought with the Afghans against the Uzbeks, but after Esfahan fell Nader split from the Afghan army and offered his services to the Safavids in 1727. He assembled an army and began the reconsolidation of the country, displaying the military genius that led some historians to refer to him as the Napoleon of Persia or the Second Alexander. After successfully expelling the Afghans from Safavid domains in 1729, Nader was the true ruler, although he acknowledged Sultan Hussein's weak son, Tahmasp II (r. 1722–32), as the Safavid shah. In 1730, Nader decisively defeated the Ottomans at the Battle of Hamadan, which he followed up with a swift occupation of southern Iraq and Azerbaijan. While Nader was quelling a revolt in Khorasan in 1732, Tahmasp led part of the Safavid army against the Ottomans and was soundly beaten. The young shah made an unfavorable peace treaty that surrendered Georgia, Armenia, and Nader's gains in the west from two years earlier. Enraged by the shah's actions, Nader deposed the Safavid monarch and then served as regent to Tahmasp's infant son, Abbas III, until 1736, at which time Nader declared himself shah.

Nader Shah used every religious and political ploy in his power to build up his position in Persia. He was a Sunni and proclaimed Sunnism as the religion of Iran at his coronation. He made various attempts to reconcile his Persian subjects' Shia beliefs with the Sunni creed and sought to get the Ottomans to recognize this new Persian Sunnism as its own sect. His motivation may have been to facilitate relations with the Sunni Ottomans, but possibly his real aim was to overthrow the Turks by uniting the Muslim world with him as its head. This would extend his domains to the ancient Achaemenian boundaries and would create a cohesive Muslim front better able to prevent the depredation of the rising Christian powers of Europe. Nader Shah's personal devotion was very shallow, however, which created doubts about his real intentions, especially among his rivals for Islamic leadership in the Ottoman capital of Istanbul. For the most part, Nader Shah's major motivation for conquest was to restore lost territory and protect his frontiers against avaricious neighbors. He also sought to improve Iran's economic position through plunder and to reassert Iran's control over the silk trade, which had been damaged by the Russian and Ottoman conquests during the latter stages of the Safavid decline.[11]

Nader Shah's military was administratively and organizationally a direct continuation of the Safavid establishment. Its ideology and resources had changed, however, which affected the army's composition and role. Most of his core troops were Afghans, steppe Turkman, and Khorasan Kurds who shared Nader Shah's Sunni beliefs. These Sunni fighters outnumbered the other members of Nader's military, the Shia Turkman and the ethnic Persian soldiers from central and western Iran who made up the Safavid partisans. In its later campaigns, the army swelled as various tribal forces, allies, camp followers, and freebooters joined it. The army Nader assembled in 1741 for a campaign in Dagestan in the northern Caucasus supposedly included up to one hundred and fifty thousand men, with Indians and Uzbeks joining the mix of nationalities. His 1743 campaign against the Ottomans allegedly involved a polyglot and multisectarian host of three hundred seventy-five thousand, which included Sunni Turkman, Afghans, Uzbeks, and Kurds; Shia Persians, Arabs, and Turks; Christian Armenians and Georgians; and both Sunni and Shia Indians. Nader Shah's large army became the main element of the state, and he subordinated the Persian economy, much diminished by Afghan and Ottoman occupations, to the needs of his growing military. His requirement for more and more funds probably was a factor driving him to his later military conquests, especially after increased taxation to support the army provoked rebellions.[12]

Organizationally, the army was composed primarily of cavalry recruited from pastoral nomadic tribes, who were lightly armored and armed with lances and broadswords. In a shift from past Safavid practice, Nader often supplied horses to his cavalry at his own expense, possibly to reduce the horsemen's reluctance to put their mounts at risk, especially against firearms. The rest of Nader's army was composed of a large force with gunpowder weapons that was trained to use them effectively on the battlefield. Infantry armed with matchlock muskets were recruited from the Persian peasantry. To preserve their newly developed skills, Nader enlisted these poor souls for life, with desertion punishable by death. Another force of musketeers, the *jazayerchis*, generally served on horseback as a mobile force and carried a larger musket, called a *jazayer*, which was fired dismounted from a rest. The Persian musketeers used a powder horn and ball rather than a paper cartridge, measuring the appropriate charge for the range of each target. This flexibility improved their accuracy, especially over longer ranges, although at the cost of a slower rate of fire.[13]

Nader Shah clearly believed in the decisive impact of firepower, but the region's rugged terrain and the absence of good roads, which had been allowed to deteriorate since Abbas the Great's reign, inhibited the use of heavy siege artillery. Instead, Nader had a small artillery force that employed the *zanburak*, the small cannon that could swivel around on its mount on its special camel saddle and fired a half-pound to two-pound ball. Nader's corps of musketeers and field artillery were well disciplined, if not always well trained. Lacking a skilled corps of engineers, Nader's various sieges were less successful than his battles.

Nader Shah recognized the importance of having his own navy, especially following his 1741–42 campaign in Dagestan, when he had to rely on mercilessly greedy Russian merchants for the transportation of supplies. He increased spending and initiated several major projects to build Caspian and Persian Gulf fleets to reduce his dependence on foreign shipping. He first ordered eleven ships from Surat, India, that were constructed of teak and known for their durability. After the first ship was delivered in 1741, Nader balked at the cost. The traditional source of lumber for the Gulf region, however, was India, and Nader Shah was forced to devise a new means to create his navy.

Ignoring the practical problems and costs, Nader conscripted thousands of his subjects and enemy prisoners of war to procure timber from the Alborz Mountains, some six hundred miles from the port of Bushehr, where the new ships were to be constructed. Much of the lumber was transported on the shoulders of the conscripted peasants because there was a shortage of wagons, and large numbers died of exhaustion in the effort to move Nader's shipbuilding material. A cannon foundry to provide arms for his ships was built at Gombroom (near Jarun and part of the area incorporated into the modern port of Bandar Abbas). In the end, however, the shipwrights and other laborers at Bushehr were unable to construct the type and number of ships Nader Shah wanted. He turned back to the Indian shipyards, and by 1745 his navy numbered some thirty ships. The Shah's demands for men and money for a navy increased popular grievances against him, and he eventually abandoned the effort to build a large fleet and instead sought an alliance with the British in an effort to get them to supply him ships.[14]

Nader Shah was a poor judge of naval talent and made serious mistakes in choosing his admirals and marine commanders. Years before the Dagestan campaign, Nader had selected Latif Khan to be his first admiral and to create a small naval force. In 1735 Latif sailed into the Shatt al-Arab to threaten the city of Al Basrah with a few small vessels and three *ghurabs,* or "grabs," a local type of trading ship used by Arabs on the coast. The local Ottoman commander commandeered two British ships and attacked Latif's small flotilla, which quickly retreated. In 1737 Latif provided transports to move troops to Oman to help the local ruler suppress rebels there. In the course of these operations, the Persian land commander, Muhammad Taqi Khan, poisoned Latif and took over command of the navy. Taqi Khan's poor treatment of his Arab seamen caused a mutiny that ended the Persian intervention.[15]

Over the next several years, new admirals fared little better, because they and their subordinate officers were unprofessional and generally incompetent. The Arab sailors, upon whom Nader Shah's navy relied, repeatedly mutinied, and in 1740 mutineers waged a war of coastal raids against Iran. Nader sent two admirals to end the raids, but they spent more time quarrelling over precedence and command. One eventually was imprisoned by his rival, Imamverdi Khan, a seriously unqualified officer. Khan was later killed when a cannon exploded after he ordered its powder charge doubled with the goal of increasing the weapon's range. In January 1742 Nader Shah inexplicably turned again to Muhammad Taqi Khan to be his chief admiral. Persian forces intervened in another rebellion in Oman later that year, capturing Oman's capital, Muscat, for Nader's Omani ally. After a lengthy siege and three thousand casualties, the Persian ground forces, under Kalb Ali Khan, captured the city of Suhar in July 1743, which put an end to the rebellion. With Oman pacified, Nader recalled most of his forces. For a second time, however, Muhammad Taqi Khan murdered his superior officer, killing Kalb Ali and then attempting to spark a revolt in Fars. Nader put down the revolt, but the disruption in the navy prevented him from supporting his garrisons in Oman, which were overrun and cost him the intervention's political gains.

In land warfare Nader's success rested on careful planning and preparations as much as on the capabilities of his armed forces. He effectively mobilized large forces for his campaigns and was careful to stockpile provisions to sustain his forces in the field. Nader paid attention to the morale of his army and did not rely just on the material improvements he made to its organization and administration. He ensured that his troops were regularly paid and fully equipped, which, along with the prospect of spoils from their successful wars, undoubtedly helped to keep them motivated. Nader maintained his officers' support and commitment with generous gifts of money, horses, and weapons.

Daily exercises to prepare the troops for campaigns were routine in Nader's army. In these exercises, according to a Greek observer, the cavalry practiced wheels and counterwheels, charges, retreats, and counterattacks while using real weapons. The *jazayerchis* also exercised together and even conducted target practice, expending expensive powder and balls to improve their skills. Nader sometimes joined in the exercises, demonstrating his skill with a bow on horseback and generally leading by example. Individual soldiers observed doing well by Nader and his commanders were often promoted on the spot, providing further encouragement for each soldier to do his best. In addition, the diversified ethnic composition of the army probably helped to encourage competition and improve military effectiveness. It also lessened the risk of disaffection spreading and offset the influence of the Safavid partisans. The large amount of resources and time put into building his army meant that Nader Shah could not allow it to be demobilized or allow the soldiers to return to their tribal homelands, as had been the Safavid practice.

Nader on the March

Nader's early campaigns against the Ottoman Empire revealed his skills as a political general but brought only mixed success. After Tahmasp was deposed, Nader repudiated the treaty with the Ottomans and renewed the war to reestablish Persia's frontiers and, perhaps, to test his imperial and religious rivals. Recognizing that partisan guerrilla warfare was wearing down the Russian occupiers of the Caspian region, Nader negotiated the 1732 Treaty of Rasht, in which Russia surrendered its claims to Astarabad (now called Gorgan) and the Gilan and Mazandaran regions. This freed the multinational Persian army to concentrate on the Ottomans. With a larger army than he had ever commanded before and an unbroken string of victories behind him, an overconfident Nader discounted Ottoman defensive preparations. After some initial victories, Nader plundered the region around the important Ottoman city of Kirkuk to draw out the major garrison at Baghdad and avoid a long and costly siege. The Baghdad garrison stayed behind the city's defenses, however. After leaving a small contingent to besiege Kirkuk, Nader moved south to blockade Baghdad. By February 1733 Nader completed his encirclement of the city with his own wall, but he lacked the heavy cannon needed to breach Baghdad's fortifications. His army settled in to starve out the Ottomans while concurrently sending contingents out to capture Samarra, Najaf, Karbala, and other towns as far south as Al Basrah. By early July, the Ottomans opened negotiations to surrender the city, only to stop when word reached them that a relief force under Topal Osman Pasha, regarded as the Ottomans' greatest soldier, was approaching the city.[16]

Reluctant to stop the siege when he appeared to be on the verge of victory, Nader made the difficult decision to split his force for the looming battle. He left twelve thousand men to keep up the blockade and then marched north with more than seventy thousand troops to stop Topal Osman and his army of eighty thousand. Unlike the low-grade provincial forces, militia, and tribesmen that had been opposing Nader up to that point, Topal Osman was bringing some of the best Ottoman soldiers from the main army stationed at Istanbul along with sixty cannon. In mid-July 1733, the two armies clashed in a savage back-and-forth battle near Samarra. Dense clouds of dust blowing into their lines and the lack of a nearby source of fresh water placed additional pressure on Nader's forces. As the day wore on, Nader, who was actively engaged in the fighting, was thrown from his horse. Before he could remount, wavering troops, believing that their commander had been killed, panicked and could not be stopped from retreating. With no other choice, Nader ordered a general withdrawal, leaving behind his artillery, baggage, and as many as thirty thousand dead. When news of the Ottoman victory reached Baghdad, the city's garrison sortied out and smashed the Persian detachment left to invest the city. This decisive defeat reversed all of Nader's gains in Iraq and for a time reduced his army's reputation. Nader was able to rally his remaining forces to hold off the enemy for the rest of the summer until reinforcements arrived and he could go back on the offensive.

Nader needed to defeat the Turks to remove them as a strategic threat, but also to discourage his political opponents at home and free his army to suppress increasing unrest over taxes and conscription. In his rematch with Topal Osman at Kirkuk in November, Nader maneuvered his army into position to assault an Ottoman force of twelve thousand that had been sent to attack him while he was despoiling the north. Once the two enemies were engaged, Topal Osman marched out of Kirkuk with another eighty-five thousand to ninety thousand men in support of the Ottoman column. After a strong charge by the Persian center successfully broke through the Ottoman line, a flank attack by part of Nader's cavalry threw Topal Osman's forces into disarray. In the melee, Topal Osman was killed, and the enemy fled from the field. Because he needed to attend to a revolt in Fars, Nader made an unfavorable treaty with the Ottomans in December 1733 that limited his victory to recovering only parts of Iraq. He then turned his army to suppress his restive subjects, who were an ongoing distraction for his remaining years. In the meantime, the Ottoman sultan refused to recognize the treaty and began to assemble an army around Yerevan and Tiflis (modern T'bilisi, Georgia) that he kept on the defensive.

In 1735, after learning of an impending Russian-Ottoman war in Europe, Nader sent a force to menace the Russian-held cities of Baku and Derbend on the Caspian coast. He threatened to join the sultan in the war, causing the Russians to negotiate an alliance and return the two cities to Nader. The general then wheeled west and invaded the Ottoman Empire, where he won several engagements, capturing Tiflis, Yerevan, and other fortified cities. At the Battle of Baghavand on a plain near the city of Kars in northeast Anatolia, Nader led an army of nearly fifty thousand in mid-June 1735 against an Ottoman force of fifty thousand cavalry, 30,000 janissaries, and forty cannon under Abdollah Koprulu. Nader lured the Ottomans into a trap where his *jazayerchis* were able to neutralize the enemy artillery. With the threat of Koprulu's artillery gone, five hundred or more camels were brought forward, and their *zanburaks* poured a devastating fire into the Ottoman center. After an additional push from Nader's infantry, a general Ottoman retreat began. During the pursuit, Koprulu and many of his commanders were killed along with fifty thousand Ottoman soldiers. After this decisive defeat, the Ottoman sultan, anxious to concentrate his attention on his Russian and Austrian enemies, agreed to recognize the earlier peace treaty in return for Nader's promise not to join Russia in a new war.

Between 1737 and 1738, Nader, now crowned shah, turned east with an army of eighty thousand men and invaded Afghanistan to reclaim the former Safavid provinces around Kandahar, Balkh, and the Baluchistan region. Kandahar was strongly fortified, and Nader did not have heavy siege artillery adequate to breach the city's thick mud walls. Left with no option but blockade, Nader's army built a ring of towers around Kandahar. The city had expected Nader's attack, however, and had stored ample provisions. Having arrived at Kandahar in March 1737, the shah was increasingly impatient as the new year arrived. He ordered new recruits to be brought forward and launched a series of frontal attacks that breached some of Kandahar's outer defenses. In March 1738 a force of three thousand volunteers concealed themselves in trenches and behind rocks near the city walls to launch a surprise attack. Although many were killed in the attempt to scale the walls with ladders, enough surged over the parapets to capture several towers. The Persian musketeers then defeated numerous counterattacks, and the Afghan commander retreated with the remaining defenders into the city's citadel. Nader turned his cannons on the stronghold, and after a short bombardment the Afghans agreed to submit. The Afghans were treated leniently, which helped to draw many into the Persian army as it prepared for its next conquest.

Nader appears to have decided earlier to conduct an army-sized raid to plunder India, perhaps in emulation of an expedition by Tamerlane more than three centuries earlier, and gather more wealth to maintain his armed forces. Because Mughal emperor Muhammad Shah had assisted the Afghans against the Persians, Nader had his justification to go to war. To secure its rear as it advanced south, Nader's army quickly occupied Ghazni and Kabul in eastern Afghanistan, which was part of Muhammad Shah's domains. On the approaches to the Punjab, a Mughal army of twenty thousand had taken up a strong position in the narrow Khyber Pass, where Nader's larger numbers would be neutralized. Leaving most of his army at the Khyber Pass to hold his enemy in place, Nader led ten thousand men along a route taken by Alexander the Great and moved over the nearby but more treacherous Tsatsobi Pass to get into the Mughal army's rear. Attacked from behind, the Mughals were defeated, and Nader advanced south into what is now Pakistan, seizing Peshawar and Lahore. In early 1739 Muhammed Shah marched from Delhi with a Mughal army of as many as three hundred thousand men and two thousand elephants to meet Nader's invading forces, which by then included about one hundred thousand fighters and another sixty thousand camp followers.

In the Battle of Karnal, Nader enticed part of the larger Mughal force to come out of its entrenched camp. Divided into two wings, the Indian forces moved toward the Persian center, where musketeers and the *zanburaks* found the elephants and the men in the howdahs on the beasts' backs large and attractive targets. Hearing the heavy fire from the battlefield, Muhammed Shah ordered the rest of the Mughal army forward, but the commander of this second contingent stopped at a nearby canal and refused to aid his hard-pressed compatriots. Nader, meanwhile, was in the thick of the fight, and his army gradually pushed the Indians back toward their camp. The Mughal forces suffered more than ten thousand casualties while Nader's army lost only four hundred dead and seven hundred wounded.

The Persian army then besieged the remaining Mughal forces and, after several rounds of negotiations, the Mughal ruler surrendered. Nader treated the emperor well and entered the Mughal capital of Delhi with the intention of keeping Muhammad Shah on the throne. The Indian monarch, however, was forced to pay a harsh tribute and surrender all territory north and west of the Indus River to Persia. Incensed by their ruler's capitulation to Nader's demands, the citizens of Delhi revolted. Nader repressed the uprising so brutally that the word *Nadirshahi* entered the Hindi language as a synonym for massacre. When he withdrew from Delhi, Nader took the equivalent of more than $100 million worth of precious metals, jewels, and money along with the Peacock Throne. The ornate dais, which includes the figures of two peacocks inlaid with precious gems, served as a symbol of Persian imperial might and the name of the Persian monarchy from that date forward. The collected booty and tribute were so extensive that Nader's soldiers took thousands of elephants, horses, and camels from India to carry it.

With so much treasure to protect, Nader moved his capital from Esfahan to Mashhad, closer to the area where he grew up and which he believed could be more easily defended. He did not rest from his conquests, however, especially when challenged by raiders from Central Asia. Within the year, his army attacked the Uzbeks of Transoxania and, in short order, captured Bukhara and annexed the region south of the Aral Sea. Nader suffered one of his few failures in 1741 when he was unable to suppress the Lez or Lesgians, a tribe occupying the area of modern Dagestan in southern Russia. The Lez were supported by the Ottomans and were unrelenting in defense of their land. Nader Shah's planned short punitive expedition turned into an ordeal when a serious shortage of supplies developed after the protracted campaign and the ravages of war denuded Dagestan of food and forage. With his soldiers becoming mutinous and unable to bring the rebels to a decisive battle, Nader Shah settled for a cease-fire.

Nader Shah's Last War

From 1723 to 1742 the Ottomans and Persians had engaged in a nearly continuous imperial conflict over territory, frontier security, and Nader's desire for a larger role in the Muslim world that contributed to the ongoing decline of both empires. Nader's setbacks in Dagestan had emboldened the Ottomans, who began moving troops toward the Persian frontier and sent the last in a series of rejections of Nader's proposals for a new Persian Sunni sect. In 1743 Nader again took up arms against the Ottomans and mobilized three hundred and seventy five thousand troops against them. Stockpiling provisions to sustain his army, Nader overwhelmed Iran's ability to support him and had to turn to the Turks, Kurds, and Arabs in Iraq to sell him the large number of horses, mules, and camels he needed. Probably as a result of these supply constraints, most of Nader's initial operations were relatively small. Contingents of ten thousand to fifteen thousand men raided into Iraq to open the campaign. In August Nader Shah assembled a large force, reportedly between one hundred thousand and two hundred thousand men, to march on Kirkuk. Four days of constant bombardment by Nader's artillery caused the city to surrender. Having secured this important fortress, Nader Shah then set out to attack Mosul, which sat at a key juncture on the trade routes emanating from Iran and could provide a base for offensive operations against Anatolia.[17]

When Nader Shah arrived at Mosul to begin the siege, the city posed a formidable challenge. Its population had grown to roughly one hundred thousand with the refugees fleeing the advancing Persian army, and the arrival of tens of thousands of able-bodied men swelled the ranks of the defenders. The city's walls also had been refortified, and a large ditch was dug to obstruct Nader's attacks. Still, the first fight of the battle was almost the last one when part of the Ottoman garrison sortied out to confront Nader Shah's main contingent and was nearly cut off. Left to face only the city's walls, the Persians brought up fourteen batteries of artillery with 390 large and small cannons and mortars. Upon examining the city's ramparts, Nader Shah built structures to allow his guns to bombard Mosul's twelve wall towers. The initial bombardment continued for eight days and nights, but this attack and subsequent shelling failed to rupture the walls. Nader Shah's next gambit was to tunnel under the walls and place gunpowder in position to blow up a portion of the barricades. The blast caused substantial damage but did not create an opening. Having failed to break through or go under the walls, Nader ordered thousands of ladders built to cross the ditch and then scale the ramparts. Once again, the attack failed because of strong resistance, which included the use of boiling oil to scald Nader's soldiers. After repeatedly failing to break into the city, Nader Shah offered to negotiate an end to the battle, and forty days after he began the siege the humbled monarch lifted it and shifted his operations south.

Beset by rebellions at home, Nader sought but did not obtain a suitable peace treaty from the Ottomans. With no other choice, he returned to the battlefield to try to get a decision but once again was unable to complete a siege, failing to take the city of Kars in the summer of 1744 even as he occupied most of Armenia. The

Ottomans resumed their support to the Lez, who attacked the Persian army's rear areas. Nader Shah regrouped his army during the winter, and in June 1745 the Persian army attacked Yerevan. Because of the city's strong defenses, fighting devolved into protracted trench warfare. Nader Shah gained victory only after a mutiny among the Ottoman janissaries gave him the opportunity to launch an attack that killed the enemy commander and put the Ottoman army, its morale shattered, into disarray. The great conqueror, still facing a deteriorating situation at home, did not press his advantage and instead sought a new round of peace negotiations, which resulted in a treaty that restored the Ottoman-Persian boundaries of 1640.

Popular revolts and plots by the Qizilbash and Persian elite increased Nader's suspicion and cruelty in dealing with real and imagined challenges. Ill health compounded by mental derangement contributed to his brutal response. Following an assassination attempt in 1746, Nader blinded his own son on suspicion of involvement in the plot. Nader also killed numerous nobles, commanders, and even commoners he feared might pose a threat to him. At the end, his own tribesmen came to regard their monarch as too dangerous to live. In 1747, two of his commanders decapitated Nader Shah.

His ignominious end did not detract from Nader Shah's accomplishments. Starting with virtually nothing, Nader took the degraded Safavid state and made it the foremost military power in Asia during the mid-eighteenth century. By the time of his death the empire stretched from the Caucasus Mountains in the northwest to the Indus River in the southeast. Nader's gains did not survive his passing, but without his brief rule Iran might have been partitioned by the Afghans, Ottoman Turks, and Russians, disappearing from the world map much as Poland did in the eighteenth century and dramatically changing the region's subsequent history.[18] At Nader's death, the empire immediately fell into anarchy and dissolution. Civil war was unleashed by various tribes, which put forward their own claimants to the throne. The Zands, a Lur tribe closely related to the Kurds, ended the Safavid dynasty and, under Karim Khan, a strong tribal leader from Shiraz, reestablished control over the terriority that makes up most of modern Iran. From 1750 until his death in 1779, Karim Khan ruled in relative peace and prosperity. Civil war then ravaged the land until 1794, when the Qajars, a Turkman tribe from Mazandaran that was the "last of the Qizilbash," claimed the throne and the Safavid legacy. Unfortunately for the Qajars, they inherited a state with no functioning machinery of government and no real military capability to deal effectively with the growing threats posed by the European powers of Russia and Great Britain.

3

Laughingstock

The Qajar Military

THE NINETEENTH AND EARLY TWENTIETH CENTURIES witnessed Iran's uneasy transition into a modern nation-state under the increasingly decrepit Qajar dynasty (1794–1926). The country solidified its contemporary boundaries during this period while its ethnic Persians, Azeris, and other peoples increasingly adopted an Iranian national consciousness. The Qajars' greatest challenge, however, was to avoid entanglements with Russian and British imperialist policies, and war was the result of the Iranian monarchs' repeated failures to do so. Qajar pretensions to retain some of Iran's imperial glory contributed to these conflicts, which, in turn, led to cycles of humiliating concessions and debts. By the turn of the twentieth century, the Qajar rulers had shown themselves to be too greedy, lazy, and unimaginative to lead Iran out of the trap of foreign domination.

The history of Iran's armed forces through much of the first six decades of the nineteenth century was one of laudable attempts at military modernization and reforms to meet the threats posed by Russia and Great Britain. But, in each instance, the Qajar reforms proved insufficient and could not keep pace with improvements among the European militaries. Politicization and corruption were rife and constantly undermined efforts to put Iranian military professionalism on par with Western armed forces. Even worse, the Qajars set dreadful precedents in the maltreatment of Iranian fighting men and wasted the benefits of their demonstrated qualities of bravery, resourcefulness, and a dogged ability to endure hardship. Toward the end of the century and into the next, the Iranian monarchs essentially gave up on creating an effective national standing army and sought instead to enlist the aid of their former Russian foes, a move that contributed to domestic political currents that left the Qajar armed forces an empty shell.

The Qajars and the West

The first Qajar shah, Agha Muhammad Khan (r. 1794–97), was a eunuch general who seized the throne of Iran and became a cruel and brutal ruler. Muhammad Khan had been castrated as a boy at the order of Adil Shah, Nader Shah's successor, to prevent him from becoming a political rival. Karim Khan, the founder of the short-lived Zand dynasty, also kept the young eunuch prisoner for many years after collaborating in the murder of Muhammad Khan's father. Not surprisingly, the future shah swore a blood feud against the descendants of Nader and Karim, and his rise to power was marked by mass murders celebrated with pyramids of skulls and the mutilation and enslavement of his surviving enemies and their families. In 1795 the last Zand ruler was betrayed and handed over to Muhammad Khan, who had him tortured, blinded, castrated, and finally murdered. Qajar fighters then conducted a campaign of rape and pillage against the major Zand cities of Bam, Shiraz, and Kerman. In the latter city, twenty thousand women and children were given to Muhammad Khan's tribal warriors or were sold into slavery while the captured men were all robbed of their sight. Muhammad Khan's last revenge was to have the remains of Nader Shah and Karim Khan disinterred. He brought their bones to Tehran, where he had moved the Iranian capital to be closer to the Qajars' tribal grazing and hunting grounds. Muhammad Khan then reburied the two former rulers under the gateway of his palace so that royalty and commoners alike walked over their remains. Formally crowned shah in 1796, Muhammad Khan's evil ways caught up with him, and he was assassinated the following year. Despite his short reign, Muhammad Khan initiated the process in which the Qajars, a minority Turkman tribe with no real power base in Iran, legitimized their rule by forming ties with other ethnic and social groups and manipulating them to work against each other.[1]

The Qajars, like the Safavids, were Turkish in race but Persian in culture. They inherited the country at a time when Iran had been severely weakened by the wars, rebellions, oppressive taxation, and economic dislocations of the preceding century. The Qajars also came to power just as Iran was becoming the focus of Russian ambitions, British concerns over the defense of India, and the schemes of Napoleon's France. Lacking any significant standing armed forces, the Qajar shahs had no centralized administration and, in fact, were "despots without the instruments of despotism."[2] The dynasty stayed in power primarily by building enormous networks of kinship and alliances that they reinforced with grandiose titles and honorifics to give military leaders a stake in Qajar society. The shahs sent princes out to rule the provinces to ensure loyalty to the state, and a contemporary complaint about the Qajars was that "everywhere in Iran there are camels, lice, and princes."[3] Despite this form of personal and patrimonial authority, the Qajars rarely ruled in areas beyond the major cities, where rural landlords or nomadic tribes dominated. Still an agrarian society, Iran's isolated villages were left responsible for their own protection against nomadic tribes and bandits. For the most part, the Qajar shahs devoted their lives to enriching themselves. Muhammad Khan's successor, his nephew Fath Ali Shah (r. 1797–1834), needed the wealth to support 158 wives, 57 sons, 47 daughters, and almost 600 grandchildren. He and his successors only halfheartedly resisted the decay from within and the encroachments from without that marked most of the nineteenth century in Iran.

To their credit, the Qajars, unlike rulers in India and much of the Middle East, avoided coming directly under European control. The Qajar experience with European imperialism, however, had a tremendous impact on Iran and made the restoration of Iranian power, measured in territory, freedom of action, and influence, the central theme of Iranian foreign and defense policies ever since. As the Qajars came to power, Russia was trying to secure its southern borders, use Iran as a buffer against the Turks and British, and gain access to a warm water port in the Persian Gulf or Indian Ocean. Concurrently, the British saw Iran as the front line of defense for their expanding empire in the subcontinent. Russia was the primary concern of the British, but, following Napoleon's conquest of Egypt in 1798, London's apprehension increased over the potential for French military forces to approach India through Iran and Afghanistan by land, or by sea through the Persian Gulf. The Qajars tried to balance the political influence of Russia and Great Britain to protect Iranian territory, but foreign interference repeatedly contributed to conflict in Iran. The Qajar shahs also were occasionally blinded by their ambitions and goaded by the clerical establishment to take actions that provoked wars with the Russians and the British. From the start, when Muhammad Khan led an expedition between 1795 and 1796 to recapture Georgia, a Russian ally, the Qajar shahs were sometimes heedless of the consequences of their aspirations. Similarly, Fath Ali's attempts to introduce France as a third power to counterbalance the British and Russians only increased outside pressure on Iran and introduced a process of foreign loans and concessions that increasingly weakened Iranian sovereignty.[4]

These foreign contacts increased the pace of modernization in Iran, especially for the military, although the process was sporadic and suffered numerous reverses. Initially, the competition between the British and French appeared to work to the Qajars' advantage. In 1801 a British mission led by John Malcolm and the Qajar prime minister signed a treaty of mutual aid that committed Iran to attack Afghanistan if the Afghans prepared for war against India and obliged the British to ally with the shah should the Afghans attack him. Meanwhile, Napoleon had learned from his Egyptian expedition that actions in the Middle East could sway politics in Europe. He sought to neutralize Russia by allying with Turkey and Iran. After years of negotiations, the French and Iranians in

1807 signed the Treaty of Finkenstein, in which France guaranteed the integrity of Iran, recognized Georgia as a part of Iran, and agreed to provide arms and military instructors. In return, Fath Ali was to break relations with Great Britain, provide support to French naval forces if they appeared in the Persian Gulf, and convince the Afghans to join them in an attack on India. Instead, the shah pulled out of the alliance after the military mission arrived and began its training because the French, who were then bogged down in Spain, were unable to help the Iranians against the Russians. He was especially angry after word reached Tehran about the 1807 Treaty of Tilsit, in which France and Russia agreed to ally against Britain.

The British continued to offer the Qajars arms, instructors, and even naval support in the Persian Gulf. British officials facilitated the dispatch of the first group of Iranian students to Europe in 1810, an important step in Iran's modernization efforts. As the French threat faded, the government in London focused more on Russian designs on the region, and, although friendly relations with Tehran would ebb and flow, the British were determined to maintain Iran's independence. As the nineteenth century progressed, however, the British established virtual semiautonomous protectorates in southern Iran to offset Russia's continued encroachment on Iranian territory in the north. Throughout the period, European business interests obtained concessions to operate Iran's mines, banks, railroads, and public utilities, enabling them to dominate Iran's economy. Over the course of the century, most of the economic benefits of increased foreign trade went to the Europeans while Iran's wealth and independence were steadily reduced.

The Qajar Military

Iran was in terrible shape militarily at the turn of the nineteenth century. Unlike the Russian military, its most immediate threat, Iran's armed forces lacked the drill discipline to shift and mass musket-armed infantry on the battlefield and had not kept up with technological improvements in artillery. Later, Iran would match up poorly against British and British Indian forces in terms of discipline, command of forces, logistics, and naval forces and coastal defense batteries. Despite efforts by various European military missions to pass along some of the tactical improvements and weapons developed during and after the Napoleonic wars, Qajar Iran lacked the resources and will to assimilate these new methods to achieve victory on the battlefield against its major opponents. The Qajars generally prevailed only in conflict with similar Ottoman, Afghan, and tribal forces.

Standing Qajar military forces in the first decade of the century consisted mainly of the royal guards and town garrisons. The royal guards, officered by Qajar nobles, contained four thousand *ghulams* armed with aging muskets. Most of Iran was ruled by tribes and landed nobles who provided levies of mounted fighters to the crown when called and, in return, got the right to collect tax revenues to cover their expenses and other needs. Little revenue made its way to the capital, and what did was usually wasted rather than invested in a standing military. In wartime, however, the regional levies could muster as many as eighty thousand generally well-prepared horsemen, who brought their own arms and kit. The tribal levies were expert horsemen and superior marksmen, capable of firing their muskets over their shoulders while galloping away from a foe. Many still used lance and bow, and all carried sabers of high-quality steel that they wielded with deadly skill. While these warriors could be assembled quickly, they might evaporate just as fast if their leader failed to hold them together. A British official observed that they had "no further discipline than that of obeying their own leaders" and accepted as their leaders only "those of their own body they deemed their superiors." Another British observer commented that the tribal contingents retained their separate identities even within the royal camp, noting that "since the army was mostly composed of men drawn from the different tribes, each tribe was encamped in separate divisions."[5] The Qajars had no functional heavy artillery at the turn of the nineteenth century and instead relied on the *zanburak*. The Iranians seem to have lost the camel-handling skills of Nader Shah's army, however, and camels often ran amok, damaging Iranian formations as much as the enemy's lines. Because the government provided so little to its fighters, the system worked well only when the Qajars were on the offensive, the opportunities for plunder were plentiful, and the campaign could be completed quickly during nonwinter months.[6]

The four Qajar shahs who ruled between 1797 and 1896 gave only slight, unsustained, and belated attention to the creation of a modern military force that might protect them from external attack and internal revolt. The first major problem was the absence of any systematic attempt to integrate the tribes into Qajar political and military organizations as the Safavids had done. Instead, Qajar policies instituted under Crown Prince Abbas Mirza after 1805 were designed to weaken tribal power. The crown prince dismissed the tribal cavalry as a rabble, despite growing European adherence to Frederick the Great's example of ending the intermingling of cavalry and infantry and returning the mounted forces to its original functions of shock action and scouting, the very roles in which Iranian horsemen excelled. One British official lamented that "to a nation devoid of organization in every other department of government a regular army was impossible . . . the tribes, the chivalry of the Empire, the forces with which [Nader Shah] overran the East, and which, ever yielding but ever present, surrounded, under Muhammad Khan, the Russian armies with a desert, were destroyed."[7] At the same time, Russian intrusions on Iranian territory in the early nineteenth century cut off Qajar access to Georgia. This made it difficult to replenish the ghulam corps that continued to serve as the shah's personal guard and remained the central government's most effective military force throughout the first decades of the 1800s.

The Iranians' second major problem in establishing a standing army was the inability to afford major military reforms. Even when the Qajars tried, they were opposed by the mullahs, who saw innovations, even Western-style uniforms, as un-Islamic or as a potential threat to their status. Similarly, many tribal leaders and other vested interests opposed military reforms, fearing that a stronger standing army would limit their autonomy. Army officers and others who profited from the corruption of the existing system also opposed modernization. Finally, despite the obvious importance of the Caspian Sea and the Persian Gulf to Iran's security and commerce, the Qajars refused to spend enough to develop a naval force. Within a few years following Nader Shah's death, his fleet ceased to exist. The Qajars did not start to think about creating a small naval establishment until 1850, years after it became clear that British naval power in the Gulf posed a threat to Iranian security. Nasir al-Din Shah (r. 1848–96), however, had to turn to his potential British foes in an effort to acquire two sloops-of-war of twenty-five guns each. The British declined to sell the warships, in part out of concern that Iran had designs on Bahrain, which would upset relations with Great Britain's Arab allies in the Gulf. Nasir al-Din approached the British again in 1868 about acquiring a steam flotilla for the Persian Gulf to be commanded by British naval officers. These were intended for use in ongoing disputes with Oman, but the shah soon lost interest and indicated that Iran wanted the British to continue to police the region's waters.

Crown Prince Abbas Mirza, the son of Fath Ali and the governor of Azerbaijan, was the first significant proponent of Qajar military reforms. With his eye on his eventual accession to the throne, Abbas Mirza may have wanted an army that owed its existence and loyalty to him and that depended on the crown for arms and pay. Faced with an ongoing conflict with an expansionist Russia, Abbas Mirza was a firm believer that Iran needed an army with more modern arms drilled along European lines. His resolution was reinforced by his knowledge of European military exploits, including the British victories in India and the French defeat of the Egyptian Mamluks in 1798. Abbas Mirza reasoned that if the Mamluks, with their renowned military prowess, were so easily defeated by Napoleon, then Iranian troops would suffer a similar fate if a European power invaded. According to a diplomatic envoy, Abbas Mirza lamented that it was in vain to fight the Russians without soldiers like theirs and without artillery. The crown prince even forced Russian prisoners of war to train his troops in European techniques and later created a Russian battalion formed of Russian deserters and Armenian and Nestorian Christians. The Russian battalion, which grew to 1,400 men in 1829, declined over time to a force of about 500 that formed a palace guard during the reigns of Fath Ali Shah and Muhammad Shah before being disbanded in 1839.[8]

Although preceded by the British Malcolm mission of 1801, the French Gardanne mission of 1807 provided the first systematic training for Qajar troops by European officers. After arriving in Tabriz, the French began drilling Abbas Mirza's battalions and erecting modern fortifications. Some of the French officers drafted maps and translated treatises on military tactics and theories of fortification. They also helped to establish a cannon foundry and arsenal at Esfahan. The British returned with thirty military instructors and engineers as part of the small Brydges mission in 1808, which, working from the unratified treaty signed by Malcolm to provide military equipment and training, drilled Abbas Mirza's troops and held classes on surveying, mapping, and geography. The Brydges mission also delivered twenty pieces of artillery and forty wagons of cartridges to Iran. In 1829 an Iranian mission was sent to Austria to obtain information on the latest methods of warfare. More military instruction was provided by the British in 1836 and the French in 1839.[9]

After the French were replaced by the British in 1808, Abbas Mirza assembled a force of twelve thousand infantrymen in twelve battalions of one thousand men each, twelve thousand cavalrymen, and an artillery force armed with the twenty British guns. The infantry and cavalry were given uniforms with vaguely French-style jackets to go with their traditional sheepskin hats and baggy trousers. The British mission had the artillerymen clothed in British style, but as good Muslims the Iranians ignored instructions for the gunners to be clean-shaven. When the crown prince witnessed an accident in which a soldier's beard was ignited by a spark from a gun, however, he saw the policy's wisdom and ordered his soldiers to shave. Abbas Mirza created a translation office for military and engineering manuals, and he established factories for cannon and muskets, but shortages of skilled manpower and equipment limited production. At Tehran, Fath Ali had his own army with regular infantry, cavalry, and horse artillery, but it was a token force that was less well trained and disciplined than the crown prince's army and was always below strength.

Abbas Mirza called his Western-style armed force the Nezam-e Jadid, or the New Order. His efforts and those of the various French and British missions to get the Iranians to copy the Europeans were only a partial success because the Iranians lacked the command, management, logistical, and technical skills necessary to fight in a European style. As important, the Qajar soldiers lacked the discipline and confidence of Western forces. Moreover, the Nezam-e Jadid was not based on correcting Iranian doctrinal and technological deficiencies because the Iranians did not have a sense of fundamental inferiority to their enemies. Another major limitation was that the army could not be transformed in isolation without introducing changes in government administration and revenue generation. Without adequate funds, the officer corps remained weak and corrupt, equipment was not maintained, and training, except when led by Europeans, was virtually nonexistent. The Nezam-e Jadid's poor performance in the second Russo-Iranian war hurt its reputation and reduced Fath Ali's support for additional costly reforms. Finally, Abbas Mirza died before his father, never became shah, and did not have an opportunity to bring his reform ideas to the entire Qajar military establishment. Abbas Mirza's reforms' longest-lasting impact was on the Persian language; *sarbaz*, a contemporary word for a Qajar enlisted man that means "he who is ready to lose his head," now is a common word for "soldier" or "private." It would be midcentury before the Iranians started to recognize that more general reforms were needed.[10]

Mirza Taqi Khan, who served as prime minister from 1848 to 1851 and came to be called Amir Kabir, or the Great Lord, because of his accomplishments in government and foreign affairs, was the next major military reformer. Appointed by Nasir al-Din Shah, Amir Kabir proposed a radical reorganization, increased indigenous arms production, new recruitment practices, and better training for the officer corps. He tried to strengthen Iran from within by asserting the government's power, assuring the soldiers' loyalty to the central government rather than landlords or tribal chiefs, and establishing military posts along the trade routes and the frontiers. His official title was Lord of the Army, and, considering himself primarily a military leader, he assumed personal control of the army, administered the provincial forces, and appointed their leaders. Amir Kabir attempted to mandate uniform training and pushed for the prompt payment of officers' and enlisted men's salaries. He invented the *bonicheh* system of recruitment, in which every village or town was ordered to provide the central government with men. By 1851 the Iranian army had a nominal strength when fully mobilized of 137,000 men, although it never assembled such a large force.

In the same year, Amir Kabir established the Dar al-Fonun (the Polytechnic School or Academy of Applied Sciences), using advisers from France and Austria-Hungary, and he encouraged education abroad in the military sciences and in industrial technology. The Dar al-Fonun was the first government-sponsored European-style educational institution in Iran and the Middle East. The school was intended to serve primarily as a military academy and was built in the royal citadel in Tehran. The third superintendent was a military officer who established strict military discipline and cemented the martial nature of the institution. Its courses included military engineering, French, medicine, sciences, cartography, military history, and military strategy and drill. Nearly half of the students specialized in military subjects, and, in addition to classroom instruction, these military students were given field training. One group accompanied their instructors on the Herat campaign of 1857, and according to an Iranian newspaper article from 1852, the institution's students were given field training in the art of commanding garrisons and combat in the desert. The school also taught Arabic and theology to legitimize itself in the eyes of the clerical establishment. Because Iran's elementary and secondary schooling programs were so poor, the Dar al-Fonun was more on the level of a French secondary school than a university. Still, the school made a start at increasing military professionalism by building on a program initiated by Abbas Mirza to translate European books and articles into Persian. Among the translated works were Gibbon's *Rise and Fall of the Roman Empire*, Voltaire's *Charles the XII of Sweden*, and *The History of Alexander the Great* as well as a few books about Napoleon Bonaparte. Over the years, other military-related books and articles translated by the Dar al-Fonun included *Treatise on the Science of Artillery*, *The Soldier's Whole Duty*, *Military Drill Book*, *The Movement of Troops*, and *The Siege of Paris*. The school also translated some works of fiction, including *The Three Musketeers*, *The Count of Monte Cristo*, *Robinson Crusoe*, and *Gulliver's Travels*.[11]

Amir Kabir's primary goals were national unity and self-sufficiency, which the shifting European alliances reinforced, especially in the area of arms production. Amir Kabir formed a garrison in Tehran staffed with men from all of the provinces to create one true national force while establishing fifteen modern armament and equipment factories to help achieve the latter goal. Earlier, Abbas Mirza, unhappy that he had to rely on European-made weapons for two wars with Russia, established factories to produce gunpowder and weapons while stockpiling other European weapons, maps, and machines. The crown prince also arranged to send Iranians as students to Europe to develop needed military, technical, and medical skills. These students put their foreign education into practice on their return as they were given high positions and great responsibilities, including roles as court physician, diplomat, head of artillery, chief army engineer, and head of the royal arsenal. The attempted reforms, however, increased the government's need for cash to buy weapons and maintain the army, which contributed to the Qajars' financial problems and increased opportunities for corruption. When Amir Kabir tried to curb the profiteering, theft, and nepotism that afflicted the military system, he developed enemies in the court. Nasir al-Din also was wary of Amir Kabir's championing of the Dar al-Fonun because he associated the school with dangerous European political ideas. As the Great Lord's achievements grew, he incited jealousy among the royal family. He was assassinated after the shah, fearful of Amir Kabir's power and efficiency, removed him from office in 1851, shortly after the Dar al-Fonun was opened.

None of the attempted reforms fully addressed the standing army's greatest need: a trained, professional officer corps. Generals were chosen by the shah, colonels and majors by the army commander, and junior officers by their regimental commanders. In all cases, no military background or special qualities besides the acquaintance of or some personal connection to the senior official making selection decisions were required. The army commander in the last years of the first Russo-Iranian war had no military qualifications and extorted money from his officers by charging them with misconduct and then extracting payments for leniency. Part of the problem was that the upper echelons of Iranian society despised military careers as low status and, except for commands where corruption and profiteering were possible, unrewarding. As a result, the officer corps tended to be drawn from families of limited means and education. Throughout the Qajar period, these officers at all levels of the chain of command pocketed the pay allotted to their troops, a practice the shahs tolerated. In turn, the unpaid soldiers had to practice a variety of full-time trades in garrison towns or nearby villages to survive, neglecting drill and training. Even if the Qajar officers of questionable capabilities had aspirations to serve honorably and well, they had no professional cadre of staff officers or noncommissioned officers to help support them in their various commands and garrisons. The Qajars did allow for a large number of aide-de-camps or adjutants to be appointed to assist the most senior civilian and military leaders and provincial governors. These officers had no real professional training, however, and, in any event, court politics and intrigues influenced most of the armed forces' policies. The nearest equivalent of a modern staff officer was the *adjutan-bashi* (chief of staff), whose job was to assemble the troops for review and act as the master of ceremonies during military parades at the palace. This officer had no other duties, however, and the position was obtained either as a result of gaining palace favor or through outright purchase.

Of all of these problems, corruption was the major bane of the Qajar military. The army existed for the most part not to be militarily effective but to transfer money to favored individuals and groups. For most of the nineteenth century the Qajar shahs sold military ranks to men and even boys to raise funds to meet their court expenses or simply used titles and ranks to reward court favorites. In 1881 Nasir al-Din Shah complained to his son and war minister, Kamran Mirza, about the promiscuous awarding of titles, offices, and medals. He lamented that Iran's prestige had been ruined because it could be charged that "the government has made such and such a child or good-for-nothing person a brigadier general."[12] Nasir's admonition was undermined by his own behavior, however, because he had made Kamran commander in chief of the army at age thirteen and had appointed a nephew of his favorite wife a brigadier general at the age of eight. Staff positions in the Ministry of War and its subordinate departments were sold to the highest bidder, who then sought to recoup the investment with interest. Service in the Pay Department was much sought after and was "a bureaucratic union for the exploitation of the military budget."[13] Arsenal Department jobs also were sold to the highest bidder with the winners then devoting themselves to making as large a profit as possible at the government's expense. Although postings in the War Ministry became less desirable as the army deteriorated and fewer arms and supplies were purchased during the later years of Nasir al-Din's reign, the corruption continued. For almost twenty years Prince Kamran Mirza's corruption as war minister was so infamous that his father finally had to remove him from office. In a memorable instance of Qajar-era malfeasance, when one minister of court was dismissed from office, it was discovered that an artillery battery was hidden in the cellars of his house with the battery horses used for the minister's private carriages and as mounts for his retainers.[14]

The Qajar army was rigidly hierarchical, disorganized, and undisciplined. It varied in size during the course of its nineteenth-century wars, seldom reaching more than sixty thousand men when fully mobilized, a process that could take several months. Following the wars with Russia the Qajar army had three main arms: the regular infantry, the artillery, and the tribal levies, most of whom were mounted. In midcentury, the army under Muhammad Shah (r. 1834–48) was in very poor shape and could put no more than twenty thousand first-line troops into the field. Transportation depended entirely upon mules, horses, and camels, and the army had few, if any, carts and wagons. There was no medical service, and wounded soldiers were left to die unless their fellow soldiers cared for them. Outside of small standing cavalry regiments from Azerbaijan, the remaining cavalry forces were raised entirely from tribal levies, who only followed tribal leaders and were often undependable. Auxiliary infantry troops were mobilized locally by regional officials and landlords. These soldiers often served unwillingly because, like their standing army counterparts, their pay was poor when it was paid at all. In both of these cavalry and infantry forces, tribal and ethnic antagonism often prevented cooperation, and in some localities the groups were actively hostile to each other. When possible, the soldiers used what little authority their position offered to extract what they could from others. One Russian observer wrote, "The rights of these defenders of the state are unlimited; they trade, steal, rob the people while moving from one province to another— in other words, do everything which can be encouraged by poverty, idleness, laziness, and impunity."[15] Except among the shahs' guards, morale was extremely low, and discipline was maintained by flogging, imprisonment, and execution.

The infantry was the most important branch in the standing army but was poorly motivated and trained. Recruits for the army "enlisted," but most had few options because of pressure on villages to provide manpower. The villagers' land tax paid a family allowance to the soldiers, who normally were enlisted for life unless they could afford to pay for a substitute. Exceptions to this form of conscription were made for *sayyids* (descendents of the Prophet), the clergy, and all non-Muslims. Because population surveys were out of date, the burden fell unequally on many areas, contributing to bribery and exploitation by recruiters. The central government also focused its enforcement efforts on areas that had historically provided the best soldiers, such as Azerbaijan. Nominal strength reported by the commanders always far outpaced the actual number of men under arms. Garrison and regimental commanders, when called into action, would bring their units up to strength by the simple expedient of spending more money to recruit new men, put them into a uniform, and give them each a firearm.

The hastily added soldiers were not significantly less skilled than their longer-serving comrades. Training was restricted to the most basic parade ground maneuvers and the perfunctory use of arms. Little or no time was devoted to musketry training on a firing range. The conscripts, some of whom were children or elderly, were generally to be found in a ragged condition with patched and torn uniforms. During the 1830s and 1840s, a Russian traveler reported that half-naked soldiers were seen busy trading and buying among the disordered multicolored tents that made up Iranian military camps. A British officer reported that an Iranian officer told him that the army did not drill in the summer or winter because it was too hot or too cold and only sometimes in the spring and autumn. The most drill occurred in the few days before the shah's birthday each year, and the soldiers were only properly dressed and shoed for the parades and displays that occurred on that day.[16]

The officers were as untrained and unskilled as the soldiers and, despite initiatives such as the Dar al-Fonun, for most of the nineteenth century neither group was encouraged to learn. In addition, their training suffered from shortages of the relevant arms and ammunition. Most of the soldiers were armed with old percussion muskets or, toward the end of the century, the Austrian Werndl, a breech-loading rifle. These rifles often rusted and deteriorated from long disuse, because the Qajar troops were given no more than five rounds per man per year for target practice. When more modern guns were added to the inventory, they were seldom if ever taken out of the arsenal for training. Many weapons did leave the armories, however, when sold by the officers in charge. The tribal infantry levies, such as the Bakhtiaris and Kurds, were in better shape because their soldiers owned their arms and developed their own fighting skills in the course of tribal conflicts and traditional banditry and policing activities.[17]

The irregular cavalry was a relatively effective fighting force throughout the nineteenth century. It was organized entirely on a tribal basis, with the men serving under their own leaders and supplying their own horses, arms, and equipment. The army favored levies drawn from Fars, Khorasan, and Azerbaijan. As with the infantry, the claimed strength of the cavalry units was almost always exaggerated. The nominal strength of cavalrymen was used by their chiefs in reports to the government for claims for subsidies in the form of tax deductions to maintain the force. Some of the cavalrymen were employed permanently to police the main roads, but most were only called up for national service when needed. The irregular cavalry units were generally judged as superior to the regular infantry because the frontier tribes were accustomed from childhood to riding and handling arms and regularly demonstrated outstanding horsemanship leaping barriers and galloping at full speed. Their horses were short, compact, graceful, and well adapted to cavalry service, although the Persian saddle was described as high, long, inflexible, and equally cruel to man and horse. The tribal cavalry were fair shots at short range and capable of offering strong resistance in their own territory. Their tactics were simple, however, and mostly involved raids against their enemies, attacks on and skirmishes with small detached parties, and interference with enemy supply lines and communications. The tribal cavalry generally only fought in their home provinces because they could not afford to support expeditions. Also their chiefs were not inclined to fight outside their domains. The prospect of plunder was needed to encourage them to help the government suppress internal unrest in other provinces or support the sporadic Qajar wars.[18]

The Qajar artillery varied in size over the course of the century, but its quality was never good. Under Muhammad Shah, the Qajars had 120 six- to twelve-pounder guns provided by the British, but the army lacked the wheeled ammunition-carrying limbers for the guns and had few trained artillerymen. During the latter years of Nasir al-Din's reign, the artillery consisted of a single regiment of four battalions with two batteries each. Two of the battalions had Austrian muzzle-loading guns, one was equipped with mountain guns, and the last had machine guns. On paper, an Iranian artillery battery consisted of six guns, but was top-heavy with officers. Each unit had a commandant, who was a general or a colonel, three section commanders, one commander of ammunition, and nine other officers to command roughly seventy gunners. To operate, the battery required thirty-nine horses for the guns and mounted men, four horses in reserve, and in the field, six ammunition wagons with six horses each were supposed to be attached to the battery along with twenty-four mules for baggage. In the 1820s, one Russian officer called a drill of Persian artillery "a satire on our infantry," while a Russian military officer who studied the condition of Persian artillery in the 1880s came to the conclusion that it "does not exist."[19]

As with the other branches, the Qajar military system seldom provided sufficient manpower, horses, or ammunition for the artillery batteries, although enough could be gathered for a few hours for parades and demonstrations. The Austrian guns were all secondhand, and no more than three rounds per gun per year were available for live-fire training. The machine gun battalion had one battery of four Nordenfelt multibarrel, lever-actuated machine guns while the other had six Mauser Maxims, the first self-powered machine guns. The Qajars, however, purchased only one hundred thousand rounds of ammunition for the rapid-firing Maxims. Like the other artillerymen, the machine gunners were poorly trained when they were trained at all. Fortunately for the Qajars, by the last quarter of the nineteenth century they faced nothing more than internal rebellions, because the Russians and British had already gained nearly all they wanted and offset each other's ambitions in the region. When advised in the latter part of his reign that he still needed to modernize his army, Nasir al-Din reportedly replied, "What does Persia want with rifles? Let England and Russia fight it out."[20]

The Wars of the Qajars

From the beginning, the Qajars were confronted with an expansionist Russia that virtually guaranteed conflict. It was the newly installed dynasty, however, that lit the fuse to war by asserting claims to Georgia, Armenia, and northern Azerbaijan to increase Qajar legitimacy. After St. Petersburg annexed Georgia in 1800, the Qajars provided assistance to Muslim tribes that were opposing the Russians. Seeking to end this support, Russia invaded Iran and captured Ganja in western Azerbaijan in January 1804, starting a nine-year war that consisted of mostly indecisive battles and raids. The Iranian army was not prepared to campaign in the winter, and Fath Ali Shah tried to avoid war but was unsuccessful negotiating with the Russians to gain their withdrawal. Crown Prince Abbas Mirza, the future military reformer, was fifteen in 1804, so an older cousin initially commanded Iranian forces. The more capable crown prince, however, soon took charge of the army facing the Russians.

The Russian army, which had conducted successful campaigns in Europe in 1799 and had a Caspian navy to maintain communications, was a formidable but flawed force. Many of its officers were well trained and brave, and its soldiers were drilled and armed along European lines. The Caucasian theater, however, was a secondary one. During the nine years of the conflict there, Russia was at war with France (1805–7 and 1812–15), the Ottoman Empire (1806–12), and Sweden (1808–9). Because the European theater had priority, out-of-favor officers were assigned to the divisions facing Iran. Russian forces in the Caucasus also had a lower priority for supplies and troops and suffered from transport problems because of the region's rough terrain. In addition, disease ravaged the Russian divisions. Czar Alexander tried to end the war with Iran on several occasions between 1806 and 1808, but his offers came with too few concessions to interest the Qajars.[21]

The Iranian army probably mustered as many as fifty thousand men for the opening phases of the war. The Iranians initially preferred to avoid direct battles and followed the tribal practice of hit-and-run attacks and raids when possible. As more European-style units entered the war following Abbas Mirza's reform efforts, the Iranians started to fight formal set-piece battles. The Iranian approach to war, however, was still very different from European concepts. Forced to live off the land, the Iranian levies not surprisingly saw battle as a type of large tribal raid. Each soldier might use the fight as an opportunity to display individual prowess, but their main goal was to take booty. Iranian forces repeatedly stopped to loot before a battle was over. Still, the Russians involved in the 1804 Armenian campaign were surprised by how well the Iranians fought. British and French observers, often the most severe critics of the Iranians they were advising, also were struck by the Iranians' courage and capacity to endure hardship.

Abbas Mirza usually faced Russian armies smaller than his own forces and blocked their advances into northwestern Iran. At the Battle of Echmiadzin (in modern western Armenia) in June 1804, the young crown prince ably commanded a predominantly Azeri force of eighteen thousand infantry and cavalrymen over three days and compelled the Russians to withdraw. The Russian commander then moved his troops to besiege Yerevan, where after a few months the six thousand to seven thousand defenders fell back to the citadel. The city was saved when a relief column under the crown prince cut the Russians' lines of communication, forcing them to retreat. During the next campaign season in 1805, the Russians invaded Gilan but were defeated by a provincial army. Sporadic warfare dragged on for the next seven years, and like the Russians the Iranians faced other conflicts involving Kurds from Ottoman territories, Turkish forces near Baghdad, and an expedition against tribal raiders from Arabia. During this period, Abbas Mirza had the French and British missions train a Western-style military force. However, as Sir Percy Sykes noted, the attempt "to drill Persians on European lines, praiseworthy as it was, contributed to the ruin of their country."[22] The Qajar military, operating under unfamiliar foreign rules, lost many of the tribal forces' capabilities. British observers reported that "internal discipline does not extend much beyond the knowledge of getting from column into line, with some awkward attempts at the formation of a square," and that Iran had forfeited its only "natural defense, her clouds of irregular cavalry."[23]

Iranian morale remained good during the war, perhaps providing an unwarranted confidence that contributed to the shah's refusal to negotiate. The Caucasus region provided good plundering opportunities for the soldiers. Georgian women, in particular, were highly valued as concubines, and the troops engaged in a brisk slave trade. In 1810 Iranian mullahs declared jihad, or holy war, against the Russians, which gave the soldiers extra incentive to fight. The Iranians were further encouraged when word reached them that Napoleon had invaded Russia. By this time Abbas Mirza had fought a few modestly successful battles with his new European-trained army. Among these was a defeat of nine hundred Russians at Soltanbud in early 1812 by a few thousand Iranians with British officers directing the infantry and artillery.

Qajar confidence ebbed in October 1812 when Abbas Mirza and his army of 5,000 men were surprised by 2,000 Russians at Aslanduz on the Aras River. Having failed to post pickets, the larger Iranian force was routed at the cost of fourteen guns and more than 2,500 men. By January 1813, the Russians were besieging the stronghold at Lenkoran, where the Iranians, defending behind walls recently rebuilt by British engineers, inflicted heavy casualties and held the Russians off for five days. On the sixth day Russian sappers blew a hole in the main wall of the fortress, and the enemy poured through the breach, slaughtering the 4,000 Iranian defenders. Soon thereafter, the Qajar government recognized that it was losing and agreed to British mediation. Iran had not been significantly less technologically advanced than Russia during the war, and Iranian commanders had not been alarmed by Russian capabilities. In the end, however, the Russian military prevailed because it was better organized, more effective, and more capable at linear infantry tactics and siege warfare. Iran agreed to the cession of Georgia and other Transcaucasian provinces to Russia in 1813 in the Treaty of Gulistan, a humiliating and poorly written settlement so unclear that further conflict was unavoidable.

Russian and Ottoman intrigue in support of rebellious tribes in Azerbaijan prompted the Qajar's next war. After the Ottoman governor of Erzerum took two Azerbaijani tribes under his protection in 1821, Abbas Mirza, now thirty-two years old and a veteran commander, led a force into the region around Lake Van against minimal Ottoman resistance. Forces under the pasha of Baghdad launched a counteroffensive into southwestern Iran, but were repelled by a force under another Qajar prince. An illness that killed the prince prevented the Iranians from capturing Baghdad, and soon thereafter cholera ended operations by the Iranian army in the south. In the course of these operations, the Qajars conquered the emirate of Arabistan, which included most of modern Khuzestan and the port of Muhammarah (Khorramshahr). The rulers of Arabistan had carved out an independent existence since the late seventeenth century by playing the Iranians against the Ottomans. Because of Qajar weakness, the Khuzestan tribes retained a large measure of autonomy.

Back in the north, Abbas Mirza and thirty thousand men defeated an Ottoman force of fifty-two thousand at the hard-fought Battle of Erzerum later that year. The Treaty of Erzerum, which was signed in 1823, ended the war, with both sides agreeing to maintain the territorial status quo. The Ottomans broke the treaty in 1837 and seized Arabistan, temporarily incorporating it into their Al Basrah province. Wary of this expansion of Istanbul's influence, Great Britain and Russia forced the Ottomans to withdraw to the western bank of the Shatt al-Arab. The second Treaty of Erzerum, signed by the Iranians and Ottomans in 1847, placed the emirate under Iranian suzerainty and stabilized the western border. Because the British wanted to keep the regional rivers open for commercial and naval exploitation, they prevented Iran from annexing Arabistan outright, and the region fell within the British sphere of influence and maintained a nominal independence for several more decades.

A boundary dispute resulting from the vague Russo-Iranian Treaty of Gulistan of 1813 led to renewed war with Russia in 1825 that resembled the earlier conflict. Fath Ali Shah was encouraged to declare war by Iranian mullahs, who also incited popular sentiment against the Russians. The Qajars were aware that the Russians were not fully ready for a conflict because of distractions from the Greek War of Independence against the Turks and the death of Czar Alexander. Abbas Mirza, his army swollen by thousands of volunteers, advanced into the Caspian region, ignoring advice that his military, only a small part of which was drilled and modernized, was still incapable of matching the better organized Russian forces. Abbas Mirza's grand uncle counseled against exposing Iran's forces to the Russians' cannon and their disciplined troops. He advised using guerrilla warfare, saying, "Their shot will never reach me, but they shall possess no country beyond its range. They shall not know sleep; and let them march where they choose, I will surround them with a desert."[24] Abbas Mirza initially followed this advice and with thirty thousand soldiers carried out large-scale raids and captured several towns and fortresses in the opening stages of war. The inevitable Russian counteroffensives, however, repeatedly defeated larger Iranian armies in set-piece battles and then pushed into Iran against minimal opposition. Inexplicably, Fath Ali refused to spend more on troops and supplies, dooming his army to eventual disintegration. After the defenseless residents of Tabriz surrendered without a fight to the Russians, Fath Ali eagerly accepted the insulting and costly conditions imposed by the war-ending Treaty of Turkmenchay. Signed in February 1828, the treaty terminated Iran's status as a regional power. Iran suffered an additional loss of territory to the Russians in 1869 when Russian troops occupied Qajar territory north of the Atrak River that is now part of modern Turkmenistan. The Russian minister in Tehran summarily informed the Qajar court that "the Imperial Government recognizes Persian dominion up to the Atrak."[25] Although Tehran lost its nominal control over the region, it benefited from the Russians ending Turkman raids into northeastern Iran.

In the first few decades of the dynasty, the Qajars also fought sporadically with various Afghan tribal chiefs and rulers over disputed territories on Iran's eastern frontiers, especially in and around the city of Herat. Fath Ali's successor and grandson, Muhammad Shah, came under the Russians' influence because they indulged his ambitions for military conquest in the east. In 1836 Muhammad Shah decided to invade Afghanistan and sent an army of thirty thousand men through Khorasan Province to Mashhad. Count Simonich, the Russian minister, and a regiment of Russian troops under a Polish general accompanied the army. Simonich, a Dalmatian who entered Russia's military ranks after serving in Napoleon's army and being taken prisoner, was an ardent Bonapartist and "hated the British with all his heart."[26] He encouraged Muhammad Shah on the campaign, but apparently was a less than objective military advisor.

At the start of the campaign Afghan cavalry scouts from Herat reported that, instead of the armed and widely dispersed mob they expected to find, the Qajar army, aided by the Russians, was advancing as a compact body protected by artillery. The disciplined march was slowed, however, by the shah's attempts to secure his northern flank against Turkman tribes. As a result, when Muhammad Shah halted his march in front of Herat in November 1837, he found the city prepared for a siege. The fighting at Herat was brutal with no quarter given, and beheadings and disembowelings were the fate of captured soldiers on both sides. The Iranians repeatedly broke through Herat's outer defenses, breached its ramparts, and even broke the main wall in June 1838. The Afghan defenders, assisted by Capt. Eldred Pottinger of the British East India Company, defeated each of the Iranian assaults. The siege dragged on into early September when the Qajar force finally withdrew. The shah apparently heeded a British warning, underscored by the landing of Royal Navy marines in the northern Persian Gulf, that Iran must abandon its aggression against Afghanistan or risk war with the British Empire. Any impression on the Qajars made by the failure at Herat and the threats from the British did not last beyond Muhammad Shah's reign.[27]

When Nasir al-Din became shah in 1848, he shared his father's favorable views toward the Russians but tried to offset their influence with help from the British, who were unwilling to allow Iran to fall completely under Russia's sway. Close ties were hindered, however, by Qajar ambitions to expand Iran's frontiers toward India. During the 1853–56 Crimea War, which pitted the Russians against the Ottomans and their British, French, and Sardinian allies over control of the Black Sea region, Nasir sought some advantage from the turmoil. When a new ruler in Herat solicited Iran's protection from his Afghan rivals, the Qajar monarch saw his chance. The shah first provoked a diplomatic dispute with the British envoy in Tehran, which gave him the excuse to break relations and have the British mission leave his capital, the better to hide his preparations for war. Then in February 1856, Nasir al-Din sent an army to aid his Afghan ally and extend Iran's hegemony in the east. Because the Qajar army behaved as conquerors rather than protectors, the angry citizens of Herat drove their ruler out and turned to the British for help against the Iranians besieging their city.

Given a British ultimatum to withdraw, the Qajars became aware of British preparations for an expedition against southern Iran from Bombay (Mumbai). The government in London believed that a repeat of the 1838 expedition against southwestern Iran would meet little resistance and cause Nasir al-Din to relent. British officials in India, however, were less certain because of challenges such as poor roads, inadequate harbors, insufficient forage and water, and long, vulnerable supply lines. Other problems confronting the British included high anti-Christian sentiment among the mostly Arab coastal tribes and concerns about the reaction of India's Muslims, who were being incited to revolt by the Iranian prime minister. The region's high heat, shamal winds, and numerous diseases also posed daunting challenges that, regardless of the Qajar's active resistance, made attacks against southern Iran by European and Indian troops a difficult proposition. In addition, many British leaders were not convinced that the 1838 expedition, during which Khark Island had been seized, had caused Muhammad Shah to abandon Herat. Officials in India were especially doubtful that the planned operation would succeed in compelling Nasir al-Din to withdraw from Afghanistan. In their view, the Qajars had few interests in the Persian Gulf, and there was a chance that they might not be impressed at all by a British expedition along the coast. Nonetheless, a force was prepared and soon sailed for the Persian Gulf.[28]

The Iranian garrison evacuated Khark Island at the British approach in early December 1856. The British turned to nearby Bushehr and landed a force of nearly 6,000 infantry, cavalry, horse artillery, and sappers south of the port. The city's garrison had prepared a series of entrenchments and had been augmented by Qajar army troops. Between 1,500 and 2,000 Iranian soldiers and local tribesmen manned the first redoubt, which had a rampart that stood thirty-five feet above a large ditch. As the battle began, half of the garrison was driven away by a thunderous British naval bombardment. The tribesmen who remained in the first line of trenches inflicted heavy British losses before falling back to the next line of entrenchments, only to be pounded again by the British warships. At this point, Iranian artillery batteries were able to return fire and did so with great spirit. Continued pressure from the British and Indian ground troops along with the British bombardment forced the Iranians to retreat from their last line of defense. The governor of Bushehr then cut down his flagstaff in token of surrender.

In response to the British victory, the Qajars offered to negotiate a peace based on their withdrawal from Herat, but British conditions were unacceptable. When the Iranian siege finally compelled Herat to surrender, the negotiations stalled. To maintain pressure on the Qajars, the British prepared for an attack on Muhammarah by sending additional infantry, cavalry, and artillery from India in early 1857. The Iranians did not stand by idly during this period, and a force of seven thousand men was assembled outside Bushehr. Qajar troops and guns moved from the north in a steady stream, and by early January five infantry regiments and one thousand cavalry had reached the area north of Bushehr. The one thousand men garrisoned at Muhammarah, meanwhile, strengthened their fortifications and were reinforced with an infantry regiment and five hundred cavalrymen. At Shushtar, a small town on the Karun River north of

Muhammarah, the Qajars deployed three thousand men while five regiments were held in reserve farther north at Kermanshah. To help stir up nationalist and religious sentiments against the British, the shah proclaimed a jihad in January and called on his Muslim subjects to gather for the defense of Islam against the Christian invaders. Qajar officials spread the claim that the British were suppressing the Muslim faith in India by confiscating copies of the Koran and forbidding Muslim women to wear the veil.

Despite their mobilization and preparations, the Qajar forces were no match for the more than five thousand British and Indian soldiers in Bushehr. The British attacked the Iranians outside Bushehr in early February and forced them into nearby mountain passes. The Qajar retreat was so precipitous that they left their ammunition stores and even their tents behind. The Iranians were not defeated, however, and their cavalry rallied and attacked the rear guard of the British as they were returning to Bushehr. The attack caused the British column to halt and hold in place for the night. The next morning, between six thousand and seven thousand Iranians had drawn up in battle order on the left rear of the British formation. Their bravery and willingness to confront the British notwithstanding, the Iranian soldiers were overwhelmed when the British launched an attack with their cavalry supported by two lines of infantry and artillery. The fleeing Iranians left most of their arms on the ground and suffered at least seven hundred killed against light British losses.

The Iranians fell back to the west on Muhammarah, where they merged into a substantial corps of thirteen thousand men, including seven thousand soldiers from the regular army with thirty artillery pieces. The artillery was placed to command the channel of the Shatt al-Arab leading from the Persian Gulf to the city. Most of the Qajar troops were concentrated on the north bank of the Karun with the rest on the south bank and on Abadan Island. The Iranians erected barriers on both shores made of solid earth twenty feet thick and eighteen feet high with casemated embrasures—armored compartments for artillery with openings facing the waterway. The Iranian positions were well planned and well prepared; they commanded the entire passage of the Shatt al-Arab and could sweep the whole waterway out to the range of their guns. The British, meanwhile, with their base at Bushehr secure from attack, started their movement into the Khuzestan region.

The Treaty of Paris ending the Anglo-Persian War was signed in early March 1857, but ten days before the news reached the British expedition nearly five thousand British and Indian troops attacked Muhammarah. The British decided that an assault on Abadan Island and any effort to clear the southern bank would be too difficult and costly. Instead, they chose to run the gauntlet of the Iranian batteries' fire and land the bulk of the troops north of the city. The British placed mortars on a raft that was silently towed into position under the cover of darkness and began the battle at daybreak with a bombardment of the Iranian batteries. The British steamers transporting the troops joined in the bombardment, and all but three or four of the Iranian guns were silenced. The Qajar forces protecting the batteries poured heavy musket fire into the British and Indian landing parties assigned to silence the Iranian guns but failed to prevent the attackers from putting the remaining Iranian gunners to flight. As the main British forces continued to the planned landing site, the remaining Qajar troops already had started their retreat after witnessing the fierce barrage and fighting to their south. The Qajar army destroyed its largest magazine and again fled without retrieving tents, baggage, stores, or guns. Iranian losses in the battle were not great; only an estimated two hundred men were killed in the initial assaults, but the demonstration of British firepower and effectiveness was enough. The Iranians continued to retreat while a large British reconnaissance force pushed farther north along to Ahvaz, which surrendered without a fight. The British ended their campaign when the news of the Treaty of Paris reached their commander. Fortunately for the Qajars, the British did not want to unduly weaken the shah. Nasir al-Din had to withdraw from Herat and renounce Iran's claims of suzerainty over several Afghan provinces. In return, the British did not demand any additional territory from Iran and did not impose an indemnity. The war, however, kept Iranian suspicions of British intentions high, and the Qajars nursed an almost pathological fear that Great Britain planned to annex Iran piecemeal as it had conquered India.

The Rise and Fall of the Persian Cossacks

One problematic aspect of the Qajar's early modernization efforts was that they saw their shortcomings as a failure to maintain traditional institutions rather than an inadequate embrace of change. They expected that the adoption of European technology and training alone would suffice to restore Iran's military effectiveness. Only after Amir Kabir established the Dar al-Fonun did the Iranians start to recognize that more general reforms and modernization were required. The Qajar shahs, however, remained unwilling to adopt the changes. The Iranian military got generally negative comments from visiting U.S. Army brevet Maj. Gen. Emory Upton, who had arranged with then U.S. Army General in Chief William T. Sherman in 1875 to take a two-year inspection tour of foreign armies. Upton, whose writings would later influence military reforms in the United States, may have let his own unhappiness with the hostility of Congress to America's small and much deteriorated post–Civil War peacetime army shape his views on Iran. He concluded his remarks by noting that "the capital of Persia, like that of all countries where military institutions are neglected, lies at the mercy of a few disciplined battalions."[29] For the most part, the Qajars relied on Iran's rugged terrain, autonomous and often hostile tribes, isolated cities, and weak lines of communication to provide protection against outside invaders. Toward the end of the nineteenth century, one Russian officer captured Iran's strengths and weaknesses with the comment that "Persia can be conquered with a single company without firing a shot; with a battalion it would be more difficult; with a whole regiment it would be impossible for the entire force would perish of hunger."[30]

The central government continued to see its immediate need for military or other domestic reforms as unnecessary because its tested tactics for ruling the country still appeared to be effective. Dividing opposing elites, encouraging factional fights, offering bribes, and holding hostages or "guests" from powerful tribes and families in Tehran kept the Qajars secure on the Peacock Throne. Except for the territorial losses to the Russians, the Qajars did fairly well in maintaining at least nominal sovereignty over the country, probably making reform seem less imperative to the ruling elite. Still, Nasir al-Din eventually came to the realization toward the end of his reign that he needed to improve his armed forces. In 1878, during a visit to Russia, the shah was so impressed by the appearance and horsemanship of the Russian Cossacks that he signed a contract for the dispatch of Cossack officers and non-commissioned officers (NCOs) to form a regiment in Iran to serve as a royal guard.[31]

In early 1879 Col. Alexey Ivanovich Dumantovich arrived in Tehran at the head of the first Cossack contingent. The Russian military mission set up, trained, and commanded two Persian Cossack brigades of four hundred to six hundred men each. The brigades were manned by detachments of *mohajers* (immigrants), who were descendants of Transcaucasian Muslims who had migrated to Iran early in the century to escape Russian rule. Colonel Dumantovich remained in overall command of the unit for three years and oversaw its initial development, making sure that discipline was strict and pay was received. The Russians abolished the practice of giving sons the ranks of their deceased fathers, prevented the selling of ranks, and established a merit system for the promotion of Iranian officers in the brigades. Most Iranians regarded the unit as an instrument of Russian influence, and at times it was treated indifferently by the Qajars. After only a few years the Cossacks deteriorated markedly because of personal rivalries between Qajar officials and inadequate funding. When the money ran out, the fourth Russian commander of the brigade chose to follow the Iranian practice of granting long leaves without pay to his men. After a particularly poor showing at drill by the resource-starved unit, Nasir al-Din ordered the brigade reduced to two hundred men.

The fifth commander, Col. V. I. Kosagovskij, arrived in Tehran in 1884 and found a much diminished Cossack Brigade. In his correspondence with his Russian superiors, Kosagovskij reported that his cash box held debts rather than money. He also noted that instead of the 500 Cossacks he expected to find in Tehran, there were only 165 horsemen fit for duty. Summing up the plight of the brigade, Kosagovskij wrote about coming upon one of the brigade's Iranian officers riding on a saddleless mule with an Iranian soldier holding on behind him. The Russian observed that, "[The] Commander and his soldier were wearing torn shoes. While still wearing their military jackets and caps with insignias . . . [their] pants were rolled up to their knees and the Captain's long underwear as well as the hairy feet of the soldier were out to see . . . both saluted me; the Captain with his left hand, and his soldier with the right one."[32]

Kosagovskij was able to turn the unit around, but not without difficulty. His initial attempts to overcome the indiscipline of the *mohajers* resulted in a mutiny. The Russian colonel was persistent, however, and over time developed a well-trained, organized, and obedient force that became virtually the sole agent for law and order in Tehran. At Nasir al-Din's death by assassination in May 1896, his eldest son, Muzaffar al-Din Shah (r. 1896–1907) ascended the Peacock Throne with the help of the Persian Cossack Brigade. The Cossacks immediately deployed to maintain order in the capital and deter two other Qajar princes from challenging their elder brother for the throne. It is a testament to the central government's weakness that one of the pretenders, Zell al-Sultan, had a private army of Western-trained soldiers that was viewed as superior to the Qajar regular army. Muzaffar was saved only because Zell al-Sultan and the other challenger, Kamran Mirza, were unwilling to take on the Cossacks and instead pledged loyalty to the new shah.

By 1899 the brigade had grown to roughly 1,500 men organized into four cavalry squadrons, two horse artillery batteries, and an infantry battalion and was led by 133 Iranian and ten Russian officers. The unit's main weapon, the American-designed and Russian-produced single-shot, bolt-action Berdan rifle, was far superior to the arms of the rest of Qajar military. The brigade occasionally raised levies of irregular tribal cavalry for support, and by late 1903 two squadrons of Shahsavan and Kurdish tribesmen were added to the Cossack formation. Most of the brigade was stationed in Tehran, but detachments eventually spread throughout northern Iran. Almost all of the soldiers were volunteers, but conscription was occasionally used. Of the estimated 1,600 men in the brigade in 1902, 1,300 were volunteers and the rest were impressed from the Shahsavan tribe. The *mohajers* continued to be an important source of recruits, and throughout the brigade's existence the majority of officers and men were Turkic speaking. In 1911 only 10 percent of the brigade's personnel were ethnic Persians, while 85 percent were drawn from various Turkic and Kurdish tribes.[33]

The Cossack Brigade's main mission was to guard the shah, maintain order in the capital, protect Europeans there, and carry out other military duties in the provinces, such as protecting governors. The brigade became indispensable for guarding and policing Tehran, especially during Muzaffar al-Din's lengthy visits to Europe in 1900 and 1902. The Russian commanders used the Qajars' over-reliance on the Cossacks at the turn of the century to ensure that the brigade was properly financed and its soldiers were paid. The Russians did not try to turn the unit into a mobile fighting formation and conducted no field training. Even parade drill was limited to the summer months while the soldiers were allowed to go home during the winter. The generous winter leave created a significant weakness for the brigade because many of the rank-and-file volunteers failed to return, and the resulting high turnover rate meant that a substantial proportion of the unit was always made up of new recruits. Despite this problem, the British in Iran judged that the Cossacks, although no match for European or Indian troops, were superior to all other Iranian forces.

Qajar control over the Cossack Brigade was weak at best. The Russian commanders chose their own officers for the brigade and controlled all of the unit's internal financial arrangements. The Russians also handled the recruitment of the brigade's soldiers, and all enlistment and discharge issues were the responsibility of the Russian commander, with no Qajar government involvement. In fact, while the shah and his ministers personally nominated all of the brigade's higher-ranking Iranian officers, the Russian commander determined who was selected and was responsible for choosing junior Iranian officers. The Russian commanders insisted on promotions based on merit and favored officers who had worked their way up the brigade's hierarchy. The bulk of the officers was not taken from prominent families but was drawn from the lower classes. As more and more men of "low birth" were promoted into the officer corps, they became personally attached and loyal to the Russian commandant. An exception was the officers of the Shahsavan, Bakhtiari, and Kurdish contingents added after 1901. These generally were men of high standing within their tribes and were recruited, in part, to increase Russia's influence with the tribes, some of which were receiving arms from the czar's agents.

Imperial Russia initially saw its interests closely linked to Qajar absolutism, and thus the Cossack Brigade received close attention and occasional support in the form of money, arms, and ammunition. Each brigade commander consulted regularly with the Russian minister in Tehran. The brigade even looked like a Russian formation: Its uniform included the Russian-style *papakha* fur hat and *cherkesska* wool long coat with the sewn-in cartridge holders across the chest. These arrangements and other actions prompted British observers to complain that the brigade was treated as part of the Russian army. The Iranian ruling class was well aware of the Cossack Brigade's subordination to the Russian mission in Tehran. But the court was impressed with the unit and understood its need of the Cossacks' protection. The Russian government was careful in its choice of commanders for the brigade, selecting men with military and diplomatic skills.

Over the years, the Russians used the brigade to place officials in nearly every district in Iran, and Russian engineers and financial agents traveled throughout the country with Cossack Brigade escorts.

By 1904 the Cossack Brigade's fortunes began to wane as it shared with the other armed forces the consequences of Iran's general decline in government revenues. Its Russian commander had to borrow money from Russian and British banks to meet his obligations. He also was forced to send more soldiers home during the winter leave period and then had to reduce the size of the brigade. These changes purportedly damaged the Iranian soldiers' morale and reduced their loyalty to their Russian officers. Meanwhile, the Russian officers were increasingly distracted by reports of political problems in St. Petersburg in the run-up to the 1905 Russian Constitutional Revolution. Eventually, Russian banks refused further loans to the commander. The growing demoralization and related inefficiency translated into less military effectiveness. Never accepted by most Iranians because it was viewed as a protector of foreign interests, the Cossack Brigade became increasingly unpopular. As Iran's own constitutional movement gained momentum, the rank-and-file soldiers became less disciplined. By late 1905 the Cossack Brigade was isolated from Iranian politics and of questionable utility to the government during the crises that soon roiled the country.

The Army at Its Nadir

Between 1885 and 1905 the Iranian military continued to suffer from all of the ills that had plagued it in the preceding decades of Qajar rule. The armed forces consisted of the irregular tribal cavalry, regular army infantry and artillery formations, and the Cossack Brigade. In addition, Iran had a small, mostly ceremonial force of royal guards to protect the shah, the crown prince, and their palaces. The morale of the army was pitiable, and the regiments were unable to defend Iran's borders and too weak to maintain internal security even by limited Qajar standards. As an institution, the Qajar military was not spared from the general popular criticism of the ruling dynasty. One of the newly established liberal journals in 1890 wrote, "Our army (is) the laughingstock of the world."[34] The various units in the armed forces, including eventually the Cossack Brigade, were woefully undermanned and lacking in the resources essential for military effectiveness. Contemporary British accounts of Qajar soldiers, however, praised their qualities as individuals despite the problems of the armed forces. As one officer noted, "They ride courageously at full speed over the very worst ground . . . [and are] remarkably hardy, patient and enduring, requiring scarcely any baggage, and able to march thirty miles a day for many successive days, while living on nothing but bread and onions."[35] A Russian observer gave a similar report in the 1890s, writing of Persian soldiers that "they are well built and of a good height and physical strength; Persians have exceptional abilities for long-distance marching. All of them are naturally good shots, extremely abstemious eaters and drinkers and are amazingly obedient and sharp; the history of the country also proves that Persians know how to be brave and martial."[36]

As in previous decades, the tribal cavalry at the turn of the century was the most powerful arm of the Qajar military. While more effective than the regular infantry formations, the general capabilities of the irregular cavalry are hard to assess. Their tactics were unchanged, and plunder was still their main motivation and means of support in the field. The provinces of Azerbaijan and Khorasan furnished most of the Qajar's irregular cavalry and, as they had for centuries, still provided excellent horsemen and marksmen. The irregular cavalry from the major northern and southern tribes increasingly fell under the influence of the Russians and the British, however, and often would not act without the foreigners' approval. As a result, the government increasingly relied on the mobilization of minor tribes, which were smaller and less effective. In the Mashhad riot of 1903, irregular cavalry assembled by the government were no more than a mob of 1,000 to 1,200 riders brought in from neighboring districts. A third of these had flintlocks while the rest were armed only with clubs.

Iranian regular army units and arms factories were mostly unchanged from the mid-nineteenth century. During his trip to Europe in 1878 the shah contracted for ten Austrian officers to go to Iran as a training mission for the army, but they had no apparent impact. The infantry continued to be poorly equipped, trained, and disciplined with few capabilities to move and fight. In 1880 the government needed three months to assemble twenty thousand men to confront a tribal revolt in Kurdistan. By the time the Iranian army was ready to move, the Kurdish fighters had concluded their raids and returned home. Pleased with the result, the regular army units returned to their garrisons where medals were lavishly distributed to commemorate the "glorious" campaign. When a regiment from southwestern Iran was sent north to help the army quell disorder in 1903, it was routed by restive Lur tribesmen between Khorramabad and Dezful. During the same year, the shah ordered the call-up of thirty thousand reservists to suppress outbreaks of unrest in Rasht but was frustrated when the various regiments refused to muster until pay arrears were addressed. Army arsenals, meanwhile, were filled with obsolete weapons and ammunition. The Tehran garrison, which had a nominal strength of forty thousand men, reportedly used at least a dozen different types of rifles ranging from flintlocks and matchlocks to British-made single-shot, breech-loading Snider and Martini rifles. At the turn of the century, Iran had arsenals in all major provincial cities, but it is doubtful that any were adequately maintained or managed. The Iranians also had added a small cartridge factory imported from France for the arsenal in Tehran. The factory's output capacity was ten thousand cartridges per day, but only half that amount was produced.[37]

At the end of the nineteenth century, corruption, inept administration, and political factionalism were major problems that reverberated into the twentieth century. In the late 1890s, Abd al-Hussein Mirza Farmanfarma's tenure as minister of war exemplified these problems. In addition to being the shah's cousin and brother-in-law, Farmanfarma was married to a daughter of the crown prince. He was closely tied to the British mission and was unabashedly ambitious and avaricious. The war minister constantly interfered in the other ministries' work, tried to weaken the Cossack Brigade because its commander did not report to him, and constantly intrigued against the prime minister. Farmanfarma resigned in May 1898 amid accusations that he took bribes and diverted military pay to his own accounts at a time when the treasury was almost out of money and signs of open revolt among the troops were spreading. Some of the Qajar soldiers had not been paid in three years, and, their patience exhausted, they began placing threatening placards near their barracks. A worried shah acquired a small local loan, paid the soldiers an installment on the arrears, and bought a measure of temporary peace and security. During this period desertion was commonplace, and half of the Qajar army was on unpaid leave at any given time. Army regiments often disbanded themselves over the lack of pay, only to be replaced by ad hoc forces temporarily recruited from local tribes. To stretch government revenues, the Qajars began to debase copper coins, the specie Iranian troops received from their paymasters. The soldiers were not fooled and transferred their allegiance to better-paying provincial governors and local commanders, which further weakened central authority.[38]

Increasingly, the degraded regular forces became incapable of executing any military missions and existed mostly on paper. Between 1904 and 1905 Prime Minister Ain al-Dawleh proposed reorganizing the army but failed to overcome the opposition of the minister of war, a Qajar prince who was following past precedent and opposing any reform that might prevent him from using the military as his private means for personal enrichment. When this war minister died, Joseph Naus, a Belgian national serving as the minister of customs, urged Dawleh to try again. Naus proposed that, rather than a large and mostly unaffordable European-style army, Iran should instead develop a small but efficient mobile force of ten thousand to twenty thousand men. The Belgian argued that this would cut the military budget in half and that the money saved could be used to address other budgetary needs. The proposal amounted to one of the first calls in decades for a modern national army and implied the need to make meaningful changes at court and in Iran's relationship with the Russians and the British. Muzaffar al-Din Shah was unwilling to take on these challenges, and the plan was dropped.

The Autumn of the Qajars

The years between Muzaffar al-Din's accession in 1896 and 1905 were marked by continued Qajar weakness, profligacy, and ineptitude and, increasingly, by internal unrest and instability, all of which accelerated Iran's decline as an independent state. The scope of British and Russian involvement in Iran's internal affairs had expanded greatly as part of the "great game" between the two empires in Central Asia. Lord Curzon, the architect of British policy in Iran, famously said of Iran and its eastern neighbors in 1889: "They are pieces on a chessboard upon which is being played out a game for the domination of the world."[39] By the start of the twentieth century the Russians and the British had established strong spheres of influence in Iran and soon reached an accommodation that eliminated opportunities for the Qajars to play the Europeans against each other. The first decade of Muzaffar al-Din's rule also was a period of great political ferment and of a complex interplay of government, popular, and external actions that were shaping the Iranian nation. As the new century approached, Iran remained a traditional society reliant on rural farming and tribal herding and, except for a ubiquitous and not very modern cotton industry, still preindustrial. It also was a failing society under great stress from economic and social dislocations, unemployment, food shortages, and oppressively high taxes. The Qajars took on more and more debt while the issuing of defective silver and excessive amounts of copper coin accelerated a serious depreciation in the value of Iranian money. Important provinces, which were difficult to control in the best of times under Qajar administration, became even more isolated from Tehran and came under British and Russian sway. Continuing economic dislocations, bankruptcy, chaos, and uncertainty led to robbery and brigandage as the only means for some to earn a living, and the lawlessness became yet another excuse for foreign intervention.[40]

Starting in the 1890s popular criticism of the Qajar shahs' despotism grew, and Iranian nationalism became an important factor in politics and views toward the Iranian military. The period between 1890 and 1910 saw the rise of opposition movements in Iran on a scale unmatched in the Middle East if not in the rest of the world. Nasir al-Din ignored earlier warnings about the growing popular sentiments against Qajar rule. In 1872 Baron Julius de Reuter, a British citizen, purchased a gigantic system of monopolies in return for a commitment to build railways, open mines, and found a national bank. Curzon commented that the deal "contained the most complete surrender of the entire resources of a kingdom into foreign hands that has ever been dreamed of, much less accomplished, in history."[41] Strong popular opposition led by the clergy and bolstered by Russian objections forced the Reuter concession to be withdrawn later that year. Toward the end of his reign, however, the Qajar ruler needed money more than he feared dissent, and the sale of concessions continued. Mass protests and a national boycott broke out over an 1891 tobacco concession granted to Great Britain. The revolt caused Tehran to cancel the monopoly but again failed to make an impression on the Qajars. These protests included intellectuals, reformists, nationalists, and revolutionaries and were supported by the bazaar merchants and the clergy, both of whom had strong nationwide networks. By the turn of the century, secret groups formed to agitate for political change. The Iranian public was receptive to such ideas and was increasingly willing to take up arms in the name of change, taking advantage of the strengths of Iranian fighting men to challenge the government and write a new chapter in Iran's military history.

4.1 Qajar Iran.

4

Nationalism Unleashed

From Revolution to the Great War

THE REGULAR MILITARY'S UNSTEADY MARCH toward modernity and effectiveness came to a virtual standstill after the start of the twentieth century, but a new popular fighting force arrived on the scene to lay part of the foundation for future improvements. These revolutionary militias, called the mujahedin, or "fighters of the holy cause," by their contemporaries, arose to battle for Western-style democratic reforms and to resist foreign domination. They were joined by tribal warriors to confront the Qajars, who remained unwilling to reform, incapable of addressing the armed forces' many problems, and oblivious to unfolding world events. While the Qajar military still relied on tribal levies, the mujahedin represented a new type of armed force. Although equipped similarly to the tribal fighters and, like the levies, organized by local leaders, the mujahedin differed in key aspects. Most were volunteers committed to a political philosophy and the fight for democratic government during the Constitutional Revolution of 1906 to 1911. They were willing to challenge the Peacock Throne and make incredible sacrifices in brave fights against invading foreign armies. These fighters faded away after the political factions they supported were unable to maintain cohesion and support Iran's democratic aspirations. Their nationalism lived on, however, and in 1912 was incorporated into another new force, the Gendarmerie, which provided a glimpse of Iran's ability to create a professional, brave, incorruptible, and effective military organization.

Ready for Revolution

At the turn of the century popular ferment against the Qajars was stirred by news from around the world. The challenge to British rule in the 1899–1902 Boer War and Japan's victory in the Russo-Japanese War of 1905 sparked great political excitement. Iranian writers applauded the Transvaal's leaders for their resistance to Great Britain. The idea that Japan, a recently backward country, could win a confrontation with a much larger and better established European nation had obvious appeal. Iranian literature abounded with praise for Japan's strong, centralized government; its powerful military; and its constitutional framework. The 1905 Constitutional Revolution in Russia provided another positive example, and Iranian mullahs were exhorted to emulate the Russian clergy in mobilizing the masses against the government.

At the same time, the Qajar court's options for resisting foreign domination grew smaller as the "great game" between Great Britain and Russia ended. By mid-decade the two powers were apprehensive over the growing strength of Germany. Ready to cooperate against this common foe, the two signed the 1907 Anglo-Russian Treaty that divided Iran into three zones of influence, with Russia taking the north, Britain the south, and central Iran designated as neutral. Russian aims in Iran were to exploit Iranian resources and prevent any changes in Iran that might influence Muslims under imperial Russian rule. The British approach was similarly imperialistic, but wavered over the amount of engagement that was necessary or wise. The strategic importance of the British zone and of Iran in general was increased by the discovery of oil at Masjed-e Soleyman in 1908 and by the British Admiralty's decision shortly thereafter to change from coal to oil as the fleet's fuel source. Concerned about stability, the British vacillated between supporting the budding democratic nationalist movement and helping to maintain the ruling elite's authority. The nationalism growing as an outlet for opposition to Qajar rule and the shahs' concessions to foreigners increased the risk of the chaos, pushing the British toward supporting the status quo. Meanwhile, hatred of the Russians and British helped to form a common bond that contributed to a nationalist outlook that linked Iranians together for the tumultuous period between 1905 and 1911, and later through the First World War. For all of the strengths of Iranian nationalism, however, it was divided. The traditionalists, especially among the clergy, sought to reassert their conception of a conservative and idealized Islamic past absent Western influences. The reformers, meanwhile, wanted to advance Iran's fortunes by incorporating Western science, technology, and political liberalism.

Iran's first national assembly and constitution and subsequent revolution took root from a quarrel between merchants and the government over the enforcement of tariffs in late 1905. The merchants were joined by leading clerics, local revolutionary councils and fighters, and other discontented elements of Iranian society. Popular protests eventually forced the shah to promise to surrender his absolute power and convene representatives of the people in a "house of justice." Muzzafar al-Din refused to keep his promise, and in mid-1906, the government exiled nationalist leaders, inciting greater unrest. When a leading cleric in Tehran was arrested, a group of theology students tried to free the mullah. They challenged Cossack Brigade soldiers sent to impose a curfew, and one student was killed in the ensuing melee. The movement now had a martyr, and the young man's bloody shirt was quickly raised by his fellow students and carried through the streets of Tehran.

Fighting men soon emerged from this turmoil who were as hardy as Iran's regular soldiers but more effective, despite insufficient supplies, training, and modern arms. All were volunteers—workers, poor city dwellers, peasants, and tribesmen with a smattering of young reformers and intellectuals. The irregular fighters were initially part of local protective forces created by nationalist political movements. As the fight for a constitution was fully joined, most became insurrectionists and guerrillas and were joined by disaffected tribes. Some of the most noteworthy were the mujahedin and fedayeen ("self-sacrificers for the holy cause") from northwestern Iran, the guerrilla fighters of Gilan and Khorasan, and the Bakhtiari tribe. In Tabriz, a volunteer army of several thousand men of all ages was formed by a revolutionary *anjuman*, an old Persian name meaning "council" or "gathering." The mujahedin's initial engagements in Tabriz were with criminal elements hired by the Qajar elite to attack the dissidents. They soon created the Secret Center (Markaz-e Ghaibi), the primary operational command for the mujahedin, to counter Qajar attacks with a program of assassinations and intimidation. Over time, the revolutionaries added explosives and bombs to their arsenals and carried out acts of sabotage against the movement's enemies.[1]

The quantity and quality of the irregulars and their arms varied widely throughout Iran. German Mauser rifles and handguns can be seen in photographs of the Tabriz mujahedin, and British and Russian firearms were available to these and other revolutionary forces. Meanwhile, similar formations were developed in other regions as *anjumans* were created in Tehran, Gilan, Khorasan, and Esfahan provinces. The peasants in Gilan, who joined the volunteer forces and became active defenders of the nationalist movement, gained a reputation as superior guerrilla fighters. In one encounter with the Gilan guerrillas, an army report noted, "We saw no one, but a hundred bullets rained on us."[2] The Bakhtiari and other tribesmen who fought with the mujahedin, meanwhile, numbered several thousand and had the same qualities and skills as shown by the tribal levies used by the Qajar armed force. Although they are unlikely to have greatly enhanced the irregulars' capabilities, some former Qajar soldiers joined with the mujahedin.

The Qajars paid for their neglect of the army during the crisis. At the height of the protests, the commander of several of the regular army regiments garrisoned in Tehran announced that his troops would not fight against the people. In other cities Qajar soldiers either refused to fire on the protestors or joined them. In a letter to the Shah titled "The Patriot's Cry from the Heart," a leading senior cleric in the Constitutionalist movement appealed on behalf of Iranian soldiers, writing that the sarbaz "is deprived of his meager rations and wages and mostly earns his sustenance by coolie labor." He claimed that many soldiers perished from hunger every day, stating, "No worse defect than this can be imagined for a kingdom."[3] Only after the government increased and distributed their pay were soldiers in Tehran willing to perform some duties, such as clearing streets and forcing shops to open.

Even the Cossack Brigade, despite its royalist leanings, was mostly passive. In any event, its capacity to intervene had been weakened by its financial problems. In addition, the unit's 1,500 Iranian enlisted men were sympathetic to the popular demands for a national assembly and a constitution, especially after mullahs joined the protests. When the new commandant, a Colonel Liakhov, arrived in September 1906, he found that the brigade was out of the Russian officers' control and was being run by a council of Iranian officers. Liakhov succeeded in abolishing the council and weeding out anti-Russian officers. He then gained the confidence of his men by defending their interests, briefly improving the unit's discipline and efficiency. Nonetheless, popular resentment of the brigade caused the Russians to keep a lower profile.

Under mounting pressure, the ailing shah consented to the formation of a national assembly, called the Majles. One of Muzaffar al-Din's last official public acts was to attend the inauguration of the new legislature in October 1906. The representatives of the First Majles, blurring their significant differences in the interest of democratic unity, quickly drafted a constitution that arranged for sharing power with the court and set out the duties, limitations, and rights of the new government. The legislature also tried to pass legislation to create a strong army and curb the monarch's power over the armed forces but failed. A dying Muzaffar al-Din finally consented to approve the constitution in December 1906, but it represented, at best, an uneasy truce between tradition and modernity.[4]

Muhammad Ali Shah (r. 1907–9) ascended to the Qajar throne determined to reverse the democratic course but lacked the military power to act decisively. The new shah was described by an American adviser to the court as "perhaps the most perverted, cowardly, and vice-ridden monster that had disgraced the throne of Persia in many generations."[5] With the help of supporters in the Majles, Muhammad Ali undermined the new legislature. Despite the Qajars' continued reliance on Russian and British support, the shah and promonarchy elements condemned the constitution as a Western-inspired and anti-Islamic document. These attacks effectively exposed rifts between the modern secularists and the traditionalists, especially among the clergy, in the constitutional movement. The Russians were adamantly proshah because, after their own recent revolution, they opposed radical reformers everywhere. The British initially favored but then deserted the reformers, fearing that only the shah could maintain stability. London also was reluctant to challenge its new Russian ally as the anti-German Anglo-Russian Treaty was being negotiated. Russia agreed to fund the Cossack

Brigade, and the payment of a special bonus and purging of anti-Russian Iranian officers restored the unit's discipline and helped assure the shah of its loyalty. Colonel Liakhov and his Russian officers began to intervene openly on behalf of Muhammad Ali against the Majles and constitutionalists.[6]

Reaction and Civil War, 1908-9

Muhammad Ali struck back at the democrats in mid-December 1907 in a failed attempt to overthrow the constitutional government by arresting the prime minister, dismissing the cabinet, and closing the legislature. As many as two thousand mujahedin assembled to defend the Majles while other riflemen scattered over the roofs of the city. Mujahedin in Tabriz, Rasht, Qazvin, Kerman, and Esfahan proclaimed that they were ready to march on the capital. The Cossack and regular army commanders in Tabriz, Tehran, and other cities backed down in the face of this popular determination. The foreign legations, frightened by the prospect of violence, joined with the democrats in demanding that the shah restore the constitutional order. With the addition of this foreign pressure, Muhammad Ali relented. He agreed to the legislators' demands to dismiss his reactionary advisers, place the Cossack Brigade and his household troops under the Ministry of War, and uphold the constitutional order. A new crisis developed a few months later in late February 1908 when a prodemocratic radical threw a bomb at the royal motorcade. The Qajar monarch was not harmed but was left shaken by the experience and determined to renew the confrontation with the constitutionalists. After receiving assurances of Russian support, the shah put in motion plans to close the legislature and arrest the constitutional movement's leaders.

The coup began in early June when Muhammad Ali and his entourage were escorted to safety outside the capital and roughly three hundred Cossacks with two artillery pieces surrounded the Majles. Other Cossacks arrested some of the nationalist leaders and seized telegraph offices to cut off communications to the provinces. Having ordered martial law, the shah made Colonel Liakhov military governor with full power over the police and military forces. In response to Muhammad Ali's ultimatum, the reformist legislators agreed to have the mujahedin disperse, providing Liakhov the opening he needed to complete the Majles' emasculation. On June 23, 1908, a thousand or more Cossacks and regular army soldiers supported by light artillery and machine guns surrounded the Majles and the nearby Sepahsalar Mosque, where some of the nationalists had taken refuge. Following some initial skirmishing between the infantry and the mujahedin defenders, six Cossack guns opened fire on the buildings. Accounts vary, but up to four hundred soldiers, including some of the mounted Cossacks, deserted rather than participate in the attack. The nationalist fighters in the two compounds were still far outmanned and outgunned. In the course of a few brave sallies, however, the mujahedin were able to put three of the six Cossack artillery pieces out of action. After nearly eight hours of bombardment, the death of 250 mujahedin, and the partial collapse of the compounds around them, the surviving fighters fled. Over the next twelve months, civil war raged in several regions as the nationalists tried to restore the democratic order.[7]

The urban revolutionary groups were unready for sustained armed resistance, and Qajar military forces soon occupied most of the major cities where fighting had broken out. Only the mujahedin in Tabriz checked the local Qajar armed forces and scratched out a toehold for the constitutionalists. There, during the previous winter, military drill and shooting practice were conducted in the city's neighborhoods, and defense squads were formed and provided homemade uniforms. Training was initially held only on Fridays, but by the spring, "every evening the sound of drum and bugle and the chanting of cadence rose from every burough."[8] All understood that the nationalist defense of Tabriz was critically important to the constitutional cause because it gave hope and time to anjumans in Rasht, Esfahan, and elsewhere to reorganize and raise the banners of revolution. Fortunately for the proconstitution forces, the Tabriz mujahedin were capably led by Sattar Khan, a former brigand with a reputation as an Iranian Robin Hood.

Fighting in Tabriz began on the same day as the coup in Tehran when reactionary clerics incited royalist forces to attack the democratic revolutionaries. After a few weeks the mujahedin had thwarted attempts by Qajar army units and Kurdish and Shahsavan tribal forces to quash the rebellion. The nationalists gradually expanded the areas under their control and held some of the key roads leading into Tabriz. Unaccustomed to street fighting, the royalist forces withdrew and placed the city under siege. The defenders, at least in the early stages, were prepared to sustain the fight and had good morale. Sattar Khan was a popular commander who consulted with others and had close relations with the rank and file of his army. Sattar organized the affairs of the revolutionaries, using theological students as staff clerks, and ensured that the mujahedin were given uniforms, arms, ammunition, and pay. He created a reserve force to guard less dangerous areas of the city and set up an effective system of patrolling and manning to maintain alert defenses against government probing attacks. Even though some mujahedin had more modern rifles than the Qajar troops, Sattar's force relied on a mix of small arms with limited supplies. In one of his most significant accomplishments for the lengthy defense of Tabriz, Sattar Khan had his troops maintain scrupulous fire control to avoid wasting ammunition. Also, after making the mujahedin swear on the Koran not to steal, he enforced strict discipline, which helped to maintain popular support for the fighters.

Sattar Khan claimed to have four thousand men under arms and the ability to raise as many as ten thousand mujahedin. Some of the volunteers flocking to the revolution were from Transcaucasia. These men were well armed, had previous fighting experience, and were politically committed, bolstering the nationalist resistance in greater proportion than their numbers might indicate. Russian, Georgian, and Armenian social democrats sent five hundred to eight hundred fighters, most of whom had fought against the czar's army, to Azerbaijan and Gilan. Among these volunteers were Georgians with experience in setting up explosive laboratories to create bombs. Another non-Iranian volunteer was a young American, Howard C. Baskerville, a twenty-four-year-old Nebraska native and Princeton graduate who was working as a teacher for a Presbyterian mission in Tabriz when the fighting broke out. Baskerville, who had served in the American military, used his experience to recruit and train a group of his students and fought courageously for months before being killed during one of the final battles. Mujahedin ranks were bolstered in early July when eight hundred Azeri infantrymen from the Qajar army crossed the barricades and joined them.

The Qajar army was commanded by Muhammad Vali Khan Nasr al-Saltanah, a major landowner in northern Iran. It may have numbered thirty thousand fighters with the addition of levies of Bakhtiari, Kurdish, and other tribesmen. Part of the Qajar troops, however, were villagers who were "caught, dressed, and armed for the occasion" with little interest in battle.[9] Colonel Liakhov disparaged the Qajar forces as "wanting alike in order, discipline, and obedience" and "a worthless lot . . . [that] can only be employed for looting."[10] In mid-October the shah sent four hundred Iranian soldiers of the Cossack Brigade under a Russian captain with four field guns to Tabriz. The Cossacks had orders to crush the constitutionalists and were told that all the wealth within Tabriz would be theirs. The shah also threatened to disband the Cossacks if they failed. In addition, Muhammad Ali released from prison a notorious brigand, Rahim Khan, with orders to punish Tabriz. After assembling about five hundred horsemen, Rahim Khan started a campaign of rape and robbery in the already suffering region. Vali Khan launched a series of attacks during the course of the summer, but each attempt to storm the city's defenses was repulsed. By October these battlefield failures and quarrels with the Qajar governor of Azerbaijan caused Vali Khan to resign, leading to a lull in the fighting during November and December.

The governor, Ain al-Dawleh, became the acting royalist commander and decided to starve the population of Tabriz by blocking the roads leading into the city. The shah dispatched a ruthless mercenary named Samad Khan in January 1909 to take command of the Qajar troops. Within a month, Samad Khan had completed the encirclement of Tabriz, but his forces still were unable to break into the city. The resistance remained strong because surrender was tantamount to death at the hands of brigands. With famine, illness, and desertions beginning to take their toll on the mujahedin, however, the constitutionalists accepted royalist offers to negotiate in April. By then, concerns about the revolution and the precedent it might set for the czar's disaffected subjects prompted a Russian military intervention. Approximately 2,600 Russian cavalrymen and infantry supported by two artillery batteries and a sapper company entered the city on the last day of April 1909. The Russians disarmed the revolutionaries, who then numbered fewer than one thousand fighters. They also disbanded the royalist forces, which probably prevented the pillaging of the city and other depredations by the tribal levies. Additional Russian cavalry and infantry formations were dispatched to protect consulates in Rasht, Astarabad, and Mashhad while Russian naval vessels steamed into Iran's Caspian ports.

The siege of Tabriz was over, but the setback to the nationalist cause was only temporary because rebellions were flaring up throughout the country. Inspired by the Tabriz mujahedin, revolutionaries were increasingly active by late 1908 in Rasht, Astarabad, and Mashhad in the north, Bandar Abbas in the southeast, and Shiraz and Esfahan in central Iran. The uprising in Esfahan gained the support of local Bakhtiari tribal khans, who with three hundred horsemen succeeded in throwing the royalist government out of the city in January 1909. After securing the goodwill of the other southern tribes to protect (or at least not threaten) Bakhtiari lands, the khans gathered an army of five hundred to six hundred horsemen for an assault on Tehran. By the beginning of March 1909, there were multiple centers of nationalist resistance, acting more or less in concert, in Tabriz, Esfahan, and Rasht. By early April, Hamadan, Shiraz, Bushehr, Bandar Abbas, and Mashhad had joined the revolt.

The insurrection in the Caspian region was the next to gain momentum. Because of its heavy woodlands and swamps, the Caspian districts were distinct from the rest of Iran, and the local peasantry was fiercely independent. Lord Curzon had assessed that any conquest of the region would be a difficult undertaking because the peasants and native militia, familiar with the land and inured to guerrilla war, would make occupation nearly impossible.[11] In the two years leading up to the 1908 coup, the anjumans and mujahedin in Gilan had already fought the government to an uneasy standstill. Gilan's governor tried to reassert Qajar control over the province in September 1908 with a force of one thousand infantry and cavalry with two cannons. The soldiers of this royal army were unenthusiastic, having been warned by the local peasants of the unpleasant consequences of being taken prisoner. After six weeks on campaign, the Qajar force reached the Tavalash region, which was known for its high and dense forests. Unprepared for either guerrilla warfare or the determined resistance it encountered, the Qajar army broke in the Battle of Tavalash and retreated in disarray, harried by the mujahedin as it fled. Freed from the threat of royalist attacks, the mujahedin went on the offensive. Yephrem Khan (Ephraim Khan), an Armenian Christian who had fought against Russia's government, commanded a force of five hundred men, called "walking arsenals" by one British eyewitness, that easily seized Rasht after revolutionaries assassinated the governor there.[12] By February 1909, Muhammad Vali Khan Nasr al-Saltanah, the former Qajar commander at Tabriz, had switched sides. Also known as Sepahdar-e Azam, or Greatest of the Marshals, Vali Khan was given command of the mujahedin army from Gilan and Mazandaran. After consolidating control over the Caspian region and collecting money, this force prepared to move against the shah.

Dethroning the Shah

In May 1909 approximately seven hundred northern mujahedin under Sepahdar and Yephrem Khan moved toward Qazvin, ninety miles from Tehran. They were joined by about one hundred mujahedin who had reformed under Sattar Khan and had been chasing royalist units back toward the capital. A British observer traveling from Rasht to Tehran came across part of the shah's army returning from Tabriz and commented that it was "straggling over five or six miles of road . . . [there were] knots of weary and dispirited but good-humored men. . . . Their baggage wagons and horses were laden with filthy rags and rotten rusted firearms, and their officers sprawled over the backs of mules in a half sleep."[13] After arriving at Qazvin, a contingent of 250 nationalists attacked the Qajar garrison, capturing one hundred soldiers and killing another twenty while only losing three mujahedin. In response, about four hundred Iranian Cossacks under a Russian commander set out with two Maxim guns from Tehran to Karaj, about one-third of the way between the capital and Qazvin, with the mission to hold a bridge on this primary avenue of approach.

Muhammad Ali Shah had no illusions about his situation. The Qajar army had approximately five thousand regular soldiers and tribal levies in Tehran and on the southern approaches to the city, while the Cossack Brigade had eight hundred soldiers in Tehran and four hundred at Karaj. The shah knew that Tabriz had fallen to the Russians and not his army while smaller rebel armies had repeatedly defeated Qajar forces. In addition, the Russians and British were advising him to compromise to avoid further violence and its unforeseeable and potentially dangerous consequences. Reluctantly, the Qajar monarch offered to restore the constitution and grant a general amnesty. The Tabriz anjuman sought to get the nationalist movement to accept the shah's concessions, but most of the revolutionaries were not inclined to trust the conniving Muhammad Ali. Despite Russian and British warnings to the nationalists against approaching the capital, the contingent of Bakhtiari warriors from Esfahan advanced against little resistance from a retreating Qajar force of 1,200 infantry, 300 cavalry, and 6 guns. The Cossacks at Karaj, in danger of being outflanked by the Bakhtiaris, withdrew back to the town of Shahabad, only fifteen miles from Tehran, opening the door for the northern mujahedin to close on the capital. The Cossacks won the initial skirmishes and slowed the mujahedin advance, which increased pressure on the nationalists as news arrived that the Russians were readying troops in Baku to intervene. Despite or perhaps because of the threats of Russian intervention, the Bakhtiari khans sent an additional six hundred mounted riflemen to join in the push to the capital.

After a series of hard-fought battles at Shahabad and other towns on the road into Tehran from the northwest, the mujahedin linked up with the Bakhtiari tribesmen to create a combined nationalist army. On July 11, 1909, Qajar reinforcements reached the frontline trenches about fourteen miles west of the capital near the small village of Badamak. At this point, the shah had a few thousand entrenched Qajar soldiers supported by a limited number of artillery pieces and three Maxim machine guns. Some Cossack Brigade units may have participated in the first day of fighting but apparently were withdrawn to police the capital against a potential popular uprising. The nationalist army, which had grown as it approached Tehran, probably was around four thousand strong with one field gun. The Qajar forces were surprisingly stalwart in the defense of Tehran, and the nationalists were unable to breach the defensive line after two days of attacks. Descriptions of nationalist actions in the next phase of the battle vary. Some historians credit the first attacks as mere feints that allowed part of the constitutionalist forces to outflank the Qajar defenses. Others suggest that it was the failure to defeat the entrenched Qajar army that caused the nationalists to attempt to bypass Badamak. In either case, the nationalists moved a substantial force to the vulnerable northern outskirts of the city.

On the morning of July 13, 1909, these nationalist forces assaulted the capital, aided by a supporting attack from three hundred mujahedin who had infiltrated the Qajar lines to the west. The revolutionaries entered the unprotected northern gates of the capital and captured portions of Tehran without firing a shot. The city's other gates, guarded by regular soldiers, surrendered after brief fights. By midday, the nationalists controlled the northern part of the city, and many Qajar soldiers and Iranian members of the Cossack Brigade deserted to the democratic side. A Qajar force that had been advancing toward the city from the northeast joined the battle late and bombarded points of Tehran occupied by the nationalist troops with little effect. By July 15, as many as three thousand Bakhtiari, mujahedin, and other volunteer fighters were in Tehran, and although the Cossack Brigade still held out in the city's central square, the battle was basically over. After the nationalists seized the city's South Gate, the last to fall into their hands, a frightened Muhammad Ali, his guard, and his attendants took refuge in the Russian legation, effectively abdicating his throne. A quickly reconstituted Majles voted to depose the shah on July 16 and established a regency for the twelve-year-old crown prince.

Muhammad Ali departed for Russia at the end of August, but Iran's troubles did not go with him. A regent ruled for young Sultan Ahmed Shah (r. 1914–26), and Muhammad Vali Khan became the prime minister and minister of war. The nationalists' attempts to consolidate the constitutional government were crippled by political divisiveness among the victorious parties, a devastated economy, inadequate government revenues, and the lack of a strong military to back government authority. The Qajar regular army was of little value, and most of the tribal levies quickly returned home. The Cossack Brigade, still the most effective military formation in Iran, was an uncertain ally at best because of continued Russian influence. When the revolutionary armies took control of the capital, Colonel Liakhov negotiated the brigade's surrender, accepted service under the new government, and agreed to act under the orders of the minister of war. Because of the threat of rioting and looting, the Cossacks' weapons were returned, and the brigade quickly restored order in Tehran. All the Cossack officers were made to pledge allegiance to the constitution, but the Russians showed little respect for the new authorities. After Liakhov was replaced in November, the Russians began to reassert themselves. The Russian and British legations, meanwhile, worked to limit the consideration of any military reforms by the new government. They also prevented the removal of Russian officers from the Cossack Brigade, the adoption of an Iranian name for the unit, and the hiring of other European military advisers who might reduce Russian and British influence.[14]

The mujahedin and Bakhtiari soldiers who captured Tehran gradually became a problem. The northern mujahedin remaining in Tehran wanted the government to address various grievances while the tribal forces grabbed power and influence. Many of the poorly paid rank-and-file fighters sought to squeeze greater rewards for their service from the new government while others turned to crime to survive. The nationalists proposed to disband these militias but had no means to enforce the action because the Cossack Brigade, despite the Russian legation's desire to see the mujahedin disarmed, refused to help. Government pension offers were met with violent protests over the payment's size, and, in one incident, Sattar Khan, the hero of Tabriz, was wounded and disabled trying to calm his veterans. Outside of Tehran, resentment of the Bakhtiaris' growing power sparked a revolt in 1910 by their Qashqai tribal rivals in Fars Province. The threat to trade from the revolt and the prospect of a British military intervention forced the Majles to agree to create a new organization to guard the roads in southern Iran, diverting men and resources from other pressing needs. In an attempt to advance critical financial reforms, the constitutional government hired an American, W. Morgan Shuster, to be the treasurer general with the mission to reorganize Iran's disordered and highly corrupt tax system and to improve its financial situation.

Shuster arrived in Iran in early 1911 to find its Treasury Department in crisis because of wasteful military spending. The American discovered that there was no budget or budgeting process and, in general, no accountability. The War Department took an estimated half of nominal Qajar revenues for the arsenals, general staff, medical corps, and combat forces. Shuster commented that the army was virtually mythical because he never encountered an appreciable number of regular army personnel except when the Treasury was approached for pay. He described the War Department as "the roosting-place for the most brilliant galaxy of uniformed loafers, masquerading as generals, commissaries, and chiefs of staff, of petty grafters, amiable cutthroats and all-round scoundrels which it has ever been my fortune to encounter."[15] Shuster battled constantly with the unrealistic demands made by Vali Khan for funds that he refused to account for. Similarly, he found that the Bakhtiari khans and others providing tribal forces to the government tried to extort exorbitant sums in return for their services. Shuster reported that even the foreign legations in Tehran tried to soak up government revenues by keeping large numbers of their citizens on Iran's salary and pension rolls. The Europeans on these lists rarely ranked less than colonel, and Shuster noted that one elderly and usually incapacitated Italian officer had managed to remain on the War Department registry with the self-awarded rank of general. Shuster's steadfast efforts to trim the rolls of deadwood contributed to Iranian and European opposition to his role and, eventually, to the Iranian leadership's willingness to submit to Russian ultimatums for his removal.[16]

One of Shuster's most important initiatives was the creation of the Treasury Gendarmerie to help collect taxes, which had significant consequences for Iran's relations with Russia. Shuster wanted to create an able officer corps for this new law- and tax-enforcement agency. He meticulously supervised the selection of officers, drawing from groups affiliated with the constitutionalists with good family backgrounds, strong character, and patriotic feelings. This approach and high pay attracted the most able, competent, and politically conscious officers, whom Shuster described as "the pick of the young Persian patriots who really desired to serve their country."[17] During its brief life, the Treasury Gendarmerie became the most effective arm of the new government.

Pushed by the liberals and social democrats of Iran's Democratic Party in the Majles, the new government attempted various reforms that increasingly brought the country into conflict with Russia. The Russian troops dispatched to Iran in 1909 had stayed to occupy and administer many of the northern provinces. With the czarist government's support, Russians bought vast tracts of land from Iranians to further secure their political and military hold on the north. When Shuster sent the Treasury Gendarmerie into the Russian zone of influence to collect taxes, the Russians and their Iranian supporters were infuriated, setting in motion the events leading to the end of the second constitutional government.

Muhammad Ali Strikes Back

In mid-July 1911, Muhammad Ali crossed the Caspian in a Russian boat carrying ample ammunition for the army he planned to gather. The former shah landed at Gumish Tepe (modern Gomishan on the southeastern shore of the Caspian) and soon assembled a few thousand tribesmen for his march on Tehran. Taking advantage of these tribes' hostility toward the Bakhtiaris, the ex-shah recruited veterans of the Qajar army from the Shahsavan and Turkman tribes of the north while his brother, Salar al-Dawleh, gathered Kurdish and Lur tribes from the Kermanshah region along the Iranian-Ottoman frontier in the west. In early August, Arshad al-Dawleh, the ex-shah's principal general and companion in Russia, put his newly formed royalist army on the road to the capital. In his first encounter with government troops at Damghan, Arshad's forces won the battle, captured two cannons, munitions, and other supplies and were augmented by defecting government soldiers. Meanwhile, Salar al-Dawleh and his eight hundred horsemen occupied Hamadan near Iran's western border without opposition.[18]

As the ex-shah's forces began their march on the capital from the north and west, the government had little more than 2,500 troops to defend Tehran. These consisted of 1,200 police and 600 gendarmes in Tehran, 500 gendarmes at Qazvin, and 200 Armenian "professional fighting men." They were augmented by a few hundred students and other volunteers raised by Shuster and democratic politicians and an undetermined number of Bakhtiari tribal contingents between Esfahan and Tehran who rejoined the nationalist cause. The government was denied the service of the Cossack Brigade as the Russian officers made excuses to refuse orders from the Iranian minister of war to confront Muhammad Ali's army. At this time the Armenian fighter Yephrem Khan was the chief of police and gendarmes in Tehran and was given the task of gathering more forces to oppose the ex-shah. The most numerous contingent, the 1,800 police and gendarmes, was needed to maintain order in the capital. Gathering the approximately six hundred Bakhtiari fighters who served as the guards and escorts of the Bakhtiari chiefs in Tehran, Yephrem Khan formed the nucleus around which the rest of the nationalist fighters assembled. The Armenian commander kept his main forces near the city to await the approach of the ex-shah's army and better identify the enemy's plans. He was not completely passive, however, and in mid-August, Yephrem Khan sent small forces of picked men to guard the mountain passes leading to Tehran from the north while others prepared to fall on Muhammad Ali's rear and cut his supply lines.

In late August, Turkman fighters under Arshad al-Dawleh set the stage for the climatic battle by defeating a smaller number of nationalist troops at Aiwan-e Kaif (Eyvanekey), roughly fifty-six miles outside the capital. A Bakhtiari contingent rode out to impede the Turkmans and kept them from advancing more than a few miles each day over the next week. Yephrem Khan, 350 picked men, and a German artillery instructor with a Maxim gun and three 75-mm quick-firing Schneider-Creuzot cannons followed close behind the Bakhtiaris. These were soon joined by other nationalist forces to form a battle line against Arshad about forty miles south of Tehran near the town of Varamin. On September 5, 1911, Yephrem Khan's force of Bakhtiaris, Armenian volunteers, and Iranian gendarmes was arrayed against about 1,400 Turkman horsemen and 600 Turkman infantry under the ex-shah's banner. Shortly before the battle began, Yephrem Khan was joined by the Bakhtiari delaying force, adding another 400 fighters and a few gendarmes to his army to bring its total strength to slightly fewer than 1,200 men. Muhammad Ali's tribal warriors started the battle when Arshad sent 300 fighters into Varamin to create a diversion. The Maxim and Schneiders, which occupied a commanding position over the town, opened on the attackers and threw them into confusion. The Bakhtiari cavalry then charged the disorganized Turkmans, who broke and fled into the lines of the ex-shah's army, carrying the rest of these tribal forces in retreat from the battlefield. Although the Bakhtiari cavalry failed to pursue the retreating army, the now fearful Turkman tribesmen dispersed back into their homelands. Arshad was wounded and captured and, unrepentant, was executed the next day.

Muhammad Ali was still safe in the north trying to rally more Iranians to his cause during the Battle of Varamin. Less than a week later, however, the ex-shah and an accompanying tribal contingent ran into a government force and were routed. Muhammad Ali and his remaining followers fled back to Gumish Tepe where they hid beneath Russian guns. Salar al-Dawleh, meanwhile, started his march toward Tehran from Hamadan in mid-September with up to six thousand Kurdish fighters and visions of installing himself as shah. Yephrem Khan and several Bakhtiari chiefs assembled about two thousand men and the Maxim guns and cannons near Qom to stop Salar. The two forces met in battle on September 27, and while details are sparse, the nationalists won another decisive victory. At a claimed cost of only two killed and six wounded, the nationalists killed or wounded five hundred of Salar's Kurdish and Lur troops and captured another two hundred along with six cannon and a large quantity of ammunition. The ex-prince and his remaining forces fled into Ottoman territory, effectively putting an end to Muhammad Ali's attempt to regain his throne.

Muhammad Ali's defeat brought no respite for the government. The Russians demanded Shuster's dismissal and sent twelve thousand more troops into northern Iran in November 1911 to back up their ultimatum. The Majles agreed to some concessions and offered future negotiations, but the prime minister and his cabinet worried that the legislature's actions were still too risky. Under orders from the regent, the Bakhtiari tribal forces closed down the Majles. Yephrem Khan and his Caucasian mujahedin force aided the Bakhtiaris because the Armenian leader, who later died while fighting the remnants of the ex-shah's forces, wanted to avert a Russian occupation. After the legislators were expelled, Russian-backed Iranians began to purge, exile, or execute the remaining constitutionalists and activists. In Tabriz, the mujahedin skirmished with Russian detachments, but the threat of a bloody attack on the city led the revolutionaries to agree to disarmament and the peaceful occupation of the city by Russian units. The Russians then systematically eliminated the proconstitution elements in the city, imprisoning and executing as many as three thousand mujahedin.

The purge of the nationalists increased foreign domination while leaving Iran more divided and weaker than ever. The Russian occupation of the north and blatant interference in the Shuster matter prompted mass protests and violent confrontations. In 1912, the Russians reacted to the assassination of one of their officers in Mashhad by bombarding and looting the revered Imam Reza Shrine. Meanwhile, the Bakhtiari khans in Tehran had taken over the government ministries and were using them to enrich the tribe. As the year ended, the provinces were being torn apart by tribal convulsions. In the north and west, Turkmans, Shahsavans, Kurds, and Lurs withheld taxes and raided villages. In the south, Qashqais, Arabs, Baluchs, and other tribes formed an alliance to stem the rising power of the Bakhtiari chiefs who had ensconced themselves in Tehran. Many tribes viewed the constitution as cover for Bakhtiari domination, and only tribal rivalries prevented the concerted action that might have brought down the government. In any event, provincial and tribal leaders increasingly ignored the central government and dealt with Russian and British officials.[19]

The Nationalists' Best Hope

In an effort to reestablish the central government's authority, the Second Majles set up the Government Gendarmerie in 1912. The Gendarmerie was envisioned by reformers in the legislature to be the efficient military force that Iran desperately needed to impose order, collect taxes, and safeguard internal trade to reduce the justification for foreign interference. It became the main focus of the Iranian constitutionalists' efforts to arm their country because regular army infantry units were beyond easy redemption and the Persian Cossack Brigade was seen as unreliable and antidemocratic. During the tumultuous years between

1914 and 1921, the Gendarmerie picked up this mantle to become a principal component of a democratic and nationalist state-building effort.

After the Russians compelled the Iranian government to dismiss the Shuster Mission and disband the Treasury Gendarmerie, its Iranian officers became the core cadre for the new Gendarmerie, bringing with them their prodemocracy, nationalist, and anti-Russian sentiments. Twenty Swedish officers were hired to serve as the primary commanders and trainers. The Gendarmerie's other leadership and staff billets were filled by the former Treasury Gendarmerie officers, regular army officers who had trained at Ottoman and European schools, and officers from the Gendarmerie's own training schools. Following the practice established by Shuster, the Gendarmerie recruited officers from families with high social standing or from families of high-ranking military officers. As a result, most Gendarmerie officers were generally well educated and came from Tehran and Tabriz. Although much experience was gained on the job, training was not ignored, and schools for officers and NCOs and a training system for enlisted men were established by the Swedish officers and their Majles supporters. The 1,100 enlisted men of Shuster's Treasury Gendarmerie also were folded into the Government Gendarmerie. To increase the nationalist disposition of the Gendarmerie, the Swedish commanders mixed troops from different regions and tribes in each regiment, although Turkic-speakers tended to dominate. The government also made sure that, at least initially, pay was issued regularly and in full, and democratic reformers indoctrinated the officers and men with nationalist and patriotic sentiments.[20]

At the end of its first year the Gendarmerie had a strength of twenty-one Swedish officers and nearly three thousand Iranian officers and men. The force structure grew from two regiments in Tehran and one for Shiraz in 1912 to seven regiments in 1914 by standing up units in Kerman, Qazvin, Esfahan, and Borujerd. At this point on the eve of the First World War, the Gendarmerie had approximately ten thousand enlisted men and NCOs, four hundred Iranian officers, and thirty Swedish officers. The majority of Swedish officers were in Tehran, while each regiment was commanded by one Swedish officer supported by a staff of at least twenty Iranian officers. Most gendarmes were mounted and armed with Mauser rifles. The force also had a small artillery detachment of four mountain guns and about a dozen machine guns spread throughout the regiments.

To accomplish their many missions, which included revenue collection, road security, and the protection of embassies, consulates, banks, and telegraph and post offices, Gendarmerie units had to overcome opposition from the local elite. The landowners and tribal khans still opposed all military reform that threatened to increase central authority. The provincial authorities, in particular, had profited from the disorder in the countryside by setting up protection rackets.

They violently opposed the extension of the gendarmes into their areas. Still, in early 1913 gendarmes dispatched to southern Iran improved road security and quelled tribal disorders, forestalling British plans to deploy forces to secure the area. The gendarmes later showed themselves as effective fighters when they suppressed a tribal uprising in Fars and, in a fight that cost them fifty dead and twenty-five wounded, stormed a rebel stronghold. Later that year, Gendarmerie units successfully disarmed and dispersed Bakhtiari tribesmen who had been intimidating the government and operating with impunity in Tehran. The gendarmes' continued success and demonstrated determination increased the organization's confidence and morale and generated more political and financial support. The Gendarmerie's expansion, however, was coming at the expense of the Persian Cossack Brigade, which, along with the gendarmes' popular support, increased Russian opposition.

The Gendarmerie's Iranian supporters and its Swedish officers had been careful in their dealings with key Iranian elites, but the force's very nature brought it into conflict with the Russians and the British. The Swedish commander made sure to conciliate the Iranian ulema, or clergy, by addressing their concerns about the Gendarmerie's role and the gendarmes' training. The clerics ended up well disposed to the force along with Iran's traders and merchants, who credited the Gendarmerie with improving security and business opportunities. These elements of Iranian society joined the democrats in seeing the force as a focus of national aspirations to eliminate Iran's subservience to foreigners. With their prodemocratic political tradition and nationalist consciousness, the gendarme rank and file had greater political awareness than the general population. Nevertheless, the Gendarmerie obediently enforced government policies and tried to keep out of politics. The Russians, the British, and their allies in the government, however, remained suspicious of the Gendarmerie and, as tensions with Germany grew in Europe, distrusted the Swedish officers.

The Swedes were undoubtedly pro-German and anti-Russian, but the British and Russians used them as a pretext to weaken the nationalist forces in Iran. The Swedish officers had a genuine sympathy for the constitutionalist movement, but beyond the administrative and technical skills they provided, their influence in Tehran was limited. Almost all the Swedish commanders could not speak Persian and depended heavily on their Iranian deputies and staff. Some Swedes were merely figureheads, with the real power in the unit held by Iranian officers, who, in turn, gave the Gendarmerie its strong nationalist cast. Despite this, in 1914 the British withheld the funds it had been providing to the Gendarmerie at its Russian ally's request in a misplaced effort to cause the Swedish officers to leave Iran. The organization was heavily dependent on the foreign subsidy, and the British action had the counterproductive result of causing Iran to look to Germany for help with funding. By the time World War I started, most of the Swedish officers had been called back home, which allowed nationalist Iranian officers to assume greater authority and responsibility. These officers were more willing to take German money, and some eventually supported activities by German intelligence operatives in Iran.

The members of the Persian Cossack Brigade resented the Gendarmerie, but the brigade was a failing military unit and no threat to the gendarmes. Between the end of the Constitutional Revolution in 1911 and the start of World War I, the roughly five thousand Iranian officers and Cossacks had poor morale, while the Russian officers compared unfavorably with the Swedish officers in energy, military qualifications, and social standing. The Cossack Brigade was organized into four cavalry regiments, four infantry companies, one field and two mountain artillery batteries, and a machine gun detachment. These units, however, were much less well trained, armed, and equipped than the Gendarmerie. On the eve of the war, the Cossack Brigade was politically unreliable, military irrelevant, corrupt, and dependent on Russian funding for its existence. As with the Gendarmerie's Swedish officers, most of the brigade's Russian officers were recalled at the outbreak of World War I. The Russians also pulled the Cossacks in Tabriz from Iranian control and made them part of a Russian army of occupation. The brigade's remaining Russian officers refused to acknowledge any allegiance to the Iranian government, and in the following four years, the unit played no significant military or political role.

The Gendarmerie had no ally in the Iranian military establishment, because the regular Iranian army during this period existed mostly on paper and was barely coherent as an organization. Its several branches differed from each other in organization, regulations, uniforms, and armament, a result of the influence of the various foreign instructors who had presided at branch formations over the years. The army had a nominal force structure of seventy-two infantry regiments of about six hundred men each. According to British military estimates at the time, however, rather than forty-three thousand men on duty, there were only thirteen thousand infantrymen scattered in posts throughout the country. Iran had another five thousand to six thousand artillerymen in sixteen detachments with a total of sixty Austrian breech-loading guns and thirty Schneider-Creuzot guns. The artillerymen, however, handled the guns poorly, and the batteries lacked horses, which forced them to borrow carriage horses from the imperial stables for exercises in Tehran. Cavalry was still provided by tribal levies, which, the British assessed, could muster up to thirty-eight thousand horsemen.

Little had changed from the pre-revolution period in the day-to-day administration of the army. Officer billets were still sold, and merit was not a factor in promotions. While the royal guardsmen were fed and quartered in a barracks near the palace, they were very seldom paid. Other soldiers in the army, almost all of whom were conscripts under Iran's unfair *bonicheh* system, fared even worse. No soldier received adequate training, some never fired a rifle, and all survived by working second jobs or by returning home on leave for large portions of the year. Even officers sometimes worked as shopkeepers in garrison towns. The end result was an army unprepared to meet foreign armies on Iranian soil and totally incapable of fighting against the numerous and better-armed tribes that constantly challenged central authority. When the gendarmes were not available, the government was forced to deal with rebellious tribes through negotiations or by mobilizing rival tribes against them.

Iran in the Great War

Iran presented a very mixed picture in the year before the First World War. Central authority was still weak, and the Bakhtiari chiefs who dominated the government refused to pursue state-building reforms at the expense of tribal power. In some regions, despite the efforts of the Gendarmerie, brigandage and tribal raiding were widespread. Yet in many respects, Iran's security and political situations were improving. The police actions in southern Iran in 1913 had shown that central authority could reach into the provinces, and much of central Iran and the Russian-dominated north were relatively peaceful. Meanwhile, British and Russian influence decreased as their interests in Iran collided. According to U.S. diplomats in Iran at the time, the 1907 Anglo-Russian agreement was becoming a "dead letter."[21] Thanks to Shuster's financial reforms, Iran's foreign debt had decreased and was becoming more manageable. Also the gendarmes had become an effective counter to the sway of the Russian-officered Cossacks. More encouragingly, Iran's democratic institutions were growing. The Iranians were able to overcome British and Russian opposition to hold parliamentary elections in early 1914 and were rewarded with a good turnout after successfully handling the registration and voting in Tehran and the provinces. The insecurity, political divisions, and tribal and provincial challenges of the Constitutional Revolution, however, were revived and intensified by the onset of World War I.[22]

The last Qajar ruler, Ahmad Shah, was crowned at the age of seventeen on the eve of war in July 1914. Ahmad Shah was hardly an inspiring monarch, with a still boyish face and his forebears' taste for personal indulgence that limited his aspirations and desire to stand up to any of the European legations constantly seeking to influence him. Popular resentment against the Russians and British was strong because of the Triple Entente (Allied) Powers' military presence and their highhanded interference in Iranian affairs. As a result, the Iranian people favored the Germans as a third force to offset British and Russian influence. Most Iranians also were sympathetic toward the Muslim Ottomans, who aligned with the Central Powers of Germany and Austria-Hungary. The government chose to remain neutral when war was declared, although ongoing foreign intrusions on

Iranian territory ensured that Iran could not avoid the conflict. At the time, the Russian military already occupied parts of Iranian Azerbaijan, Gilan, Golestan, and Khorasan with more than fourteen thousand troops, including about seven hundred soldiers at Qazvin. The British had troops in Khuzestan, a cavalry detachment in Shiraz, and a naval presence in Iran's Persian Gulf ports. Turkish troops, meanwhile, had occupied some of the border districts of northwestern Iran since 1910. Iran announced its policy of strict neutrality in a royal firman (decree) on the first day of November 1914, but the Ottomans rejected Iran's position so long as the Russians refused to remove their troops from eastern Azerbaijan.

The war came to Iran shortly after Turkey's entry into the conflict in late October. As the highest-ranking Turkish Sunni cleric issued a fatwa (religious ruling) declaring jihad against Russia, Great Britain, and France, an already shaken imperial court in St. Petersburg, reeling from its armies' defeats in East Prussia and Poland, now faced the prospect of war in the Caucasus and the loss of Black Sea transit routes for essential war supplies from its British and French allies. At the same time, the western allies were anxious to maintain access to Ukrainian grainfields, making it essential that Iran be kept out of the Central Powers' control. Respected Shia scholars in the holy cities of Karbala and Najaf in Ottoman Iraq supported the call to jihad, and some Iranians responded with attacks on British interests and assaults on Iranian opponents of Turkey. Former Tabriz mujahedin, exiled since 1909, entered Iran's Azerbaijan Province in late November 1914 under the command of Amir Hishmat Nisari to attack Russian military outposts. In December 1914 the Ottomans launched an offensive against the Russian stronghold of Kars in Transcaucasia that forced the Russians to call on troops from Iranian Azerbaijan. Seeing an opportunity, the Turks extended the front south and, with the help of irregular forces provided by Iranian Kurds, captured Tabriz without a fight in early January 1915. Turkish defeats in the north, however, were followed by a strong Russian counteroffensive in Azerbaijan. By the end of the month, Russian forces had reoccupied Tabriz, and the Turks had retired to the western side of Lake Urmia while the Iranian Kurds dispersed back to their mountain strongholds and Hishmat Nisari's mujahedin returned to Ottoman territory.

Serious hostilities did not begin in southwestern Iran until a short-lived Turkish invasion around Ahvaz in early 1915. A British Indian brigade had captured the Al Faw Peninsula in southern Iraq in early November and, after being augmented by another brigade and two cavalry squadrons, the British force occupied Al Basrah. A Turkish cohort of perhaps 1,500 infantry, 100 cavalrymen, 2 field guns, and 3,000 Arab auxiliaries crossed into Iran in late January 1915 to get behind the British position. The Sheikh of Muhammarah, with London's backing, ruled most of oil-rich Khuzestan (or Arabistan as the British and local Arabs called it) and was supposed to defend the region. The sheikh, however, pleaded that the tribes were unwilling to fight their Muslim brothers on behalf of the infidel British. The British Indian command could spare only a platoon-sized detachment with two mountain guns to stiffen the sheikh's resolve, but this force was ambushed during a reconnaissance shortly after entering Iran and was severely mauled. The loss forced the British to send reinforcements, which, after the Turks withdrew because of defeats in Iraq, spread out to establish a protective ring around Abadan, its oil refinery, and adjoining oil installations with the help of local Arab and Bakhtiari tribesmen. The British also set up a base of operations in Ahvaz to help protect the Mesopotamian (Iraqi) theater's communications. Farther south, a British contingent landed at Bushehr and, along with a cavalry detachment already in Shiraz, moved to establish control over Fars Province. London's main objective was to arrest German officials and their networks of agents, but the Tangistani tribe, which had attacked Bushehr in August and September, resisted the British forces and was soon joined by mutinous gendarmes.[23]

British concern focused on the security of its oil, the Iraq theater's rear areas, and communications to India through telegraph stations at Bushehr and at Jask in far southeastern Iran. These worries were aroused by German attempts to incite the tribes, sabotage oil installations, bring Afghanistan into the war on the Central Powers' side, and destabilize Iran. The Germans sponsored a major anti-British propaganda campaign and encouraged the assassination and kidnapping of pro-British and pro-Russian Iranian politicians. Wilhelm Wassmuss, sometimes called the German "Lawrence of Arabia," and other German and Turkish agents in Iran engaged in espionage, sedition, and sabotage. The Germans were successful in the early months of the war in getting the Qashqai and other tribes hostile to the British to attack and rupture the southern oil pipelines in several areas. The British response was harsh, and punitive operations suppressed the tribes and allowed the pipelines to be repaired. The cost was increased anti-British sentiment and a further decline in the Iranian government's reputation.[24]

A Nationalist Call to Arms

As 1915 began the Iranians were not so much pro-German as anti-Russian and anti-British. Seeing an opportunity to bring Iran to an anti-Allied stand, Berlin's minister in Tehran, Prince von Reuss, and German agents worked with Iranian democrats, clerics, tribal leaders, and the Gendarmerie. Count Kaunitz, the German military attaché, appealed to the tribal chiefs and provincial governors, stimulating their ethnic and sectarian hostility toward the two "partitioning partners" of Russia and Britain. The Prussian nobleman even planted a rumor

that Kaiser Wilhelm had converted to Islam and spread the claim that the German race had its origins in Iran's Kerman Province. The few remaining Swedish
Gendarmerie officers were promised German army commissions with corresponding status and privileges to support the nationalist cause. German agents
also inflamed Iranian nationalists to kidnap, injure, and murder British and Russian officials; the Russian vice-consul in Esfahan and the British vice-consul in
Shiraz were assassinated as a result of this German agitation. Similarly, the Germans encouraged the nationalists and tribes to threaten British and Russian citizens living in Iran, and the British consul in Shiraz along with other British men
and women were taken prisoner by a mix of Qashqai tribesmen, gendarmes,
and nationalist volunteers in early 1915. After gaining the cooperation of local
democratic committees and Gendarmerie commanders in the south, Wassmuss
conducted attacks with the Qashqai and Tangistani tribes against British positions in the Bushehr region. Later in 1915 the nationalists helped a large German
mission under Oskar Niedermeyer move through southeastern Iran to Afghanistan. The German expedition entered that country in mid-August, but only 37
of 140 men completed the desert crossing with just over a third of their pack
animals. Lacking sufficient men and resources, the Afghanistan mission failed.
British retaliation against the tribes that supported Niedermeyer was swift and
brutal, and the deployment of British Indian and Russian troops to defend the
eastern border as the East Persia Cordon increased domestic support for the
democrats.[25]

The Iranian government tried to use the war to slip out from under British
and Russian thumbs, but the German activities increased the Allies' determination to control Tehran. This resolve was doubled after the Allies' Gallipoli
campaign failed between April and August 1915 to secure a passage through the
Dardanelles to the Black Sea and restore a critical supply line to the Russians.
Following heavy, yet indecisive, Russian-Ottoman fighting during the winter
and early spring in the Caucasus, a large Russian force landed at Iran's Caspian
port of Anzali in May 1915 and then moved to Qazvin for the purpose of intimidating the shah and his government. As part of this effort the Allies tried to
eliminate the Gendarmerie and remove the allegedly pro-German Swedish officers. The Gendarmerie by this time had expanded to seven infantry regiments,
five mounted regiments, and several field gun and machine gun units with approximately ten thousand men and four hundred Iranian officers. Anti-Allied
sentiment permeated the ranks because of the British and Russian violations of
Iranian neutrality, and large numbers of gendarmes were actively supporting the
Democratic Party. Although the Swedish officers are sometimes presented as
pro-German mercenaries or dupes of Iranian nationalists, most remained loyal
to the government in Tehran. Some even served as a restraint on Gendarmerie
actions against British and Russian interests, and the British minister in Tehran
in March 1915 reported that their presence was needed for this purpose.[26]

Recognizing Tehran's vulnerability to the Russians, democratic leaders had started to create fighting forces to defend a new government to be set up in Esfahan. The plan was to build the army around Gendarmerie units, supplement it with tribal forces and urban volunteers, and rely on the German military mission's help with operations, supplies, and administration. By May 1915 the leaders of Iran's Democratic Party, with German support, had gathered a mixed force of more than seven hundred tribal levies and irregular volunteers at Kermanshah in western Iran. This small army established control over the area between Kermanshah and Qasr-e Shirin on the border with Ottoman Iraq. It then tried to expand eastward to Borujerd to link up with the Gendarmerie regiment there, which commanded approximately three thousand trained and equipped men dispersed in regional garrisons. Anticipating a Russian advance on Iraq to outflank the Caucasus Front and support the British expedition just then starting to move up the Tigris River toward Baghdad, the Germans guided the nationalists to control the Borujerd region to block the main routes through the mountain passes leading from central Iran. The Gendarmerie officers in Borujerd and their Swedish commander cooperated with the Germans and already had set up an intelligence network to support the democrats and pass along coded telegraphic communications between all Gendarmerie outposts.

Despite British and Russian pressure on the Iranian shah and prime minister that had led to the reshuffling of a series of cabinets, a German-leaning government was formed at this critical moment. The new prime minister, a democrat, held secret talks with the Germans, who promised to defend Iran's territorial integrity and independence if Tehran participated in the conflict against Great Britain and Russia. At roughly the same time, Count Kaunitz and Major DeMare, the Swedish commander of the Borujerd Gendarmerie, met with Nizam al-Saltanah, the governor of Luristan and Khuzestan, and obtained his agreement to become the commander in chief of the nationalist army. The first German supplies and money were soon delivered to Kermanshah, and the governor began enlisting Lur tribesmen into his army. Mustering the Lurs and fostering a modicum of intertribal cooperation enabled several hundred warriors from pro-German Bakhtiari tribes to travel unimpeded through Lur territory to Borujerd to join the nationalist forces there.

Iranian Democratic Party and German plans for a defense of Tehran were threatened with preemption as Russian expeditionary forces appeared ready to move before preparations in the capital were completed. In addition to the nationalist army being created at Kermanshah, the democrats had formed armed mujahedin units from Gilan to Semnan to harass the Russian troops entering Iran from the north. Most of the northern fighters came from Gilan and followed Kuchik Khan, the leader of the Jangali insurrection. (*Jangal* means "forest" in Persian and entered the English language from India as *jungle*. The *jangal* in Gilan at the time, however, consisted of dense temperate-zone hardwoods, not tropical trees.) A former clerical student and a mujahedin during the Constitutional Revolution, Kuchik Khan had started a mixed pan-Islamist, nationalist, and leftist rebellion against the northern landlords, the central government, and the Russians in early 1915 and easily repulsed the Persian Cossack units and tribal forces sent to suppress him. At home in Gilan's forests, the Jangalis established training camps and were joined by some Gendarmerie officers and Kurdish tribesmen. It was autumn, however, before these forces began to raid Russian supply detachments using the small amounts of arms and ammunition supplied by the Germans and Ottomans.

As rumors about an Iranian-German pact spread, the British asked the Russians to send more troops to Iran and then warned the shah's government against joining the Germans. The growing number of Russian troops poised to move on the capital caused the nationalists to understand that no pro–Central Powers government could survive in Tehran for long. Although Iranians reportedly were quietly collecting arms and ammunition for active resistance, the nationalists prepared to leave the capital because Berlin failed to provide most of the promised arms, munitions, and money in a timely manner. This fateful lag allowed the Allied powers to avert an Iranian declaration on behalf of the Central Powers. On November 7, 1915, Russian forces marched on Tehran to stop the democrats and their allies.

The nationalists fled to Qom, in what was called the Muhajirat, or Emigration, to establish a new government beyond the Russian army's reach. At the time expectations of a German victory in the war were high because of German battlefield successes in the preceding year and the failure of the Allies' Dardanelles operations. The democrats hoped that the shah would follow them to Qom and declare war on Russia and Great Britain. Ahmad Shah's natural caution and Allied pressure, however, caused the monarch and most of his ministers to stay in the capital. The Majles disbanded in late November, and Iranian appeals to the United States to defend Iran's neutrality went unheeded. By December, a cabinet favorable to the British and Russians was formed, and the government agreed to a new treaty in which Iranian neutrality became a de facto alliance with the Allied powers. The nationalists and their German and Ottoman allies, meanwhile, prepared to continue their resistance in central and western Iran.

When the Muhajirat began, the nationalists and their supporters were joined by many Gendarmerie officers and men and members of the German, Austrian, and Ottoman legations. Once in the holy city of Qom, the nationalists set up the Committee of National Defense as a provisional government. While declaring obedience to the shah, the nationalists declared war on the Allies and continued to recruit local Iranians to join the gendarmes and mujahedin. Gendarmerie and other nationalist forces seized control of Shiraz, confiscated notes and silver from the banks, and arrested all British citizens in the city. The British women were soon released, but the men would remain prisoners in a nearby fort until August 1916. Elsewhere in western and central Iran British and Russian citizens were expelled as the gendarmes took possession of Hamadan, Kermanshah, Soltanabad, Yazd, Kerman, and Esfahan. In the latter city, 1,500 men mutinied to remove their Swedish regimental commander, who was discouraging the nationalist officers' plans. After raising funds by looting British banks and trading firms, the regiment recruited an additional one thousand men to help defend the city. When a detachment of Persian Cossacks entered Hamadan, they were quickly routed by gendarmes and volunteers. The Iranians were led by a Gendarmerie officer, Maj. Muhammad Taqi Khan Pasyan, who was so impressive that the British consul suggested that he should be killed to rob the nationalists of his leadership.[27]

The War in Iran

The main threat to the democrats was the sixty thousand to eighty thousand Russian troops spread across northern Iran, which greatly overshadowed the small British detachments in the south. Most of the Russian forces, however, were committed to fighting the Turks or to occupation duties. The Russians needed a few weeks to feed more units into Iran for an offensive against the provisional government. In the meantime, Russian Cossacks conducted raids on some nationalist-held cities while the Persian Cossack Brigade was designated a division and filled out with more Russian officers and NCOs, hastily recruited Iranians, and a few more Russian artillery pieces and machine guns. Despite the new leadership and equipment, the Persian Cossacks were held back for policing missions behind the front lines, especially after the nationalists chased local Cossack detachments out of Hamadan and other cities. At the same time, the Jangalis in Gilan began skirmishing with Russian Cossacks to delay the Russian advance. The nationalists also established a small band of mounted irregulars under the command of a German military advisor to upset Russian rear area operations. By the end of November, however, General Baratov, the senior Russian commander at Qazvin, had twenty thousand men ready to march. The main column headed toward Hamadan to disperse the nationalist army there while a smaller secondary column moved to outflank the National Defense Committee in Qom.

In the holy city the democrats and their German advisors were supervising the preparation of defensive lines while the German military mission deployed Gendarmerie units along the route through the strategic Sultan Bulaq Pass between Hamadan and Qazvin. The nationalist forces built trenches and fortifications in a front stretching from the town of Avah, north of Qom. Around 3,000 Gendarmerie and a little more than 1,500 mounted fighters under German commanders defended this Avah front against nearly 15,000 Russian soldiers through early December. Many of these fighters were funded by the German mission, which also arranged for the manufacture of uniforms and other supplies for the defenders. Weapons and ammunition, however, had to be laboriously delivered to the front on pack animals over mountain trails. While both armies had to contend with severe cold in the high mountain passes, the bulk of the Iranian forces had no winter clothing. In addition, the nationalists' defensive works offered insufficient protection against the artillery and dogged assaults of the more numerous and heavily armed Russians. The Iranians eventually were forced back and left the Russians in control of the Sultan Bulaq Pass. Leaving a small rearguard in place, the Gendarmerie and tribal forces withdrew to the mountain passes to the west and south of Hamadan. By mid-December, Hamadan had fallen to Baratov's army.

After several more defeats north of Qom, the nationalist forces followed the Committee of National Defense southwest to Kermanshah. At German urging, Nizam al-Saltanah reestablished the provisional Iranian government with himself as leader and continued to build an army. Despite the earlier setbacks Iranians from all walks of life flocked to the nationalist banner, and the Iranian leader recruited four thousand to five thousand tribal fighters to help approximately three thousand gendarmes defend the mountain passes leading to Kermanshah. Hismat Nisari's mujahedin, who had spent much of the past year inciting Kurdish and other tribes against the Russians, added a few hundred more experienced fighters to the provisional government's army. The Gendarmerie continued to recruit and train local volunteers in other cities held by the nationalists. Despite being pushed out of Qom and Hamadan, the nationalists controlled, if only briefly, all of southwestern Iran except for the Persian Gulf ports and the oil fields of Khuzestan. In addition, a small number of Turkish units were starting to arrive around Kermanshah to support the nationalists. The Germans, whose arrogance was a serious detriment to collaboration, still took a dim view of the situation. In January 1916 Field Marshal Colman von der Goltz, the German commander of the Ottoman army, reported after a visit to Kermanshah that Iran was in a state of anarchy. He complained that Germany's vast expenditures were not generating the desired results in diverting British resources and protecting the Turkish flanks against a Russian push into Iraq.[28]

The assessment of the nationalists' problems by Goltz Pasha, as the Turks called him, was overly negative. The smaller Russian column that occupied Qom had continued south to capture Kashan and Esfahan. About one thousand Bakhtiari tribesmen and some seminary students provided only limited resistance to this part of Baratov's force, which quickly seized its objectives. Through February, however, the mixed force of gendarmes, mujahedin, and tribal fighters kept the Russians from advancing after a series of fierce battles in the snowbound mountains. The gendarmes and mujahedin fought well, but, as Goltz observed, the tribal forces were unreliable and often disappeared despite having accepted German gold. An important part of Goltz's "vast expenditure," the arms and ammunition promised by the Germans, had not been delivered, however, and the resulting serious shortages had an even more harmful effect on the nationalists' defense than the tribes' performance. Finally, despite Nizam al-Saltanah's designation as commander in chief, the nationalist army lacked a functioning chain of command, and mutual distrust among the Iranians and their German and Turkish advisors made the execution of defensive plans difficult. These shortcomings, exacerbated by demoralization, virtually ensured the nationalists' ultimate defeat. Although unable to stop the Russians, the gendarmes and their fellow Iranian fighters, aided by unusually severe winter weather and Russian transportation problems, still held up Baratov's forces outside of Kermanshah through most of February. This delay bought precious time for the Turkish forces in Iraq and allowed the provisional government to stay a step ahead of the Russians.

By March 1916 the remaining nationalist forces, backed by increasing numbers of Turkish infantry and up to a dozen pieces of artillery, had established new defensive lines in the mountains east of the border city of Qasr-e Shirin. Content with having dispersed the provisional government, Baratov was wary of continuing the fight. The Russians had suffered heavy losses during the campaign, and their supply lines stretched more than four hundred miles over rough terrain from the front at Kerend, roughly halfway between Kermanshah and Qasr-e Shirin, back to the port of Anzali. In addition, Kuchik Khan's partisans continued to attack Russian troops and supply convoys along the Anzali-Qazvin road, and winter snows still made the roads and tracks leading to Kerend nearly impassable. Baratov questioned his superiors on the advisability of pursuing his offensive into Iraq , but Great Britain was urging its ally to drive to Baghdad to draw away some of the Turkish army besieging the British forces trapped at Kut al-Amara. The British had captured the city in late September 1915. After overextending their inadequately supplied units in an advance to Ctesiphon, however, the exhausted British force had retreated to Kut in early December to wait for supplies and reinforcements and were invested by the Turks.

On April 10, 1916, Baratov gathered up his remaining reserves and with roughly 7,500 troops and twenty guns launched renewed attacks on the Paitak Pass. This gateway into the Iraqi frontier was held by one thousand gendarmes and as many as one thousand tribal horsemen and, according to British claims, as many as six thousand Turkish soldiers, although most of these apparently were spread out behind Kerend's defenses or in reserve closer to the border. The nationalists held on for nearly a month before being driven back, suffering up to 50 percent losses among the Gendarmerie units. The Iranians had inflicted heavy casualties on the Russians and, more important for the future prospects of the nationalist cause, delayed Baratov's invasion.

The provisional government was forced to retreat again, this time crossing into Iraq and settling in Baghdad. The Russians did not reach Qasr-e Shirin until early May, however, more than a week after starving British forces at Kut had been forced to surrender unconditionally to the Turks. This Ottoman victory marked a temporary turning point in the military balance in the Iraqi theater because it would take seven months for the British to gather enough strength to resume offensive operations in Mesopotamia. By halting the British drive up the Tigris, the Ottomans freed a large portion of their army for a counteroffensive against General Baratov. The Russians, still preparing to launch their own offensive against the Turks, were in a perilous position with Baratov's logistic lines running 450 miles over difficult terrain and his exhausted units short on manpower and critical supplies. For the moment, the Iranian nationalists had reason to hope that the provisional government and its armed forces could soon return to Iran and resume military efforts to restore a democratic government.

Between late 1915 and mid-1916, German influence among the southern Iranian tribes was at its height, but it soon ebbed with just a small push from the British. By encouraging rebellion among the Bakhtiari, Qashqai, and Tangistani tribes, Wassmuss and his agents briefly eliminated British control in all but a few areas in the south. The tribes diverted British troops from Iraq to Khuzestan and blocked British lines of communication between Tehran and the Persian Gulf ports. After the nationalists departed Tehran, the British reached an agreement with the shah's government to establish a new Iranian force with up to eleven thousand men to maintain order in southern Iran. Gen. Sir Percy Sykes was put in command of the unit, which came to be called the South Persia Rifles. Sykes, a few British officers and NCOs, and a company of Indian soldiers landed at Bandar Abbas in March 1916 with a large load of arms and ammunition to begin operations.[29]

Sykes immediately started to recruit Iranians to fill the ranks while various pro-British tribes and provincial officials helped to pacify the south. After the provisional government fled to Ottoman territory, most of the nationalist forces withdrew from Shiraz, and roughly eight thousand pro-British fighters armed by Sykes and led by the former governor of Fars Province, Qavam ol-Molk, met little resistance as they recaptured the city in the last week of April. Meanwhile, in March the Germans had left Kerman, their primary base for agents in the east, and Bakhtiari tribesmen and local officials there, sensing the improving British position, disarmed the nationalists and welcomed Sykes and a small rifles detachment when they arrived in June. Sykes then conducted a series of mostly uneventful marches, reaching Yazd in August, Esfahan in mid-September, and Shiraz by November. Having gained the Iranian government's formal recognition,

Sykes planned to recruit local men and create brigades for the Shiraz, Kerman, and Bandar Abbas regions. Col. J. N. Merrill, an American who had helped establish the Treasury Gendarmerie for Shuster and then advised the Government Gendarmerie, was recruited to help build the South Persia Rifles and later served with the Kerman brigade. At the start of December Sykes reported that he had 2,000 infantry, 450 cavalry, 2 artillery pieces, and a machine gun in Fars Province; 1,100 infantry and cavalry and 4 guns around Kerman; and 150 troops at Bandar Abbas.

After the fall of Kut in late April 1916, some of the southern tribes, spurred by Wassmuss and his agents, were briefly emboldened to go after British interests. The British conducted what they considered mopping up operations through the summer and fall, but many tribes continued to resist. The Qashqai attacked a Rifles garrison at Kazerun, between Shiraz and Bushehr, and stripped it of its weapons in mid-December. Tangistani, Shahkutan, and Borazjani tribesmen captured another Rifles' outpost a week later and closed the mountain road between Shiraz and Bushehr. The Qashqai could field at least 5,000 fighters while other nearby tribes could provide several thousand more to threaten and harass the 2,500 men of Syke's Fars Brigade and prevent it from opening the road. When pressed, the tribes fell back to their mountain redoubts, which were marked by sheer cliffs and honeycombed with caves. British forces dispatched to the Kazerun region could not dislodge them.

The Imperial General Staff in London was reluctant to divert resources from the British drive to Baghdad and advised Sykes to focus on holding Shiraz. Sykes gained a breathing space when winter weather reduced the number of attacks by the tribes through February, and he used this period to concentrate on training his forces. In the spring of 1917 the British crafted an agreement to end Qashqai raids, which freed Sykes to turn against the other tribes. The South Persia Rifles' operations became more punitive, directly attacking the tribal strongholds, destroying crops, and seizing livestock to deprive the tribal chiefs of the means to sustain conflict. Nearly all of the restive Iranian tribes then made peace with the British, but raids and severe outbreaks of anti-British violence continued through the end of the war.

The Nationalists Return

The fate of the democrats was in the hands of the foreign powers by mid-1916. The British continued to urge the Russians to extend Baratov's offensive into Iraq to relieve the pressure on the British Army, still reeling from the loss at Kut. The Turks, meanwhile, sensed an opportunity to extend Istanbul's influence over the Turkic-speaking people of Azerbaijan and Iran. Two Turkish divisions supported by German artillery, machine gun detachments, signal units, and pilots were placed under General Ali Ihsan and prepared to capture Kerman-shah. In operations in which the remaining Iranian nationalist forces played only a minor role, the Turks defeated Baratov's advance and forced the Russians back to the Paitak Pass in Iran. Disease and casualties had depleted Baratov's forces while attacks by Kurdish raiders on Russian supply convoys left him with criti-cal material shortages. After several days of intense fighting in which both sides suffered severe losses, the Turks occupied Kermanshah on July 1, 1916, as the Russians withdrew to Hamadan.[30]

Nizam al-Saltanah's provisional government followed the Turkish army into Iran to cooperate in reactivating and expanding the nationalist army to supple-ment the Turkish spearhead and protect the Ottoman flanks. With German sup-port, the nationalists called back gendarmes, trained new recruits, dispatched troops for garrisons in the liberated cities, and incited the Bakhtiari tribes around Esfahan to attack Allied forces there. After Ali Ihsan forced the Russians out of Hamadan in mid-August, the Ottoman-Iranian forces expanded the front to the northwest and southeast, establishing their control over a large part of the central border region. The Turks, however, faced their own problems with long supply lines and a less favorable balance of forces after the Russians bolstered Baratov's defenses in the Sultan Bulaq Pass with more troops. Ali Ihsan lacked the ability to sustain the large attack needed to push on to Tehran, so the two enemies settled into a static front from Bijar in the north to Borujerd and Sol-tanabad (Arak) in the south until February 1917.

During these five months the provisional government built up its Gen-darmerie and tribal cavalry forces to a strength of perhaps ten thousand men. The restored army still was heavily dependent on Turkish units that were soon needed elsewhere. A new British offensive in Iraq in December 1916 forced the Ottoman high command to recall the Turkish divisions in Iran. In late January, the Turks started to withdraw, and the Russians quickly seized Hamadan and then Kermanshah. By the end of March the Russians and Turks were again fight-ing on the Diyala River to the northeast of Baghdad, which had just fallen to the resurgent British. The provisional government left Iran just ahead of the Rus-sians and sought asylum in Turkey, where the movement, weakened and demor-alized, expired. Many Iranian Gendarmerie officers left for exile, but others went back to their homes and eventually rejoined Iran's postwar armed forces. Peace, however, had not yet come to Iran.

Resisting British Domination

The Iranian nationalists still in Iran had their hopes for independence revived by the two Russian revolutions in March and October 1917, and even members of the shah's government saw opportunities to shift their sympathies away from the Allied Powers. When the new Bolshevik government started to withdraw from the war, Russian armies throughout the region disintegrated. Although a few of the Russian formations under Baratov resisted the general breakdown, many troops headed for home, abandoning or selling their weapons on the way to the benefit of Iranian tribes and the Jangalis.

A nervous Great Britain sent more forces to southwest Asia to close the gaps left by the Russians in northwestern Iran and in the East Persia Cordon. In Tehran, the cabinet that had given its official recognition to the South Persia Rifles fell in June. Despite the government's desperate need for British financial support, the new prime minister and his cabinet refused to confirm the agreement and even encouraged opposition to Sykes' force. Hostility to the South Persia Rifles, including from its Iranian members, was so intense in late 1917 that the British approached the United States to take over the unit and substitute American officers for British ones to mollify the Iranians. Lacking officers with the language skills and area knowledge to take on the task, Washington declined the request. In January 1918, the new Soviet government renounced czarist policies on Iran, ordered the remaining Russian forces out of the country, and revoked all of the agreements and concessions that limited Iranian sovereignty. The removal of these elements of Russian influence and the subsequent decline in the threat from the Central Powers made Great Britain, at least temporarily, the dominant power in Iran and the focus of Iran's nationalistic anger.

As word of the great 1918 German offensives in France spread, desertions from the South Persia Rifles grew and tribal resistance to the British forces in the south increased, roused by the government and a still active Wassmuss. Sykes noted that tribesmen were armed with German Mauser rifles and fought bravely, using their remarkable mobility and invisibility in the hills to good advantage. The U.S. legation also reported that the Qashqais were excellent fighters and determined in their resistance. A large force of as many as 8,000 Qashqai, Kazerunis, and other tribes were especially aggressive in attacking Rifles' outposts, convoys, and British-dominated towns. In mid-May the Qashqai surrounded a Rifles detachment and cut off its water supply, prompting the unit's Iranian soldiers to kill their British commander and surrender their weapons to the tribesmen. British forces at the time consisted of perhaps 2,200 regulars at Shiraz, 2,000 men under Qavam ol-Molk, and between 7,000 and 8,000 South Persia Rifles troops. Fodder for horses was a critical handicap for the Rifles and inhibited their activities. Meanwhile, the troops had enough food amid a general famine in the region to support themselves, but this only increased Iranian resentment. Through midsummer Iranians demonstrated against the British presence, and Shia mullahs began issuing written orders authorizing the killing of anyone dealing with the British. An uprising in Shiraz and mutinies at a few Rifles' garrisons were suppressed, and as the British began to feed more regular regiments into the fight, the tide began to turn decisively against the tribes. In October 1918 Wassmuss was captured, and the British inflicted a final defeat that broke the back of the Qashqais' resistance. The British opened the Shiraz-Bushehr road in January 1919 by sending a force of 20,000 men through snow-filled mountain passes to occupy Kazerun and disperse the tribal forces threatening the highway. Although a semblance of order was restored in the south, the tribes and provincial leaders continued to resist British and later Iranian government attempts to assert central authority.[31]

During the last year of the war the desire for independence by the Iranian government, the northern tribes, and the Jangali guerrillas clashed with London's concerns about the Central Powers' threat to the Caucasus and about Russian bolshevism. Still burdened with other military commitments in the Middle East, the British decided in late 1917 to send small political-military missions into northwestern and northeastern Iran to determine where local resistance forces against the Germans, Turks, and Bolsheviks could be created. Gen. L. C. Dunsterville led a motor caravan from Baghdad into Iran in February 1918 with twelve officers in touring cars accompanied by thirty-six Ford vans with their gear, rations, and money. The rest of the mission, referred to as Dunsterforce, consisted of approximately 150 officers and 300 NCOs who followed behind Dunsterville's small procession. To the east, an expedition from India commanded by Gen. Sir Wilfrid Malleson occupied Mashhad in March 1918 and established bases in northern Khorasan Province that later supported anti-Bolshevik White Russians and Turkman tribes against the Soviets. After Dunsterville passed through Gilan Province and arrived at Anzali, he found that the Jangalis and hostile Russian soldiers and sailors dominated the region. Forced to withdraw back to Hamadan, Dunsterville reported that it was useless for the British to return to the Caspian port "until we either fought or came to an agreement with Kuchik Khan."[32] By April more British forces had arrived in Iran and occupied Kermanshah, Hamadan, and Qazvin. Now headquartered at Qazvin and designated the North Persia Force, or Norperforce, Dunsterville's mission prepared to return to Gilan with reinforcements that included 4 armored cars, 2 airplanes, and 1,200 Russians under General Bicherakov, who was still a willing British ally.

The Jangalis had become more cautious after suffering their first major defeat in early 1917 in a battle with seven hundred Russian Cossacks armed with artillery and machine guns. Under increased pressure, Kuchik Khan's guerrillas had been saved when the czar abdicated and the Kerensky government recalled Russia's armies from Iran. Kuchik Khan met with Dunsterville during the British officer's first passage to Anzali, but unimpressed with the small detachment and perhaps encouraged by the German and Austrian advisors still with his movement, the guerrilla leader refused to cooperate. Kuchik Khan ignored British ultimatums for safe passage for Norperforce units moving through Gilan and instead established a defensive trench line manned by 2,500 to 3,000 Jangalis armed with rifles and a few machine guns at Manjil, seventy miles north of Qazvin in June 1918. In the subsequent battle, British artillery and airplanes began the attack by bombarding the Jangali positions. The British and Russian cavalry struck the rebel right flank, the armored cars hit the left, and Russian infantry advanced slowly against the center of the trench. Kuchik Khan had foolishly placed his lines in front of a bridge joining two sides of a deep canyon. Fearful of being cut off, the Jangalis fell back across the span rather than make a determined stand in their trenches. Unable to destroy the bridge, the Jangalis then fled into nearby forests to avoid the British pursuit. With the road to Anzali open, British forces quickly occupied the port and the nearby city of Rasht.[33]

Despite growing demoralization among the guerrillas, Kuchik Khan assembled between one thousand and two thousand men for an attack on the roughly one thousand British troops in Rasht in late July. The Jangalis' main assault on the British headquarters was driven back with heavy losses while secondary attacks against the British consulate, a British bank, and the telegraph office were partially successful in forcing the British to abandon these facilities. The Jangalis dug trenches and felled trees across the streets to block British counterattacks led by armored cars, and the fighting continued for four days. British air and artillery attacks on Jangali positions eventually caused the guerrillas to retreat with losses of two hundred killed and wounded. After this defeat, Kuchik Khan made peace with the British, although the Jangalis continued to harass the Iranian government and the rich landowners of Gilan.

Aftermath

As the Great War came to its close in the fall of 1918, Iran's plight was woeful. The war had created an economic catastrophe, invading armies had ruined farmland and irrigation works, crops and livestock were stolen or destroyed, and peasants had been taken from their fields and forced to serve as laborers in the various armies. Famine killed as many as two million Iranians out of a population of little more than ten million while an influenza pandemic killed additional tens of thousands. The shah's government was virtually bankrupt and was reduced to paying civil servants with its only valuable commodity, the bricks from the rubble of old buildings. Iran was almost totally under the control of the British military, which was trying to restore order in the country but was poorly situated to address the disunity tearing at the fabric of Iran's still unrecovered sovereignty. Because the Allied and Central Powers had used local Iranian levies to support their operations, many tribal leaders and influential local leaders seized the opportunity to assert their independence. Qajar Iran, in its waning years, amounted to Tehran, the region surrounding the capital, and a few other large cities. Iran's other regions were controlled by whichever provincial noble or tribal chief had the power to enforce his rule. Thanks to his British support, Sheikh Khazal of Muhammarah was virtually independent in the oil-rich and ethnically Arab region of Khuzestan. Elsewhere, Iranian tribes in pursuit of power and booty disrupted trade and communications, isolating most villages as social chaos spread throughout the country.

To add insult to injury, despite the Iranian government's coerced alignment with the Allied Powers, Iran gained nothing from their victory. Tehran sent a delegation to the Paris Peace Conference of 1919 with exorbitant or superfluous demands. These included the abrogation of the 1907 Anglo-Russian Treaty; the abolition of the remaining capitulations; the restoration of Iran's former imperial boundaries to the Oxus River in the northeast and to Baku, Yerevan, and Mosul in the northwest; and millions of dollars in war reparations. Ignoring the warring nations' violations of the Iranians' declared neutrality, the victors considered Iran a neutral power and deemed its representatives ineligible to sit at the negotiating table. Despite some sympathy and support from the American delegation, Iran and its demands were ignored at London's behest. And British interference continued to set the parameters for Iran's future security and military developments through the middle of the 1920s.

5

Two Paths

The Birth of the Modern Iranian Armed Forces

FOLLOWING THE FIRST WORLD WAR the character of the two main contestants to become Iran's dominant military force presented very different paths to the emerging modern nation-state. On one path was the promonarchy and authoritarian Persian Cossack Brigade, which had no tradition of being answerable to Iranian authorities or the Iranian people. On the other, the prodemocratic and nationalist Gendarmerie was allied to reform-minded liberals and had a good reputation from its battles against the Russians and British during the war. All things being equal, Iran's earlier history suggested that the country's modern armed forces would spring from an amalgamation of the positive and negative traits of these two forces. The catalytic impact of Russian intrigues and British dominance in Iran, however, propelled the Iranian military down the less promising and authoritarian path represented by the Cossacks and, in particular, by one Cossack officer, Reza Khan, the future shah of Iran. The subsequent unification of the armed forces avoided a potentially divisive split into two military services. Professionalism, sensible budgeting and procurement, and concern for the soldiers' welfare, however, once again were ignored.

Gendarmes and Cossacks

As fears of Bolshevism grew in the West, Tehran was bullied by Great Britain into signing the Anglo-Persian Treaty of August 1919, making the country a British protectorate. At the start of 1920, Iran's various military forces purportedly had twenty-five thousand men and depended almost exclusively on British financial support. The Persian Cossack Division, commanded by fifty-six anti-Communist White Russians, represented roughly a third of the armed forces and had received a windfall of arms and ammunition from the departing Russian troops. The Gendarmerie was reconstituted after the war from the two regiments that had remained in Tehran and stayed loyal to the government. It retained a handful of Swedish officers and made up another third of the Iranian military. The final third was comprised of the South Persia Rifles and the regular army, which had been reduced to the Central Brigade in Tehran with approximately 2,200 officers and soldiers on its rolls, if not in its barracks.

A mixed Anglo-Persian military board recommended dissolving the Persian Cossacks and merging the remaining military forces into a national army based on the South Persia Rifles under the Ministry of War. The gendarmes and other police forces were to be combined into a national police force under the Interior Ministry. Two of the four Gendarmerie officers on the commission refused to sign the final report, however, and a third committed suicide in protest. The proposal died as Russian interventions in the north and problems in Great Britain combined to reduce London's control over events in Iran.

Ahmad Shah and his ministers remained committed to the Gendarmerie concept, if only because some force was desperately needed to restore order. The Gendarmerie's prestige was high among Iranians, and its officers maintained their anti-British attitudes despite the reliance on British subsidies. The British, also desirous of stability, overlooked the gendarmes' nationalist sentiments and supported the rebuilding effort, even providing the service captured Turkish rifles. The organization grew rapidly during the two years after the war to fill the void created by the Russian collapse in the north. By 1921, the force had nearly ten thousand officers and men organized into fourteen regiments and independent battalions. Its recruits were all volunteers, and the officers were promoted from the ranks or commissioned from reestablished officer schools. The Anglo-Persian military commission reported that the Gendarmerie had "acquired an appreciable degree of efficiency, and is probably the most useful force, controlled solely by the Persian Government, which exists in the country."[1]

The Gendarmerie was able to improve security along the roads and suppress banditry. It fared less well in military operations against tribal insurrections because of training and equipment shortcomings. Despite the gendarmes' best efforts, order in the countryside relied on groups of dozens to a few hundred fighters belonging to the provincial nobles. Called sowars, these men were supplied to the nobles as needed by their village chiefs. Most were excellent horsemen and well armed but generally preferred to avoid direct confrontations. The sowars' principal duty was collecting taxes for the landowner, but when not policing bands of thieves these men-at-arms often competed with the criminals by raiding caravans.[2]

The Persian Cossack Division had been undergoing its own transformation since the 1917 Russian Revolution. When the Bolshevik government stopped subsidies, Great Britain took over the Cossacks' financial support amid concern about their political reliability. The Kerensky government assigned a liberal-minded colonel named Clergi as commander, but the second in command, Colonel Starroselsky, was an ambitious and unscrupulous White Russian.

In early 1918, Starroselsky plotted with the British to replace Clergi, bringing in an Iranian lieutenant colonel named Reza Khan to help. Reza got other Iranian officers to join him in forcing Clergi's resignation. In return, Reza was promoted to brigadier general and given command of an infantry regiment. He later ran afoul of Starroselsky for advocating Iranian control of the unit and lost his command and promotion. Starroselsky, meanwhile, used his new powers to staff the division with White Russian officers and to reassert the division's traditional independence. Mixed brigades called *atriyads* with an infantry regiment, cavalry regiment, and field or mountain artillery unit were established in Iran's eight largest northern cities. Two military schools for training Cossack officers and NCOs also reopened. Unhappy with the unit's independence and its overall performance, the British still were wary of quarrelling with Starroselsky because they were unsure which side the Gendarmerie would support.[3]

With the two main Iranian armed forces settling into their postwar form, London became unwilling to devote the resources needed to secure an increasingly unstable Iran. Bolshevik-incited Azeri nationalists and socialists declared an independent republic of "Azadistan" (land of freedom) in April 1920 and demanded democracy for Iran with provisions for Azeri autonomy. Cossack forces attacked the rebels and suppressed the revolt after several months by killing the leaders and reoccupying Tabriz. Following provocative White Russian and British forays into Russia from Iran, the new Soviet government conducted an amphibious invasion in May 1920, capturing Anzali, seizing Rasht, and establishing with Kuchik Khan an independent Communist republic in Gilan. During the invasion, a Cossack detachment of about eight hundred men surrendered to a force of Jangalis and Bolsheviks, handing over their weapons without a fight. The depleted British forces in the country could offer no meaningful resistance to the Soviets and withdrew south to avoid a direct confrontation. Ahmad Shah and his government then wanted a revived British presence to meet these threats. In London, however, the postwar government was short of funds, bogged down in efforts to pacify Iraq, and lacked public support for military operations in Iran. Instead, the British announced their intention to withdraw all military units from Iran by April 1921.

Still wanting to maintain their influence the British arranged to remove the now troublesome White Russians from the Cossacks. The shah's government had turned to Starroselsky to restore the situation in the north at the cost of naming the Russian commander in chief of all Iranian troops and the de facto dictator of the Caspian provinces. Assembling his Cossack units, a large part of the Gendarmerie, and the Central Brigade in June, Starroselsky first marched into Mazandaran Province and forced the Iranian Bolsheviks there to retreat. Political negotiations between the government and Kuchik Khan split the Jangalis from the Bolsheviks, and Starroselsky was ordered to take advantage of

Jangali neutrality and attack the Bolsheviks around Rasht and Anzali. Crossing British lines at Qazvin in the middle of August, the Cossacks alone marched through the Manjil Pass and entered Rasht without a fight. Overconfident, the Russian colonel moved his unit north with inadequate preparations and little appreciation of his enemy's strength. The Cossacks assaulted Anzali in September but stiff resistance by Bolshevik and Soviet troops with Red Navy gunfire support caused the division to flee in panic back to British lines.[4]

At the beginning of October, Gen. Edmund Ironside took command of Norperforce and started arranging for Starroselsky's removal. The Cossacks had returned to Rasht, which the Iranian Bolsheviks had left undefended, and then moved against the defensive works around Anzali. Ironside had tapped the telegraph wires and knew that the Cossacks were demoralized and suffering from malaria. He saw that a likely Cossack retreat would provide the excuse and opportunity to get rid of Starroselsky. When the unit collapsed as anticipated and withdrew to the British lines, Ironside's soldiers divided the Russians and Iranians into separate camps. Reza Khan, the Hamadan *atriyad* commander and a British ally since Starroselsky demoted him, helped keep the Iranian Cossacks passive while Ironside successfully negotiated with the shah to discharge Starroselsky and his Russian officers. The British used their newly established control over the division to reorganize the Cossacks and lay the groundwork for the next important development in the political life of the nation and the creation of Iran's modern armed forces.

The Rise of Reza Khan

Reza Khan, a tall and powerfully built forty-two-year-old colonel, had a reputation for extraordinary leadership, intelligence, and willpower. Ambitious and hard working, Reza also was uneducated and often brutal. A native of Mazandaran Province, he was born into a humble Turkic-speaking family with a tradition of military service. Enlisting in the Persian Cossack Brigade at the age of fourteen, he taught himself to read and write and rose through the ranks. He also had the good fortune to be in the right place at the right time to make himself useful when Starroselsky and then the British needed help. General Ironside and other British officials increasingly viewed Reza and the Cossacks as the best force to fill the gap left by departing British units. Worried about bolshevism, the British had grudgingly determined that Tehran needed a strong nationalist government, if only to withstand Soviet threats and machinations. They recognized that the South Persia Rifles were not acceptable to the Iranians as the basis for a national army while the Gendarmerie was too nationalistic and anti-British for London's tastes. Reza's desire to make Iran more independent was well known to the British, but they continued to assist him and cultivate the Cossacks, who then numbered 3,500 men garrisoned at Qazvin. To ensure the brigade's loyalty, the shah chose a favored senior officer and St. Cyr graduate, Sadr Homayoon, as commander. Homayoon was unable and mostly unwilling to assert his authority, however. The British officers advising the Cossacks saw Reza as efficient and energetic and selected him to be Homayoon's deputy, making him the de facto commander.

Fortune continued to smile on Reza Khan. At the same time that Iranian Cossack officers saw an increasing need to replace the weak postwar Iranian government, Iranian nationalist politicians, including a group led by Sayyid Zia al-Din Tabatabai, felt a similar urgency to take over the government to preserve the monarchy and create a strong anti-bolshevik state. After gaining support for a coup from the British and the Gendarmerie's commanders in Tehran, Zia approached Homayoon, but failing to win him over turned to Reza Khan. Reza agreed, and with British encouragement, arms, and other supplies, he prepared a Cossack force to march to the capital to force the government to resign. Claiming loyalty and devotion to the shah, he entered Tehran against virtually no resistance after midnight on February 21, 1921. His roughly three thousand Cossacks imposed martial law and arrested potential political opponents to prevent a countercoup. The government collapsed as the soldiers spread out through Tehran, and Ahmad Shah asked Zia to form a government. Reza Khan was made the commander of all armed forces, receiving the title of Sardar-e Sepah along with a jewel-studded golden sword. Appealing to the Iranians' most basic desires for security, unity, and freedom, Reza declared, "Our aim is to establish a . . . strong government, which will create a powerful and respected army, because a strong army is the only means of saving the country from the miserable state of its affairs."[5]

Reza Khan's actions following the coup demonstrated that his ambitions for himself and Iran went well beyond control of the Iranian military. Political power in the capital appeared to belong to Prime Minister Zia and two Gendarmerie offices serving as Minister of War and military governor of Tehran. Real power belonged to Reza Khan and the Cossacks, however. A personal rivalry between Reza and Zia began immediately, and the old animosity between the Cossacks and gendarmes caused Reza to try to undermine the Gendarmerie. By April, the minister of war, frustrated by Cossack disobedience, resigned and created an opening for Reza to occupy the post. Less than a month later, Reza forced Zia to put the Gendarmerie under the control of the War Ministry, which increased Reza's day-to-day control of the service. The change was part of Reza's plan to build a unified, centralized national army officered by Iranian Cossacks. Reza's goals collided with Zia's plans to invest British officers with more authority to direct operations in Gilan against Kuchik Khan, who was again challenging local and national authority. Seizing the opportunity to undercut his rival,

Reza declared that Zia's plan amounted to selling out the army to foreigners, and he colluded with Ahmad Shah and disgruntled politicians to force Zia out of office.

One potential challenger to Reza's attempts to consolidate power put into greater clarity the two paths available for Iran's political and military development. In Mashhad, Gendarmerie colonel Muhammad Taqi Khan Pasyan, a key commander of the Muhajirat provisional government's forces during the war, was serving as military governor. The Gendarmerie colonel was a born leader and formidable opponent, as noted by the British official who suggested during the war that Pasyan should be killed. Like many Gendarmerie officers, Pasyan was from a high-ranking family and well educated. He had been promoted rapidly during his prewar service and fought bravely during the war. While in exile in Germany after the collapse of the provisional government, he had trained with German air and ground forces, which added to his reputation as a military commander.

Both Pasyan and Reza Khan were nationalists, secular, and opponents of the traditional Qajar elite. The Gendarmerie colonel, however, shared the strong democratic sympathies of his service. After returning to Iran in 1920, Pasyan was given command of the Khorasan Gendarmerie with the mission to rebuild the regiment and establish security in the region. Pasyan supported the 1921 coup and in early April, after following orders from Tehran and arresting the corrupt provincial governor, Qavam al-Saltanah, he took control of Mashhad for the new government. In a short time Pasyan restored order, reformed local government, and improved financial management. At the end of May he was shocked when Qavam, who had been sent as a prisoner to Tehran, was named the new prime minister, with Reza Khan's help, to replace Zia. Seeing this shift as an attack on democratic political aspirations, Pasyan anticipated the worst.[6]

Within days Pasyan received an order from Tehran relieving him of his command, but after checking with his subordinates and being assured of their loyalty he chose to defy the government. He started his rebellion by arresting local notables he believed were likely to collaborate with the government against him. He then began recruiting local irregulars to join the gendarmes in what became a force of four thousand armed men. Because of the ongoing fighting in Gilan, Tehran had no military forces to confront Pasyan, so Reza encouraged the landlords and tribal chiefs who had prospered under Qavam's corrupt rule to revolt. By the end of September, Pasyan's forces were overstretched, and the colonel left Mashhad to lead a small force of gendarmes combating pro-Qavam Kurds. A much larger group of well-armed Kurdish fighters surrounded this Gendarmerie unit in early October, and Pasyan was killed in the subsequent battle. After his death, the gendarme-led government in Mashhad disintegrated. Pasyan's insurrection highlighted the tension between the Cossacks and Gendarmerie that continued for years, with new rounds of mutinies occurring in 1922 and 1926. More important for Iran's future, by removing a viable alternative to Reza Khan's leadership, Pasyan's death freed the minister of war "to adopt unchallenged the mantle of nationalism among the military and to fashion the army in his own image."[7]

Reza Khan's next most pressing need was to end the challenge posed by the Gilan Republic and the Jangali movement. Although the Bolsheviks and leftists and the more conservative forces represented by the native Jangalis were divided, the Gilan Republic had several mostly untroubled months to govern itself after Starroselsky's failed campaign because Iran had insufficient forces to oppose it. Following the coup, Reza maintained friendly relations with the Soviet Union, and after obtaining the Red Army's evacuation he assembled a large Cossack contingent in Mazandaran Province to assault Gilan from the east. Kuchik Khan responded by splitting his Jangalis into three groups to defend key passes and valleys, but this only allowed the Cossacks to defeat them in detail. After crushing the rebels in Mazandaran in July 1921, the Cossacks routed a second army of roughly three thousand Jangalis in Gilan. News of the defeat weakened morale and spurred dissension among the guerrillas, causing Jangalis in Rasht to surrender without a fight. Reza joined the Cossacks and arranged a cease-fire with Kuchik Khan, but after a group of Jangalis, who may have been unaware of the truce, killed three Iranian officers and fifteen soldiers, the furious minister of war ordered a merciless assault on the rebels. The Jangali leader and his remaining forces retreated and then dispersed, effectively ending the rebellion and the Gilan Republic. Kuchik fled to the Tavalesh Mountains but was caught in an unexpected snowstorm and froze to death. The rebel leader's decapitated head was sent to Tehran to prove his demise.

Unification

Reza Khan believed that gaining a monopoly on the use of force was the only way to build a strong and united country. To gain this monopoly, he set out to create a national military force that combined the strengths of the Cossacks and the Gendarmerie. By late 1921 the Gendarmerie was widely respected, well trained, and disciplined and was Iran's largest service, with more than 700 officers and cadets and nearly 9,300 other ranks after Prime Minister Zia incorporated Iran's regular military units into the organization. In contrast, the Cossacks had 300 Iranian officers and 7,000 men and, despite its success against the Jangalis, a generally poor reputation. The South Persia Rifles, meanwhile, were disbanded by the British, who were unwilling to have it merged into a new army. During the spring Reza had combined the Cossack, Gendarmerie, and regular military officer schools in Tehran into a single military college, which had a pro-Cossack, anti-gendarme, and anti-foreign military orientation. The war minister also recruited an additional 10,000 men for the Cossack Division, making sure that these soldiers, at least initially, were paid regularly. Because he desperately needed the Gendarmerie's skills and numbers to build a strong military, Reza did not want to drive them out of the service. His solution was to move Gendarmerie officers into staff positions throughout the new army while appointing only Cossack officers to command billets and other positions of authority. Former Iranian officers and NCOs of the South Persia Rifles also joined the new armed forces. In early December 1921, Reza Khan issued Army Order Number One, which combined the two forces, put the Gendarmerie headquarters under the command of a Cossack officer, and dismissed the few remaining Swedish officers in the organization. The minister of war used appeals to nationalism to win the gendarmes' grudging acceptance of this momentous change, and by the start of 1922 the Gendarmerie's political and military influence had been almost totally suppressed.[8]

Between 1922 and 1926, Reza Shah continued to consolidate his military and political dominance over the Iranian government and the country at large. As the army commander and war minister, Reza set up a general headquarters in Tehran composed of the General Staff and the Higher Military Council, a group of senior officers who advised on plans and policy and prepared training manuals. The General Staff was divided into departments for operations, personnel, intelligence, ordnance, veterinary services, and medical services. As part of the unification plan, the new army was organized into five divisions with plans to grow to forty thousand men. The divisions were headquartered in Iran's five largest cities, Tehran, Tabriz, Hamadan, Esfahan, and Mashhad. Reza later established the Northern Independent Regiment at Rasht to help control the still restive Caspian region and the Western and Southwestern Forces Headquarters in response to tribal unrest in those regions. Each division created staffs for operations, recruiting, supply, ordnance, and engineers, but there was only a minimal effort to develop combat support units such as medical services, engineers, and transportation. The 1st, or Central, Division in Tehran was gradually set up as the largest formation with approximately eleven thousand men. In addition to securing the capital, the 1st Division was the on-call reserve force for the rest of the country. By late 1922, the unified army's rolls carried nearly two thousand officers and twenty-eight thousand soldiers, and its reported strength would jump to nearly fifty thousand by the end of 1925. These numbers, however, were grossly inflated as commanders tried to draw extra pay and rations. A more accurate count of thirty-three thousand men was made in 1926 following large numbers of desertions during campaigns against rebellious tribes and the discharge of numerous soldiers to avoid disbursing pay arrears.

Reza Khan sought greater control over the government and its revenues to pay for the army's expansion, taking steps that put him ever closer to supreme power in Iran. He appointed loyal Cossack officers as provisional governors, and Cossacks in civilian dress were assigned to represent him in the other government departments. Appreciating Reza's strong nationalist stance and appeals for modernization, Iran's politicians rewarded him with increased authority and budgets and acquiesced in press censorship and the imposition of martial law in some provinces. In October 1923, Reza Khan arranged to have himself appointed prime minister by the shah, who soon departed for Europe, purportedly for health reasons. This left Reza the de facto ruler of Iran. Looking at Ataturk's Turkey, the new prime minister briefly considered making Iran a republic but backed down in the face of strong opposition led by Iranian clerics and merchants fearful of republican secularism. To reestablish his power, the wily soldier resigned to go into a self-imposed internal exile, but only after arranging for army commanders throughout Iran to threaten to march on the capital if he were not reinstated. A fearful Majles relented and reappointed Reza, who abandoned republicanism but gained the latitude to continue his harsh tactics to stifle political dissent.[9]

In July 1924, the U.S. vice-consul in Tehran, Robert W. Imbrie, may have been the victim of one of Reza's schemes. While observing a demonstration instigated by the government to divert antiregime anger over the murder of a dissident writer, Imbrie was attacked by the mob with Cossacks from Reza Khan's household regiment allegedly participating. The American vice-consul was taken to a hospital in a nearby police headquarters, but the mob, possibly with army and police connivance, murdered Imbrie in his bed. A U.S. Army major sent to investigate the incident and the British military attaché reported that Imbrie's death was deliberate and had been conducted to provide the pretext for Reza Khan to declare martial law, censor the press, and clamp down on political activity in the capital.[10]

Reza's next move was to usurp the monarchy for himself. Using the military to manipulate the 1925 legislative elections, Reza made his supporters the majority party in the Majles. After a military-led propaganda campaign and the passage of several laws to reduce royal power, Reza had the Majles abolish the Qajar dynasty in October. Two months later, the Majles voted to make Reza Khan the new shah. In April 1926, Reza, like Napoleon, placed the imperial crown on his own head, inaugurating the new Pahlavi dynasty and confirming his six-year-old son as crown prince. When accused later of taking the throne from the Qajars by force, the new shah purportedly replied, "Not so, I found the Crown lying in the gutter."[11]

By the time Reza became shah, he was already the military dictator of Iran. Now called Reza Shah Pahlavi, the new ruler embarked on a major modernization program in close association with the military. Reza saw the army as the keystone of his authority and the focal point around which he planned to raise up the Iranian nation. To cement the relationship, Reza gave career officers a standard of living far above that of other salaried government employees, placed them in charge of government factories, and sold them state lands at discounted prices. Reza continued to wear military uniforms to all public occasions, and many of his modernizing economic programs were directed toward providing the army with transportation, uniforms, and equipment. The most costly infrastructure project of Reza's reign, the Trans-Iranian Railroad, which was started in 1927 and eventually ran from the Persian Gulf to the Caspian Sea, was partially funded through the defense budget. A hallmark undertaking by the shah, the railroad was justified by national security requirements for moving troops to suppress revolts and stop a potential Soviet invasion. The Pahlavi shah built thousands of miles of new roads to support economic interests but also to ease the movement of army units enforcing domestic order.

During the early years of his reign, many of Reza Shah's faults were ignored or endured because of widespread support for his accomplishments in freeing Iran from foreign political and economic domination. All foreign capitulations were abrogated in 1928, and many other concessions were eliminated by 1933. Only the British continued to be a strong force because of their past economic penetration and control of the southwestern oil fields. The new shah tried to balance Soviet and British influence with the United States and later Germany. An American financial advisor, Dr. Arthur C. Millspaugh, spent five years from 1922 to 1926 trying to eliminate graft and create fiscal responsibility in Iran. Millspaugh's and Reza's inflexibility over the size and budget of the armed forces led to disagreements that resulted in the American being asked to leave the country. Afterward, the United States retreated from an active role in Iran, and Reza Shah turned to Germany as the balancing power. Toward the end of his reign, Reza cooperated with Turkey, Iraq, and Afghanistan to help improve Iran's security. In July 1937, the four neighbors signed a treaty of friendship and nonaggression at the shah's palace at Saadabad recognizing existing borders and pledging greater cooperation. The Saadabad Pact's most important feature was an agreement by Iran, Iraq, and Turkey to stop using the Kurds to foment trouble for each other and instead to work together to stifle Kurdish dissent.

Although Reza improved Iran in many ways, the arbitrary power, brutality, and greed he showed in pursuing the elimination of all challenges to central authority and the creation of a large national army overshadowed his accomplishments. Like Ataturk and Mussolini, Reza aspired to be a modernizing dictator and was increasingly enthralled by European fascist movements. After meeting Ataturk in 1934, the shah became frustrated with Iran's pace of change and became more determined to strengthen his country. With the army's help, Reza continued to rig elections and censor newspapers, while the military's supervision of the Majles turned it into a rubber stamp for the shah's policies. He established a secret police network throughout the country and intimidated, arrested, tortured, and even murdered his political opponents. The shah's thirst for wealth proved insatiable, and he confiscated land, extorted money, and diverted state revenues for his personal use. By 1941, he was the richest man in the country and reportedly owned 15 percent of Iran's productive land. Not surprisingly, as his reign wore on, Reza's authoritarian nature, personal greed, preferential treatment of the army, and harsh methods in dragging Iran into modernity caused his popular support to evaporate. Concurrently, the armed forces were tainted as an arm of autocracy and mechanism for the dynasty's aggrandizement.

Imposing Reza's Iron Hand

Reza Shah had started to bring order to Iran while still minister of war with pacification and disarmament campaigns that temporarily brought an end to brigandage and armed intertribal hostilities. The degree of security, if not perfect, was unprecedented, and it enabled long abandoned lands to be brought back into cultivation and allowed peasants to return to their villages without fear of tribal raiders. Reza had larger ambitions for the nomadic tribes, which he saw as the bastions of alien cultures and languages, allegiance to hereditary chiefs, and primitive ways of life he wanted to change. Although it would take the rest of the 1920s, Reza managed to defeat and largely disarm the major tribal groups, including the Kurds and Shahsavan in the northwest; the Arabs of Khuzestan; and Turkman, Qashqai, and other tribes throughout the country.[12]

Reza's army did not cover itself in glory in these operations. The tribes repeatedly got the best of government forces and inflicted heavy casualties in ambushes and other attacks. In addition, the army set the course of its future alienation from the Iranian people by its large-scale looting of the countryside and its arbitrary and unrecompensed requisitioning of men, horses, grain, and money from the villagers while on campaign. The American vice-consul in Bushehr reported in 1924 that because the troops' pay was six months in arrears, the soldiers were penniless or in debt, and so their undisputed power was their chief source of income. Goods were openly stolen, and the army replaced the tribes in demanding payment for safe transit on the roads. He also noted that officers seized houses, commandeered vehicles, and impressed men for work gangs without compensation. A British official reported that the "arrogance and indiscipline towards the civil population of the officers and men of this new army are growing more marked. The Persian soldier today carrying his rifle does not hesitate to level it at any civilian on the slightest provocation, real or imagined."[13]

One of the first tribes targeted by Reza before he became shah was the Shah-savan in northwestern Iran. When Reza made a strong show of force with 1,800 infantry, cavalry, and artillerymen in early 1923, most of the Shahsavan quickly offered their submission, but others continued to resist, posing tactical chal-lenges that would be repeated in the Iranian army's other campaigns. A Rus-sian commander who participated in earlier operations against the Shahsavan described their tactics, which were similar to other tribes' fighting styles. Shah-savan combat rested on their familiarity with the terrain, which allowed them make use of every rock and hollow, and on the ability of their light mobile forces to cover long distances through the mountains on their sturdy horses. The Rus-sian noted that the Shahsavan did not mass their forces but split into groups to divert and outflank their enemy, thrusting and retreating as needed to avoid being fixed in one position. They used sharp, brief skirmishes and sniping to divide the government forces into smaller groups that the tribesmen could de-stroy. The tribe also had learned to deal with machine guns by using one team to draw fire while another observed the enemy position. When the gunner stopped to reload, the Shahsavan teams would charge the position. The Shahsavans' te-nacity in battle varied, but they fought stubbornly if their camps were nearby and their options for retreat were limited. The few Shahsavan tribes that resisted Reza's forces were eventually brought to battle and defeated. Thereafter the cen-tral government relied on the Shahsavan tribal chiefs' cooperation to maintain regional security.[14]

In general, Reza's tribal policy was an extension of previous Iranian military campaigns. Throughout the period, the army relied on traditional tactics in which negotiations or ploys were favored over fighting. Army outposts were ex-tended into tribal regions, and a decisive factor in defeating the tribes probably was the construction of major roads along the nomadic tribes' migration routes. Between 1923 and 1938, Reza Shah built more than fourteen thousand miles of new roads, over three thousand miles of which were classified as first-class roads or highways. Taking a patient approach, the army refrained from having its units march into the tribes' nearly impenetrable mountainous home territories and refuges. Instead, a focus on tribal migration routes allowed the army, with the aid of a few spotter planes, to confront the tribes at the most advantageous points during their journeys from winter to summer pastures. The commanders also relied on bribes to divide the tribes and stir up internal conflicts. As nec-essary, Reza offered concessions and government positions to tribal leaders to gain their loyalty.

The Iranian monarch did not shy away from trying to terrorize the tribes into submission when other tactics failed. Massacres and looting were common fea-tures of the pacification campaigns. As control was established, military gover-nors were appointed over the tribes, the tribal warriors were disarmed, and the young men were conscripted into the army. As Iranian rulers had done for centuries, Reza forced tribal leaders and other hostages to reside in Tehran, sometimes imprisoning or killing them in response to their tribes' behavior.

Unlike his predecessors, Reza Shah adopted policies that sought to destroy the social and economic foundation of nomadic tribes by forced settlement in fixed locations or by restricted annual migrations. The tribes appear not to have recognized that Reza represented a new type of ruler and, much to their own detriment, continued to indulge their long-standing rivalries and cooperate with the government against their neighbors. The shah initially tried to use small government detachments to quell restive tribes, but the army's failure caused Reza to call up larger tribal levies, which continued to be Iran's most effective fighting force. Tribal recruits, both individuals and contingents, were merged into larger units of mixed composition but were now led by commissioned officers rather than their chiefs. The British minister commented after Iranian campaigns in 1927 that tribal levies had done most of the successful fighting and that when the army operated without these tribal allies "the results were a record of incompetency, hesitancy, and lack of energy."[15] Reza even suspended later attempts to disarm the tribes because their warriors were needed to protect the frontiers from tribes in neighboring countries. Still, by the end of 1927, Reza had broken the power of the main tribal chiefs. He stopped his efforts there to preserve the unity of the smaller tribes and subtribes, which he needed to augment the army and avoid anarchy.[16]

Iran's most persistent tribal opponents were the various Kurdish tribes, the most troublesome of which were led by the warlord Ismail Agha, commonly known as Simko. Leading the second largest Kurdish confederation, the Shakak tribe, Simko had thousands of armed tribesmen to enforce his rule over much of western Azerbaijan Province in the immediate aftermath of World War I. The Kurdish chief had a reputation as a daring warrior and bold raider, and when the Russians withdrew from Azerbaijan, Simko captured many of their rifles, machine guns, and artillery pieces. Several hundred Ottoman soldiers also joined Simko's army, bringing field guns and machine guns that made Simko's forces more than a match for the ill-trained government troops in Azerbaijan following the armistice. Simko exacted tribute from a broad region of western Azerbaijan to help maintain his army, capturing and looting towns and occasionally massacring Azeris who refused to recognize his authority and pay his taxes. Simko sparred repeatedly with Gendarmerie, Cossack, and Azeri tribal forces in 1920 and 1921, winning numerous battles but falling back to his mountain stronghold of Chahriq when pressed too hard. The Kurdish chief kept his fighters mobilized by constant raiding but also appealed to Kurdish nationalism and the prospect of independence to keep them motivated.[17]

After the army's unification at the end of 1921, Reza devoted several months to preparing a campaign against Simko. A more resolute and better trained and supplied army of eight thousand Iranian troops under Gen. Habibullah Shaybani, one of the former Gendarmerie's most promising officers, confronted Simko's army, which could not sustain its heavy weapons in repeated battles. Simko's fighters melted away after the first few reverses to no more than a thousand loyal followers. At the same time, the Iranian army commanders got rival Kurdish tribes to join in the government attack. After heavy fighting in July 1922, Simko's warriors retreated to Chahriq. With the addition of Kurdish irregulars, the Iranian expedition captured the fortress for the first time in August, dispersing Simko's warriors and causing their leader to flee to Iraq. The Kurdish chief returned to Iran several times to try unsuccessfully to regain the power and autonomy he once had. Fearing that Simko was becoming a tool for Turkish pressure, Reza Shah offered him amnesty in 1929 but then had government troops ambush and kill the Kurdish leader. Despite Simko's passing, tribal unrest in Kurdistan continued until the late 1930s.

Another potential separatist challenge was squelched by the subjugation of Sheikh Khazal of Muhammarah, the ruler of Khuzestan. In the summer of 1922, contingents from the Southern Division at Esfahan were sent into Muhammarah and nearby areas to recruit men and give the central government a foothold in the region. A column of four hundred men was attacked en route to Ahvaz by Bakhtiari tribesmen, who killed one hundred soldiers; captured the detachment's weapons, animals, and baggage; and stripped the survivors. An enraged Reza Khan sent Brig. Gen. Fazlallah Khan Zahedi and forty specially selected officers to take over the division in early 1923 to prepare it for a major operation to secure the southwest. Meanwhile, Sheikh Khazal, still a British protégé and partner in protecting the oil fields, sought to safeguard his autonomy against Reza Khan's revival of central power by aligning with the neighboring Bakhtiari khans and Reza's political opponents. In 1924, the sheikh invited Ahmad Shah to return from Europe and offered to help restore his authority, but the monarch turned down the invitation and remained in self-imposed exile. The sheikh continued to risk Reza Khan's anger by trying to stir up opposition to the war minister in the Majles.[18]

The sheikh had fatally misjudged Reza Khan and, more importantly, British support for the Arab emirate. Reza ordered three thousand Iranian soldiers to march on Khuzestan in November 1924. Two task forces were established, with one to advance south from Dezful while the second, under General Zahedi, was to move from Esfahan through the Zagros Mountains to the Khuzestan plain. The latter force defeated a Bakhtiari tribe allied with Sheikh Khazal and cowed the other Bakhtiari chiefs into submission. Reza traveled to Bushehr, and his saber-rattling along with the concentration of Iranian soldiers around

Ahvaz were sufficient to get Sheikh Khazal to request a negotiated settlement. The sheikh looked to London to protect him, but the British saw his position as untenable and favored Reza as a bulwark against Soviet Communism. When he realized that the British had abandoned him, the sheikh disbanded his Arab forces and retired to Muhammarah. Reza pardoned Sheikh Khazal in return for his submission, and Iranian troops occupied Ahvaz and military governors took posts in that city and Abadan. The forced amity between Reza and the Sheikh did not last long, however. In April 1925, Reza ordered General Zahedi to embark a detachment of fifty men on the yacht *Khuzestan* and waylay the sheikh's yacht on the Karun River in the middle of the night. Sheikh Khazal and his son were captured and sent to Tehran, where they were kept under house arrest for eleven years. After ignoring British demands for the sheikh to be exiled to Europe, Reza Shah ordered him strangled in 1936.

The new Iranian Army was constantly engaged in operations to restore order and gain the submission of the tribes. After Reza became shah he provoked new rebellions by the Qashqai, Lurs, Kurds, and Bakhtiaris with policies compelling tribes to submit to conscription into the army and to become settled farmers. The Qashqai tribes continued to resist central authority until the construction of new roads and the addition of tanks, armored cars, and aircraft gave the army sufficient strength in 1933 to stop tribal migrations and force the tribes to settle in existing cities, towns, and pastoral regions. Similarly, the Lurs regularly defeated army units and were not subdued until the early 1930s. Despite several campaigns against the Turkmans in the mid-1920s, the government was unable to bring the tribesmen to battle. Instead, the Turkman tribes withdrew into Soviet territory, from which they continued raids into Iran for many more years. The Baluch in eastern Iran were pacified only after the arrest and execution of their chief, Dust Muhammad Khan, in early 1929. In the end, the forced settlement of the tribes shattered their economies and, as the shah hoped, undermined their traditional social structure. Tehran provided little help to the tribes, and, ill prepared for sedentary life, the tribe members and their herds died in large numbers for many years.[19]

With the tribes increasingly passive, Reza Shah's next step to increase his and the government's authority was to undermine the power of the Iranian clergy. Reza sought to weaken the ulema by castigating them as symbols of Iran's weakness and subjugation in contrast to his deliverance of the country from foreign domination. To match Islam's strong influence on Iranians, Reza tried to connect his countrymen to a glorified image of ancient Persia. The shah extolled the Achaemenids and notable shahanshahs such as Shapur the Great, who humbled the Romans, and Chosroes I, who had established pre-Islamic concepts of justice and kingship. Reza also revived the use of Zoroastrian symbols in government architecture and required schoolchildren to memorize sections of the

Shahnameh that emphasized Iranian glory and its dependence on monarchy. He ordered that ancient Persian or Farsi words replace Arabic ones in the language to correspond with a simultaneous attempt to relate the military to its historical antecedents by giving Persian names to the units and ranks. He also altered the names of Iranian cities from Arabic to Persian, and among these changes Muhammarah became Khorramshahr and Soltanabad was renamed Arak. In 1935 Reza Shah demanded that foreign countries stop calling the country Persia and refer to it by its true name, Iran.

As Reza Shah extolled Iran's past glory, some of the ulema tried to resist this and Reza's social policies. The Iranian religious establishment, however, lacked a senior cleric with enough moral authority to mobilize the faithful during this period. So the clergy retreated temporarily from politics. Over time, Reza's orders to impose European headgear and dress, ban public mourning rituals, and forbid the veiling of women incensed the clerics, along with most Iranians, and spurred violent opposition to these laws. Iran's autocrat then seized this chance to suppress the ulema ruthlessly and ensure their silence for the remainder of his rule.

The most violent confrontation began when a cleric at Mashhad's Imam Reza Shrine, angered by the shah's rejection of a request to exempt the city from the veil prohibition, denounced the shah's policies and the court's corruption in July 1935. Antiregime rioting broke out, and local police and army contingents in the city refused to violate the sanctity of the mosque. Reza called up more troops and ordered the mob to be dispersed by force. Army and other security forces surrounded several thousand Iranians assembled at the shrine, but some troops refused to fire on the rioters. Officers summarily executed two soldiers, then watched a third commit suicide rather than shoot the protestors. Disaffection among the local army units was so high that the commanding officer ordered many of his men disarmed and placed under guard during the second day of the protests. The resulting standoff lasted another two days, during which more regular troops from outside the region, including machine gun sections, arrived at the mosque. With a force of two thousand soldiers surrounding the shrine, the commander ordered rifle and machine gun fire over the heads of the crowd. When the protestors stood their ground, the soldiers' aim was gradually lowered and a massacre began. Estimates of the killed and wounded vary, but British reports, which may have been intentionally kept low, related that civilian casualties were 128 dead with 200 to 300 wounded and more than 800 arrested.[20] The army lost two officers and eighteen soldiers in suppressing the riot. Once again, Reza Shah had shown that he had the will to pursue mercilessly a strong and modern state, but the gulf between the shah and his army and the Iranian people had grown irredeemably wide.

A Growing Yet Hollow Military

To strengthen the main prop of the regime, Reza Shah was unstinting in the attention he gave to the armed forces, but problems with manpower, professionalism, corruption, and material resources continued to plague the military. Like other dictators, Reza's suspicious nature hampered the development of the armed forces and left its structure fragile. Undiscouraged by the military's earlier setbacks with growth, Reza set a goal after becoming Iran's monarch for expanding his army of thirty-three thousand men in 1926 into a one-hundred-thousand-man force, which was reached a decade later. The army's budget increased more than fivefold between 1926 and 1941, and over time the military acquired new weapons, equipment, and specialized capabilities, obtaining at least the appearance of a modern military with air and naval arms.

The army's ground forces were the source of the shah's greatest pride. As early as 1927 Reza and the General Staff determined that the realities facing the Iranian military required a change in force structure. Only the Central Division in Tehran retained brigades, regiments, and batteries. Except for a few cavalry regiments, all of the other divisions became composite forces of infantry, cavalry, and artillery whose strength varied according to local conditions. The change was made to meet the demands for internal security and because the army could not mobilize additional forces quickly to provide each military region with a self-contained force under a unified command and administration. The Central Division was the best and most reliable unit and was directly responsive to Reza. Its troops served as a strategic reserve for the army and frequently supported other divisions engaged in combating tribal insurgencies.

By 1930, the army had eighty thousand men and could count on the cooperation of the twelve thousand men belonging to a reestablished Gendarmerie service called the Aminiyyah. The army did not buy many new weapons through the 1920s and early 1930s because of Iran's general destitution, and it lacked any significant mechanized forces. According to an American legation report, after the 1921 coup, Iran received ten small tractors and four small tanks from France while Germany provided thirty-two trucks. Iran also took delivery of four Rolls Royce armored cars from Great Britain. These vehicles do not appear to have been used in the field but were a fixture in annual military parades until 1941.[21]

After Reza renegotiated the oil concession with the British-owned Anglo-Persian Oil Company (renamed Anglo-Iranian at the shah's request) in 1933, more money became available for the army and its mechanization. The following year, Iran bought nineteen heavy trucks from the Indianapolis-based Marmon-Herrington Company and another thirty-six trucks and twelve armored cars in 1935. Shortly thereafter, Iran ordered fifty-six Czechoslova-kian Skoda light tanks, reportedly canceling orders with Marmon-Herrington because the shah was angry about American press articles that referred to his humble origins. In the late 1930s, the American ambassador reported that all of Iran's infantry units possessed machine gun batteries and growing numbers of automatic rifles. Some new motorized light and medium field artillery pieces and eight motorized antiaircraft guns had been procured, but much of the army's artillery was still the horse-drawn Schneiders or the Qajar-era mountain guns that were transported disassembled on mules. In 1938 the U.S. ambassador reported that Iran's armored forces consisted of one hundred Czechoslovakian light and medium tanks plus the four Rolls Royce armored cars, twelve Marmon-Herrington armored cars, and twenty-eight German armored trucks. The cavalry, mounted on sturdy and well-groomed horses and armed with carbines or lances, was still Iran's major striking arm for maneuver and shock effect on the battlefield.

Iran's ground forces continued to grow, passing 105,000 men in 1937 and reaching 126,000 men by mid-1941. Organized into sixteen divisions, the army still followed the earlier practice of varying troop and equipment levels. Some divisions had as many as 8,500 men while others had only 3,000 troops. Interestingly, given Iran's concerns about the Soviet threat, none of the divisions in the north held any modern artillery while only eight antiaircraft guns were distributed among them. Iran's armored vehicles, meanwhile, were consolidated into one mechanized brigade with three mechanized regiments in Tehran. The mobility of other army units rested on 50 Belgian and 16 Harley-Davidson motorcycles, 300 trucks, and 150 other vehicles and tractors. Iran's army had been designed to focus on internal security rather than external defense, and in mid-1941 it faced no serious challenges from the tribes, while the Saadabad Pact seemed to guarantee peace along the borders with its non-Russian neighbors. The U.S. embassy, less sanguine about the challenges potentially posed by the wars in Europe and Asia, reported that the Iranian army's reliability had not been tested, and its well-known shortcomings crippled its effectiveness.

Reza Khan and Iran's other military leaders immediately understood the benefit of airpower for their own tribal pacification plans after noting the success of the Royal Air Force in suppressing Iraqi tribes in 1920. By mid-1924, sixteen French, Russian, and German biplanes had been delivered to Iran. Three of the seven French aircraft were out of commission shortly after arriving in Iran because of the wear and damage suffered from mishaps during their flight to the country. The Russian and German planes proved sturdier and were used for reconnaissance, maintaining communications between the capital and forces in the field, and occasional bombing missions during the campaigns against the Bakhtiaris, Lurs, and Turkmans.

The army-dominated leadership did not see a major role for the air service other than supporting ground units with internal security missions. For several years the air force had insufficient pilots and technically knowledgeable officers and mechanics to administer and operate its growing inventory of aircraft. European pilots were hired to fill the gap, but the Iranians' lack of experience and inability to plan resulted in serious sustainment problems. The maintenance complications caused by the diversity of airplanes were aggravated when Iranian officers regularly failed to stock adequate spare parts, fuel, and oil. The air force also had no wireless radio capability or meteorological service, which may have contributed to the spate of accidents that slowed the service's growth.

Despite using European pilots, the air force lost aircraft almost as quickly as new ones were purchased and delivered. By 1930, Iran had only twenty planes in flying condition. After eighteen new British Hawker biplanes were delivered to Bushehr and assembled there, two were lost on the subsequent flight to Tehran; one was lost and never found, while the other crashed and its Iranian pilot was killed. In March 1935, five Hawker aircraft, which had been shipped to and assembled in Ahvaz, encountered storms while flying to Tehran. Two of the biplanes landed safely and eventually made their way to the capital, while two others were severely damaged when they landed and had to be trucked to Tehran. The fifth plane, piloted by a Belgian, got so far lost that it ran out of fuel and landed in the Dasht-e Lut desert between Tehran and Mashhad. Upset by the mishaps, the shah had the chief of the air service confined for two days. Afterward, fear of Reza's displeasure and the high cost of aircraft procurement caused the new air arm to avoid taking risky actions. The Iranian military was open to some experimentation, however, and bought one hydroplane in response to Turkman raiders using boats to attack villages along the Caspian coast.[22]

The shah eventually decided that one supplier for the air force would simplify logistics. Despite lingering anti-British sentiment in the country, Reza turned to London because its aircraft manufacturers already dominated Iranian aviation. By the end of 1934, Iran had 145 serviceable airplanes on hand or on order, mostly de Havilland and Hawker biplanes with a few other British, German, and American aircraft. The government planned to build a force of 200 planes, but Iran lacked the proper facilities and trained personnel to effectively exploit their existing air forces. By 1937 the Iranian air force had 1,000 personnel but retained a little more than 130 serviceable aircraft. In an effort to build infrastructure and increase Iran's inventory, Reza ordered an aircraft production factory to be built and managed by the British. It was constructed near Doshan Tappeh outside Tehran, and the first planes produced in Iran were rolled out in early 1938. Nearly three years later, the Americans reported that the Iranian air force's order of battle had a total of 245 aircraft, nearly all of which were British biplanes designated as fighters, light bombers, and trainers.[23]

Reza Shah initially created an Iranian navy to combat pirates menacing Iran's maritime trade and smugglers depriving him of needed custom revenues. In addition to curbing the pirates, he wanted to suppress the regional slave trade, if only to strengthen his contention that British naval patrols in the Persian Gulf were unnecessary. Reza's long-term goal was the exceedingly ambitious one of reducing the Gulf Arabs' reliance on the Royal Navy and substituting Iranian for British influence around the region. The Iranians, however, had to start from virtually worse than scratch to build a navy. In 1925 the American vice-consul in Bushehr reported that Iran's two largest vessels were the *Persepolis,* which had been acquired in 1885, and the *Muzafferi,* which had been added to the inventory at the turn of the century. Both were unseaworthy, and their small crews conducted regular pay strikes and often had to be forced to stay on board the ships. Reza made his first major naval acquisition while minister of war in 1924, purchasing a small German ship, which was renamed the *Pahlavi.* The American vice-consul reported that when this motor launch was delivered the following year it ran out fuel and had to be rowed the last few miles into port at Bushehr. At this time, Iran lacked trained naval personnel. With no qualified officers available, the Iranians promoted a German deckhand to captain and gave him an Iranian crew. In short order, the unpaid sailors began to sell the ship's fittings in the bazaar, forcing the army to place an armed guard on board to protect the ship. The *Pahlavi* was ordered to Muhammarah and was nearly lost by its untrained crew in the Bushehr channel before eventually reaching its destination. The shah's navy added another vessel in 1925 when an Iranian resident of Al Basrah purchased a small British craft, later named *Khuzestan,* and presented it to Iran as a gift. Iran belatedly sent the first party of naval cadets to Italy for training the next year.[24]

More money was allocated to the navy in 1927, and new ships were ordered from Italy. As these were being delivered, Reza Shah issued the orders establishing the naval service in November 1932. The Italian vessels were the 950-ton sloops *Babr* and *Palang* and the 350-ton gunboats *Shahrokh, Simorgh, Karkas,* and *Chahbaaz.* Sold to Iran as new, the Italian ships actually were reconditioned. Iran lacked the technical experts to discover this misrepresentation, however, and accepted the vessels. The sloops and gunboats joined four smaller vessels and the *Ivy,* Sheikh Khazal's former yacht, which served as a training ship, to form Iran's Southern Navy. This force operated out of the ports of Bushehr, Bandar Shahpur, and Muhammarah (Khorramshahr). Iran also had a Caspian flotilla with four small 28-ton vedette or scouting boats and the royal yacht, *Shahsavar.* A former Cossack officer, Golam Ali Bayendor, was made a rear admiral and given command of the Southern Navy, which continued to struggle with inadequate personnel and insufficient funding. When operations against smugglers finally commenced, the Iranian crews survived by levying and then immediately collecting fines and by treating the smugglers' boats and goods as prizes, the proceeds of which were distributed among the officers and sailors.

After all of these efforts to expand the size and inventories of the armed forces, the Iranian military had only a "veneer of modernization" and "was a parade-ground army, largely untried in battle and led by complacent and corrupt officers."[25] This outcome was a direct result of Iran's inability to address the military's major shortcomings, starting with the provision of the personnel needed to build a modern force. While still minister of war, Reza proposed compulsory military conscription for every adult male to address the problems of the *bonicheh* system and provide the manpower for the armed forces' envisioned growth. Conscription also was seen as a way to transform Iran by integrating society and spreading literacy, nationalist sentiment, and a romantic vision of Iranian history through military service. In addition, the new system was a means to reduce the government's reliance on tribal levies, although it failed to meet this objective. The conscription bill passed in 1924 called for two years of compulsory military service for all men reaching the age of twenty-one. After two years of active duty, the conscripts were to remain in reserve status for twenty-three years with progressively declining obligations for service. Objections from the mullahs to the bill were neutralized by exemptions for clerics and religious students, and to demonstrate Reza's emphasis on nationalism over religious and communal identity, non-Muslims were included in conscription for the first time in Iran's modern history.[26]

Throughout the decades of Reza Shah's rule, conscription never quite delivered on its promise for any of the shah's goals while it generated occasional violent opposition from the parts of Iranian society that the government was trying to unify. The government initially limited its imposition of conscription to Tehran, Qazvin, and Hamadan but was met with hostility everywhere. The most significant resistance occurred in three waves in Iran in the late 1920s: first in Esfahan and Shiraz in 1927, then Tabriz in 1928, and finally among the tribes in 1929. Protests and opposition were particularly strong in the south, where the *bonicheh* system had not been enforced, and it was led by clerics concerned about the secularizing impact of military service. Corruption followed in the wake of the resistance, and recruiters focused on the poorest and most defenseless sectors of society. Many "volunteers" were recruited by bribes or by convincing former soldiers to return to duty. Corrupt census officials entered false ages to allow the enlistment of middle-aged men or help younger men avoid the draft. In some instances, domestic servants were kidnapped and then ransomed for an eligible recruit from their household. Other coercive measures included forcing body washers and coffin makers to demand proof of registration for conscription of young men from the families of deceased persons before providing their essential services. Minorities became a special target of the recruiters. In Shiraz about 10 percent of those called to serve were Jews, a proportion far greater than their presence in the general population. In Kerman the conscription committee reportedly took every available Zoroastrian. Iranians in the countryside could bribe their way out of service, but many chose flight to avoid conscription. Among the tribes, where military service in the levies was accepted and even desirable, the chiefs opposed having their young men removed from tribal authority and given a nontribal identity. In the face of occasional violent resistance, the government was forced to exercise extreme caution as it gradually took recruits from the tribes during the 1930s.

Conscription produced a larger Iranian army for the shah, but it failed to produce a strong and efficient one. Despite Reza Shah's professed care for his army, Iranian conscripts were not treated well and were poorly paid, fed, and housed. Even in the Tehran garrison, purportedly under the shah's eye, the conditions were so bad that disturbingly high death rates for recruits eventually caused Reza to appoint special medical officers to supervise the soldiers' treatment. The attendant poor morale and the soldiers' inadequate training were major factors in the government's continued reliance on tribal levies throughout the 1930s. As the tribal levies were phased out, the army probably became less effective because the conscripts were not comparable fighters to the tribal warriors. Most of the conscripts entered the army illiterate, and literacy programs, when actually conducted by often indifferent officers, took time away from other duties and training. In general, military skills were developed while on campaign against the tribes and bandits. Still, reading instruction and the indoctrination given to all recruits were indispensable elements in Reza's nationalization campaign and had some impact as rural and tribal recruits took home their modern ways. By failing to address the poor treatment of the troops and other critical problems, however, a huge emotional and financial gap developed between the officers and soldiers.

The lack of professionalism was a serious deficiency of the Iranian military throughout Reza Shah's rule. In the mid-1920s, many of Iran's officers had no real experience with modern warfare and made no attempt to learn from Europe's experience in the Great War. Lacking knowledge and skills, Iran's officers were poor trainers and bore much of the responsibility for their soldiers' rudimentary proficiency at standard tasks. Reza recognized the need to reform military education to provide more and better officers to lead the new platoons, companies, and battalions in his expanding army. After combining the existing officer schools into a single military college for officer basic training, Reza established a military education program that included a primary school for seven- to twelve-year-old boys and an intermediate school for thirteen- to nineteen-year-olds. A military academy that commissioned young men as second lieutenants upon graduation was the final step in the program. Reza also set up a type of officer candidate school to train NCOs selected to become officers and later, as funding allowed, established medical, aviation, and communications schools. Despite his distrust of foreign influence, Reza sent many junior and midlevel officers abroad, mostly to the French military schools of Saumur, St. Cyr, and École Supérieure de Guerre for professional training. Reza Shah also established an Iranian staff college in 1935 to provide instruction on military history, cavalry tactics, and military geography among other topics for midgrade officers. By mid-1941, when Iran's army had 126,000 men on its rolls, slightly fewer than 2,100 officers were graduates of the military academy and just more than 1,000 NCOs had completed training to become officers.

Over time this education and training might have improved the army's efficiency. The senior Cossack officers running the shah's military, however, were conservative men uninterested in the application of new military methods. The senior commanders were more comfortable with the old Cossack Brigade practices. They made poor use of the military academy graduates and limited the impact of the French-trained officers. Thus they squandered the opportunity to initiate improvements in staff work and administration.

The former Cossack officers dominating the army had other practices that seriously weakened the army, particularly financial mismanagement and corruption. Dishonest officers confiscated tribal treasuries, falsified rosters to draw more funds and rations, stole taxes, and commandeered materials almost without restraint. Reza even winked at the officers' continuation of the Qajar practice of keeping a share of their subordinates' pay. The shah's own abuse of power to enrich himself and his cronies set a bad example. With their monarch's help, the former Cossack generals became rich, acquiring fortunes in real estate and, with their new status, mixing their fortunes with those of the old Qajar elite through marriage. Financial mismanagement and corruption were facilitated by Reza's control over all of Iran's revenues, including its oil royalties. The shah even set up a special bank, called Bank Sepah, which was owned by the army's pension fund, catered to the armed forces, and provided additional opportunities for shady deals. With losses due to graft and mismanagement, government funding and other financial arrangements were never enough to support the army's growth. The easy short-term solution to the problem was to hold back the soldiers' pay, which contributed to the various mutinies and desertions Reza's army suffered in its first decade. Reza Shah partially restored the military's financial situation by eventually correcting some of the worst abuses, but the army's overall reputation had been indelibly stained as corrupt.

The Iranian officer corps was generally unequal to the task of linking its growth and its operational goals to supply and other services essential to the armed forces' proper functioning. Iran was slow to develop its combat service and combat service support elements, such as the signal, transportation, and quartermaster branches. The General Staff set up a logistic system for the purchase of supplies and services, but mismanagement was an ongoing problem. The multiple types of weapons in Iran's arsenal complicated the supply of arms and ammunition. With European help, Reza established a small defense industry to correct these problems, but the effort was hindered by the absence of a larger industrial base. German firms were given most of the contracts for building and modernizing defense factories and small arms and vehicle repair facilities. A German officer was placed in charge of the Tehran and Bushehr arsenals. At the beginning of Reza's rule the Tehran arsenal had British, French, and Austrian machinery, most of which was underutilized, and powder for fireworks was its major product. After improvements were made, the arsenal could produce fifty thousand rounds of rifle ammunition and twenty-five rifles daily. Later, production lines for German machine guns, bayonets, and grenades were added, and a facility was set up at Parchin, sixteen miles southeast of Tehran, to produce cordite and high explosives.

Solving the army's problems with transportation, communication, and other services initially was accomplished by imposing on Iranian citizens and civilian infrastructure, adding to the list of popular grievances against the armed forces. In 1924 most of the goods imported from Europe were still being moved by animal power from Bushehr to Tehran, and there were few motor vehicles in Iran. One of Reza's first acts after he became minister of war was to seize the automobiles of the nobility against payment of their tax arrears. From these he formed a Motor Transport Service. Well into the 1930s, the army relied on civil transport, usually from private caravan owners, whenever the troops were required to deploy. Similarly, military communications relied on the existing civilian telegraph services or on messengers traveling by foot, horse, car, and airplane. The signal service was part of the army's engineer regiments, but these elements were small, slow to expand, and limited in their technical knowledge. The army also lacked capable cartographers and relied on Russian and British maps. For many years, food was taken by force from nearby villages and towns when units were in the field. While military hospitals were better than their civilian counterparts, the army medical service was understaffed and poorly equipped, and few doctors had any modern medical training.

The nature of the relationship between Reza Shah and his commanders and the army at large was perhaps the key impediment to Iran's modernization and professionalization. Most of the army remained loyal to Reza throughout his reign, especially the most powerful senior commanders who owed their position to the shah. An undercurrent of dissent in the new army never subsided, however, springing first from the Cossack-Gendarme rivalry, then from promonarchy and republican sentiments, and finally from economic and religious grievances that coincided with the broader popular disenchantment with the shah. In particular, the soldiers, although little interested in politics, tended to be ideologically dominated by the clergy, who increasingly despised their monarch.

Reza's response to these challenges was to allow his mistrust to undermine the military and its role as a national force. Military effectiveness was less important to the shah than loyalty, and Reza surrounded himself with Cossack officers he knew and trusted. Army officers and other government officials learned to report only favorable information and withhold any that might contradict the expectations of the shah. In addition, Reza was wary of capable and ambitious men, tended to promote mediocre but dependable officers, and dealt harshly with even the hint of disloyalty. One commander of the Central Division was arrested and suspended merely because the shah suspected he was trying to acquire too much influence. In such an atmosphere, independent-minded officers kept a low profile, and the motivation to build innovative and self-reliant units was sapped from the army.

Being a suspicious man, Reza relied on intrigue, blackmail, and, as needed, physical force to eliminate potential and actual foes. Jealousies within the senior leadership, political factionalism, and, until 1936, an absence of standardized promotion procedures contributed to an officer corps more focused on personal interests than those of the armed forces. This selfishness led to bad-tempered soldiers who often refused to drill, regularly deserted, occasionally abused their officers, and flirted with communism. The indiscipline, in turn, increased Tehran's anxiety about mutinies and contributed to the harsh treatment given to soldiers when their protests collapsed. Rumors of plots real and imagined against Reza by ex-gendarmes and army officers continued to spread, although many regime allegations were propaganda or part of the shah's efforts to secure his control over the government.

In one instance, after anonymous leaflets were distributed in Tehran criticizing the recently crowned monarch, the chief of police was pressed by Reza to find the ringleaders. Several army officers and civilians were arrested, and Col. Mahmud Khan Puladin, a regimental commander who had been Reza's aide-de-camp, was accused of being a member of the dissident faction. The police chief was a skillful intriguer and in a bitter feud with Puladin, however, and probably fabricated the evidence. The former aide-de-camp, who apparently was guilty of nothing more than being approached by a politician trying to set up a coup, was tried and executed by firing squad. Puladin's treatment and execution cast a chill over other army officers, who feared that if Puladin was vulnerable, then anyone could be arrested and convicted on a baseless charge. The resulting impact on morale and effectiveness almost certainly contributed to the fragility of the army and to continued dissension. In late 1939, reports surfaced that hundreds of army officers were arrested for coup plotting, and in early 1941 one of the airplanes participating in the annual military parade flyby broke formation and flew on to the Soviet Union.[27]

The Costs of Greatness

Over the course of nearly two decades Reza Shah succeeded in maintaining order and defending the nation at a time when external threats were minimal. Reza Shah can be credited with numerous accomplishments that modernized Iran and, to varying degrees, improved the national infrastructure supporting the military. In addition to greatly expanding the amount of roads and railways, the shah's efforts resulted in the construction of power plants to ensure that by the late 1930s all of Iran's cities had electricity and were connected by six thousand miles of telephone lines. Backed by the development of Iran's oil resources, he led the transition from virtually total dependence on farming and herding to a nearly equal mix between agricultural and nonagricultural sectors.

The cost of Reza's programs for most Iranians was high, and poverty, corruption, and injustice remained as bad as during Qajar times. In fact, the shah's repression became so severe that an American official described the country in 1934 as being strongly reminiscent of Soviet Russia in the period of militant communism from 1917 to 1921.[28] Many of Reza's reforms were cruel and inefficient, as they concentrated wealth in fewer hands and impoverished all Iranians earning a living from the land. On the eve of World War II, Iran was in bad shape economically, inflation was rife, and many Iranians were living at subsistence levels. In addition, with war clouds forming on Iran's horizon in 1941, the Iranian armed forces were still ill prepared for any mission larger than the suppression of Iran's tribes. The bill for Reza Shah's absolutism, greed, distrust, and overall failure to take the modern structure of his army and make it a genuinely effective military would be national humiliation and personal exile.

6

Sidelined

The World at War in Iran

FROM THE TIME GERMANY AND THE SOVIET UNION invaded Poland in September 1939 until the Soviets and British invaded Iran in August 1941, Reza Shah and his country were the subject of intense great power concern and operational planning. The shah had proclaimed Iran's neutrality in early September 1939, but the sum of Allied fears was an exaggerated picture of the real but still limited German influence in Iran. Reza Shah for once found himself on the wrong side of history, and the consequences of the unprovoked Allied invasion in World War II were significant for Iran. Its army was crushed, its monarch left the country, and the Red Army, saved from defeat by supply lines running across Iran, undermined Iran's sovereignty and territorial integrity. Perhaps most important for the future of Iran's armed forces, the United States was drawn inexorably into Iranian affairs. The Americans provided another opportunity for Iran's military leaders to embrace reform and address their long-standing problems with professionalism, training, and other aspects of military effectiveness. Old habits died hard, however, and the baleful effects of Reza Shah's domination of Iran's military survived the shock of invasion, occupation, and abdication. For most of the world war, Iran's armed forces remained on the sidelines, eagerly accepting military aid while grudgingly adopting Allied-recommended changes, as Iranian military leaders marked time until the occupiers left and they could regain control of their own destiny.[1]

Reza Raises West's Suspicions

Without question, Iran had sought strong relations with Berlin since the turn of the century to offset British and Russian influence. Following World War I, the Weimar and Nazi governments reciprocated this interest and tried to increase all ties, especially through propaganda disparaging "colonial" powers and trumpeting Aryan and Nazi superiority. Berlin helped Iran by lending its technical skills, building docks, roads, and parts of the Trans-Iranian Railroad, and sending advisers to the Iranian government and professors to the Iranian school system. The Germans made an exception for the Iranians as "pure Aryans" in the Nuremberg Racial Laws and emphasized use of the Nazi swastika, which also was an ancient Zoroastrian symbol, to highlight the two countries' common interests and racial ties. In 1941, however, Iran was only hosting roughly one thousand German residents, a far cry from the two thousand to seven thousand claimed by the Allies. A little more than three hundred were German officials and their families, including a few Gestapo and military intelligence officers. Most of the other German residents worked for the Iranian government. Despite this fact, Iran's vulnerability to invasion increased markedly once London and Moscow became allies against Hitler because, in addition to protecting oil installations in Iran and Baku, the Allies needed to open supply corridors to Russia. This, in turn, required the Allies to uproot Nazi influence in Iran to eliminate potential German threats to these interests. Memories of Wassmuss's espionage and seditious activities in World War I and developments such as a short-lived German-incited coup in Iraq in early 1941 heightened the Allies' fears about a German "fifth column" in Iran. Tehran's position was not helped by Reza Shah's unpopularity, his increasing resort to violence to control the political opposition, and his perceived pro-German sympathies.[2]

The Germans were actively collecting intelligence on the Allies and promoting rebellion and anti-Allied actions in Iran, but Allied perceptions of Reza Shah's sympathies were, to a large extent, fearful distortions of the cautious ruler's steps to maintain Iran's neutrality. For the most part, anti-British and anti-Russian sentiment probably outweighed pro-Germany sympathies in Tehran's decisions. In the years before the war, Reza refused repeated requests by Berlin to allow the Germans to set up a military mission, and he limited contacts between Iranian army officers and the Germans. Unhappy with the German-instigated coup against the Iraqi monarch in April 1941, the shah denied German requests to send weapons through Iran to the Iraqis and contemplated intervening. The government in Tehran later assured the British that Iran was doing all it could to reduce the number of Germans and prevent any subversive activities. Reza Shah and the Iranian military even offered in 1940 to cooperate with the British in developing defensive plans against the Soviets, who were then aligned with Hitler.

After the British and Soviets became allies, Reza Shah could not bring himself to make the compromises needed to forestall an invasion. The Iranians viewed Allied demands for the expulsion of Germans as a pretext for invasion and unsuccessfully sought American help to protect Iranian neutrality. The British and Soviet governments gave Iran their final demand in mid-August, but Reza lacked a clear picture of events, because he saw only his own officials, who had learned not to provide him with displeasing news. Unable to reject the

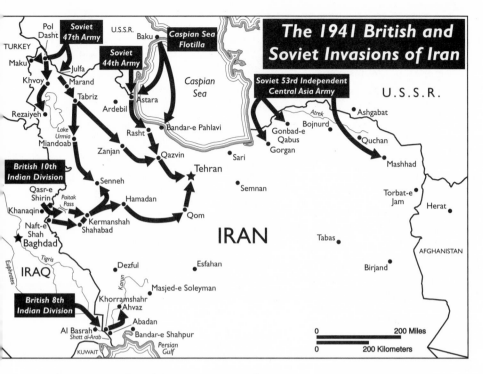

6.1 The 1941 British and Soviet Invasions of Iran.

ultimatum for fear of provoking an attack, the Iranian monarch also was wary of agreeing to Allied demands. He believed that a capitulation would only prompt more demands and would infuriate the Germans, who were then inflicting horrible defeats on the Russians and threatened to have armies on Iran's borders within months. The shah sought to buy time, rejecting the demands while trying to reassure the Allies. Fatefully, Reza delivered an address to graduating military academy cadets on August 20, 1941, telling them they must be ready for sacrifices and then announcing that the customary graduation leave was cancelled. The Allies interpreted the speech as a call for mobilization and set the date for their invasion.[3]

The Unhappy Event

Iranians called the British-Soviet invasion of August 25, 1941, the "unhappy event of Shahrivar (August)," but the Iranian army's inadequate preparations contributed greatly to the unhappiness. As early as July 1940 Iran had started to construct new fortifications, call up a few reserves, and move some additional troops to join the six ill-equipped and understrength Iranian divisions facing the

Soviet border. Ordered by Reza Shah to prepare a detailed defensive plan against a Soviet attack, Brig. Gen. Hassan Arfa judged Iran's northern frontier indefensible and proposed that troops and supplies be pre-positioned in the difficult mountain regions of central and southern Iran. In his plan, light forces would delay the Soviet advance by demolishing roads, bridges, and railroads, forming a screen to allow the government to retreat to a mountain redoubt. Maj. Gen. Ali Razmara proposed instead that the army defend the entire northern border and engage the Soviets as they crossed the frontier. Arfa claimed that the other generals favored Razmara's approach because they feared admitting to their ruler that they could not defend the north. Reza accepted the latter plan, and Arfa later concluded that the shah did not believe Iran could resist a Soviet attack but hoped to discourage a Red Army advance by displaying a willingness to fight. By the summer of 1941 British offensive preparations were increasingly evident, and the shah agreed to concentrate additional forces along the main approaches from Iraq. Iran's 5th and 12th divisions were moved to defend the mountainous central border frontier, and tank units from the 1st Pahlavi Infantry Regiment in Tehran were belatedly sent to Ahvaz.[4]

Although the government claimed it had 180,000 men under arms, the Iranian army probably was not much larger than the 126,400 troops reported by the U.S. legation in mid-1941 because of the belated call-up of reservists. The army's sixteen divisions were spread across the country in their home garrisons, and only some of the western divisions had received any significant reinforcements of infantry and artillery. Maj. Gen. Hassan Mogaddam, the 5th Division commander, was put in charge of all western forces. To the south, the 6th Division, augmented by two regiments from the 1st Division and another regiment from the 15th Division, was dispersed throughout western Khuzestan Province. Mogaddam had these troops improve their defenses by digging antitank ditches around Khorramshahr and constructing entrenchments to block the approaches from central Iraq and Al Basrah. Elsewhere, most of the northern divisions obeyed orders to remain in garrison, and the divisions in central and eastern Iran went about their normal routines.

As war approached, the readiness of Iran's 1,100 air force personnel and roughly 250 mostly obsolete biplanes was unchanged. No redeployments were initiated for the regiment, three squadrons, and training detachment at Tehran or for the three squadrons at Tabriz, Mashhad, and Ahvaz. At best, Iran probably had 125 operational combat aircraft with bomb racks and gun mountings and 250 to 300 pilots. Ten modern and capable American-built Curtiss P-36 Hawk fighters had recently arrived at Ahvaz, but nine remained in their crates. The Iranian navy, with two 950-ton Italian sloops, four 350-ton Italian gunboats, several auxiliary craft, and perhaps 1,000 officers and sailors, similarly took few steps to improve its readiness.

Rear Adm. Golam Ali Bayendor was appointed to direct the defense of the Khorramshahr-Ahvaz region, taking charge of his sailors at the naval yards plus a brigade from the 6th Division. Along with beefing up defenses at the Abadan refinery, a line of machine gun, antiaircraft, and artillery positions was established between the two Iranian ports, with the sloop *Palang* and its four-inch guns securing the Abadan end and its sister ship, *Babr,* at Khorramshahr. Maj. Gen. Muhammad Shahbakhti, the 6th Division commander, was responsible for defending the rest of Khuzestan Province. His unmotivated and poorly trained units suffered from a shortage of officers, and NCOs led many of the division's companies. He was backed by the Fourth Air Regiment, a squadron-sized force with eighteen to nineteen biplanes at Ahvaz, which failed to scramble aircraft to chase off British reconnaissance flights in the days before the attack. The 6th Division was augmented by infantry, eight medium and eight light tanks, and ten armored cars from Tehran. The armored vehicles were dubious additions because the crews, especially the drivers, were poorly trained.[5] Shahbakhti reinforced Abadan as best he could, gathering all available conscript soldiers and gendarmes for the task.

On the eve of the invasion, Iranian forces were only at a medium state of alert. Iranian soldiers were deployed in trenches and prepared positions, but were generally unaware of the looming attack. At Abadan, the key posts along the waterfront were continuously manned, but most of the garrison was in their barracks east of the town with their weapons locked in the armory. One regimental commander entertained his officers well after midnight with tales of campaigns against the mountain tribes. Along the central western border, the artillery from the Central Garrison had moved into positions to support the 12th Division along the Qasr-e Shirin-Kermanshah road. Iran's northern garrisons remained in their barracks that night and displayed no unusual vigilance. Iranian soldiers stationed at Bandar Pahlavi spent the evening cleaning their barracks in preparation for an inspection by their commanding officer on the following morning.[6]

At a quarter past four in the morning on August 25, Iran's prime minister received the British and Russian ministers at his home and was informed that Iran was being invaded. As the European officials urged that Iran not resist the invasion, the attacks already were under way. The Red Army was launching one hundred twenty thousand men and more than one thousand tanks in two powerful thrusts on either side of the Caspian Sea against the estimated thirty-seven thousand Iranian infantrymen in the north. To the west, the 47th Army was advancing on Julfa and headed for Tabriz, while a second column formed by the 44th Army was marching through Astara toward Rasht. To the east, the 53rd Independent Central Asia Army was preparing to invade Khorasan Province. The Soviet Caspian Sea Flotilla sortied out to capture Iran's northern ports with gunfire and amphibious assaults while nearly five hundred combat aircraft flew in support of the Red offensive. The British, in contrast, had nineteen thousand men and fifty light tanks aiming to outmaneuver the roughly thirty thousand Iranians entrenched along the border with Iraq. In the south, the 8th Indian Division and its nine infantry battalions, armored car regiment, artillery regiment, and Royal Navy support attacked to secure the southern oil fields and ports. Along the central border the 10th Indian Division, under Maj. Gen. William Slim, one of the war's most effective commanders, sent two armored brigades and one infantry brigade into Iran to secure the oil fields near Khanaqin. It also readied itself to push through the Paitak Pass to Kermanshah and, if necessary, farther into central Iran. Ever timid, Iran's prime minister refused to wake the shah with the news and waited ninety minutes while Reza finished breakfast before informing Iran's ruler of the Allied invasion.

The War in the South

As morning approached, no Iranians observed the British vessels moving into position in the Shatt al-Arab near Abadan and the Khowr al-Musa channel leading to Bandar Shahpur (now called Bandar Khomeini). The Iranians at Abadan were surprised when the British sloop *HMS Shoreham* opened the battle by firing on *Palang,* causing the Iranian vessel to erupt in a massive fireball. The *Palang*'s gunnery officer ordered terrified crewmen to return fire, but secondary explosions killed him and injured the *Palang*'s commander, who then led the survivors ashore. At Bandar Shahpur, the attacking force of an Australian and Indian sloop, a British corvette and gunboat, and a few other smaller vessels caught eight Axis merchant ships off guard, capturing seven while one was scuttled by its crew. British boarding parties also assaulted two nearby Iranian gunboats, the *Chahbaaz* and *Karkas.* The *Chahbaaz* was attacked first and its crew was quickly captured. On the *Karkas,* the commander of Iran's naval forces in the port tried to have his crew scuttle the boat but was stopped by the British. The Iranian garrison commander surrendered the port soon thereafter when confronted by the British Indian landing force. Two platoons of the Iranian 18th Infantry Regiment fought briefly before retiring into nearby marshes and leaving the port in British hands.[7]

Back at Abadan, the Iranians put up stronger resistance. The first explosions alerted the garrison, and soldiers manning the waterfront posts trained their guns on the British vessels approaching in the light of the blazing *Palang.* Although the firing and explosions caused many Iranians at the garrison to panic, those soldiers stalwart enough to try to fight found the armory locked. The buzz of British aircraft overhead then caused the milling and unarmed Iranians to seek cover in a nearby palm grove. As the British Indian troops disembarked, an Iranian machine gun position on the pumping station roof pinned down one British company along the main jetty. Intense Iranian fire elsewhere on the waterfront forced another British company to shift its landing downriver in an attempt to use moored merchant ships for protection. But it also was pinned down for a short while. At one landing site, a company of sixty to seventy Iranians stopped a company-sized British Indian assault force in its tracks for ninety minutes before being compelled to withdraw. Iranian soldiers west of the refinery continued to resist the British advance despite coming under heavy mortar fire. Elsewhere around the refinery, the Iranians fought fiercely using antiaircraft guns and machine guns to pour concentrated, close-range fire into the advancing Indian infantrymen.

The Iranian commander at Abadan, Colonel Nakhjevan, arrived shortly after sunrise to assess the situation and found few options to salvage the defense. Nakhjevan was out of contact with both Bayendor at Khorramshahr and Shahbakhti at Ahvaz. Most of the Iranian troops fled without their weapons as British aircraft attacked the barracks area. The colonel ordered the armory doors broken open but then had no way to distribute the weapons and ammunition. Deciding that an organized defense was impossible, Nakhjevan ordered all available trucks loaded with ammunition and staged for a withdrawal to Ahvaz. The colonel assembled as many men as he could for the retreat along with the brigade's truck-mounted antiaircraft guns. Iranian soldiers in their waterfront posts, meanwhile, continued to defend well into the day, and rooftop machine gun posts in the port fired until silenced by 50-caliber machine gun fire and four-inch rounds from the *Shoreham*. Eventually all fell back except for a few snipers. To avoid British mopping-up operations, Colonel Nakhjevan began his retreat before he had enough trucks to transport the ammunition, leaving a small rearguard to screen his move. Although the British War Office later judged that the Iranian soldiers around the Abadan refinery "fought with tenacious gallantry," by day's end all resistance in the city had ceased.[8]

At Khorramshahr, some Iranian officers and sailors were awakened by the gunfire from Abadan but had no inkling of the scope of the imminent British attack. In addition to a naval flotilla moving up the Shatt, a British Indian infantry brigade split into three columns had crossed the border undetected shortly after midnight and was converging on the city. The British flotilla consisted of two warships, and the British commander initiated his attack by shelling the *Babr*, Iran's other 950-ton sloop. The *Babr* was pounded with ten rapid salvos, and its quickly spreading fires kept the Iranian gun crews, who had rushed to their mounts, from returning fire. Now alert to the danger, Iranian sailors and soldiers on shore began to direct rifle and machine gun fire from the barracks and the naval staff building at the British ships. This Iranian resistance was ended, however, after a three-inch shell smashed into the barracks. Farther downstream, the Iranian training ship *Ivy* opened fire on a British sloop, which used its twin

50-caliber machine guns to rip the *Ivy*'s wooden superstructure to bits. In the city, Rear Admiral Bayendor rushed to a waiting motorboat and sped to the small pier above his two gunboats, the *Shahrokh* and *Simorgh*, in time to witness their loss. The gunboats were prime examples of Iran's unpreparedness; the *Shahrokh* was undergoing a refit and had no ammunition on board on that morning while the officers of the *Simorgh* were on shore leave. Crewmen on the *Simorgh* tried to fire on an approaching British sloop but were either killed or chased away by the ship's machine guns. The two gunboats and an armed Iranian tugboat were captured by boarding parties, and as the sun was rising British Indian troops were landed to clear the Iranians from the waterfront.

Bayendor retreated to a nearby army post on the Khorramshahr–Al Basrah road to try to reorganize the city's crumbling defenses. In addition to the fighting along the river and near the naval station building, the Iranians had engaged the British Indian forces attacking from the north. Bayendor ordered the available troops divided into two contingents. One was sent to defend the outer approaches to Khorramshahr while the other was withdrawn to protect the main munitions depot and a ferry crossing needed for a retreat to Ahvaz. Bayendor and the 6th Division artillery commander then drove to a nearby wireless station to inform Tehran. In a palm grove running between the station and the river, Iranian troops deployed into prepared fighting positions that included a two-meter-wide antitank ditch. The Iranians stopped the enemy infantry's advance temporarily here, pinning them down until British armored cars moved forward with artillery and mortar fire in support. After some close quarters fighting along the antitank ditch, the Iranians were in danger of being overrun, and Bayendor's soldiers began to withdraw. Bayendor also tried to flee the compound, but his car was stopped by machine gun fire, and when the admiral left the vehicle to try to escape on foot he was shot and killed. The Iranians, aided by effective fire from an artillery battery, made another strong but brief stand inside a nearby army post. As the British Indian forces converged on the position, the Iranian captain commanding the defenders came forward and surrendered, adding 150 Iranians to the several hundred prisoners of war the British had already captured.

With Khorramshahr lost and Abadan abandoned by all Iranian forces except for a few snipers and isolated defenders, the defense of Ahvaz became the focus of Iran's efforts. The city had already been attacked by the Royal Air Force at daybreak. Colonel Gilanshah, the commander of the Fourth Air Regiment, ordered three aircraft scrambled to oppose the British. As the Iranian pilots warmed their motors for takeoff, however, British fighters roared in at low level and strafed all three planes. A few minutes later, six British bombers dropped three thousand pounds of bombs on the airfield, destroying two hangers and five planes and damaging two other aircraft. The sole assembled P-36 fighter was saved by an American technician, who jumped into it as soon as the British aircraft departed and flew to safety in Iraq. To the south of the city, soldiers from Abadan were moving toward Ahvaz and joined with a battalion of the 1st Pahlavi Infantry Regiment from Tehran to defend a nearby police fort. The fort had high walls and concealed entrenchments, and a nearby 75-mm howitzer battery supported the defenders. A British Indian brigade tried to outflank the fort but was forced to withdraw after the Iranians engaged the two lead battalions with artillery and machine gun fire. The Iranian fire was less effective at stopping a third British Indian battalion, which inflicted heavy losses on the Iranians. With the outer defenses lost and suffering heavy casualties inside the fort, an Iranian captain surrendered the position along with the remaining three hundred defenders, removing the last major obstacle on the road to Ahvaz.

By the morning of the invasion's second day, most of the Iranian soldiers in the south had abandoned their posts, deserted their units, or were struggling to reach garrisons far from the front lines. Two Iranian biplanes from Ahvaz took off, possibly for a reconnaissance mission, but were jumped by British fighters, which downed one of the Iranian aircraft and forced the other to retreat. General Shahbakhti had entrenched his remaining forces along the various approaches to the city with fortified positions covered by artillery set up in the hills facing the British approach. These fixed defenses were backed by patrols of tanks, armored cars, and truck-mounted infantry. The Karun River Bridge was rigged for demolition, but the General Staff in Tehran, providing the only guidance received from a higher command, ordered the general to halt any infrastructure destruction. Shahbakhti threatened to "break the teeth" of anyone talking about retreat, but British air attacks and the Abadan survivors' stories undermined Iranian morale. As British forces closed on the city during the afternoon, Iranian units mostly held their fire while the 6th Division's patrolling tanks and other vehicles withdrew in front of the advancing British Indian reconnaissance units and infantry battalions.[9]

The fighting in the south was basically over. The next day the British moved cautiously toward Ahvaz, establishing a line outside the city and conducting reconnaissance missions against the Iranian defenses. On August 28, the British started to advance on the city, and Royal Air Force bombers attacked barracks and troop concentrations there. At 6th Division headquarters, General Shahbakhti received a cease-fire order from the shah, which was being transmitted to all Iranian commands. Shahbakhti fired back a cable to Tehran claiming that he was winning and should continue fighting. The general had a good defensive plan with an infantry regiment, backed by a reserve battalion, entrenched along a ridge west of Ahvaz and a similar force dug in on the east bank of the Karun River. He also had a force of tanks and cavalry northwest of the city ready to counterattack the British flank. The Iranian soldiers, however, were unable to execute Shahbakhti's plan, and it quickly fell apart. The Iranian tank and cavalry contingent was dispersed by British antitank gunfire while artillery peppered other Iranian force concentrations. After sepoys stormed into the Iranian lines and overran the main trench, killing or wounding fifty Iranians and taking 250 prisoners, the remaining Iranian soldiers fled to the rear. Many piled into trucks and buses and drove away while their officers did the same using cars and cabs.[10] Shortly thereafter white flags began to appear over the Iranian lines, and an envoy from Shahbakhti approached the British with an offer to surrender. The British commander was greeted by an honor guard when he arrived at Shahbakhti's quarters in Ahvaz, and after brief negotiations the Iranian commander agreed to British terms. In four days of operations, the resistance cost as many as six thousand Iranian casualties while the British suffered the death of only sixty men.

The War in the Western Mountains

Despite their earlier preparations, most of the Iranian army and Gendarmerie units in the central border region around Khanaqin were asleep when Major General Slim's division crossed into Iran. An Iranian detachment at the Naft-e Shah oil field quickly surrendered to a British Indian battalion. In Kermanshah, Major General Mogaddam was awakened by a call from the regimental commander at Qasr-e Shirin reporting that British forces were invading. Mogaddam assembled his staff and correctly assessed that Slim's forces would advance toward the Paitak Pass, which was defended by General Puria's 12th Division, and would try to bypass Puria's defenses by taking a more southern route through the mountains to Shahabad (modern Eslamabad). Mogaddam had deployed a full infantry regiment supported by antitank guns and artillery on the ridges along this southern route, and he and his staff drove west to join the forces there. At Qasr-e Shirin, heavy Iranian fire targeted the approaching British trucks, forcing the British Indian soldiers to dismount to seize the surrounding high ground before pushing the Iranian defenders back into the city. Around midmorning, as the British infantry and tanks entered Qasr-e Shirin, the Iranian soldiers fell back into the hills along the Iraqi border. Shortly after noon, the British column cautiously started to ascend the series of hairpin curves to the six-thousand-feet-high Paitak Pass. At roughly the same time the southern British column began its climb into the Zagros Mountains. From concealed positions, the Iranian regiment along the ridgeline initiated its ambush, and machine gun, antitank gun, and artillery fire swept over the British Indian soldiers. As the lead British elements pulled back and set up their artillery to return fire, tanks were sent forward to try to knock out the Iranian positions. In the first and only Iranian victory of the day, intense Iranian fire drove the British tanks back after each of three separate attacks. As nightfall approached, the British withdrew to await reinforcements.[11]

On the next morning, Slim's forces were stymied by the Iranian defensive positions, but the defenders were faltering. On the southern route, the British probed and harassed the Iranian lines, but heavy Iranian fire deterred a major push. Mogaddam was personally directing Iranian operations there but realized that his soldiers were hungry, demoralized, and rapidly exhausting their limited supply of ammunition. When he sighted the dust from the British units marching to augment the attacking forces, Mogaddam ordered his troops to withdraw, instructing those soldiers who could not be transported by truck to disperse into the mountains. After directing that the road to Shahabad be demolished at various points to delay the enemy, the general rushed back to Kermanshah to organize a new line of defense. The withdrawal was executed quietly, and the British did not realize that the ridge was deserted until a few hours had passed. The northern British column, meanwhile, continued its cautious advance, harassed but not slowed by Iranian artillery. The British responded with counterbattery fire, and later in the day twelve bombers pounded the summit of the pass. As night descended, the British column closed on the summit but was stopped by machine gun fire. The Iranians also succeeded in delaying the southern British column with undefended obstacles; one well-placed demolition blocked all vehicle movement and caused British engineers to work fervidly through the night to clear the road.

By the start of the third day of the invasion, Iranian defenses in the mountains were crumbling. Probably in response to the heavy bombing they had received the previous day, Iranian units had withdrawn from the Paitak Pass during the night, abandoning large amounts of ammunition and some soldiers, who surrendered to the British battalions that scrambled through the pass. The southern British column was now behind the Paitak Pass, sending units on a fruitless quest to catch the retreating Iranian troops. While other Iranian soldiers continued to withdraw east, an Iranian cavalry patrol caught the British advance guard by surprise, taking a few prisoners and forcing the British to fall back temporarily. Mogaddam, meanwhile, used the day to assemble as many as eight thousand soldiers and much of the artillery of the 5th and 12th divisions, augmented by units from Tehran, in defensive positions around Kermanshah. As the day ended, the British consolidated their gains and prepared for the next morning's assaults.

At daybreak on August 28, Iranian artillery began shelling the lead elements of Slim's forces, which were moving through the mountains toward Kermanshah. The 105-mm artillery Mogaddam had deployed outranged the British eighteen-pounders with Slim's forces. An Iranian cavalry brigade was deployed to threaten the exposed British left flank and rear, which compelled Slim to divert part of his attack force to shield the main column. The battle was aborted at virtually the last minute, however, when the shah's cease-fire order reached Mogaddam. The Iranians sent a major under a white flag to propose a cease-fire to the British while their governments negotiated. Slim refused and demanded that the Iranians withdraw from the Kermanshah region, allow British troops into the city, and hand over any British subjects in their custody. During heated negotiations, the major rejected Slim's request to meet with Mogaddam by announcing, "It is not the custom in the Iranian Army, as it appears to be in the British Army, for the general to be in the front line!"[12] Soon thereafter, the Iranian major agreed to Slim's terms on behalf of General Mogaddam and the fighting was ended. Slim later permitted Mogaddam to leave a two-hundred-man garrison in Kermanshah to help him save face with the shah, and the Iranian 5th and 12th divisions began withdrawing by foot the next day.

The War in the North

Shortly before dawn on August 25, a regimental-sized element of the 63rd Georgian Mountain Infantry Division of the Soviet 47th Army secured the border crossing at Pol Dasht and, led by light T-26 tanks, advanced west toward Maku, where the Iranian 17th Infantry Regiment was garrisoned. The Iranian soldiers were already getting ready for the day's duties when Soviet bombers swept over Maku and loosed their loads on the city. An Iranian company commander managed to restore some order among the frightened soldiers and led them to the armory to distribute rifles and ammunition. Other officers and men gathered trucks to transport the unit and available supplies to defensive positions overlooking a wide river valley that provided the most likely Soviet avenue of approach. Once there, the Iranians hurriedly dug foxholes and prepared to meet the advancing Red Army infantry. The rest of the 63rd Georgian Division moved south from Pol Dasht toward Khoy and Rezaiyeh (now called Orumiyeh), which were already under attack by Soviet warplanes. The 1,800 Iranian cavalrymen in Khoy mounted their horses and fled toward the Turkish border as the Soviet ground forces approached. At Rezaiyeh, the main barracks of the 4th Infantry Division was bombed after antiaircraft fire revealed the garrison's location to the Soviet pilots. The division commander, Major General Moini, was short of troops, weapons, and ammunition, and most of his men were so scattered in outlying garrisons that preparing a coherent defense was out of the question. He sent out a call for army reservists to report for duty and waited in vain for a convoy of fourteen trucks with munitions from Tehran to arrive.[13]

As the Pol Dasht attack was occurring, a small Iranian border post to the east was surprised by Soviet troops dashing across the one-hundred-foot wooden bridge over the Aras River at Julfa. Soon the left wing of the 47th Army, consisting of an infantry division, cavalry division, and elements of two tank divisions, was driving south into Iran. At the Iranian 3rd Division's barracks in Tabriz, 8,500 soldiers were in morning formation when waves of Soviet bombers flew over the garrison and dropped bombs that did little damage. The Iranians broke ranks and sought cover while antiaircraft gunners blasted away at subsequent waves of Soviet warplanes, hitting one and causing others to veer off and dump their bombs outside the city. After the attack ended, the Iranian soldiers formed into their units, gathered their equipment, and prepared to march to their battle positions. The division armorers and quartermasters, however, had only five rounds of ammunition for each man and no rations.

Major General Matbooi, the 3rd Division commander, ordered Colonel Shaybani, the commander of the Second Air Regiment, to send reconnaissance flights north to determine the strength and direction of the Soviet advance. Shaybani decided to fly the mission himself and, with another pilot to accompany him, flew north. In the narrow four-mile-long Daradis Gorge south of Julfa, Shaybani beheld hundreds of tanks and other vehicles accompanied by infantry marching unopposed toward the city of Marand. Shaybani reported his observations to Matbooi, who knew his situation was dire. Five miles beyond Marand was the fortified but unmanned Yam Pass, where the Soviets might be delayed. Matbooi had no hope of reaching the pass before the Red Army's advance guard and had insufficient artillery and ammunition to make a stand there. The division's main defense line at the Shibli Pass was a better choice. The pass was fortified, the road was mined, and the artillery observation posts were connected by telephone. Word that another Soviet force had crossed into Iran farther east near Ardebil, however, convinced Matbooi that his line of retreat to Tehran was at risk, causing him to view the defense of Tabriz as untenable. Matbooi ordered the 3rd Division to withdraw southwest around Lake Urmia's southern shore and then toward the Turkish border. After withstanding several more Soviet bombing runs against Tabriz, the 3rd Division soldiers marched out around noon with pack mules carrying the mountain artillery trailing behind them.

Matbooi's withdrawal was forced by the onrush of Russia's 44th Army. Its advance guard had crossed into Iran north of Ardebil around dawn and engaged a small Iranian cavalry patrol on the Astara-Ardebil road. Soon thereafter, Soviet bombers hit Ardebil, causing little damage but prompting the 15th Division headquarters and two infantry regiments with about three thousand men to start preparations to deploy out of garrison. The commander of one regiment assembled his troops and marched them south to the village of Nir, an easily defended bottleneck on the road through the foothills of Mount Sabolan, which dominates the Ardebil plain. The other infantry regiment followed behind in relatively good order. The 15th Division had only twenty light and fifteen heavy trucks to transport its artillery, ammunition, food, and water, which were being loaded for the retreat. In one of the most selfish incidents of the brief war, the division commander, Brigadier General Gaderi, ordered some of the vital ammunition removed to make room for his personal furniture and household goods. The two infantry regiments arrived at Nir in late afternoon and began constructing defensive positions. When Gaderi arrived, he directed the units to withdraw to a more defensible position eight miles farther up the winding mountain road. After promising to send food and supplies, Gaderi then drove away and abandoned his unit. Fortunately for the men of the 15th Division, the Soviet 44th Army was not moving in their direction but was instead marching unopposed to the south toward Rasht.

While most Iranian soldiers in the north remained in their barracks, the Soviet Caspian Sea Flotilla, carrying a regiment of infantry troops, steamed from Baku at first light with gunboats, torpedo boats, and subchasers in escort. After the flotilla split into two groups, the transports of the first ran their bows into the sand just offshore from Astara and off-loaded their troops and equipment into small launches and fishing boats to ferry them ashore. By afternoon, this small amphibious force had linked up with the ground forces entering the city from the northwest. At Anzali, renamed Bandar Pahlavi by Reza, the Chief of Staff of the Iranian 36th Infantry Regiment was warned that eight Soviet ships had been sighted off the coast and were ferrying soldiers ashore in small boats. The Iranian officer notified the 11th Division headquarters at Rasht, but was only told to watch these activities. When the regiment's commander, Lieutenant Colonel Iranpur, arrived an hour later, the troops were prepared to march out of garrison. Iranpur gave a situation report to Iran's naval commander for the Caspian, Capt. Morteza Daftari, who hurried to his headquarters to alert his command. Shortly thereafter the Russians bombed the port, and Iranpur ordered his regiment away from the barracks. By early afternoon the Iranian soldiers were hunkered down in a forest near the beach. The port's fortified shore batteries lacked coastal guns, and, to compensate, a four-gun army artillery battery was positioned to cover the approaches to the harbor. Captain Daftari took the few defensive measures available to him, scuttling a dredger between two long concrete moles to block the harbor entrance and ordering the antiaircraft guns on his three patrol crafts to be armed and ready. When the second group of Soviet transports and escorts arrived after nightfall, two volleys from the four Iranian 75-mm guns greeted them. After briefly returning fire, the Russian flotilla turned away because the Soviet commander did not want to attempt an opposed night landing.

As the day ended the Iranian forces in northwestern Iran started to fall apart. While the Red Army moved into night encampments, the fatigued and hungry soldiers of Iran's 3rd Division were still marching toward Turkey. Their line of march was increasingly ragged as the tired men had begun to throw away equipment, including the cumbersome mountain artillery pack guns. The unit's junior officers maintained enough control to prevent the troops from deserting or turning into a mob, but Matbooi and the other senior Iranian officers had disappeared. Near Maku, the Iranian 17th Infantry Regiment opened fire on the approaching Soviet infantry and light tanks and prompted the Soviets to launch an attack during the late afternoon. When the fighting subsided a few hours later, the remaining Iranian troops used the cover of darkness to retreat across the mountains to Rezaiyeh. To the east of Tabriz, the soldiers of the Iranian 15th Division marched through the night to reach their new defensive position at the Sain Gaduki Pass. A search of a nearby town for food and ammunition was unproductive, and many dispirited soldiers dropped their rifles and deserted to search for provisions. A few remained, unaware that the Soviets had bypassed Ardebil, but their ranks would thin from desertion with each passing hour.

Back at Tabriz, Colonel Shaybani, unaware that the ground units had departed, had waited hours for orders until finally cabling the Army Chief of Staff in Tehran for instructions. Told to evacuate his regiment to Zanjan, Shaybani faced a dilemma; the Russians controlled the air, making a daylight evacuation suicidal, but the Tabriz airfield lacked field lights for night operations. The Iranian pilots were given the option to flee by car, but all volunteered to try to save their aircraft from capture. A takeoff was planned for just before dawn on the following day with the goal of reaching Zanjan shortly after sunrise. After a long night, the thirteen biplanes of the Iranian Second Air Regiment warmed their engines for takeoff in the predawn darkness of August 26. Colonel Shaybani flew the lead plane, and when sufficient light was available to take off, his and the rest of the Iranian aircraft raced down the runway and rose sharply to avoid the surrounding mountains. Eleven of the thirteen pilots landed their aircraft at Zanjan while the other two pilots survived crashes into the mountainside and eventually made their way to Tehran. After refueling his aircraft, Shaybani led his regiment to Tehran, barely getting away from Zanjan before it was bombed by the Soviets.

North of Zanjan the Soviet 44th Army was moving unopposed from Astara down the Caspian coast where poor roads and numerous streams were the main obstacles to a more rapid advance. On the same morning, the Caspian Sea Flotilla resumed shelling Bandar Pahlavi but made no attempt to land troops because of the blocked harbor entrance and the unlocated Iranian artillery. Soviet aircraft, unable to find the Iranian guns because the crews held their fire, bombed the naval station instead. Iranian antiaircraft fire from the three patrol boats kept the Soviets from bombing the base with impunity but did not stop the attacks. Iranian 11th Division troops in Rasht stayed in their barracks as ordered while Soviet planes above them dropped leaflets. Farther to the west, Soviet tanks and infantrymen were mopping up the few Iranian snipers and machine gun nests in Tabriz. At Rezaiyeh, the 4th Infantry Division's scattered detachments had collapsed or deserted, although the Soviets were still north of Khoy at the end of the day on August 26. The 3rd Division, meanwhile, was barely holding together on its march to Turkey.

In the predawn darkness of August 27, the Soviet 53rd Independent Central Asian Army opened a new front that ran from the eastern shore of the Caspian to the Afghan border. Iranian border guards alerted the Iranian 10th Division, under the acting command of Colonel Motazedi, that the Soviets were crossing the Atrak River into Iran. The 10th Division, headquartered in Gorgan, had its infantry regiments dispersed in posts along the border, where, outnumbered by the Soviet attackers, the Iranian infantrymen were already dropping their weapons and fleeing. The 58th Soviet Infantry Corps advanced on two axes, one leading almost due south to Gorgan and the other slightly to the east to Gonbad-e Qabus. In Mashhad, Major General Mohtashemi, commanding the 9th Division, was alerted to the Soviet invasion. Even though Iran had been under attack for two days, the Iranian general had received no guidance from Tehran. On his own initiative, Mohtashemi had started preparations to secure and defend the vital Mazduran Pass west of the city. At the time, the 9th Division was comprised of two infantry and two cavalry regiments at Mashhad, a cavalry regiment at Bojnurd, and a cavalry regiment at Torbat-e Jam opposite the Afghan border. The general placed the Mashhad units into two mobile groups. Each group had an infantry and a cavalry regiment along with a mix of 75-mm and 105-mm artillery batteries. When reports of the Soviet invasion were received, the first column under Colonel Dollow was sent to the Mazduran Pass while Lieutenant Colonel Afshar was directed to go northwest with the second mobile group to engage the Soviets wherever he found them. After seizing civilian vehicles to help move the columns, Afshar sped along a paved highway while Dollow made good time over a dusty secondary road.

Despite this promising start, Iran's ground and air units in Mashhad were overmatched by the large Soviet invasion forces. The Red Air Force bombed the Mashhad airfield and the Iranian Third Air Regiment throughout the morning. One direct hit on a hangar destroyed six of the unit's twenty-two aircraft, killing four and wounding eighteen men. During the afternoon, Dollow's column was detected by Soviet air reconnaissance, and Soviet fighters and bombers hit the packed trucks and buses on the open road, killing many. Dollow ordered the survivors back to Mashhad, leaving the road open to advancing Soviet forces. Similarly, Afshar's troops came upon a Soviet infantry division in Quchan that bombarded his column with artillery fire. Afshar ordered a general retreat back to Mashhad, during which many of his officers deserted their units to make a faster getaway. After nightfall, a telegram from the capital instructed the forces in Mashhad to retreat to Tehran in an effort to withdraw units for the defense of the capital. By this time, however, Mohtashemi's division was in disarray as the soldiers who had bravely sallied forth against the invaders came flooding back to the city. Iranian officers tore off their uniforms, filled vehicles with gas, and then drove south. Mohtashemi gathered the remaining troops and began a night march toward Tehran, heading first, after some confusion, for the desert oasis of Tabas to link up with a detachment coming from Birjand. In Gorgan Province, the Iranian 23rd Cavalry Regiment started its withdrawal to Tehran after midnight, with many of the seven hundred officers and soldiers weeping over the shame of having to retreat without fighting.

Consternation in Tehran

After the prime minister informed Reza Shah about the invasion on August 25, the Iranian ruler gathered his senior advisors to consider the generally accurate reports filtering in from the fronts. The monarch was clearly surprised by the invasion, but turned aside Allied requests that Iran not resist. Before the shah's government took any actions, British bombers dropped on the capital thousands of leaflets alleging German subversion in Iran. Radio Tehran broke the first official news and tried to reassure the people that Iranian forces were defending the country. While the shah ordered Major General Zarghami, the Army Chief of Staff, to deploy the Central Garrison to defend the capital, he offered no instructions for the divisions under attack. The next morning, Zarghami and a newly formed war council heard reports that the Soviets had occupied much of northwestern Iran. The council also was told that the British were in control of the southwestern ports and an area near Masjed-e Soleyman where British paratroopers had landed 120 miles behind Iranian lines to protect Anglo-Iranian Oil Company employees there. The only bright note was the British failure to cross the Paitak Pass. General Arfa, then serving on the General Staff, later wrote that he learned that front line units had gotten no operational instructions other than a command prohibiting the destruction of bridges, railways, and roads and that rearguard actions had not been ordered. Arfa speculated that the shah had no intention of conducting a true defense and only wanted to demonstrate token resistance so that Iran would not be treated as hostile if occupied later by the Nazis. Arfa again proposed that important bridges should be destroyed and that the powerful Tehran garrisons withdraw to a mountain redoubt west of the capital, but Reza rejected this advice.[14]

Reports on the expanded Soviet offensive in the northeast and on the loss of Tabriz and Rezaiyeh reached the capital on August 27. A new government was formed later that day and, in a move aimed at allowing negotiations to begin, Reza agreed to order his military forces to cease fire and withdraw toward Tehran the following morning. Although the cease-fire was handled well by the units facing the British, its execution among other divisions contributed to the Iranian military's disintegration over the next two days. The Iranian 15th Division, isolated east of Tabriz and unable to withdraw, chose to disband. Its troops were released to their homes, and the officers were told to get to Tehran as best they could. In Rasht, defiant Iranian soldiers of the 11th Division fired anti-aircraft guns at Soviet planes dropping leaflets, provoking Russian bombers to attack the barracks and kill almost one hundred soldiers. Many of the surviving soldiers then took weapons from the armory and dispersed into the Gilani forests. The 10th Division accepted the cease-fire order but had few units under its control. The 23rd Cavalry Regiment, after offering to surrender to the pursuing Russians, disbanded when most of the Iranian officers and soldiers discarded their uniforms, donned civilian clothes, and went into hiding. The Iranian 9th Division negotiated surrenders for itself and Mashhad, where Russian infantry quickly occupied the city and disarmed local security forces. To the west, the 3rd Division was overtaken by a Soviet column near Miandoab on August 29 and, still unaware of the cease-fire, tried to organize a hasty defense. Having earlier abandoned their heavy weapons, the soldiers were unwilling to take on Russian tanks with rifles and surrendered. General Puria's 12th Division and the attached troops from Tehran continued their march to Hamadan, but General Mogaddam, after discovering that the Soviets were pushing on Senneh, turned the 5th Division northwest into the mountains of Kurdistan.[15]

Fear of revolution was palpable in Tehran as British and Soviet propaganda against the shah fed popular resentment against Reza and led to major misjudgments by the military leadership. Army units were needed to put down a mutiny by pilots at an airbase near Tehran. Later, the General Staff, without the shah's approval, ordered the release of all conscripts. The 2nd Division commander complied immediately, ordering his conscripts to turn in their weapons and ammunition and leave the compound before the martial law curfew began that evening. After gathering up weapons, General Puria ordered the 12th Division soldiers to return home, a course followed throughout the army by units whose conscripts had not already left. The following day Reza Shah discovered that the soldiers had been released and angrily ordered the Tehran garrison's conscripts rounded up and returned to duty. Over the first few days of September, the release of the conscripts and desertions by the police and many military officers fueled instability in Tehran. Soldiers who returned to their barracks found little order or food and deserted again, although some stayed long enough to loot army warehouses and steal the artillery's horses, which were then sold in the bazaar. In Kurdistan, armed rebellion and raiding broke out as the Kurds drove the few Iranian army detachments still on duty into the major towns. General Slim's forces had to quell the worst of the Kurdish attacks, delivering the final blow to the military's ruined honor, which, in turn, crushed Reza Shah's remaining prestige.[16]

After the shah's cease-fire order was broadcast over the radio, most Iranians were happy that the fighting had ended, but many soon decided that Iran's
rapid and humiliating capitulation was worse than the war itself. Shortly after
the cease-fire, Reza ordered all senior general officers to meet with him. At the
appointed time, only the minister of war, Army Chief of Staff, and two other
generals appeared. Always a physically violent man, Reza Shah began hurling
obscenities and abuse at his generals, whipping the war minister and Chief of
Staff with his cane while accusing them of treason. Still furious, he ordered the
two men stripped of their rank and arrested. The shah then ordered immediate
courts-martial for five leading generals. While some Iranians were initially happy
to see the arrogant and often brutal Iranian military officers shamed, more felt
betrayed by their ruler. An American Presbyterian minister serving in Tehran at
the time reported that many Iranians were angered by Iran's rapid submission
after people had endured years of exorbitant taxes and other sacrifices to build
the Iranian armed forces. They resented the fact that Reza Shah had exhorted
the military to be prepared for the ultimate sacrifice but then had prevented it
from fighting. The reverend noted that many Iranians now felt that their country
had been disgraced.[17] Iran accepted the Allied terms on August 31, but unwilling
to stay under Allied political constraints on his power, Reza abdicated in favor
of his son, Muhammad Reza Shah Pahlavi, on September 16, 1941. The former
monarch left Iran and eventually settled in exile in South Africa, where he died
in July 1944.

The new shah ascended the Peacock Throne without the central foundation
of his father's rule. Although only eight divisions were engaged by Allied forces,
the Iranian army was reduced from sixteen to nine divisions during the last week
of August. The army never was a match for the Soviet and British forces, especially in terms of firepower, mobility, communications, and logistics. Some
Iranian units' willingness to fight and their few temporary successes in holding
off much stronger Allied forces supported by airpower showed the potential that
Reza Shah and his senior officers wasted by their inattention to morale, training,
communications, and logistics. Iran's people were well justified in their resentment of the armed forces' failure. Nationalist politicians stripped Muhammad
Reza of many powers, and the army, now in disgrace, was subjected to more government scrutiny. Over the next several years, government officials whose formative political experiences were during the Constitutional Revolution fought
with the young shah to bring the armed forces under civilian control.

The Silent Partner

The new shah and Iran were conscripted into the war against the Axis, becoming the fourth partner in the British, American, and Soviet effort to keep the Red
Army supplied for the gargantuan struggle in Russia against Hitler's war machine.

In his history of U.S. Army operations in Iran during the war, Thomas V. H. Motter described the country's situation in these terms: "Although its sovereignty was reaffirmed . . . the normal exercise of sovereignty was so circumscribed by the demands of the war as to be virtually suspended for the duration. As the essentially passive partner, Iran contributed in proportion to its acquiescence in Allied purposes."[18] The Allies sought to limit the Iranian army to internal security duties while the politicians in Tehran worked to prevent the military from regaining its former role in politics. The shah's goals for himself and the army were directly opposed to the Allies and dominant Iranian political groups. The twenty-two-year-old Muhammad Reza recognized, however, that care was needed in reasserting royal authority. Because his first goal was survival, he accommodated the Majles, allowed more power to flow to the prime minister, and returned much of the wealth amassed by his father to the state.

The new monarch retained control of military matters because, like his father, Muhammad Reza saw the army as the bedrock supporting the dynasty and Iran's independence and modernization. The young shah considered himself a soldier, having attended military primary and secondary schools, graduated from the military academy as a second lieutenant in 1938, and served as Inspector of the Army until he became shah. He was encouraged in this by his father's most important bequest to him: a cadre of senior officers who transferred their personal loyalty to the young monarch. The old chain of command was retained, and orders flowed directly from the palace through the General Staff to the field. The War Ministry, meanwhile, was packed with royalists who worked to advance the shah's policies. Despite the Iranian military's humiliation and reduction in size, it was still the largest and best organized government institution and a strong foundation for Muhammad Reza's plans.

Although many younger officers resented Reza's senior commanders and cronies for their failed leadership, the army rallied to the new shah because it also was being attacked by the Majles and the British and Russian occupiers. The shah worked aggressively but quietly to regain the officer corps' loyalty by protecting the field commanders who had deserted their posts during the invasion from public hearings. He also showered his officers with promotions, creating twice as many colonels and generals in twenty months as his father had made in twenty years. In addition, Muhammad Reza took a personal interest in the military, organizing army maneuvers, taking inspection tours, and attending graduation ceremonies at the military colleges, where he never failed to remind his audience that the Imperial Army owed its existence to the Pahlavi dynasty. The payoff for this careful cultivation came in late 1942 when the prime minister made a bid to take control of the army and tried to purge royalists from the War Ministry. The shah arranged to have armed thugs turn ongoing public protests into violent riots that the army prevented the police from stopping. British troops had to restore order, and the Allies, unwilling to divert military resources to the capital, sided with Iran's sovereign, who was confirmed as the Supreme Commander of the Armed Forces.

In a break from his father's policies, Muhammad Reza was convinced that Iran needed to be in alliance with the West rather than remain neutral. He correctly judged that the wartime and postwar security challenges he faced would require foreign assistance and decided that Iran should align with the United States. Early in 1942, Iran was given promises in the Tripartite Treaty of Alliance with the Soviet Union and Great Britain that the Allies would defend Iran from aggression by other powers, respect its territorial integrity, sovereignty, and political independence, and withdraw six months after hostilities with Germany ended. In return, Iran pledged to cooperate with the Allies, allow free passage and use of its harbors, railways, and roads, and limit the Iranian army's role to internal security. The Soviet occupation, however, already had revealed Moscow's intentions to establish its influence and control over northern Iran. The Soviet zone was closed to foreigners, lands were seized, and food products were diverted to Russia while other parts of Iran faced serious shortages.[19]

The shah had no desire to link Iran again to the British and now looked to the United States for help in reorganizing, retraining, and reequipping his armed forces. After Iran was declared eligible for U.S. Lend-Lease aid in March 1942, Muhammad Reza and his ministers, hoping that Iran's centrality to the war effort would result in significant American aid, submitted requests for help to rebuild the army and even expand its prewar strength. At this point in the war Iran was the only safe way to move war materiel to the Soviets, but Washington already faced enormous challenges in managing scarce resources. The U.S. military had no interest in trying to build up Iran's military when the Nazis were still advancing toward the Caucasus, and resentment over the invasion among Iranian officers made the armed forces a suspected font of pro-German sentiment and fifth column activity. The importance of protecting the supply lines, however, required some improvements in the Iranian army and Gendarmerie, and the United States agreed to send two advisory missions to Iran to overhaul its military.

The American missions focused on internal security operations, which Washington saw as key to maintaining Iran's unity and stability. External defense was made the responsibility of the British and Russians, who regularly meddled in the U.S. advisors' work. The interference and intriguing of the shah and the army command, opposition from entrenched Iranian interests, and the political instability in Tehran that resulted in the creation and fall of eleven governments in the five years between 1941 and 1946 also hindered the missions. The Gendarmerie's American advisory team, led by Col. H. Norman Schwarzkopf, was the first to arrive in August 1942. Schwarzkopf, a 1917 West Point graduate, had helped to create and then led the New Jersey State Police, which gave him an excellent background for restoring the Gendarmerie. (Schwarzkopf had gained national fame for leading the investigation into the Lindbergh baby kidnapping and was the father of Gen. H. Norman Schwarzkopf Jr., the commander of U.S. and coalition forces in the Gulf War of 1991.)

Starting slowly, Schwarzkopf studied the Gendarmerie before developing and submitting a two-hundred-page reorganization plan in March 1943. Many Iranians opposed the American's ideas, including the Gendarmerie's commander, who withheld information, failed to support the mission's suggestions, and carried on a whisper campaign against Schwarzkopf. Other Iranian officials wanted to see these reforms implemented and arranged in late November 1943 for the establishment of the U.S. Army Military Mission with the Imperial Iranian Gendarmerie, known as GENMISH. The Gendarmerie was put under the Ministry of Interior, and Schwarzkopf was given the authority he needed to push through his plans. The shah opposed the broad powers given to Schwarzkopf while many senior officers continued efforts, without success, to return the organization to the military's control.[20]

From late 1943 until the end of the war, the roughly twenty thousand Iranian gendarmes were reorganized, trained, armed, and directed by GENMISH. Within a year, GENMISH achieved considerable progress despite the succession of ministers of interior during this period. By August 1944 training schools for sergeants, motorcycle riders, and truck drivers were established. Despite limitations placed on Lend-Lease supplies for Iran, Schwarzkopf reported steady progress in the delivery of trucks and other essential items for the force. GENMISH also installed a communications system for the dispersed Gendarmerie outposts. Under the leadership of the American mission, the Gendarmerie steadily reestablished central government authority in urban areas and parts of the Iranian countryside. By December 1944, the U.S. military attaché in Tehran reported that the Gendarmerie, backed by the army, had improved to the point where Allied troop withdrawals would not jeopardize the security of the central government. The most striking change brought about by GENMISH was the "improvement of the condition of the ranks and the creation among them of an *esprit de corps*. . . . Starting with human material handicapped by illiteracy and opium addiction, Colonel Schwarzkopf was in time able to report progress against ills long associated with abuse of office. The Gendarmerie rank and file moved steadily toward a better sense of discipline and a respect for businesslike, honest, and efficient procedures."[21] GENMISH had helped the Gendarmerie to remain independent, but many reforms recommended by the Americans, such as a separate and adequate budget, pensions, and the elimination of graft and red tape, fell by the wayside at war's end.

The Iranian army's leadership was less open to change and tried to rationalize their defeat by blaming inadequate equipment. In 1942, the minister of war
claimed the army's lack of mechanization was at fault and, in an apparent refer-
ence to France in May 1940 and Russia in the summer of 1941, compared the
August debacle to similar reversals suffered by other armies.[22] The Iranians were
understandably pleased when the first American adviser to the army, Gen. John
Greely, arrived in July 1942 and immediately began proposing a major buildup
to bring the Iranian army into the war against the Germans. Greeley's ambitions
ran afoul of the U.S. War Department's priorities, however, and Maj. Gen. Clar-
ence Ridley arrived in Tehran in October to replace him and bring the Iranians
down to earth. Although proscribed from any actions that interfered in Iranian
politics or impinged on Iranian sovereignty, Ridley was empowered to recom-
mend the promotion, demotion, and removal of army officers to the shah and
notionally had access to all records and information he needed to perform his
mission.

Ridley found numerous problems with the army as he began his work. There
were serious equipment shortages, compounded by the Russian demand that
Iran surrender the one hundred thousand rifles, three thousand light machine
guns, and one thousand heavy machine guns in its armories in 1943. In addition,
the lack of motor or other means of transport was a crippling shortcoming. The
organization and functioning of the supply and auxiliary departments, which
had never been developed by Iran, also were unsatisfactory to the American.
Finally, inflation had rendered officer salaries and the army budget inadequate.
Ridley judged that the Iranian army's tactical methods and training were sufficient for the internal security missions it was to be given for the course of the war.
He then set out four principles for the army's reorganization: the total strength
needed to be limited to eighty-eight thousand men, only the best officers should
be retained on duty, a reasonable pay scale should be established, and adequate
motor transport needed to be acquired. The shah promptly approved the recommendations, but Iran was slow to carry them out.

Ridley initially focused on the supply and auxiliary branches. At the time the
Iranian system procured and distributed centrally only the soldiers' clothing and
basic equipment. Everything else, including the distribution of pay, was administered locally through each regiment with the attendant inefficiency, graft, and
corruption. By early 1944, the mission set up a depot system for supply with
centralized responsibility for procurement, distribution, and troop payment.
The new system included financial accounting measures, the standardization of
procurement, and a reorganization of the Offices of the Quartermaster General
and the Chief of Finance to improve management. Training schools in administration, engineering, medicine, finance, and quartermaster operations were

established and run by the mission. Ridley had less success with reforms for recruitment and the administration of military justice. According to Motter's history, Ridley "took no hand in the unsavory recruiting department of the Army, where exemption of those who could buy themselves off, faking medical examinations, and enlistment of unfit persons were among 'widespread practices that seem impossible to correct until the whole law-enforcement policy and moral sense of the country are radically revised'... (while) [t]he Justice Department of the Army also seemed ... to offer no hope of accomplishing results."[23]

The Ridley mission's most prominent achievement was "motorizing" the army, the one reform that the Iranian officers recognized as valuable. Ridley found the Iranian army "practically immobile," with almost no vehicles, equipment, or drivers. The Americans were frustrated by the competition for trucks in 1943, with first priority going to the Red Army and the few remaining vehicles being spread among the army, Gendarmerie, and the agricultural sector, which desperately needed help with the fall harvests. Under pressure from Ridley, arrangements were made in mid-1943 to adjust truck production schedules to sandwich roughly fifty trucks for Iran into the Russia-bound assemblies every twelve days. By May 1944, the mission also had arranged for the delivery of six hundred Lend-Lease trucks and opened training schools for drivers and mechanics. The Iranian army's Transport Department was reorganized, and a new motor transport organization with regular operating schedules and repair and maintenance facilities at Tehran, Esfahan, and Kermanshah was established. The army's administrative functioning, discipline, and armament clearly had improved with American help by 1944, and the military was assessed as capable of putting down tribal disorders and urban unrest. The Iranians wanted more help, but with the disappearance of the German threat to Iran after mid-1944 the U.S. War Department saw no military necessity for the mission. Strong pleas from the shah, backed by the State Department, got the War Department to agree reluctantly to extend the mission past its original March 1945 termination date.[24]

The Iranian military's most intractable problem remained its budget, which was complicated by the shah's unrealistic vision of a large army. In January 1943 the American financial mission arrived in Tehran under the leadership of Dr. Arthur Millspaugh, making his second attempt to put Iran's financial house in order. Unfortunately, Millspaugh's second assignment was no more successful than his first mission. Iran's royalists and nationalists objected to his proposals and his control over Iran's financial affairs. More important, Muhammad Reza, like his father, was enraged by Millspaugh's attempts to cut the military budget. Millspaugh supported proposals to balance the budget by reducing military expenditures and lowering compulsory military service from twenty-four to twelve months. The British military attaché commented that reduced terms of service would make the army a farce because one-fourth to one-third of the conscripts spoke only Turkic and needed six to twelve months to learn enough Persian to understand orders. In mid-1944 Iran's monarch wanted the army increased from roughly 60,000 to 108,000 men while the prime minister, encouraged by Millspaugh, proposed a force of 30,000 men. The American told the shah that if the army budget was increased, little could be done for agriculture, education, or public health, to which the Muhammad Reza replied that those things would have to be postponed. General Ridley's earlier proposal for an 88,000-man army, which was supported by the British, strengthened the shah's position. Refusing to change his stance, Millspaugh was dismissed from Iran for a second time. After he departed, the Majles agreed to start increasing the army to 90,000 men and in the fall of 1945 passed a bill that hiked the military budget, improved officer salaries and benefits, and expanded the force by another 12,000 men.[25]

Problems with America

Following the Allied invasion, Iran received a growing number of U.S. Army troops sent to help move supplies to the Soviet Union to ensure that the Red Army survived its battle against the Germans. After the Japanese attack on Pearl Harbor, Iran became the safest all-year route for Allied aid and was the closest to the main battlefields in Russia. The route also was the longest one, involving a twelve-thousand-mile sea voyage from the United States around Africa to the British-controlled port of Al Basrah, Iraq. From there, Russian-bound cargo had to travel more than one thousand miles, starting on a narrow-gauge railroad in Iraq and then switching to a standard-gauge railroad in Iran that followed a treacherous path through the Zagros. After reaching Iran's central plateau, the line headed back north to Tabriz, where it was switched a third time to a Soviet-gauge railroad for the final leg. Goods delivered to Khorramshahr, which was not linked to the Iranian railroad, had to be moved across the desert to reach the first all-weather road at Dezful or transported by shallow boats up the Karun River to Ahvaz for transfer to the railroad. Bandar Shahpur, the Gulf terminus of the 808-mile-long Trans-Iranian Railroad, was connected to Iran's Caspian Sea ports, but these smaller ports' prewar needs were limited, and the railroad's capacity was similarly small.[26]

In 1942, restrictions on transport capacity and flow were aggravated by slow ship turnaround times, factors that drove the decision to commit a large American force to Iran. These troops were eventually placed under the Persian Gulf Command, whose overall impact on Iran's situation eventually contributed to anti-American attitudes in the military and the public at large. After a period when American civilian contractors aided the British in running supply operations, five thousand U.S. troops landed in Iran in December 1942 under Brig. Gen. Donald Connolly as the Persian Gulf Service Command. The American force included port battalions, railway operating battalions, road maintenance groups, truck regiments, and engineer battalions and reached its final strength of thirty thousand troops by August 1943. Connolly depended heavily on Iranians for the labor needed to make the huge supply effort work, which, along with the Trans-Iranian Railroad, made the shipment of war materiel to the Soviet Union feasible. The command improved the ports of Khorramshahr, Abadan, and Al Basrah, reducing the average time to unload a ship from fifty-five days in January 1943 to only eight days in September 1944. Iran's railroad system was expanded with new trunk lines to the ports, rolling stock was increased and improved, and maintenance was upgraded, which helped to reduce accidents. In October 1941 Iran's rolling stock was capable of carrying only six thousand tons each month, but two years later monthly capacity had been increased to one hundred and seventy-five thousand tons.

Renamed the Persian Gulf Command, the Americans also put together un-assembled aircraft and trucks for the Soviets. All of the vehicles were loaded with cargo and driven north, many with Iranians behind the wheel. The Americans trained more than 7,500 Iranian drivers by the end of 1944 when the massive flow of supplies began to subside. In all, the Americans and Iranians delivered nearly 150,000 vehicles and 3,500 planes, including 1,400 bombers, to the Red Army, which helped the Russians defeat the Nazis at Stalingrad and begin the drive on Berlin. Of the 17.5 million long tons of U.S. Lend-Lease aid provided to Moscow during the war, 7.9 million long tons, estimated as enough to equip sixty Red Army combat divisions, were sent through the Persian corridor.[27]

Although Iran's leaders appreciated the improvements made to their country's infrastructure, Persian Gulf Command and Allied operations created many problems. Popular resentment toward Great Britain and Russia was easily transferred, sometimes at the instigation of opportunistic politicians and clergy, to the Americans. The Allies had commandeered much of Iran's economy along with its transportation system, which upset commerce and created serious food shortages and local famines. In December 1942, after a bad wheat harvest caused, in part, by Soviet impressment of farm workers for its own labor gangs, a bread protest in Tehran overwhelmed the police and led to the occupation of the Majles, which required the call-up of Iran's 2nd Division to clear. During this period, massive Allied spending for goods and services in Iran unleashed a severe inflation that was accompanied by speculation, hoarding, and black market operations. Despite these problems, the Iranians initially saw the American troops as dynamic, cheerful, and friendly, not aloof like the British or fearsome like the Russians. Viewed as powerful and worthy of respect, the image of the United States was gradually tarnished as real and imagined American interference in Iran's governance and society increased and other outrages offended Iranian pride.

Policing the convoy routes was a major source of tension. Every twist in the road that forced drivers to slow down gave bandits the opportunity to jump on trucks, slit tarpaulins, and throw off the goods to waiting compatriots, sometimes with the drivers' connivance. American military police were forced to patrol the convoy routes, creating a much more visible presence in the countryside. They also angered the locals by actions such as entering native huts during search-and-seizure operations to recover stolen goods or by the accidental deaths of peasants unaccustomed to sharing the roads with fast-moving jeeps and trucks. In addition to the deadly traffic accidents, incidents of drinking and brawling upset the Iranians, who found insult added to injury because U.S. personnel enjoyed de facto immunity from prosecution under Iranian law. Amid the general poverty of Iran, large and well-supplied encampments housed American troops, where "muffled booming [was] heard that marked, day after day, the detonation of antipersonnel mines set off by native prowlers attempting the barriers enclosing the foreigners' stores of goods and food."[28] Even young Iranian military officers, despite the American support given to the Iranian armed forces, were irritated by rules about saluting Allied officers, the presence of American and other Allied soldiers in the towns, and Allied soldiers' contacts with Iranian women.[29]

Negative attitudes toward the Allies resulted in greater pro-German sentiment, especially in the army, but the Nazi threat in Iran remained a minor one. A pro-German Resistance Movement of Iran was created in 1942 by nationalist politicians and Iranian army officers, the most prominent of whom was Gen. Fazlallah Zahedi, the captor of Sheikh Khazal in 1925. In January 1943, six Germans, including a wireless operator, landed by parachute to join forces with Franz Mayer, a Nazi agent stationed in Iran who had avoided the earlier expulsion of Germans. Two months later, three more were landed in southwestern Iran to aid Berthold Schultze-Holthus, another effective Nazi agent who had arrived in Fars Province in 1942 and was advising a Qashqai tribal insurrection. As fifth column activity increased through the summer, British counterintelligence officers expanded operations against the German networks in Iran. In August, the British captured one of the principal German officers along with a gold mine of information files that led to the arrest by Iranian police of 170 suspected or proven Iranian collaborators, including Zahedi and up to forty other army officers, Majles deputies, and journalists. Citing these German subversive activities, Iran declared war on the Third Reich in September 1943, which guaranteed Iran a place among the United Nations. More importantly, the act ensured that Iran would not be denied, as it had been in 1919, a seat at the table of conferences dealing with the postwar peace settlement. Following on the heels of these developments, Stalin, Churchill, and Roosevelt met in Tehran in November, issuing a Tri-Partite Declaration that acknowledged Iran's contribution to the war and supported Iran's independence, sovereignty, and territorial integrity.

Minorities and Communists on the March

A final cost to Iran of its "silent partnership" with the Allies was the increased instability caused by the Allied invasion's removal of government authority from the tribal areas when the security forces and other government elements collapsed. The British consul in Shiraz reported after the invasion that southern tribes rejoiced in their new freedom, dug up and cleaned buried weapons, bought new rifles from arms traffickers, seized weapons from army outposts, or simply added the rifles kept by tribal conscripts when they left the army. In the northwest, the Soviets supported the region's separatist ambitions and allowed the Azeris and Kurds in their zone to ignore Iranian laws on dress and language, take over provincial administration, and create armed militias. The various chiefs held hostage in Tehran escaped or were released to rejoin the tribes, increasing the impetus for demands for autonomy and the prospects for unrest.

The rearmed Qashqai left their settlements in Fars Province after Reza abdicated and their chiefs returned, moving quickly to reclaim their former pasturelands. In October 1942 the government tried to disarm the tribe but after a few minor clashes in which few weapons were taken, the army declared victory and ended its campaign. The German mission under Schulze-Holthus encouraged the Qashqai to go on the offensive and raid Allied convoys and trains, which forced army units to return in May 1943. Staging from Shiraz, the army planned to use its few truck-mounted units to control the road between Esfahan and Shiraz while six infantry brigades drove the Qashqais into the deserts to the east. The tribe, however, held the mountain passes leading to its pastures against the Iranian attackers, withdrawing only after Tehran recruited the Khamseh tribe to attack the Qashqais from the rear. By June, the Qashqai were back on the offensive, and in July a force of a few hundred Qashqai warriors overran the fortified garrison at Semiron, south of Esfahan. The Iranians lost two hundred men in the battle, and as many as one thousand Iranian soldiers surrendered along with eight hundred rifles, sixty-three machine guns, two mountain guns, and large quantities of ammunition. The victory led neighboring tribes to rally to the Qashqai cause, which forced Tehran to offer a truce and begin negotiations. The government agreed not to interfere in tribal territory and left the chiefs responsible for the region's security. As a hedge against the Qashqai's good behavior, small army garrisons and Gendarmerie posts were established in areas around the tribe's territory.[30]

After 1941 the British and Soviets allowed a vacuum to develop in the Kurdish lands between the fringes of their two areas of occupation. The Kurdish

tribes in these inaccessible mountain redoubts were out of Tehran's control
but did not pose a separatist challenge, because of their focus on fights for local
power and control. The Iranian government tried to negotiate a settlement, but
the chiefs' demands for autonomy, the return of confiscated lands, and a role
in the central government prevented agreement. The region became so unruly
because of intra-Kurdish rivalries and sectarian violence among the Azeri Shia,
Armenian Christians, and Kurdish Sunnis that Tehran armed the Shia peasantry
to protect themselves before removing most of the Gendarmerie units from the
Kurdish heartland. Following past practice, the Iranian army used Kurdish rivalries to control the tribes and maintain a rough stability. In general, tribes that
did not oppose the government but only reverted to their former autonomous
ways were left alone. Tribes that revolted were confronted by government forces
and sometimes treated harshly once defeated. After one Kurdish tribe captured
Saqqez in February 1942, the army sent a 1,200-man force of infantry, cavalry,
and artillery on a predawn assault against the town. Taken by surprise, the Kurds
were hit by artillery and machine gun fire while the cavalry cut off their retreat,
allowing only a few to escape. It was not uncommon during the war for one
Kurdish chief to enter government service only to attack a neighbor. The army
would side with the aggressor but would then turn against that tribe if conditions favored such a move.[31]

Russian interference in Kurdistan and Azerbaijan was setting the conditions
for the political and security crises that would grip Iran in the years immediately
following the end of the war. The Soviets actively worked to make the Kurds
more hostile to the British and Iranian governments and in May 1942 used Red
Army troops to prevent Tehran from sending a detachment from the 6th Division against Kurdish rebels around Rezaiyeh. Moscow also tried to dominate
Iran through economic pressure and its occupation troops, secret police, labor
unions, sympathetic leftists, and ethnic separatists. Most important, the Soviets supported the Iranian Communist Party, Tudeh ("Masses"), which was reorganized in 1941 and expanded rapidly during the war. Reza Khan had pushed
the first Iranian Communist Party underground, but its imprisoned members
were released after the invasion. Jafar Pishevari, the president of the short-lived
Gilan Republic in 1920, was a key leader of the new Tudeh Party and was prominent in the Soviet-supported Azerbaijani autonomy effort. Tudeh was active
throughout Iran and set up a military network centered around a core group of
Communist officers that had formed during 1930s, establishing new cells between 1943 and 1944 that tried to exploit class differences in the army's ranks.
Militias associated with Pishevari were observed in 1945 carrying the weapons
confiscated by the Red Army from Iran's armories in 1943.[32]

When General Arfa became Chief of Staff of the Army in December 1944
after yet another cabinet shake-up, he was given a list of one hundred names of

Iranian officers with Communist ties or sympathies. The army, however, was a center of strong anti-Communist feeling and benefited from the shift of other antiroyalist parties away from the Tudeh Party as their legislators called for increased defense spending to prevent Communist uprisings. It was a shock then when the first but ultimately unsuccessful Communist revolt in Iran was led by young army officers in Khorasan Province in late summer of 1945. The group from the 9th Division tried to incite the rest of the province to rise but only recruited a few small army detachments before being defeated. Six of eighteen seditious officers were killed, and the rest were captured and later tried and imprisoned. Twenty-four other officers were purged from the 9th Division over their suspected Tudeh sympathies and transferred to units in the south, away from the Red Army and Soviet agents.[33]

When the war ended the Iranians were anxious for the Allies to abide by their earlier pledges and leave Iran. Following Hitler's defeat, the Americans and British removed their forces by the end of 1945. Stalin, however, insisted that Soviet troops remain until six months after Japan's defeat, delaying their departure date to March 1946 and setting the stage for new crises. Although smaller, Iran's revived army had become more mobile and, backed by a more effective Gendarmerie, was better prepared for the internal security challenges to come. The restoration of the ties between monarch and military ensured close attention to the armed forces' procurement and training needs, which would be enhanced by the new shah's decision to seek U.S. aid. At the same time, Muhammad Reza's turn to his father's generals guaranteed that the prewar Iranian army's problems with politicization, lack of professionalism, and greed and corruption would have their own revival during the following decades.

7

Cold War Pillar

The Rise of the Imperial Armed Forces

DURING HIS REIGN, MUHAMMAD REZA surpassed his father in lavishing attention and resources on Iran's armed forces. Over the course of the three decades
following World War II the country recovered from war and internal turmoil and
was blessed with a windfall of oil revenues that allowed the monarch to achieve
most of his material ambitions for a large, well-armed, and modern military. But
the Pahlavi shah, even after he firmly established himself as Iran's leader after
1953, allowed his fears and ambitions to override advice on developing a sus-
tainable and effective military. The result was uneven growth, wasteful spending,
and an incoherent procurement program for weapon systems that his military
had difficulty using and maintaining. Following his father's example, he linked
his fate to his generals, allowing their worst instincts of abusive power, politicization, and corruption to continue to flourish and undermine the Iranian military's effectiveness. By the end of his reign, Muhammad Reza, having survived
serious internal and Cold War challenges, had the largest and best-equipped
armed forces in the Middle East. All the monarch's soldiers, sailors, and airmen,
however, were unable to offer protection from the political tidal wave forming
as a result of his autocratic behavior, out-of-control defense spending, and economic mismanagement.

The First Battle of the Cold War

During the last part of 1945, the Soviets, with an estimated thirty thousand
troops in Azerbaijan and another seventy-five thousand Red Army soldiers
spread across the rest of northern Iran, encouraged communists and sympathetic nationalists in Iran's Azeri and Kurdish areas to seek greater autonomy.
In October, the Red Army started to reinforce its commands in Iranian Azerbaijan, prevented Iran's military from entering the province, and forced the Iranian Gendarmerie and army units already there to stay in their barracks. In a
revolt later that month Tudeh members neutralized the remaining elements of

the Iranian government, army, and police in the province. After incorporating a few other political factions and renaming itself the Democratic Party, the Tudeh dominated elections to create a national assembly with the backing of its armed party members and the Soviets. In mid-December, these so-called Democrats proclaimed the establishment of the Autonomous Republic of Azerbaijan and selected Jafar Pishevari to be prime minister.

One of Pishevari's first goals was to create a "peoples' army" with as many as ten thousand men under arms. Conscription was introduced to build this army, which was provided with Soviet uniforms and equipment. Iranian officers from the Tudeh military network were called to Tabriz to help organize the Peoples' Army, but their effect was limited because trust never developed between the Farsi-speaking officers and the Turkic-speaking Azeri fighters. The Azerbaijani regime, which quickly became an unpopular police state, remained dependent on the Red Army for its survival, and Pishevari kept tensions high with Tehran, possibly to give the Soviets a reason to stay.[1]

The Soviets simultaneously were encouraging the Kurds to seek greater autonomy, funneling support to the Kurdish Communist party, Komala (Committee for the Revival of Kurdistan), which had formed in late 1942. In the fall of 1945, the Kurds formed the Kurdish Democratic Party of Iran, which absorbed Komala. The new party was bolstered by the influx of one thousand experienced Iraqi Kurdish fighters under Mullah Mustafa Barzani, who had fled to Iran after a failed rebellion against the Iraqi government. Braced by Soviet advisors, the Kurdish leadership declared independence just days after the Azerbaijani republic was announced. With Soviet help and advice, the Kurds formally established the Kurdish Republic of Mahabad in late January 1946.

The new government appointed a minister of war and tried to set up an army that would be independent from the often unreliable tribal forces by recruiting Kurdish nationalists from the cities and mixing them with Barzani and other tribal fighters. Soon thereafter, the Mahabad army had some seventy officers, forty NCOs, and 1,200 soldiers dressed in Soviet-style uniforms with captured Iranian government weapons provided by the Russians and the new Azerbaijani republic. A few defectors from the Iraqi military advised the new army and were soon joined by a Soviet mission to organize and train the force. The training was rudimentary, however, with a focus on drill, rifle and machine gun marksmanship, and the use of grenades. Despite these preparations, the Mahabad army continued to rely on tribal fighters under their respective chiefs' commands and, when augmented by other tribal forces, might field up to three thousand men. Military decisions, however, still required the approval of all the fractious tribal leaders, including the Barzanis, which limited the scope of the army's independence and actions.[2]

The Iranian government responded to these developments as best it could given the uncertainty and fear created by the Soviets and their proxies. In December 1945 the Army Intelligence Department uncovered a Soviet scheme to take over the Iranian government using the Azerbaijani Peoples' Army, armed Tudeh partisans from Tehran and northeastern Iran, and Red Army elements.[3] After deploying army and Gendarmerie units to protect the capital and furnishing arms, ammunition, and radios to various tribes to enlist their support, these loyal forces stopped several thousand Communist fighters marching toward the capital in January 1946. This incident and the failure of negotiations with the Soviets and Pishevari caused the Iranians, with Washington's and London's encouragement, to take their complaint to the recently created United Nations Security Council, making it the first issue brought before this body.

Later in January, Ahmad Qavam al-Saltaneh, who had been exiled shortly after helping quell the Pasyan mutiny in 1921, was again made prime minister and started a more determined effort to deal with the Soviets. To appease Moscow, he fired General Arfa and replaced him with Gen. Ali Razmara, a pro-Russian officer with connections to the Tudeh military network. In March, Moscow upped the ante and deployed as many as fifteen Red Army combat brigades with hundreds of tanks, motorized infantry, and heavy artillery into Azerbaijan and other Soviet-held regions. An advanced guard of Russian tanks pushed forward to Karaj, twenty-six miles west of Tehran. In Washington the Joint Chiefs of Staff warned that Soviet pressure against Iran might well lead to World War III, and President Truman remarked to Averell Harriman, "We may be at war with the Soviet Union over Iran."[4] Truman wrote to Stalin threatening that Washington would send troops to Iran and naval forces to the Persian Gulf unless the Soviets withdrew.

In early April, the American threats, an Iranian arrangement to drop its UN complaint and give the Soviets an oil concession, and Moscow's hopes of bolstering Qavam as a pro-Soviet Iranian leader produced a Soviet policy reversal. Russian troops evacuated Azerbaijan and other parts of Iran in May. By June the crisis subsided after Azerbaijani claims to independence were abandoned. In moves to placate or ingratiate himself with the Soviets, Qavam made numerous concessions that gave the Azeris considerable autonomy, allowed the Peoples' Army to be incorporated into the Iranian army, and brought Tudeh members and other pro-Soviet factions into his government.

Muhammad Reza and the Iranian officer corps opposed Qavam's dealings with the Russians and Pishevari and his growing closeness to the Tudeh and labor unions. Reclaiming some of their lost political power, army field commanders instigated border incidents, and members of a joint military commission refused to recognize the Azeri fighters as legitimate members of the Iranian armed forces. Elsewhere, the British encouraged rebellion by the Qashqai and other tribes in Fars and Khuzestan to offset the pro-Soviet provincial governments in the north. Taking advantage of this, the opportunistic Qavam leaned back toward the West, using the Qashqai uprising to justify removing Tudeh ministers and provincial officials.

With the Soviet withdrawal, the fate of the two autonomous republics was sealed. The Iranian army's initial operations along the borders of the Kurdish republic, however, did little to weaken the Kurds. In late April, the Barzanis ambushed a column from Saqqez with six hundred Iranian troops, cavalry, and artillery. The Kurds defeated other Iranian probes, and fighters led by the Barzanis made plans to surround and capture Saqqez. The Mahabad army participated in these operations, but its main role was to keep the tribal contingents supplied with food, which kept them from foraging and plundering within the republic's territory. In the Saqqez garrison, General Razmara took command and conducted a successful attack in mid-June on nearby Kurdish positions to reduce the threat to the city, restore troop morale, and give heart to progovernment Kurdish tribes in the region. After Russian officers told them that they could not count on the Soviets restraining the Iranian army, the rebellious Kurds drew the appropriate conclusion. The Mahabad republic asked for a truce and began negotiations to return to Iranian control as most of the Kurdish tribes withdrew from the region and the Mahabad army evaporated.[5]

The Iranian army's preparations to attack the rebellious regions, in which the shah took a large role, stayed on course. Muhammad Reza had started the process earlier by ordering a full-scale study of the two republics' military strength. The general staff collected intelligence provided by government sympathizers in Azerbaijan while senior officers involved in the talks with the Kurds in Mahabad used their trips to make estimates of Kurdish military strength. During the summer General Razmara sent Iranian army officers and other ranks who were Kurds and Azeris into the region secretly to arrange for the defection of enemy troops. The finished intelligence report correctly assessed that Azeri morale was low and that the government in Tabriz could muster few of its ten thousand fighters. After getting the study, Muhammad Reza, Qavam, and Iran's military leaders met in a secret planning session. To create a pretext for sending army units into the republics, the government scheduled a Majles election and announced that the armed forces would supervise the vote. In November, the army resumed arming the tribal opponents of the Tabriz government. After the Iranian monarch gave a speech to his officers, the Iranian army moved to occupy Zanjan with Muhammad Reza supervising the operation from the air.

On December 10, 1946, the Iranian Army mounted a three-pronged attack into Azerbaijan and toward Mahabad. The Azeri militia destroyed a key bridge on the Tabriz road, but the army's main column forded the river and pushed ahead against limited resistance. Pishevari called for a "fight to the death" by the Azeris, but armed crowds of locals instead attacked Tudeh members while the Peoples' Army and other fighters retreated to Tabriz. On the next day, the second government column won a small skirmish, and the retreating rebels, aware that the population was rising against the Communists, dispersed into the mountains to escape across the border into the Soviet Union. Hundreds were caught and massacred by the people while the Shahsavan tribe, armed by the army earlier in the year, attacked the Communist militias near the Soviet border. Pishevari fled to the Soviet Union, where it was reported that he later died in a car accident. Two days after the start of the operation, the main column reached Tabriz and was welcomed into the city as liberators. Simultaneously, the second column entered Miandoab and then turned west to hook up with the third column from Saqqez, effectively surrounding most of the Mahabad government.

The rapid collapse of the Azerbaijan Republic demonstrated to the Kurds that the Soviets were unlikely to save them. Most of the chiefs had already decided to switch sides, and as Iranian forces advanced they were joined by local Kurdish tribesmen who wanted to demonstrate their loyalty to their monarch, get a chance to plunder Mahabad, and take revenge on their enemies. Facing these conditions, the Mahabad leaders judged that submission was the best option. After short surrender talks, the Iranian commander had the Kurdish leaders prepare Mahabad for the arrival of Iranian troops while he delayed the column with its Kurdish augmentees to prevent violence. Mahabad was entered quietly a few days later on December 17, 1946. The crisis ended after many of the Kurdish leaders were tried and executed and the army reestablished government authority in the Kurdish region.

Although Qavam's nimble political maneuvers, American pressure, and Soviet policies were the essential elements in reestablishing Iranian sovereignty, the widely publicized entry of the shah and his military into the provinces greatly improved the status of both. Bolstered by his "victory," Muhammad Reza began to assert himself. Before forcing Qavam into retirement in early 1947, the shah maneuvered the prime minister into helping gain a reluctant Majles' approval for a powerful army and additional American military assistance. As a consequence of the crisis, Washington became more amenable to Iranian military aid requests. The Joint Chiefs of Staff wanted strong unified states in the region as a buffer against the Soviets, and the American military chiefs believed that token assistance to Iran would create goodwill and a more solid alliance. The supply of substantial military aid to Iran was authorized in October 1946, foreshadowing the Truman Doctrine of 1947, which stressed U.S. readiness to contain Communism and defend nations threatened by it. Using the leverage gained by American concerns about Soviet expansionism, the shah worked hard to build a closer security relationship with Washington. His efforts were rewarded in October

1947 when the American mission to the Iranian army was followed by a larger advisory effort known as ARMISH, which extended the Truman Doctrine to Iran to prevent Soviet domination of Middle East.

By 1949 the still young shah had developed ambitions to make Iran a major regional power and recover the absolute power his father held. This required, in Muhammad Reza's view, a large, strong, and loyal military, preferably armed with state-of-the-art equipment. He recognized that he first needed to control his domestic political opposition and overcome obstacles to reasserting his authority. But, by late 1949, nationalist opposition to the monarch's power was gathering strength around the issue of British control of Iran's oil resources. Also, building the larger Iranian military he desired required a level of American support that Washington was reluctant to provide. The shah floated proposals to more than double his army's size, but the ARMISH commander advised Washington that Iran was barely able to support the current force of 113,000 men. With a push from Cold War developments and the dramatic growth of Iran's oil production and exports, the Shah and his army gradually overcame all these challenges.

Reign and Rule

The period between 1949 and 1953 was one of political turmoil and intrigue that inevitably drew in the Iranian military. In February 1949, an alleged Tudeh member fired five shots at point-blank range at Muhammad Reza at a public event, managing only to wound the monarch slightly. The shah used the attack as a pretext to clamp down on his opponents. He declared martial law, outlawed the Tudeh Party, strong-armed the Majles into giving him new powers to dissolve the legislature and control the media, and tried to rig the 1949 Majles elections. At the same time, he was facing stronger opposition from the Nationalist Front, a proreform, anti-British, and antiroyalist coalition led by Muhammad Mosaddeq. An elder statesman of Iranian politics, Mosaddeq had served in the first Majles, held various cabinet positions and governorships, and briefly partnered with Reza Khan before becoming a fierce opponent of Pahlavi autocracy and foreign entanglements. The National Front was incensed by the blatantly unfair terms offered by the British in a proposed agreement covering oil production and royalties, the horrible treatment by the British of Iranian employees in the oil industry, and the shah's toleration of both. In 1950, Mosaddeq and the National Front called for the nationalization of the oil industry.

A worried Muhammad Reza nominated his Army Chief of Staff, Gen. Ali Razmara, as his new prime minister to push the agreement through the Majles. Razmara was a risky, but also clever, choice by the shah. The general, a forty-seven-year-old career soldier, was energetic, intelligent, ambitious, and notoriously independent. He also was pro-Soviet, had links to the Tudeh, and was suspected of having had a role in the 1949 assassination attempt. Appointing Razmara, however, helped the shah by removing a potential competitor from the armed forces' chain of command and putting him in a position to draw popular anger away from the court. As anticipated, Razmara's advocacy of the flawed oil agreement cost him popular and clerical support while his refusal to send Iranian troops to the Korean War and restrictions on U.S. military advisors' movements in Iran alienated Washington. In March 1951, a member of a radical Islamic group assassinated Razmara.[6]

The army's involvement in politics continued to grow, and control of the armed forces became the focal point in the contest for power between the shah and his opponents. Faced with growing turbulence in Iran, Muhammad Reza reluctantly made Mosaddeq prime minister, and the oil nationalization problem grew into an international crisis. The eccentric and mercurial Mosaddeq arranged to have Iran nationalize the oil industry and repeatedly bested the British in the court of world opinion. A national hero, Mosaddeq tried to weaken the monarchy but was stymied by royalists in the Majles, who had gained a majority with the help of the army in the 1951 elections. In July 1952 Mosaddeq demanded that Muhammad Reza surrender control of the war ministry and allow Mosaddeq to appoint himself minister of war. When the shah refused, Mosaddeq resigned, sparking protests in Tehran and other major cities that quickly escalated into violent unrest.

The military was called out, but its response was uncertain. A year earlier, the shah had dismissed Gen. Fazlallah Zahedi, the same general arrested by the British in 1943 for pro-German activities, from his post as minister of interior after security forces killed thirty people in quelling an anti-American protest. The memory of Zahedi's dismissal made the commanders reluctant to use lethal force, despite occasionally bloody fighting between the protestors and the military. One senior ayatollah issued a fatwa calling on soldiers to join the public's struggle against the government, and young military officers, appalled by the violence, began talk of mutiny. Seeing that he was losing control, the shah relented, asking Mosaddeq to return and giving him control of the war ministry. Without hesitation, Mosaddeq set out to undermine the shah's power. He cut the military budget by 15 percent, transferred 15,000 men from the army to the Gendarmerie and established commissions to investigate corruption, procurement, and promotions. Mosaddeq also purged the army of 136 officers, including 15 generals, and spoke of ending the U.S. military missions.

Army officers, already apprehensive about Mosaddeq's seeming indifference to Tudeh involvement in the nationalist protests, were upset by the budget cuts and other actions that undermined their influence. Soon, disgruntled royalist officers began military coup planning. The British intelligence service also was considering Mosaddeq's removal, and by summer's end many Iranian officers were working with the British on coup plots that the Americans eventually joined. The key figure in the primary plan was General Zahedi, who was selected by the British as the best man to lead the coup, despite his generally poor reputation as an unscrupulous opportunist, because he was personally acquainted with almost every Iranian officer. Other prominent military figures involved in the plot were the current Gendarmerie commander, a former army chief of staff, the chief of the air force, the secret police chief, and the commanders of the Imperial Guards.

The planning gained momentum as turmoil increased through the first half of 1953. Mosaddeq was losing popular support because of an economy seriously weakened by British sanctions and embargoes and because of the harsh measures he used to control anti- and pro-government demonstrations. In late June, Washington gave its go-ahead to the Iranian conspirators and the Central Intelligence Agency (CIA) officials who had taken charge of the coup plot, now called Operation Ajax. After spurring more protests to make the prime minister's position untenable, the plotters were to have the shah replace Mosaddeq with Zahedi while mobs and military units on the CIA payroll stood ready to crush any attempt by the prime minister's supporters to resist. When the time came in mid-August, however, Muhammad Reza showed his indecisive nature and vacillated for several days before eventually agreeing to issue the royal decrees dismissing Mosaddeq.

The delay was nearly fatal, and the initial stage of the coup miscarried because the plan had been compromised. Shortly after midnight on August 15, 1953, army units loyal to the prime minister arrested the Imperial Guard commander, Col. Nematollah Nassiri, when he tried to deliver the decrees to Mosaddeq. Nassiri blundered into a trap after an earlier attempt to seize Chief of Staff Gen. Taqi Riahi came up empty. Not realizing that the general had learned of the coup and was away directing loyal troops to thwart it, Nassiri proceeded to Mosaddeq's house and his capture and incarceration. Other officers in the plot learned of the compromise and aborted their missions. As loyal units fanned out through Tehran, many of Nassiri's confederates were arrested and the remainder, including Zahedi, went into hiding. Hearing of the failure, the shah fled to Baghdad and then to Rome.

The CIA team, led by Kermit Roosevelt, refused to give up and amid the tumult in Tehran improvised a new strategy that rested on the military's support. At Roosevelt's direction the remaining conspirators publicized the decrees, characterized Mosaddeq's actions as the real coup, and sent out calls for the military to back the shah and Zahedi. The U.S. military mission distributed supplies to pro-Zahedi military units, and the mission's head, Gen. Robert McClure, was enlisted by Roosevelt to recruit Iranian commanders for the coup. McClure's overtures were rejected by Riahi and a division commander in Esfahan, but by offering money and future promotions the American general was able to suborn a tank battalion commander and two infantry regiment commanders in Tehran.[7] Col. Teimur Bakhtiar, the Kermanshah garrison commander, was persuaded by other conspirators to lead a column of tanks and armored cars to the capital. Simultaneously, a large crowd pretending to be Tudeh members was hired to protest against the shah with the goal of provoking fears among Iranians about a Communist takeover. As the unrest mounted, the American ambassador helped to convince Mosaddeq to send the police to restore order. After subduing the Tudeh and asking the nationalists to stay off the streets, however, Mosaddeq was confronted on August 19 by large throngs of CIA-sponsored pro-Zahedi demonstrators marching through Tehran.

In the climax of the coup, hundreds of soldiers, some in trucks or on top of tanks, joined the pro-Zahedi protestors, who attacked and burned pro-Mosaddeq newspapers and organizations. Midranking military officers soon emerged as the leaders of the protestors. While some were suborned, many were truly loyal to the shah. They and the soldiers lent the uprising an air of legitimacy, which, along with the firepower from their tanks and artillery, encouraged the proshah forces and discouraged the troops loyal to Mosaddeq. Nasiri and other plotters from the earlier coup attempt were freed from prison, and the colonel immediately assembled the Imperial Guard to help the protestors. By late afternoon, word arrived in Tehran that Bakhtiar's division was marching on the capital, and the tide began to turn against Mosaddeq. Zahedi was escorted from his hiding place to Radio Tehran to declare his assumption of the prime minister's post while military and police units took control of the capital, seized the telegraph office, and arrested General Riahi. As this was happening, loyal soldiers guarded Mosaddeq, fortified his house, and emplaced a few machine guns and Sherman tanks for its defense. During a nine-hour battle in which approximately three hundred people were killed, the loyal troops defeated wave after wave of assaults by the proshah forces. When tanks joined the anti-Mosaddeq forces, the pressed defenders, running low on ammunition, fought on just long enough for the now ex-prime minister to escape. Not wanting to be a fugitive, Mosaddeq later surrendered, was tried for treason by a military tribunal, and sentenced to three years in prison followed by house arrest for life.

The shah returned to Iran, and even though his own role had been very small and uninspiring, he had overcome the Mosaddeq challenge and was ready to consolidate his power. Although the monarchy's residual popularity contributed to Operation Ajax's success, Mosaddeq's overreaching and attendant unpopularity with the military were the key factors in his downfall. A *New York Times* reporter wrote at the time that Mosaddeq's big mistake was to push the army and the nation to choose between him and the shah; it cost him the military's support when the chips were down. Kermit Roosevelt agreed with this judgment. He wrote years later, "We believed—and were proven right—that if the people and the armed forces were shown that they must choose, that Mosaddeq was forcing them to choose, between their monarch and a revolutionary figure backed by the Soviet Union, they could, and would, make only one choice." Most army officers purged by Mosaddeq were returned to their posts, and the shah, Zahedi, and Bakhtiar, who was promoted to general and made military governor of Tehran, began to suppress demonstrations, purge pro-Mosaddeq officers, and round up the political opposition. One ironic outcome of the crisis was that, thanks to Mosaddeq's efforts, the shah gained more control over Iran's oil industry and greater oil revenues with which to build up the military and cement his rule over the country. He next moved to eliminate the remaining Tudeh threat to the military's loyalty.[8]

The Renewed Communist Challenge

The shah had been wary of the Communists since the war when Soviet intelligence used the Red Army's occupation to establish its largest presence beyond Soviet borders at the time. The Russian service, later renamed the KGB, had nearly forty residencies and subresidencies with more than 115 operations officers in Tehran alone during the war. The Kremlin's intelligence officers' principal task was neutralizing anti-Soviet elements in Iran, and Soviet influence declined after the Red Army withdrew. The Tudeh Party, however, remained active, especially among trade unions, students, intellectuals, and, to a lesser degree, the military. After it was outlawed following the 1949 assassination attempt against the shah, the Tudeh still managed to create and expand a clandestine military network. Led by a Gendarmerie colonel and a former army captain, the network grew from one hundred to as many as six hundred members in the early 1950s. During the oil nationalization crisis, the Tudeh resumed more open activities, including its unsuspecting participation in the CIA-sponsored antishah protest during the coup against Mosaddeq. After Mosaddeq's ouster, the Tudeh Party participated in anti-Zahedi demonstrations, and a Tudeh sabotage squad, aided by members inside the military, destroyed aircraft being readied at the Shiraz airbase for use against rebellious pro-Mosaddeq Qashqai tribesmen. Another Tudeh team tried to sabotage several naval vessels at Khorramshahr in October 1953 while a third group led an antigovernment uprising in Esfahan in November. As the government cracked down in the coup's aftermath, the party was subjected to intense repressive measures, and active Tudeh membership was cut in half by the end of year.[9]

During this period a new intelligence unit was established under General Bakhtiar with CIA help and in August 1954 it was instrumental in the discovery of the Tudeh military network. Helped by the capture of documents that revealed the extent of the organization, Iranian security forces arrested more than 450 military personnel, ranging from colonels to sergeants and cadets. In his biography, Muhammad Reza expressed his resentment and distrust of the Communist infiltration of the military, claiming that "even the commander of the most trusted battalion of my Imperial Guard was a hard-core Communist."[10] Most of the Communist officers, however, were found in the military schools, air force, Gendarmerie, and police rather than in key combat units capable of threatening the government. The Tudeh officers were treated harshly for allegedly plotting to overthrow the government; 27 were executed and 144 were sentenced to life in prison. The network and the Tudeh were broken and would never be more than a nuisance during the rest of the shah's reign.

Another consequence of the fight against the Communists was Muhammad Reza's decision to expand Bakhtiar's intelligence unit in 1956 into a larger agency, the National Intelligence and Security Organization, better known by its Persian acronym, SAVAK (Sazman-e Ettela'at va Amniyat-e Keshvar). Provided CIA training on spycraft, counterintelligence, and analysis, SAVAK worked to uncover and combat domestic and foreign threats to the shah's rule as a single organization that would not be hampered by the poor coordination that plagued the separate army, Gendarmerie, and national police intelligence units. For the military, the result was a division of labor that freed the armed forces from most internal security duties. Although the army continued to be tasked with occasional interventions when the police and other agencies could not deal with domestic unrest, the armed forces were allowed to turn their focus toward external threats.

Building the Pillar

Over the course of the next quarter century the shah and his army alternately struggled and cooperated with Washington over the Iranian military's role in the country and within a Western-led alliance. Well into the 1960s, the Americans held that the solution to Iran's security problems was economic development and political reform, but Muhammad Reza proved more persistent in pressing for the Iranian military's growth. The U.S. military mission was reorganized in 1950 as the U.S. Military Assistance Advisory Group (MAAG) to train and assist the Iranian army in using the increased flow of U.S. military aid and equipment. The Joint Chiefs of Staff reported that keeping the natural defensive barrier provided by the Zagros Mountains under Allied control was essential to regional defense plans. The Americans then sought to adjust the Iranian military's mission from internal to external security, leaving the former to the Gendarmerie and national police. The shah welcomed the shift in U.S. policy to adjust the Iranian military's mission to external security, which led to ever growing quantities of more modern arms for the armed forces. Over the next few years U.S. military planners concluded that the defense of the Middle East required effective military collaboration between Turkey, Iraq, Pakistan, and Iran, which led to creation of the Baghdad Pact or Central Treaty Organization (CENTO) in 1955. Muhammad Reza, in turn, used CENTO commitments as a new justification for expanding his military. The United States agreed to provide Iran with its first jet fighters and other modern equipment but tried to limit the deliveries based on Iran's ability to absorb the new arms.[11]

Events in the region bolstered the shah's ambitions. Declining British influence in the Middle East after the 1956 Suez War contributed to the creation of the Eisenhower Doctrine, which committed U.S. economic and military assistance to regional countries threatened by Communist subversion or invasion. Iran was one of the few states to endorse the Eisenhower Doctrine and, in return, received additional aid and arms. After the July 1958 overthrow of the Iraqi monarchy by pan-Arabist and pro-Soviet military officers, Iran's importance to the West's Middle East defense strategy increased. Not only were Iranian oil resources essential for Western economies, but also Iran became an indispensable base for staging air and ground attacks against the Soviet Union in wartime and for intelligence activities against the Russians in peacetime. In March 1959, Iran and the United States signed a bilateral defense agreement that guaranteed a strong American military commitment. From Iran's perspective, it was finally receiving the equal status with Turkey and Pakistan that it deserved. As some Iranians put it, "No longer would America treat Turkey as a wife and Iran as a concubine."[12]

In 1961 the shah found the new Kennedy administration unsympathetic to his goals because it saw Iran's requests for military assistance as excessive. According to one U.S. official, "In Iran, the Shah insisted on our supporting an expensive army too large for border incidents and internal security and of no use in an all-out war."[13] With the strategic missile threat overshadowing the menace of the Red Army's ground forces, the defense of Iran against external attack seemed less important than preventing its internal collapse. Under the Kennedy Doctrine, Washington saw internal subversion and guerrilla conflict as the main threats and wanted the Iranian military reconfigured for counterinsurgency operations. Later, the shah's insecurity was fed by the Johnson administration's "flexible response" doctrine to deter Soviet aggression while negotiating to reduce tensions. Muhammad Reza feared the possible compromise of Iran's interests in the superpowers' accommodations to avoid war. This apprehension was heightened—and the Shah's faith in CENTO shaken—when the organization gave no support to Pakistan during its 1965 war with India. The shah was especially unhappy that Iran was prevented from offering bilateral support to

Pakistan because Washington refused to approve the transfer of weapons originally given to Tehran. U.S. war plans' recommendations that Iran's main defensive line start at the Zagros Mountains rather than Iran's northern border was another contentious issue. Fearing a rapid Soviet incursion followed by calls for a truce to forestall a U.S. response, the shah worried that the surrender of northern Iran and Tehran was likely to have a very negative effect on Iranian troop morale, undercutting their will to fight and possibly dooming any defensive plan.[14]

The shah took various domestic and foreign policy actions to minimize American pressure for political, economic, and military reforms and later, because of Washington's Vietnam distraction, to hedge his bets on Iran's alliance with the West. In particular, the shah pursued better relations with Moscow and diversified his arms suppliers. Iran had pledged to the Russians in 1962 not to allow foreign missile bases to be built on Iranian soil, and after years of talks Iran purchased $110 million worth of Soviet weapons in 1967. During roughly the same period, American deficits aggravated by the cost of the war in Vietnam caused U.S. aid to drop to just a few million dollars. Using their increased oil revenues, the Iranians began dealing with the British, French, and Italians for weapons and other systems for Iran's army and navy. When the British government announced in 1968 that it was withdrawing its military forces "east of Suez" by 1971, the shah saw another reason to increase procurement to prepare to achieve his goal of replacing the Royal Navy in the Persian Gulf.

In the early 1970s three events came together that freed the shah to pursue his grandest military ambitions. First, the Tehran Agreement of 1971 between the Persian Gulf members of the Organization of Petroleum Exporting Countries (OPEC) and twenty-two major Western oil corporations gave Iran and its neighbors greater control over oil production and the ability to set prices and increase oil revenues. Iran's oil revenues doubled in just one year as a result, increasing from $885 million in 1971 to $1.6 billion in 1972. Next, with the completion of the British withdrawal in 1971, the U.S. government sought to apply to Iran the Nixon Doctrine, which announced that, while faithful to its treaty commitments, the United States expected its regional allies to assume responsibility for their own defense and well-being. The Nixon Doctrine dovetailed with Muhammad Reza's goals of greater independence and power and provided greater access to the weapons he wanted. Finally, following the October 1973 Arab-Israeli War, the shah worked with Arab oil exporters to cut production and more than quadruple oil prices. Iranian oil revenues jumped from $1.6 billion in 1972 to $4.6 billion in 1974 and then to $17.8 billion in 1975. Awash in cash, the shah was ready to build his "great civilization," with the Iranian armed forces in the starring role. From 1950 to 1972, Iran's various purchases of arms amounted to $1.5 billion. After the dramatic increase in oil prices in 1973, the value of arms transactions in the first year alone was twice that total. Between 1970 and 1977, the Iranian defense budget surged from just under $900 million to $9.4 billion, a staggering tenfold increase.[15]

Iran was posed to be the new "policeman of the Gulf" after the United States announced that it would not replace Great Britain in the region. Washington also described Iran as one of the "twin pillars" in a regional security system, a fiction created because American reliance on Iran was viewed as a threat by the Arab states. The Twin Pillars policy, which identified militarily weak Saudi Arabia as a second and coequal regional power, was intended to assure the Arabs that they would not be abandoned to Iranian hegemony. In declaring Iran the new power in the region, Muhammad Reza also tried to salve Arab sensibilities by resolving several outstanding boundary disputes, supporting Kuwait against Iraqi intimidation, and sending troops to fight with Oman against militant insurgents. The Gulf Arabs remained antagonistic, however, because of Iran's seizure of the disputed Persian Gulf islands of Abu Musa and Greater and Lesser Tunbs on the day before the British departure in 1971. American claims of evenhandedness aside, it was to Muhammad Reza at the end of a May 1972 meeting that Nixon said, "Protect me."[16] The last American constraint on the shah's appetite for arms was loosened when National Security Advisor Henry Kissinger announced to a reluctant American bureaucracy in 1972 that purchasing decisions would be left primarily to the shah's government, giving Iran access to virtually any conventional American weapon system it wanted. This policy was reemphasized in 1974 when President Ford's secretary of defense, James Schlesinger, stated that, because of Soviet nuclear parity with the United States, Western deterrence would be greatly strengthened by "regional military balances in critical areas of the world."[17]

The shah had genuine concerns that the vacuum left by the British was being filled by other powers. Senior Iranian commanders watched with alarm as Soviet ties with Iraq improved, Soviet naval forces increased their presence in the Indian Ocean, and Soviet subversive activities in support of radical groups in the Arabian Peninsula, Pakistan, and Iran grew. During the early 1960s Soviet sabotage and intelligence groups operated with local Communists and other partisans in Iran, where more preparations for wartime sabotage were made than in any other non-Western country. Between 1967 and 1973, a series of landing sites, bases, and weapons caches were selected, photographed, and reconnoitered by Soviet officials and agents in Iranian Kurdistan, Azerbaijan, and around Abadan. The Soviets also supported the expansion of Iraq's armed forces, which spurred an arms race the shah was determined to win.[18]

For the most part, it was the shah's ambitions to be regarded as a world statesman and have Iran respected as a great power that drove his military buildup.

The British and American governments accepted the need to equip Iran to meet its new responsibilities under the Nixon Doctrine, but they worried about the shah. A British foreign minister judged that Muhammad Reza was more auda-cious than shrewd, suffering from delusions of grandeur. He even suggested that the shah might not be an ally, an understandable view given the negative impact on Western economies of the "oil shock" the shah had helped create. The U.S. State Department also warned the Nixon administration about the shah's gran-diose ambitions while a CIA psychological profile reported that the shah was a dangerous megalomaniac.[19]

Even with Iran's oil-boom-generated wealth, defense expenditures consumed a third of the government's budget, with much of this spending wasted or si-phoned off by corrupt officials. The pace and volume of Iran's defense buildup competed with the civilian economy and imposed severe stress on the country's already stretched infrastructure. Inflation, economic dislocations that ruined agriculture and created a restive urban underclass, and constant power interrup-tions caused by Iran's inadequate and overwhelmed generating capacity created an economy that seemed out of control. Ironically, as the shah affirmed his in-dependence from the United States in policy matters, his procurement program made the armed forces ever more reliant on American personnel to maintain and operate the military's equipment. A 1976 U.S. Senate committee staff report noted that popular opposition to the regime was aggravated by the socioeco-nomic problems created by the large number of American technicians flowing into Iran to help the armed forces absorb the new sophisticated weapons sys-tems. Even Iran's role as regional "policeman" reinforced many Iranians' view that the shah was a lackey of the United States. The 1976 Senate report con-cluded that U.S. arms transfers were a runaway program and that virtually unre-stricted arms sales increasingly were not in Iranian or American interests.[20]

The Imperial Armed Forces

Despite the immense surge in resources devoted to the Imperial Armed Forces, known in Iran as the Artesh, no distinct Pahlavi military system developed. The Iranian military was based on the U.S. and British armed forces, and organiza-tions from the service staffs down to the squad level mimicked their Western counterparts. The ARMISH and MAAG missions worked with the Iranians to translate U.S. Army military manuals and regulations and provided a steady stream of advice and suggestions to the senior Iranian leadership. Their efforts gave a strong American cast to the Artesh's tactics and administration, but emu-lating a Western force structure proved much easier for the Iranians than adopt-ing American leadership and management styles. In addition, the ground, air, and naval services went through almost constant reorganization following the

1953 coup, with numerous ups and downs in funding and growth. The regular addition of new weapon systems and evolving internal security operations and Cold War missions contributed to the turmoil. As Iran acquired more weapon systems following the oil boom, the Artesh increased in size from roughly two hundred thousand at the start of the decade to four hundred and ten thousand by the late 1970s, making it the largest military in the Middle East. The two constants throughout this period were Muhammad Reza's favored treatment of the upper echelons of his military establishment and his tight personal control over the armed forces.[21]

The Imperial Iranian Ground Forces was the largest and most established of the three services. The army had been steadily upgraded through the mid-1960s, gradually changing from a light infantry force still reliant on pack animals supported by a few World War II–surplus armored vehicles to a mechanized force with contemporary U.S. armored vehicles and self-propelled artillery. After 1965, the Army relied less on American systems and shifted its orientation from the Soviet threat to Iraq, counterinsurgency, and power projection missions. By the late 1970s, the army had two hundred and eighty-five thousand men, including the Imperial Guard, an infantry division of eight thousand men that protected the capital. The members of one brigade, called the Javidan, or Immortals, were carefully vetted and swore special allegiance to protect the shah and his family. In the event of war, the army could call on the Gendarmerie's seventy-four thousand men, who had some basic military skills. Iran also had a reserve force with a nominal strength of three hundred thousand, but between the 1950s and 1970s the American military missions regularly lamented Iran's lack of preparations to maintain its reservists' capabilities or establish a suitable mobilization system. As 1978 began, the army had three armored divisions, three infantry divisions, and four independent brigades consisting of one armored, one infantry, one airborne, and one special forces unit. The army emphasized firepower, and 30 percent of its personnel were assigned to artillery units, organized into divisional artillery groups of four to eight battalions each. An Imperial Iranian Army Aviation Command was created to manage the more than six hundred helicopters used for the service's growing transport, fire support, and command and control needs. Shortly thereafter, a Sky Cavalry Brigade based on American air cavalry was established for rapid deployment missions.

With its expanding inventory of upgraded and more modern weapon systems, the army had significant firepower and mobility. Iranian infantry units were equipped with more than 800 U.S. and Soviet armored personnel carriers. In addition to modern rifles and machine guns, Iranian infantry units had various antitank guided missiles, including the U.S. TOW (Tube-launched Optical-tracking Wire-guided) system. Iran's armored units were equipped with roughly 860 older American M-47 and M-60 Patton tanks that had been improved with the addition of gun stabilizers and laser range-finders that made them a match for Iraq's newer Soviet tanks. The heart of Iran's expanding armored forces, however, were 760 new British Chieftain main battle tanks, which had a 120-mm gun and a powerful twin engine system that made it an excellent counter to the Soviet T-72 tanks just entering Red Army and Iraqi inventories. Iran's tank units also had a few hundred British light tanks and scout cars, which improved the mix and mobility of forces for Iran's rugged terrain. With another 1,450 Chieftains on order, Iran's projected tank inventory would become as large as France's armored formations and twice as large as the British Army's tank force. The infantry and armored units were backed by more that 1,500 contemporary U.S. and Soviet artillery pieces, and, for local air defense, the army acquired 1,800 Soviet-made antiaircraft guns and first-generation shoulder-fired surface-to-air missiles (SAMs). The Army relied on four U.S. I-HAWK (Improved Homing-All-the-Way-Killer) SAM battalions for medium- to high-altitude air defense and in 1978 had ordered mobile British SAMs. The new army aviation command, meanwhile, included 220 U.S. helicopter gunships and nearly 400 other helicopters for troop transport, medical evacuation, aerial reconnaissance, and command and control duties. The new command vastly improved Iran's air mobility, which enabled the army to overcome Iran's harsh geography, long distances, and still inadequate lines of communication.

The Imperial Iranian Air Force became a separate service in 1955 and rapidly became the favorite of Muhammad Reza, who was a pilot and loved to fly. During the two decades following the end of World War II, the service had graduated from motor-powered American fighter-bombers to jets. Air defense and close air support to the ground forces were the Air Force's main focus until the mid-1960s, however. Then the shah's decision to devote more money to the air force and the addition of the F-5 Tiger in 1965 marked the beginning of a slow but steady expansion. The air force grew from seven thousand personnel and seventy-five combat aircraft in 1965 to fifteen thousand men and two hundred combat aircraft in just three years. The new warplanes, including the recently added F-4 Phantom fighter-bomber, gave Iran a clear edge over Iraq's Soviet fighters and long-range bombers. Under Gen. Muhammad Khatami, the Shah's brother-in-law and a competent leader, the air force was patterned on the American model and changed its orientation from close air support to become Iran's main striking arm. The air force relied almost totally on American aircraft, air-to-air missiles, television-guided bombs, and ground equipment to simplify logistics and maintenance. Because of Iran's limited transportation grid, its far-flung borders, and harsh terrain, the air force devoted some of its resources to expanding its transport and tactical airlift capabilities, nearly tripling the number of transports in its inventory between 1965 and 1968.

Given the highest priority in Iran's defense budget after 1970, the air force grew at an explosive rate. By 1978, the air force had nearly five hundred combat aircraft, including state-of-the-art F-14 Tomcats—sometimes called "Ali-Cats" by the American technicians—that were armed with Phoenix long-range air-to-air missiles. In becoming the only country in the world to purchase the swing-wing fighter, Iran had saved the F-14 program by loaning Grumman, its troubled manufacturer, the money to finance the production to fulfill the Imperial Air Force's order. The F-14 was so sophisticated, however, that even the U.S. Navy had problems absorbing the system at the time. Another major addition was a squadron of thirteen tankers for in-flight refueling, which greatly increased the Phantoms' and Tomcats' operational ranges. The air force's transport inventory continued to grow, expanding from eleven to seventy large jets. At its height in 1978, the shah's air force was the largest and most sophisticated in the Persian Gulf and was even larger than the French and West German air forces. Most remarkably, the service's manpower grew to one hundred thousand personnel by 1978 in response to the overwhelming technical, logistical, managerial, and maintenance needs of the seven major systems and hundreds of aircraft added to the inventory. During this period General Khatami created the *homafars*, technicians similar to American warrant officers, to try to improve maintenance, but their role was not firmly established as the air force's growth posed virtually unmanageable challenges. A nationwide base expansion program was still inadequate for the air force's growing size and missions, and Iran only belatedly started to establish an early warning command and control system to use Iran's air power more effectively.

The Imperial Iranian Navy was the smallest of the services and was virtually ignored until the mid-1960s. After World War II, the navy had received a reconditioned frigate and a number of torpedo boats, minelayers, and minesweepers from the United States and Great Britain. Iran began to acquire contemporary naval equipment after it joined the Baghdad Pact in 1955. Still, it was 1965 before the navy's manpower expanded from one thousand to six thousand personnel to man two corvettes, four coastal minesweepers, two inshore minesweepers, six patrol boats, two landing craft, and other support vessels acquired from the Americans and the British. Even before London announced its plans to withdraw from the region, the shah had started planning to supplant the British in the Persian Gulf. He purchased four British frigates armed with "sea-skimming" antiship missiles and SAMs in 1966. Later, the shah created the world's largest fleet of military hovercraft to patrol and support operations around the shallow areas and islands of the Gulf. At the time the new ships were ordered, none of Iran's naval bases could accommodate them, and new construction and expansion programs were rushed toward completion. Toward the end of the decade, the navy moved its naval headquarters and main operating bases from Khorramshahr to Bandar Abbas, where it would be less vulnerable to Iraqi attacks and interdiction. A base for Iran's twelve hovercraft was established at Khark Island, where Iran's primary oil export terminal had been developed to replace Abadan, which could not accommodate modern tankers.

On the Navy's fortieth anniversary in November 1972, the shah announced the expansion of Iran's security perimeter beyond the Persian Gulf and Gulf of Oman into the Indian Ocean. He told the assembled seamen that the navy's striking power would increase several times over within the next two years, promising qualitative and quantitative changes for the service.[22] In fact, over the subsequent six years the navy grew from nine thousand to twenty-eight thousand men while its major warships increased from one to three destroyers and from two to four frigates. Twelve La Combattante missile boats armed with Exocet and American Harpoon antiship missiles were purchased from France. Iran's hovercraft fleet added two more vessels while the navy's light forces included seven large patrol craft, five minesweepers, two landing ships, two landing craft, and two logistic support ships. Iran's navy had twenty-four helicopters for various duties in 1972; by 1978 it had established a naval aviation organization with forty-six helicopters for anti-submarine warfare (ASW) operations, protecting tankers, and aerial transportation needs. The organization included a maritime reconnaissance squadron with six P-3 Orion patrol aircraft and an ASW squadron with twelve Sea King helicopters. The P-3s had the range to conduct patrols well over the Indian Ocean, where, because the Persian Gulf is too shallow for most submarine operations, the main subsurface threat was to be found.

The shah repeatedly expressed concern about guerrilla attacks against shipping and oil platforms in the Gulf. He justified Iran's occupation of Abu Musa and the two Tunb islands as a move to prevent them from serving as bases for guerrilla attacks.[23] In response to this fear, the navy created an amphibious capability with three units designed to deal with insurgents, border incursions, and guerrilla attacks on oil installations, tankers, and oil platforms. One unit was a marine battalion capable of being deployed by helicopter, hovercraft, and landing craft. The second was a small specialized naval unit called the Khark Special Strike Force, which had the antiguerrilla mission. The third unit was a special forces group, modeled on the U.S. Green Berets, which served as a fast-reaction unit for multiple contingencies.

By 1978, Iran's naval forces were more than large enough to ensure Iran's dominance of the Persian Gulf littoral. Although the Iranian navy was not comparable in size or quality to Western navies, it was the only Middle Eastern navy with modern missile-armed destroyers and frigates. The shah's naval expansion plans stretched well into the 1980s with the goal of increasing the Iranian navy's reach. Iran had ordered helicopter support ships along with more ASW helicopters, logistical ships, mine sweepers, patrol boats, and long-range maritime patrol aircraft. Four modified American Spruance-class long-range destroyers, which were more sophisticated than those being procured by the cash-strapped U.S. Navy, were on order, and Washington had agreed to sell Iran three Tang-class diesel attack submarines to guard the Indian Ocean approaches to the Persian Gulf. The U.S. destroyers would give Iran the ability to patrol as far away as the Cape of Good Hope at the southern tip of Africa, and the shah's government obtained berthing rights for Iranian ships in Mauritius, the island nation off Africa's eastern coast. The Iranians also were negotiating with West Germany and other European countries for purchases involving six diesel submarines and German-Italian frigates. Construction was started on the expansion of the small port of Chah Bahar, just fifty miles west of the Pakistani border, which the shah planned to turn into the largest military base in the Middle East. When finished, Chah Bahar was to have the naval and air facilities to give the navy direct access to the open ocean and enable it to better counter potential deep water threats. The naval facilities were being built to accommodate the new American destroyers and submarines that Iran had ordered and were to include capabilities to service U.S. nuclear submarines.

Following the example of his father, Muhammad Reza sought to develop Iran's indigenous defense industries and maintenance capabilities. Iran turned to the British for help in creating a military-industrial complex to service and maintain the Chieftains and to produce spare parts and ammunition for the tanks. With American help, the Iranians set up licensed production for helicopters at Esfahan at the major maintenance facility and training center colocated with the Aviation Command's headquarters. By the late 1970s, Iran also had coproduction contracts for computer terminal products and sophisticated anti-tank, surface-to-air, and air-to-surface missiles. The Iranian Electronic Industries, established in 1971, maintained, repaired, and produced electronic components of various weapon systems and manufactured electronic switching systems for military and civilian telecommunications. In 1970, Iranian Aircraft Industries was established to manufacture spare parts and develop technicians and managers with the long-term goal of licensed production of more sophisticated components and the overhaul of aircraft. Throughout the decade, Iran's military factories manufactured fairly large quantities of explosives, small arms, ammunition, rockets, mortar rounds and fuses, and vehicle batteries and tires. Other assembly plants produced Jeeps, Land Rovers, and trucks and trailers for military and civilian use. In addition to working with Americans and Europeans, the shah's defense establishment cooperated with Israel on Project Flower, which involved various missile-related projects, to include plans for a missile assembly facility and a test range. Flower's main focus was the development of antiship missiles, but a document taken from the U.S. embassy in 1979 indicates that Iran and Israel envisioned the introduction of surface-to-surface missiles into their joint project.[24]

A Majestic or Mediocre Military?

Imposing on paper, the Imperial Armed Forces' capabilities were much more modest. As with any military force, the Iranians were capable of doing some things very well, others well enough, and some not well at all. A review of reports prepared by the U.S. training mission to Iran, its higher commands, and the U.S. Army between 1946 and 1970 indicates that the Iranian military made progress in many areas, especially at the individual soldier and small unit level.[25] Sustaining improvements seemed to be a major obstacle, however, as unit performance varied over time when new commanders and other leaders were reassigned, new equipment was introduced, and the force structure was repeatedly reorganized. In the early 1950s, ARMISH reported that some Iranian divisions responded quickly to practice alerts and had successful driver and mechanic training programs, well-maintained facilities, and tanks and artillery in good condition. In early 1953, the American advisors identified a long list of Iranian army officers who had demonstrated notable professional capabilities. On this list a number of Iranian army, air force, and navy generals and colonels were described as aggressive, efficient, and cooperative and touted as excellent commanders and commendable instructors, managers, and engineers. A group of lieutenant colonels and majors were praised as intelligent, hard working, and forceful with some singled out for being effective under pressure, resourceful, industrious, and energetic. In his memoirs, one American colonel who advised an Iranian division between 1958 and 1959 commented on the unit commander's good qualities and his willingness to relieve incompetent battalion commanders and give younger officers a chance to lead. He also praised the division's ability to improve its readiness rate dramatically, singling out a dedicated colonel who was willing to get his hands dirty and get on the ground to show mechanics how to make repairs. As a result the division kept 85 percent of its mostly World War II–surplus vehicles operational. Although other outstanding Iranian officers would be recognized over the years, systemic problems with the officer corps limited the contributions such officers could make.[26]

Throughout the quarter century following Mosaddeq's ouster, U.S. advisors and other U.S. government agencies judged that the Iranian military was able to handle internal unrest. While it never was seen as proficient for conducting more than a brief delaying action against any Soviet attack, the Artesh was assessed as being capable of defending Iran against any regional threat. Both judgments were proved correct in southern Iran, along the Iraqi border, and in Oman during the 1960s through the mid-1970s. The Artesh's major internal challenges occurred in 1963 when attempted land reforms generated violent tribal and clerical opposition. Starting in February, the Qashqai, Bakhtiari, and other southern tribes rebelled, storming Gendarmerie posts to capture weapons. In March, air force jets strafed some tribal encampments while a Southern Expeditionary Army, with four army divisions, an air force squadron, and Gendarmerie forces, was established to restore order. After army units invaded tribal territory in Fars Province and arrested one of the main tribal leaders, it suffered the loss of nearly fifty officers and soldiers when a battalion was ambushed. The army persisted, however, and the rebels were forced back into their mountain strongholds. The rebellion collapsed as more chiefs were arrested or killed, allowing the expeditionary army to be disbanded by July. Except for sporadic small-scale unrest, the tribes did not challenge the army again. During the same summer, the army was still robust enough to send a paratroop battalion to suppress dissident clerical students in Qom. When the subsequent arrest of Ayatollah Ruhollah Khomeini, then emerging as a vocal and influential critic of the regime, sparked three days of the worst riots Iran had ever seen, the Tehran garrison was still able to restore order in the capital. The soldiers of the Tehran garrison, which had sent many of its units to the expeditionary army, obeyed orders to use lethal force, killing as many as three hundred Iranians and wounding several hundred more in quelling the unrest.[27]

The Artesh demonstrated its capacity in several areas during steadily worsening tensions with Iraq from the mid-1960s on. The shah, who had long been concerned about radical Arab nationalism, had tried to weaken the Iraqis by supporting Iraqi Kurdish rebels with arms, aid, and haven in Iran. In April 1969 Baghdad tried to enforce the 1937 Saadabad Treaty and assert its control over the Shatt al-Arab waterway by threatening to block access to Iran's ports. In response, the shah abrogated the treaty and provided naval and air escorts for merchant shipping. Baghdad reacted to this show of force by expelling Iranian residents and pilgrims from Iraq, calling for the liberation of Khuzestan Province, and supporting Baluch separatists in eastern Iran. Tension became so high that the Iranian and Iraqi armies mobilized in 1969 and 1970. The ARMISH commander praised Iranian actions during the border incidents with Iraq in 1970, noting that the army executed a crash program to prepare its personnel and equipment for deployment to the border. He reported that the army moved units the length and breadth of the country in "a highly professional manner" and met their mission requirements. The U.S. Intelligence Community judged that, although Iranian armed forces were larger than Iraq's military, the two sides were about evenly matched in tanks while Iraq had a slight edge in artillery, armored personnel carriers, and operational aircraft. The American intelligence analysts also assessed that Iran's logistics deficiencies were a major constraint on offensive movements into Iraq.[28]

Border clashes continued as Iraq tried to stir up the Arab world against Iran in November 1971 when the shah had his navy seize the three disputed islands that sit astride the western approaches to the Strait of Hormuz. The successful amphibious operation using Iranian hovercraft and marines was unopposed on Abu Musa Island, while token resistance on the Tunbs was quickly overcome with the loss of only four soldiers on both sides. After the signing of the Soviet-Iraqi Friendship Treaty of 1972 and the start of deliveries of new and more modern Soviet weapon systems to Iraq, the number of armed incidents grew. Sniping became a daily occurrence and, in a couple of minor incursions, raiding parties from Iraq blew up an oil pipeline, took three gendarmes hostage, and attacked four border posts with armored personnel carriers, artillery, mortars, and small arms. In February 1973, Pakistani police raided the Iraqi embassy in Islamabad and seized approximately three hundred machine guns and sixty thousand rounds of ammunition smuggled in under diplomatic pouch for passage to Iranian Baluch tribesmen. In the same year, Iran helped the Pakistanis crush Baluch rebels whose territory spanned their mutual border.

When fighting resumed in 1974 between the Iraqi government and the Kurds, Iran renewed and then greatly expanded its military support to the Iraqi Kurdish tribes. The army sent Iranian Kurds to assist and deployed regular forces, dressed in Kurdish garb, to advise and fight. Light artillery and antitank guided missiles were furnished to the Iraqi Kurds, and Iran's long-range artillery provided indirect fire support from Iranian territory. In response, Iraq sent aircraft to conduct reconnaissance flights over Iranian territory and bomb Kurdish guerrilla camps there. Iran retaliated on behalf of the Kurds by sending aircraft to fly combat support missions that strafed targets in Iraq. At the end of 1974 an Iranian HAWK battery shot down two Iraqi MiG-23 fighters. In January 1975, Iran posted two regiments inside Iraqi territory to protect its frontier towns. Such military pressure succeeded in forcing Iraq to agree to Iran's terms on control of the Shatt al-Arab waterway in the Algiers Accord of 1975. In return, Iran ended its support of the Iraqi Kurds, which contributed to the rapid collapse of their rebellion.[29]

Except for the skirmishes with Iraq, the Artesh was not tested in combat until a few ground, air, and naval units were sent to help the Sultan of Oman defeat an insurgency in 1973. Aggrieved tribesmen in Dhofar, an isolated and long-neglected province of Oman along the border with South Yemen, had started an armed rebellion in 1963. Over time the rebel forces grew and became radicalized, aided by ideological and logistical support from South Yemen, China, the Soviet Union, Iraq, and various Palestinian organizations. By 1969 much of western Oman and the major coastal town of Rakhyut were under insurgent control. Rebel actions spurred the overthrow of the Omani sultan by his Sandhurst-educated son, Bin Said Qaboos. The new sultan built up his military, the Sultan's Armed Forces (SAF), which was commanded by British officers and manned primarily by Baluch soldiers from Pakistan. After successfully containing the rebels with British assistance, Qaboos turned to Iran for help in 1973 to put an end to the insurgency. The shah responded favorably because of his long-standing concerns about communist penetration on his southern flank and the potential security threat posed should Oman or any Gulf state fall to revolutionaries.[30]

Iranian troops and support played an important part in the latter stages of the Dhofar rebellion. An Iranian special forces battalion with 1,500 men arrived in the spring of 1973 to help the Omanis establish the Hornbeam Line, a defensive barrier of wire, minefields, and block houses stretching some thirty-five miles from the coast to the mountains. In December 1973, the 1,200-man Imperial Iranian Battle Group arrived in Dhofar. Its first mission was Operation Thimble, the opening of the Midway Road, a key supply route running between Dhofar and Muscat, the Omani capital, that was regularly targeted by the rebels. From their staging area at Thamarit, Iranian troops reportedly seized key positions in the mountains overlooking the road under the cover of darkness. These units entrenched themselves on the ridges and then harassed the rebels with heavy mortar fire and intensive patrolling. Backed by ample artillery, warplanes, and helicopter gunships, the Iranians secured the strategic road and in the process transformed the airbase at Thamarit into a major military complex. Iranian troops were rotated every three months to allow as many soldiers as possible to gain combat experience, although this policy contributed to higher losses among Iranian personnel; the rapid turnover meant that veteran units left just as their skills had improved. Between fifteen thousand and seventeen thousand Iranians rotated through Oman during the 1973 to 1976 deployment. To ease Arab sensibilities, Iran's troops were kept isolated, even from the most casual contact with Omanis, and the Iranians had all their supplies, including food and water, flown in directly from Iran.[31]

In December 1974, between 3,500 and 4,000 Iranian troops with artillery, aircraft, helicopters, and naval support began a pincer movement from north and south of Rakhyut to seize this symbolic rebel capital. Iranian inexperience and caution coupled with strong enemy resistance caused the operation to bog down. Plans were revised and the campaign resumed, isolating and then capturing the city in early January 1975. Later in the year, as Omani forces launched a campaign to clear more areas along the Yemeni border, the Iranians worked to establish the Damavand Line, another barrier of barbed wire and sensor devices to cut off the flow of men and materiel from rebel camps in South Yemen. The

Iranian contingent staged a concurrent series of diversionary feints to tie down the guerrilla forces while the Omanis deployed along the border. The shah also provided Oman with Iranian air defense units to guard against intruding South Yemeni aircraft. With this Iranian support, the Omanis pushed the last rebels across the border, and in mid-December 1975 Sultan Qaboos declared the Dhofar war officially over.[32]

Generous observers held that the Iranian forces, which had lost five hundred men during the fighting, gave a good account of themselves in Oman and gained important experience in counterinsurgency operations and in handling the logistic requirements of expeditionary warfare. The British commander of the sultan's armed forces during the Dhofar campaign, Maj. Gen. Ken Perkins, had the Iranian units under his overall command and was in an excellent position to observe their performance. Perkins noted several years later that the Iranian army's discipline withstood the test of operations in Dhofar, morale was good, and the Iranian troops "wanted for nothing" in terms of supplies and spare parts. The Iranian commanders were careful not to overtax their conscript soldiers, and each company had a detachment of better-trained special forces soldiers to assist them. The Iranian army's field surgical support, according to Perkins, was as good as he had seen anywhere. The British general was more impressed by the leadership of the Iranian naval contingent. He wrote that the fleet's commander was knowledgeable of modern combat and naval operations and that navy discipline was very good. Perkins commented that, unlike most other Iranian naval units, the ships sent to Oman were manned completely by Iranians. The naval squadron performed effectively in the Rakhyut amphibious operation with no prior rehearsals.

Perkins's major criticism of the Iranian ground and naval forces was that each applied massive firepower as a substitute for tactical skill. Other British officers were less generous, saying that the Iranians showed inexperience and an over-reliance on American training and tactics by trying to use firepower against guerrillas when dedicated pursuit was needed. In particular, Iranian helicopter pilots were characterized as rash and the Iranian infantry as trigger-happy. Even the critical British officials were impressed, however, by the surprisingly smooth logistical effort.[33]

The Crippled Giant

Despite its impressive order-of-battle and various accomplishments in Oman and along the Iraqi border, the Artesh in the late 1970s was a troubled military. A U.S. congressional report in 1977 found that Iran's armed forces were unable to use U.S. weapons effectively without excessive American technical assistance.[34] The report also judged that the new weapons did little to enhance Iran's defensive capabilities. Some observers expressed doubt about the Iranian military's ability to defend against Iraq, much less deter the Soviet Union, without continued American support. The Artesh's problems included a politicized officer corps, skilled manpower shortages, and inadequate infrastructure. All were obvious and a subject of constant advice and proposals by the MAAG as the 1970s wore on and the consequences associated with the shah's arms-buying spree became manifest.

Perhaps the original sin of the shah's armed forces was that political considerations took first priority in managing the officer corps, even if this meant removing capable officers or promoting mediocre ones loyal to the court. American military advisors consistently complained about most Iranian officers' unwillingness to show initiative and strong leadership to avoid gaining unwanted attention from Muhammad Reza and the senior commanders. Subordinates regularly hesitated to act on routine matters without approval from their superiors. Not wishing to risk mistakes or raise suspicions, unit commanders showed a marked lack of interest in collective training or in developing their abilities to handle larger combined forces. The senior leaders were a tight-knit group of men close to Muhammad Reza. They tended to share common values, were finely attuned to the monarch's wishes, and wanted to do nothing to risk the cozy arrangement—and accompanying corruption—between them and the shah. The senior officers' example trickled down to the midgrade and junior officers, who, as inflation ravaged Iran in the 1970s, felt that their pay and living conditions were insufficient and turned to petty graft, extortion, and shady business deals.

The weakened officer corps was not well served by other elements of the military establishment and saw its ties to the crown fray. Iran never developed the necessary cadres of trained, relatively honest, and effective military managers and civil servants to handle the logistic, maintenance, procurement, medical, financial, and operational requirements of a modern military. For thirty years U.S. advisors complained that Iran often wastefully put expensively trained specialists in unrelated jobs and appeared unable to force some officers with needed skills and experience to serve in posts outside the capital where life was harder and opportunities for dishonest financial gains smaller. A related problem was that the military establishment never provided sufficient capable junior commissioned and non-commissioned officers. The army and air force suffered from a shortage of well-trained midgrade staff officers able to plan large-scale maneuvers and then move and maintain forces in the field. The introduction of new technology and massive new amounts of equipment overwhelmed the limited pool of qualified personnel, forcing the services to shift trained manpower from old to new systems without leaving behind any cadre to maintain and use the older equipment. During the 1970s expansion, the advancement of large numbers of individuals without thorough training or an understanding of the military altered the identity of the officer corps. This problem and the change in the composition of the class-conscious officer corps widened the gap between the junior and senior officers, weakening the younger military leaders' links to the regime. The air force *homafars*, high school educated and technically trained, had a social background and outlook on life very different from that of the officers. They became a source of dissidence within the military when the air force refused to meet the *homafars'* demands to be amalgamated into the officer corps.

The Iranian armed forces never closed the gap between the services' requirements and the country's ability to provide men able to learn many of the necessary technical and advanced skills. Because several major languages and numerous dialects were used by the conscripts, some training time during the first part of the two-year term of service had to be devoted to Farsi language skills. For many officers and all pilots English was required, which added to the demands on officer education. As for technical knowledge, even into the 1970s many conscripts lacked experience with mechanical devices and cars that might have given them a better sense of how to use and maintain military systems. Without sufficient numbers of adequately trained personnel, the Iranian military was simply unable to assimilate the high-tech equipment pouring into Iran in a timely or systematic manner. The challenge was magnified by the absence of a coherent procurement strategy, which resulted in a mix of equipment from various foreign suppliers with few common components, which made maintenance and resupply more difficult. The almost total dependence on foreign know-how, technicians, and technical trainers required the presence of tens of thousands of foreign advisors, who contributed to the growing rumbles of civil and military dissent. The congressional assessments of the era noted that Iran might not be able to absorb and operate a large proportion of its sophisticated equipment even with the support of American technicians. The Iranians disproved these assessments during the war with Iraq, but the effort to manage and operate foreign equipment without advisors was time-consuming, difficult, and incomplete.[35]

Shortages of military training facilities, a central logistic system and warehouse system, military communication networks, and even major roads were significant problems. Iran's civilian and military infrastructure had improved steadily during the postwar decades but was still inadequate. Part of the problem was a lack of planning and administrative capabilities to support the expansion and maintenance of infrastructure in line with the military's growth. In early 1975, the helicopter gunship pilots were not gunnery qualified because Iran had neglected to program the construction of suitable firing ranges when it ordered the system. In fact, most military training in Iran was limited by the lack of suitable training areas. One American advisor reported that nearly twenty years of negotiations were required to purchase land for a training range near the army aviation airfield. At the same time that the shah was ordering the expansion of indigenous production capabilities for arms, ammunition, and spare parts he also was trying to develop the civilian economy. Given Iran's limited industrial base, these numerous projects increased the competition for qualified administrative talent and resources between the many critical military and civilian infrastructure needs. In the air force, an estimated ten thousand trained managers and technicians were required to maintain just the fighters, and, of these ten thousand, approximately one-fourth needed skills that generally required five to ten years of training and hands-on experience to develop.[36]

The acquisition of the F-14 Tomcat perhaps best summed up the range of leadership, maintenance, and training problems in Iran's rapid military expansion. At the time the first Tomcats were delivered, air force mechanics were not fully proficient in maintaining the airframes, engines, and weapon systems of Iran's less sophisticated F-4 and F-5 fighters. Although roughly 120 ground crewmen were trained on the F-14 by 1976 and another 100 were in training, the Iranians were not allowed by the Pentagon to maintain or repair any of the Tomcat's sensitive systems, requiring such components to be sent to the United States for maintenance. Experienced F-4 and F-5 pilots were transferred to F-14 transition training, leaving a gap in their old squadrons. Air force commanders, wary of displeasing the shah by losing one of his expensive new aircraft, restricted the use of the Tomcats in training. Aircrews, sensing their leaders' unease, became reluctant to fly in any conditions that might increase the risk of accident. As a result, although Iranian Tomcat pilots later distinguished themselves during the Iran-Iraq War, during the last years of the shah's reign one of the world's most sophisticated and combat-capable aircraft was flown almost entirely in daylight hours and in good weather as it conducted simple missions, with no dogfighting. Much of Iran's other new equipment faced similar problems in the process of being absorbed by the armed forces and could not be used to its full capabilities in 1978. The Chieftain tank, in particular, had recurrent maintenance problems because its engines and cooling system were not designed for optimal performance in Iran's harsh climate and terrain. Even as the demand for resources and time for new weapons increased, Iran's older air and ground systems continued to suffer from the services' uneven maintenance practices and ongoing supply problems.[37]

The Artesh's Deadly Defect

Of all the Artesh's problems, the fault that probably doomed the Pahlavi dynasty was the shah's overbearing system of control. Determined to prevent the military from becoming a challenger to the regime, Muhammad Reza applied diverse methods to check the armed forces. He gave the senior officers attractive salaries, generous benefits and pensions, great housing, modern medical facilities, frequent travel abroad, and low-priced department stores. In addition, senior officers were assigned to run provinces, important government ministries, and large state enterprises, particularly major industrial installations. The motto *Khoda, Shah, Mihan* (God, Shah, Fatherland) was a byword for the Artesh, and at every morning formation all military units recited a prayer for their ruler's welfare. Muhammad Reza never let the officers forget their dependence on the monarchy or on him personally. From time to time, he publicly scolded high-ranking officers to ensure that everyone understood that no one was immune from his system of reward and punishment. He quickly penalized officers suspected of disloyalty or political unreliability. Finally, he used multiple organizations, including SAVAK, his own secret intelligence bureau, and military intelligence, to watch the armed forces and each other, ensuring that officers could not confidently make alliances with each other or regime opponents.[38]

The shah's continued involvement directly in the armed forces' day-to-day operations was another means of control, even as he acquired greater foreign policy interests and domestic development duties. As the constitutional commander in chief, the shah led the Artesh through the Supreme Defense Council (SDC; also called the Supreme Commander's Staff). He alone chose the service chiefs who made up the SDC, but seldom used them in a joint advisory role and limited their input into their services' fates. In fact, the SDC was not a true joint staff. Between 1978 and 1979, for example, all but a few of its two thousand personnel were from the army. Instead, Muhammad Reza held weekly audiences with his service chiefs and other senior offices, almost always meeting with them individually rather than as a team. The Iranian monarch selected the major unit and military school commanders, made all senior officer promotion decisions, and even insisted on approving the promotions and school selections of junior officers. Competitive and jealous men, sometimes even personal rivals, were placed in charge of the intelligence organizations and in senior commands to induce competition between the services. Muhammad Reza also frequently shuffled commanders to ensure that they could not form power bases or enduring alliances. Under his micromanagement, no regular chain of command developed. Every general viewed himself as responsible to no one other than the shah, and the field commanders regularly bypassed the SDC and their service chiefs to contact Muhammad Reza. At the same time, officers were not allowed to feel irreplaceable and, with spies and rivals looking over their shoulders, no one dared withhold information for fear the shah might get it through another channel.[39]

Under the shah's system no individual military leader was given a chance to establish a reputation that might allow him to create an independent power base. Muhammad Reza quashed ambitious military men, starting with his transfer of

General Razmara from the chief of staff job in 1951. Within days of Mosaddeq's ouster in 1953, discord erupted between the shah and General Zahedi, when the former started issuing orders to the military and promoting officers without consulting with his prime minister. The result was Zahedi's "exile" with a diplomatic posting eighteen months later. The head of the army's intelligence branch in 1958, Gen. Valiollah Qarani, was arrested for plotting to take over the government. During a political crisis in 1961, another army intelligence chief and the head of the SDC were dismissed in a conciliatory gesture to the opposition, demonstrating to all that no one was indispensable to the throne. Despite being related to Muhammad Reza by marriage, General Bakhtiar was replaced when he became too powerful as chief of SAVAK and was accused of planning to overthrow the regime. He later fled into exile and was assassinated by SAVAK in Iraq. When the armed forces chief of staff from 1969 to 1971 asked for more authority than the shah was prepared to grant, the general was immediately sent to Spain as an ambassador.[40]

Because of the shah's controls, critical judgment and professional independence remained underdeveloped in the Iranian armed forces and led to a military system that worked only when the shah was fully functional. Increasingly overwhelmed by trying to run the Artesh single-handedly, Muhammad Reza asked the United States in early 1978 for help in setting up a modern and automated command and control system, indicating that the principal requirement was a foolproof system to protect against coups and maintain absolute control.[41] As 1978 began, the obstacles to coordination and the promotion of tensions among Iran's senior officers and between the services allowed them to ignore the benefits of cooperation and joint operations for military effectiveness. As a result, the Artesh was inflexible and mentally unprepared for dealing with the political crisis that was then gaining momentum. Seemingly incapable of even conceiving of widespread domestic dissent, the Iranian armed forces had no plans, no training, and no equipment for riot control. As the shah desired, the military was divided and led by men unlikely to seize power for themselves. It also was a military unwilling or incapable of rescuing its monarch when the man at the top, dying of cancer, was increasingly unable to save himself.

8

Old Guard, New Guard

Iran's Armed Forces in the Islamic Revolution

BY 1978 THE IRANIAN MILITARY BUILDUP had given Muhammad Reza "the capability to patrol the sea as far south as Madagascar and the skies as far west as Cairo."[1] With his armed forces becoming even more powerful, the shah had declared a new Persian Empire. Blinded by his grand plans, he ignored numerous warning signs about the fraying of his dynasty and armed forces. The shah failed to build the bonds that ensured the historical strengths of Iranian fighting men would be used in his service. In contrast, Ayatollah Khomeini, the people's Imam, kept a clear view of his goals and his plans for the armed forces, and it was among the various revolutionary groups that a sense of Iranian patriotism, resourcefulness, and tenacity in the face of the Pahlavi police state became most pronounced. Once Khomeini rose to be the preeminent leader of the revolution against the shah, he began to bend the Artesh and later the various armed revolutionaries to his grand design with dramatic consequences for Iran's military force structure, roles, and effectiveness.

Mounting Challenges

Although the Islamic Revolution lasted little more than a year, challenges to Muhammad Reza's rule had surged back and forth for most of the preceding decade. In the years leading up to 1978, the shah's regime and its opponents engaged in sporadic battles fomented by a revived Tudeh Party and other leftists and, to a lesser degree, by Islamic militants. The guerrilla groups were decentralized, compartmentalized for security, and fractious. Some were financed by money from mosques, and the major groups, the Fedayeen-e Khalq and Mujahedin-e Khalq (MEK), received assistance from the Palestine Liberation Organization (PLO) and probably Libya. They used guerrilla warfare to provoke regime repression and show that it was possible to act against Pahlavi autocracy. Operating from Gilan's mountains and forests, the Fedayeen-e Khalq initiated a period of intense activity with an attack on a Gendarmerie post in Siakal in February

1971 that left several gendarmes and guerrillas dead. The radicals, using bank robberies to fund their activities, followed the subsequent regime crackdown with a campaign of assassinations and bombings. The MEK, which came from the religious wing of the Tudeh Party and wanted to link Shiism with modern ideas, also fought with security forces and conducted bombings, assassinations, kidnappings, and attacks on American citizens. The MEK assassinated four U.S. military officers between 1973 and 1976, killed an Iranian employee of the embassy mistaken for a U.S. diplomat, and in August 1976 gunned down three civilian employees of Rockwell International.

SAVAK was generally effective in countering guerrillas, although it took them several years to stop the violence. With four thousand full-time agents and scores of part-time informers, SAVAK cooperated with the army, Gendarmerie, and police through the Joint Anti-Terrorist Committee created in 1972 to coordinate antiguerrilla operations nationwide. The security services conducted virtually unrestrained operations against the guerrillas and surveilled government bureaucracies, censored the press, and interfered with and monitored university classes in going after the young intelligentsia, especially college students, teachers, and engineers, who manned the guerrilla groups. However, while SAVAK had dossiers on many if not most of the secular revolutionaries, it failed to penetrate their networks. The security forces also knew little about the religious opposition. Between 1971 and 1977, nearly 200 guerrillas and members of armed political groups died in gun battles while another 165 were executed, tortured to death, shot while trying to escape, or allegedly committed suicide. By early 1976, these heavy losses forced the guerrillas to reconsider their tactics and reduce violent activities. The groups remained intact, however, and added new members, kept their weapons stored, and were ready to provide muscle to the popular revolution when it began in early 1978.[2]

Other opposition to the shah was fragmented, demoralized, and nearly depoliticized during the early 1970s, but discontent was growing. In particular, the conspicuous consumption of the newly affluent angered the poor, while the lower and middle classes seethed over unmet expectations and the government's poor economic performance. Popular alienation against the throne and the perceived influence of foreign powers increased because of the shah's emphasis on Iran's royal heritage over its Islamic history, his ties to Israel, and the seeming subordination to U.S. interests and Western culture. By May 1977 Iran faced a major recession, increased unemployment among the millions of urban poor, and the inflation-induced collapse of the value of professional salaries. In the middle of these troubles, the shah made small gestures of political freedom in response to Carter administration and international pressure that only succeeded in bringing opposition activities into the open. The mullahs, especially the exiled Ayatollah Khomeini, became a focal point for popular antagonism against Muhammad Reza. As 1978 began the monarch had lost the support of the major landowners, the merchants, and just about every other segment of society except for the military and senior regime officials.

The Fuse Is Lit

When it came, the revolution spread quickly as the initial violence fed a series of incidents at regular intervals throughout Iran that the shah and his security services failed to contain. Strong repressive responses in early 1978 were followed by regime attempts at reconciliation and appeasement that ultimately gave way to indecision, paralysis, and mutiny in the Iranian armed forces. The government ignited the popular rebellion on January 7, 1978, when it placed an anonymous editorial in a major newspaper that blamed recent protests on Communists and Islamic extremists, including Khomeini, who was described in an obscene way to suggest he was a British agent. Enraged religious students protested the next day in the religious center of Qom. The police fired on the crowd, wounding hundreds and killing more than a dozen, including two mullahs whose blood-soaked turbans were displayed outside the main mosque. After the riots spread to Tabriz, the shah declared martial law, but a cycle of violence was already in motion. Among the Shia and some other Muslims, mourning ceremonies are held for the dead at prescribed intervals, and *arbain,* the forty-day anniversary, is the most important. Senior clerics declared that the dead protestors were martyrs and called for a national observance of *arbain* for them. The ceremony resulted in more protests, violence, and death, which was then repeated through the year as new martyrs were created.

During the rioting in Tabriz, the army had its first major clash with antigovernment forces since 1963, bringing in tanks to restore order. The demonstrations continued with violent clashes in Yazd in late March and in Kermanshah and seven other cities in early April. Tehran University students refused to attend classes and held sit-ins, clashing with army paratroopers in early May on the *arbain* for Yazd's martyrs. In mid-May in Qom, army commandos shot followers of Grand Ayatollah Muhammad Kazim Shariat-Madari, a moderate cleric, who then joined the opposition and took most of the other religious moderates with him. Iran's network of mosques joined the opposition, transmitting messages and instructions throughout the country. Soon thereafter, the first chants of "down with the shah" were heard. In July, Mashhad, Esfahan, and Arak erupted in serious violence. Some cities were put under martial law with nighttime curfews, and the army, stationed on Iranian city streets for the first time since 1963, was seemingly unable to adapt to the large-scale disorder.

By late summer 1978, the Iranian monarch decided to accommodate the more moderate elements at the revolution's margins as striking workers in key industries joined the protestors. Muhammad Reza removed General Nassiri as the head of SAVAK, sending him to Pakistan as ambassador. He then fired nearly three dozen other SAVAK officers, severely demoralizing the security services. But the shah's carrot-and-stick approach failed to buy peace. Instead, the opposition saws signs of weakness and indecision that caused them to increase their demands. On August 19, 1978, the twenty-fifth anniversary of the 1953 coup, nearly four hundred people were killed in a fire at the Cinema Rex movie theater in Abadan. It was later determined that Islamic militants, who had conducted earlier arson attacks on theaters showing "sinful" films, were responsible for the fire. At the time, however, the public blamed SAVAK and local security forces because Abandan's police chief had been in charge in Qom during the January riots and the movie was about antigovernment guerrilla activities. The public was enraged by the seeming cold-blooded murders, and by the end of August soldiers watched as marches of tens of thousands of Iranians in Tehran grew into massive rallies of hundreds of thousands. These events caused the government to resign, and the shah formed a government of national reconciliation while hard-line military commanders seethed.

The attempted reconciliation was stillborn amid the confusion caused by Muhammad Reza's spasmodic switches between violence and accommodation. In early September large peaceful demonstrations demanding free elections, the release of political prisoners, and observance of the 1906 Constitution took place in Tehran and other cities. During these marches, the protestors made a special effort to establish rapport with the soldiers lining the streets, putting flowers in gun barrels and encouraging the conscripts to join them. Worried by these developments, the shah declared martial law, ordered more troops into the streets, and made Maj. Gen. Gholam Ali Oveissi, a strident promonarchy officer, governor of Tehran. The government failed to broadcast the martial law declaration, however, and the next morning, on September 8, 1978, students and other Iranians took to the streets unaware of the decree. When the protestors failed to respond to orders to disperse, security personnel enforced the new law. In the ensuing encounter, up to two hundred people in Jaleh Square and a few hundred more across the city were killed in what became known as Black Friday.

The Jaleh Square massacre reportedly horrified the shah but also caused the revolutionaries to pause briefly and consider the consequences of their actions. The government then mishandled what possibly was one of its best opportunities to reassert control. Some revolutionary leaders were arrested but soon were released as the regime tried to find the right balance between repression and compromise. The security forces were ordered to fire only into the air unless they were attacked, and unpopular security officials were dismissed to appease the public. The revolutionaries, who repeatedly became more cautious when the military appeared resolute, constantly probed for signs of weakness and acted boldly when convinced the army and police would not. In late September the government arrested more SAVAK officers, and General Nassiri was recalled from Pakistan and jailed. Such concessions only made the regime appear weaker, and the mixed approach of civilian government offering conciliation while the military was confrontational solidified the opposition and undermined the shah's credibility. In a fateful mistake, Muhammad Reza demanded in early October that Iraq expel Khomeini in a fruitless attempt to silence him. The Imam went to Paris, where press exposure and better telecommunications gave him even greater prominence inside Iran as he urged the monarchy's overthrow and the establishment of an Islamic republic.

The Army Steps In

The shah's military options may not have been as great as the revolutionaries feared, but the possible outcomes of a stronger application of Iran's armed forces to save the monarchy remains a great "what if" of Iranian history. As events played out, the imposition of martial law in early September 1978 marked the beginning of the bloodiest phase of the revolution. Still, the Artesh and other security services were unprepared. The focus on external threats and projecting imperial might had degraded readiness for internal security. The weapons and training for crowd control were unavailable. Police clubs, twenty-five thousand canisters of tear gas, and other riot equipment were finally purchased from the United States in November, but the delivery came too late to help. The shah and many of his commanders were unconvinced that military action could do more than increase the government's unpopularity. In the aftermath of Black Friday, the Iranian ruler had rebuked his generals, creating divisions within the government and raising doubts about his will to keep power. Similarly, the armed forces may have lacked the determination to prevail regardless of the generals' actions. The economic and political divisions among the various ranks were widening, morale sank, and soldiers often refused to fire on crowds while some fraternized with the revolutionaries. Worst of all, the indecisive shah for too long nursed the unrealistic hope that he could bargain with the revolutionary leaders. Khomeini, meanwhile, was willing to create martyrs by the tens of thousands to prevail.[3]

The shah's mix of political concessions with martial law, aggravated by restrictions on the military, had a debilitating effect on security. Muhammad Reza's top commanders were men desperately seeking strong leadership from the throne. The chief of staff of the armed forces, General Azhari, was a loyal but unambitious soldier. According to the American ambassador, the other senior flag officers reflected their services. General Oveissi, the hard-line army commander, was solid, unimaginative, and conservative. General Rabii, the air force chief, was dashing and enthusiastic. The navy commander, Admiral Habibollahi, was a serious intellectual, professionally competent, dedicated, and loyal to the shah. General Qarabaghi, the head of the Gendarmerie, was a personal favorite of the shah and very political.[4] The service chiefs were unaccustomed to working as a team and, absent strong direction, the selfishness and rivalry nurtured by Muhammad Reza over the years became an additional hindrance to military efforts to deflate rising revolutionary sentiments. As martial law was extended to Iran's other major cities in September, the shah repeatedly scolded Oveissi for fatal shootings and reprimanded commanders for ordering their men to shoot to kill in self-defense. Not surprisingly, the security forces became increasingly incapable of making decisions at the local level and wavered between inaction and harsh responses, an inconsistency that emboldened the revolutionaries.

On November 4, 1978, the anniversary of Khomeini's exile in 1964, a student protest turned into a major riot in Tehran. Oveissi ordered the army not to intervene, allegedly hoping that the shah would be forced to set up a military government with the army commander as its head. The violence did convince the beleaguered monarch that a military cabinet was needed, but he named the middling General Azhari as prime minister. This government soon was revealed to be military in name only. The service commanders retained their respective commands and left day-to-day administration of the ministries to their civilian deputies. More important, the increasingly withdrawn monarch was still in charge of policy, and the new military government was not given new powers to apply martial law more effectively. The military government probably was the regime's last chance to stem the tide of revolution; the shah could make significant compromises to isolate and undercut the Islamic militants or unleash the armed forces and put Iran's fate in their hands. Both options were unpalatable to the autocratic ruler, and he precariously continued to straddle the widening divide.

The Revolutionaries' Tactics

Khomeini and other antishah leaders identified the armed forces as the key to the revolution's success early in 1978. From the beginning, they wanted to neutralize the military. The more far-seeing Khomeini anticipated that he would need the military to prevent leftists and autonomy-seeking ethnic minorities from undermining the Islamic republic he intended to establish. So he promoted violent and peaceful means to nullify the military's influence while maintaining its cohesion. On the one hand, leftist guerrilla and militant Islamic groups attacked army patrols and checkpoints. They also mixed in with peaceful protests to try to provoke the security forces into firing into the crowds to incite more anger and chaos. On the other hand, fraternization, propaganda, and psychological warfare were used to present military personnel options beyond obedience to their commanders. Khomeini famously ordered his followers: "Do not attack the army in its breast, but in its heart. You must appeal to the soldiers' hearts even if they fire on you and kill you. Let them kill five thousand, ten thousand, twenty thousand—they are our brothers, and we will welcome them."[5]

The revolutionaries' tactics to disarm the military were much less forgiving than Khomeini's order suggested. Behind invitations to join the revolution were religious edicts and threats designed to disconcert and endanger the conscripts and professionals. Military personnel were told they had a religious duty to desert and were threatened with being declared unbelievers for serving the regime. Parents were used to persuade their sons to abandon their posts. Khomeini threatened jihad against the military and denounced the Artesh as being under American command, a threat and charge sure to upset the mostly religious conscripts who feared being branded as fighting for infidels. Prodded by Khomeini, the religious opposition stepped up the protests in late 1978, constantly confronting the troops with the prospect of being forced to take violent action against other young Iranians. The chant of "God is Great" from rooftops and the protestors' wear of white burial shrouds helped unnerve the soldiers. Midlevel and senior officers, meanwhile, faced constant harassment and intimidation.

To supplement these coercive tactics, the revolutionaries tried to persuade military personnel to join their cause. Soldiers' grievances were included in the demonstrators' slogans and speeches. The antishah forces tried to split the less prosperous junior officers and poor enlisted men from the relatively affluent senior officers, reminding them that their families were suffering from economic difficulties along with all Iranians. In dealing with the air force, the opposition played up the class differences between the *homafars* and the commissioned officers. Military personnel also were reminded of the religious sanctions given to opposition activity, and mullahs addressed conscripts from their provinces using local languages and dialects to elicit support. In addition to placing flowers in rifle barrels and garlands on tank guns, the revolutionaries occasionally offered civilian clothes and bus fare to the soldiers. In contrast, the shah's hesitant government provided no clear guidance and no vision of the future. Not surprisingly, Iran's military personnel increasingly sympathized with their fellow citizens and were attracted by opposition promises of a better future. As enlisted personnel deserted in droves or disobeyed orders to fire on demonstrators, the officer corps became frustrated and divided. By the end of the year, concern over their senior leadership's inaction and the reliability of their troops caused many officers to become passive observers or, if able, to submit retirement papers. Desertions and absenteeism increased at an alarming rate, jumping from one hundred to two hundred per day in early 1978 to more than one thousand each day by the end of the year. In December, the army division at Mashhad was virtually disbanded by mutinies and desertions.

The dwindling military services faced an "enemy within" as leftists, Islamic militants, or their sympathizers penetrated units at all ranks. In late December, some of the troops assigned to protect the U.S. embassy shouted pro-Khomeini and anti-American slogans as a mob burned an official car at the embassy gate. Sympathetic soldiers, NCOs, and junior officers distributed leaflets, tapes of Khomeini's speeches, and news reports about violence in the provinces to arouse fear and goad fellow soldiers into desertion. In addition, following the initial incident of subversion in which a helicopter was destroyed at Esfahan in October, prorevolution military personnel increasingly engaged in sabotage at military bases. Later, the regime was confronted by the prospect of disloyalty in its most elite units when a small group of officers and enlisted men from the Imperial Guard attacked the officers' mess hall. The early December assault killed more than a dozen officers and wounded a few dozen more officers and NCOs.

New Governments with No Answers

The military government created in early November was no match for the revolutionaries. To stifle unrest, the new cabinet expanded press censorship and closed the universities, high schools, and even the bazaar. Uncertainty over the change bought the regime a few weeks of peace, but by late November strikes and demonstrations had resumed. Tanks roamed Tehran's streets, but the loss of electricity, water, and oil paralyzed the capital except for the daily clashes between troops and protestors. Qom and Mashhad slipped out of government control. Marches were banned, but the regime was unable to enforce its rules as crowds grew into the hundreds of thousands. In this environment the lackluster General Azhari, with no real following in the military, had no stomach for confrontation. The shah's unwillingness to appoint a strong military leader over a mediocre loyalist was further sabotaging his prospects for survival. With an eye toward reestablishing the status quo at some point, Muhammad Reza could not break his habit of using rivalry and resentments among his senior commanders to prevent the rise of a potential alternative to his rule. The result was a senior command structure unable to coordinate action to stop the revolution.

The new government was divided and indecisive over increasing its repression. The two most senior air force officers, Deputy Minister of Defense Hassan Toufanian and General Rabii, refused to cooperate with General Azhari on grounds that he had given most of the government posts to army personnel.[6] All the senior officers continued their direct contacts with the shah to influence his decisions. The primary promoters of firm actions were Oveissi and Major Generals Manuchehr Khosrowdad, the commander of Iran's army aviation units, and Abbas Ali Badrei, the commander of the Imperial Guard. Despite backing from Washington, Muhammad Reza remained reluctant to use decisive force against his people. Instead, he listened to Azhari and others who advocated the arrest and punishment of former officials as the only way to mollify the public and restore calm. This convinced many senior officers that loyalty to the throne did not guarantee safety and added to their demoralization. After suffering a heart attack in late December that allowed him to resign, a despondent Azhari told the American ambassador, "This country is lost because the King cannot make up his mind."[7]

As 1979 began Muhammad Reza still lacked the will to order a serious crackdown. Suffering from lymphomatous cancer, which he had kept secret from everyone, the shah's medical situation had deteriorated during 1978. He was increasingly lethargic, withdrawn, and depressed and was looking to Washington for guidance. Yet he rejected repeated American entreaties to take more decisive action. Instead, he ended martial law, removed the military government, and asked Shahpour Bakhtiar, a liberal elder statesman whom he disliked, to form a new government. Once again Muhammad Reza chose poorly. Bakhtiar led the revived National Front, the successor to Mossadeq's coalition, but he lacked a popular following, had no ties to the clerics and militants, and had no support in the armed forces. Bakhtiar agreed to form a government in return for concessions from the shah, including assurances of military support, the retirement of some hard-line generals, and the power to name the minister of war. The ailing monarch also agreed to appoint a regency council and leave the country "on vacation" after the Majles approved the new cabinet. The compromises and agreements started to break down almost immediately. Oveissi, Rabii, and Khosrowdad, the hard-liners Bakhtiar wanted out, resigned as agreed in early January but stayed on duty because no replacements were named. Bakhtiar then appointed Feridun Jam, a former army chief of staff, as war minister, but when the shah rejected Jam's demand that the service chiefs report directly to him, the retired general withdrew from the cabinet. The Bakhtiar government was seen by many Iranians as merely a fig leaf for the shah's departure, which, in turn, signaled significant erosion of the military's political power.[8]

As Iran's military government collapsed, the U.S. government recognized that the shah's days were numbered. In early January President Carter sent U.S. Air Force General Robert Huyser, the Deputy Commander of the European Command, to persuade Iran's senior military leadership to remain in Iran, prevent the military's disintegration, and support a strong and stable constitutional government. In addition, Huyser, who had close ties with Iranian air force commanders, was to work with the generals on contingency plans for a military takeover. None of the shah's military leaders, however, was prepared to take the reins of power. Even the most dynamic among them showed little initiative, and Huyser found the senior commanders thinking about leaving rather than planning to support or replace a postshah Bakhtiar government. Gen. Abbas Qarabaghi, the new SDC Chief of Staff, complained that he had no experience with planning because the shah had always handled plans. The service chiefs also appeared unable to act without the detailed guidance they were accustomed to getting from the throne. In blunt terms Huyser encouraged Qarabaghi and the chiefs to accept responsibility for sustaining the military's cohesion and to work together on plans to deal with the crisis. The senior Iranian commanders, however, tried to get the Americans to do most of the planning while they remained unsupportive of Bakhtiar because of the prime minister's antimonarchy views.[9]

When Muhammad Reza announced that he would leave Iran, the hardliners pushed without success for more authority to facilitate greater repression or a military takeover. Despite some differences in views, the generals worked with Huyser and other American officers on a contingency plan to take over if the Bakhtiar government fell. Fearful of the impact of the shah's departure on the military, Qarabaghi begged his sovereign not to leave, making support for Bakhtiar contingent on the shah's presence in Iran. Bakhtiar's authority already was waning after one general publicly said that the army would not follow the prime minister and then was not reprimanded by Muhammad Reza. During his last weeks in Iran, however, the shah had become resigned about military matters and did nothing to clarify control of the armed forces or delegate any of his authority. The lack of clear instructions set the stage for later divisiveness among them and with the civilian government. Qarabaghi had to deny military coup rumors to the public and warned that the armed forces would deal harshly with any takeover attempts by subordinate units.

Muhammad Reza Shah Pahlavi spent the day before he left Iran forever saying good-bye to the Immortals and his senior military officers. After his plane took off on January 16, 1979, Tehran erupted in celebrations with mobs attacking statues of the shah and his father and, in the words of General Huyser, "symbolically killing him."[10] The Iranian commanders executed plans for a military show of strength by putting more soldiers on the streets, conducting air force overflights of Tehran, and printing press pieces about the Imperial Guard's willingness to fight. But the postshah government was beset from all sides with strikes and protests threatening to shut down the country, while the armed forces were not up to the job of stabilizing Iran. Their proclivity toward inaction solidified around their uncertainty about the loyalty of their troops, their mixed views about supporting Bakhtiar, and their deep divisions over taking control or trying to deal with the revolutionaries. Despite assurances to Huyser, even the hard-liners showed no real capacity or willingness to plan for a military takeover.

The generals were in full agreement that allowing Khomeini to return to Iran would be disastrous, but after Bakhtiar reluctantly gave permission for the Imam to fly to Iran the officers split again. Qarabaghi threatened to resign but was prevailed upon to remain, in part by promises from American officials that the United States was quietly working to prevent Khomeini from returning. The chiefs used their very real concerns about protecting Khomeini and the potential for a bloodbath if anything happened to the ayatollah to justify the closure of the Tehran airport, which temporarily delayed Khomeini's arrival. In the meantime, senior military officers contacted Khomeini's lieutenants in Iran. Although the focus was on the Imam's security, the talks also were the start of the military's acquiescence in the revolution's victory. Soon thereafter, a declaration of solidarity with Khomeini by some senior and lower-ranking military personnel was being publicly distributed.

Huyser's attempt to keep the military loyal to Bakhtiar and prevent their flight or defection to Khomeini had only marginal success. His mission seemed to have been misperceived by all Iranians. The generals wanted Huyser to tell them what to do, the shah came to believe that the American general was responsible for arranging a deal between the revolutionaries and the military to end the monarchy, and the revolutionaries were convinced Huyser was in Iran to promote a coup. The leftists and Islamic militants exploited Huyser's dealings with the Iranian military to portray Iran's military leaders as puppets to increase the alienation of the rank and file from the commanders, hastening the Artesh's collapse from within. Until nearly the end, Huyser thought that the Iranian armed forces were capable of taking control if Bakhtiar gave the order and was convinced that Generals Rabii, Toufanian, and Badrei were ready to act. In saying farewell to Iran's military leaders, however, Huyser claimed that he questioned their will to act and warned that if they did not act soon they would still face a crisis when the Bakhtiar government inevitably collapsed. The Iranians were stoically silent in the face of the implied criticism of their courage. However, many of these officers followed Huyser's advice, bravely stayed in Iran, and were among the first to be tried and executed by the Islamic Republic.[11]

Surrender

When Khomeini arrived from Paris on February 1, 1979, the military's collapse became imminent. The armed forces allowed the revolutionaries to provide the Ayatollah's security, and the only uniformed presence at the airport was pro-Khomeini air force technicians. A show of strength in the capital backfired when the opposition used the opportunity to fraternize with the troops and claim that the armed forces had turned out to welcome the Imam. The decision to allow Khomeini back also influenced many officers and their subordinates to accept the idea of accommodating the revolutionaries. In the days before the Imam's return, Qarabaghi met with Khomeini's lieutenants to try to negotiate an end to the increasing violence in Iran. Turning aside requests to align the military with the revolution, Qarabaghi reminded Khomeini's supporters that

Iran's officers and soldiers had taken an oath of loyalty on the Koran to protect the constitution and support the legitimate government. His refusal to switch sides possibly contributed to a resumption of armed attacks on the military during a general breakdown in law and order as the revolutionaries stole automatic weapons from government armories and occupied government buildings.

On his first day back in Iran Khomeini dismissed the importance of the military's oath by declaring the Bakhtiar government illegitimate and announcing the creation of the Islamic Revolutionary Council, a de facto provisional government. Mehdi Bazargan, the leader of a movement of secular students and political activists that grew out of the Khomeini-inspired protests of 1963, was the head of the council. Bazargan had recognized Khomeini's appeal early on and aligned with the grand ayatollah to counter communism and promote social justice in a liberal, nationalistic, and Islamic Iran. The hapless Bakhtiar struggled to assert his authority, in part because the armed forces, freed from the shah's control, were increasingly unresponsive and unsupportive. As the two rival governments sought to win over the once formidable Artesh, Khomeini addressed the armed forces, praising the military personnel who had joined the revolution, promising protection to defectors, and threatening prosecution of those who failed to break from the regime. The army began to reduce its presence in Tehran as the increasingly isolated armed forces lost their will to fight. Growing numbers of military personnel joined the revolutionaries, mutinied, or deserted. On every base and garrison, the shah's loyalists and defectors to Khomeini vied for control as orders and counterorders flowed from the two governments.

The Iranian air force, arguably the service closest to the United States, led the switch of allegiances from the shah to Khomeini. Ten days before the ayatollah's return, more than eight hundred *homafars* declared their fidelity to Khomeini and took over air force bases at Dezful and Hamadan in the first mass mutiny by military personnel. A few days later, General Rabii reported the arrest and transfers of hundreds of dissident *homafars* and commissioned officers. Following the Imam's arrival, increasing numbers of military personnel and civilian employees of the military establishment declared their solidarity with the revolution. Officers at all ranks expressed a willingness to serve under Khomeini, and even Qarabaghi started to waiver. After addressing graduating military academy cadets on nonintervention in politics, support for the constitution, and support for the legitimate government in early February, the chief of staff omitted the pledge of loyalty to the shah from the commissioning oath. Two days later, dozens of air force officers in full dress uniform paid their respects to the Imam and switched allegiance to the Islamic Revolution.

Iran's armed forces then collapsed in a matter of days. On the evening of February 9, 1979, a television rerun of Khomeini's arrival in Tehran excited the emotions at air force bases in the capital. Fighting broke out between pro-Khomeini *homafars* and cadets and progovernment officers, NCOs, and airmen. At Doshan Tappeh fistfights led to gunfire as the *homafars* tried to take control of the airbase and elements of the Imperial Guard joined the battle. At Faraha-bad airbase, mutineers joined by civilian revolutionaries eventually forced Imperial Guard units to retreat. They then seized a nearby machine gun factory and distributed the captured weapons to antiregime fighters. At roughly the same time, the *homafars* at Doshan Tappeh were handing out weapons taken from the base armory. Thus armed, leftist guerrillas and Islamic militants spread the fighting into the city. Khomeini denounced a government-proclaimed curfew and warned that any moves by the armed forces to oppose the revolution would cause him to proclaim holy war against the Artesh.

Iran's military leaders still were unable to come together to respond to this new crisis. Part of the Imperial Guards' Javidan Brigade, the Immortals, was sent to reinforce progovernment units at Doshen Tappeh. The column, which included as many as thirty tanks, was stopped by thousands of revolutionaries, who set up barricades and shot the column commander and several other officers. Consideration was given to ordering the air force to bomb the machine gun factory, but Rabii refused because armed revolutionaries and unarmed civilians were mixed at the site. Qarabaghi also contemplated using elite paratroopers to recapture the factory, but the commander of the Aviation Command and his deputy could not be located. The military's hollowness was revealed further as desertions soared and officers switched their units' allegiance to Bazargan's provisional government. U.S. ambassador Sullivan and the American military attaché reported that some Imperial Guard tanks and other members of elite units defected to the revolutionaries or mutinied. As the government's defenses crumbled at day's end, armed guerrillas attacked military bases, overran U.S. facilities, and captured the notorious Evin Prison to release the political prisoners there.

After nightfall the government belatedly discussed taking harsh measures to control violence and enforce martial law. With most units already struggling with law and order missions, the army commander was reluctant to call on the Immortals. Badrei still believed these soldiers were so dedicated that they might undermine the armed forces' cohesion by clashing with mutinous units. He allowed the bulk of the Javidan Brigade to remain unused at palaces and other buildings around the city. Infantry units from Qazvin were ordered to Tehran, but revolutionaries blocked the main highway and prevented their arrival. Badrei issued an order putting the Imperial Guard at SAVAK's disposal, apparently unaware that the organization had already collapsed. Instructions to set up barricades and shoot-to-kill orders for violators of the curfew also were dispatched.

The security forces, however, were in no shape to respond and were hampered, in part, by standing orders designed to prevent coup attempts and limit access to ammunition for heavy weapons.[12]

The end came the next day when the Artesh's ranking officers chose to move to the sidelines to salvage the armed forces. After daybreak on February 11, the revolutionaries and mutinous military personnel captured more police stations and army barracks to confiscate weapons. Others seized the state radio to transmit instructions and propaganda. Fighting flared up again at Doshen Tappeh, and General Rabii capitulated. Before the day was out, General Badrei was assassinated outside his headquarters, and General Mehdi Rahimi, the Martial Law Commander, declared that he could no longer resist the revolutionaries. That morning Qarabaghi convened a meeting of the senior military leadership to discuss their next actions. Twenty-seven flag-rank officers reported on the dire security situation and the breakdown in military discipline. Their discussion then turned to a proposal to declare neutrality in the political struggle. One by one each man stated his support for such a declaration either to maintain the armed forces' unity or to join the people in backing Khomeini. A statement was prepared and signed by twenty-four of those present. Issued at midday, the pronouncement reaffirmed the armed forces' duty to defend Iran's independence and territorial integrity but declared neutrality to avert further chaos and bloodshed. The senior commanders then ordered all military units to return to their barracks. As the generals anticipated, the declaration was the death warrant for Bakhtiar's government. The prime minister went into hiding, and his government disintegrated.[13]

Because Qarabaghi did not offer to support the provisional government, it was slow to stop the assaults on military facilities. Although the generals had intended that military bases would be protected as the troops returned, the revolutionaries continued to confiscate weapons and equipment. Qarabaghi's own headquarters was besieged and his deputy was forced to surrender by early evening. As night fell nearly two dozen military installations were in the revolutionaries' hands. Admiral Majidi, the navy's deputy commander, ordered his personnel not to fire on crowds, basically joining the revolutionary side. Others had already accommodated the new order, including at least three army generals and the chief of SAVAK, who had cooperated with Khomeini's provisional government before the military's collapse. General Hossein Fardust, perhaps the shah's closest friend, abandoned the regime, allegedly sharing secrets with the Soviets and leftists groups in case the latter seized power, while also cooperating with Khomeini's followers. (Fardust later was rewarded by being entrusted with turning SAVAK into a new prorevolutionary security organization, the Organization of the Iranian Nation's Security and Information, or SAVAMA.) The fighting lasted until February 12, when the fiercely defended Imperial Guards barracks were finally captured and Khomeini and Bazargan appealed to the people to stop attacking military installations. Iranian newspapers reported that roughly 650 were killed and 2,700 wounded in the three days of fighting. For the entire revolutionary period from January 1978 to February 1979, as many as ten thousand Iranians may have died in the violent protests and other dissident activities.

The new revolutionary government immediately issued orders to uniformed and civilian members of the armed forces to return to work, including those who had deserted during the preceding year. Khomeini announced that the Artesh and police were now part of the revolution, and his officials stated their desire to rebuild the military. Despite these professions of support, many enlisted men and officers failed to return. They apparently had a better sense of Khomeini's ultimate goals and will to power than the generals, who probably hoped that the revolution could be moderated when they stood aside at a key moment. Khomeini and his militant supporters, however, had little use for the Artesh's senior leaders as they worked to consolidate their control over the country.

The Revolutionary Guard

The Islamic Revolution succeeded in large part because of its unprecedented mass participation, but the lack of shared goals beyond the shah's removal created major problems for regime consolidation and the postrevolution military. By mid-February 1979 competition between leftists and Islamic militants had become deadly, while the armed forces, weaker by the day, were hardly a factor. Despite their political differences, the revolutionary groups agreed that the Artesh's political influence should be ended, its size reduced, and senior officer privileges removed. Gen. Muhammad Vali Qarani was appointed chief of staff by Khomeini to replace Qarabaghi, who had fled into exile, and Admiral Madani was made defense minister. Qarani complained that he had "inherited an army that did not have a single soldier in Tehran."[14] His immediate contribution to the situation hardly helped matters as he dissolved the Imperial Guards and retired more than 120 generals and admirals. Indiscipline was rife in the undermanned and sometimes leaderless commands. Under the influence of radicals, some soldiers formed revolutionary councils to bring charges against their officers and oversee unit operations. To ease public resistance to the draft, which was not being enforced, the tour of duty for conscripts was reduced from twenty-four to twelve months, and men were allowed to serve in their home provinces. The new government also cancelled contracts for weapons and military construction, expelled foreign advisers and technicians, and brought home Iranian soldiers serving in Lebanon and Oman.

With the military dispirited and mistrusted, Khomeini's new Islamic Republic needed its own organized armed forces to establish the emerging clerical regime's monopoly on power. At the time, the MEK and Fedayeen had between fifteen thousand and twenty thousand armed guerrillas, while the Tudeh Party had about seven thousand armed men and women in Tehran alone. Militant Islamic groups aided by cadres of Lebanese Shia and Palestinians had nearly twenty thousand fighters while another twenty thousand or more armed Iranians were in the streets after the military's armories were looted. Many of the Islamic militants had formed *komitehs,* or revolutionary committees, around mosques to handle local security and enforce their interpretation of Islamic law. Some *komitehs* were called Hizballah (Party of God) or Ansar-e Hizballah (Partisans of the Party of God), but were more popularly known as the *chomaqdars,* or club wielders, because of their violent methods of exerting authority. The clerics around Khomeini understood that discipline needed to be imposed on these various Iranian fighters and selected the *komitehs* to be the nucleus of the new organization.

In early May Khomeini issued a decree creating the Islamic Revolutionary Guard Corps (Sepah-e Pasdaran-e Enqelab-e Eslami) to channel the *komitehs'* energy to restore order and enforce Islamic law. One of its primary missions was to serve as a counterweight to the regular armed forces during the chaotic birth of the Islamic Republic. As important, the Guard, also known as the Pasdaran, tried to absorb as many of the other armed revolutionary groups as possible to prevent them from becoming a threat to the regime. Although its members eventually were given military fatigues without insignia or rank to wear, the Pasdaran's first loyalty was to the clerics and not the new government. The Guard initially enlisted six thousand men drawn from those who had fought against the shah's regime before 1978 and had received some guerrilla training with Palestinian and Lebanese groups. The first group, which provided the Guard's leadership, tended to be better educated and politically sophisticated. Later recruits were zealous volunteers drawn from the urban poor. Behzad Nabavi and Mohsen Rezai, two of the Guard's early senior leaders, were former MEK members who had split from the leftists because of the group's emphasis on Marxist philosophy over Islamic theology. Their splinter group, the Mujahedin of the Islamic Revolution (MIR), strongly supported the Islamic character of the revolution, fought fiercely against the shah's security forces, and then helped to secure the streets after the monarchy collapsed. MIR members were instrumental in the Pasdaran's creation, serving as the core around which the rest of the Guard formed.[15]

The Revolutionary Guard quickly developed into a central pillar of the regime. The Guard's first task was to restore order and dislodge other revolutionaries from government buildings and military bases, but it soon faced ethnic rebellions and leftist attempts to usurp power that fueled the expansion of the Pasdaran's size, responsibilities, and its national command structure. The

Pasdaran also was given law enforcement authority, ran prisons, protected government facilities, and served as bodyguards for regime leaders. The strong resistance by Kurdish and other rebellious ethnic groups led to the creation of more conventional Guard military units, and the Guard's leaders grudgingly began limited cooperation with the Artesh in training and operations. At the same time, the battles with leftists and the clerics' distrust of the regular military led to the creation of Pasdaran intelligence and counterintelligence offices. Guard military units set up their barracks near garrison exits to ensure that regular army units did not move without proper authorization from Khomeini. Later, the Basij (Basij-e Mostazafan, or mobilization forces of the oppressed) was created as a popular militia and reserve component for the Guards. A National Mobilization Staff with representatives from the Guard, *komitehs*, clerical groups, and the army was created in late 1979 and arranged for basic military training and political indoctrination for the *basijis* to be provided by Pasdaran members and regular army junior officers and NCOs.

From the start the Pasdaran was a political force in Iran, involved in regime in-fighting and confronting political divisions within its own ranks. Its mission to defend the purity of the Islamic Revolution, later enshrined in Iran's constitution, allowed for participation in politics. Guard leaders considered themselves free from civilian political authority other than the Supreme Leader and fought against Bazargan's attempts to control them. They also felt free to use force as they saw fit. Khomeini, who wanted to strengthen the organization, saw that some checks on the Pasdaran were needed, if only to stem growing popular dislike of the Guards' arbitrary behavior. Mostafa Chamran, appointed defense minister in May, was ordered to work with a newly established Supreme Command and the ruling Revolutionary Council to centralize authority. At his behest the Pasdaran's chain of command was formalized, and clerical supervision was arranged for all Pasdaran units down to the local level. Future Iranian presidents Ali Khamenei and Ali Akbar Hashemi Rafsanjani served as Khomeini's clerical representative to the Guard, a relationship that became a major factor in the ascendancy of the pro-Khomeini Islamic Republican Party (IRP) over other factions in the new government.

Before the Pasdaran's factionalism receded, it played an important role in the political battles between the IRP and the first elected president of the Islamic Republic, Abol Hasan Bani Sadr. A secular intellectual and respected moderate, Bani Sadr had joined with Khomeini in Iraq, served as finance minister for the Revolutionary Council, and received the Imam's backing for the January 1980 presidential election. In February Khomeini delegated to Bani Sadr his powers as the armed forces' commander in chief, including authority over the Revolutionary Guard. The new president wanted to reorganize and restore traditional institutions, including the Artesh, Gendarmerie, and police, and absorb or abolish the revolutionary organizations, including the Guard. The Pasdaran's leaders quickly coalesced to oppose Bani Sadr and undermine his authority. When Bani Sadr made Abbas Zamani, a veteran of the revolution and the Lebanese civil war, the new Guard commander, other Guard leaders opposed him. Zamani resigned after a month, citing his inability to administer the Pasdaran. The Guard forced Mohsen Rezai on Bani Sadr as the new Pasdaran commander, and after this success Guard leaders were no longer responsive to presidential authority. The new Guard leadership, unlike their predecessors, offered full-throated support for Islamic consolidation and acquiesced in the ruling clerics' campaign of religious and civic indoctrination for all Pasdaran units. This effort was accompanied by purges of leftists, and as the Guard expanded to twenty-five thousand members, or *pasdars*, by mid-1980, other clerical opponents and undesirable elements were expunged from the service. During this period the committed and capable commanders who were distinguishing themselves against restive minorities were being promoted and exercising influence that strengthened Guard cohesion along with the clerics' monopoly of power.

Consolidation

The Artesh was the main target of the new regime's efforts to settle scores and eliminate potential counterrevolutionary challenges. Iran's new leaders executed the shah's top military leaders to satisfy the public clamor for retribution, but the revolutionary government was divided on the scope of planned military purges. The leftists and Marxists wanted to abolish the armed forces and establish a "peoples' army" while Khomeini's followers favored purifying the Artesh with purges and a merger with the revolutionary militias. Bazargan's provisional government and even Khomeini saw a need to retain the regular military's structure and personnel in anticipation of future challenges to the Islamic government. They recognized that discretion was needed because there was no ready cadre of capable pro-Khomeini senior officers to replace the shah's discredited commanders. Eventually, the revolutionary council settled on the goal of consolidating regime control over the Artesh, preventing Islamic militant groups from interfering in military affairs, and creating a smaller standing regular military supported by a large popular reserve force. The Pasdaran and Basij were groomed to help guarantee the military's loyalty, or at least its deference to the new rulers. The mullahs were confident that a divide-and-rule policy would keep the armed forces in line as they built a military with the same political and social characteristics as the clerics. Officers who had family ties with the clergy or who belonged to religious families were promoted while all ranks were heavily indoctrinated.[16]

The purge tribunals started immediately after Bakhtiar's government fell, and punishment was swift and deadly. The first generals to die were martial law commander Rahimi, former SAVAK head Nassiri, Aviation Command chief Khosrowdad, and the military governor of Esfahan. More than four hundred military, Gendarmerie, national police, and SAVAK officers were executed between February and September, many of whom had been involved in martial law enforcement or suppression of revolutionary activities. Other officers were imprisoned, sentenced to internal exile, or simply retired. Scores were assassinated by leftist groups or became victims of personal vendettas. At the same time, Islamic societies within the military had become de facto control boards with veto power over leadership appointments and other military activities. Some of the groups appeared intent on destroying the military from the inside, which caused the Revolutionary Council to regularize judicial proceedings for military personnel accused of antirevolutionary activity. By July, an estimated two hundred and fifty thousand military personnel had not returned to duty. The need for manpower coupled with problems caused by the subversive Islamic societies led Khomeini to announce an amnesty for all military and security personnel except for cases of murder and torture. The Imam specifically pardoned the armed forces, Gendarmerie, and police and asked the Iranian people to forgive them.

The amnesty did not end the purges, and after generals, colonels, and majors were removed, the process was extended to lower ranking personnel. Investigations of the thousands of officers and servicemen who had trained overseas produced a stream of trials, dismissals, and retirements. The focus also shifted from shah loyalists and officers alleged to have committed crimes against the people to those judged potentially disloyal because of participation with disfavored political groups. Sinful behavior or sympathy for foreign ideologies also were grounds for dismissal. After Defense Minister Chamran declared the purges over in February 1980, another purge committee was established to continue the process, dismissing roughly one hundred officers a day through the summer. The pace of purges slowed only as tension with Iraq increased and the need for technically and professionally competent leaders and pilots trumped regime distrust. Although many retired and even imprisoned officers were allowed to return to duty after Iraq invaded Iran in September 1980, sporadic purges of the armed forces continued into the second half of the decade.

Although data on the purges vary, the Islamic Republic's own statements indicate that by mid-1980 between ten thousand and twelve thousand military personnel had been removed from service. The great majority was from the ground forces, and officers accounted for 65 to 90 percent of those removed. Most of the shah's flag-rank officers were executed, imprisoned, or forcibly retired or emigrated from Iran. Only senior officers who had fallen out of favor with the shah or who had cooperated with the revolutionaries avoided the purge. The regime's figures do not include the large number of military personnel who deserted or left the country, and the Iranian officer corps may have lost as much as 40 percent of its strength by the eve of the war with Iraq in mid-1980.

The Imperial Army was top-heavy, so the loss of many deadwood colonels and majors minimized the purges' overall impact. Still, the deprivation caused by the discharge of many technically proficient men was significant. The army suffered the worst losses, but the air force, despite its early change of allegiance to Khomeini, was too closely identified with America to elude serious reductions. The navy alone escaped significant purges, a result of its limited presence in Iran's main urban centers and Admiral Madani's ability as a member of the revolutionary government to protect his home service. Not surprisingly, the purges had a negative effect on the armed forces' ability to conduct combat operations and created an unhealthy atmosphere of distrust and anxiety that made officers unwilling to challenge questionable regime policies and, later, its wartime strategies.[17]

The new Islamic government established a political control system for the military. To institutionalize its authority, the Islamic Republic's new constitution, passed in an October 1979 national referendum, made Khomeini the *rahbar,* or leader, of Iran and the constitutional commander in chief of the armed forces. (Khomeini also was called the supreme leader, which refers to his theory of religious leadership, *valiyat-e faqih,* which means the comprehensive or supreme authority of the jurist.) Khomeini's government set up several agencies with parallel and overlapping responsibilities to oversee the armed forces. In addition to Khomeini's representatives assigned to the Pasdaran and the other services, a Political-Ideological Directorate (PID) was established under the Ministry of Defense. The PID, however, was primarily accountable to the IRP's top leadership, and its personnel were mostly clerics. These "Islamic commissars" were assigned to the joint staff down to the platoon level with bureaus and subordinate elements attached to divisions down to companies. The PID was responsible for the ideological and political education of the troops, evaluated candidates at all ranks for promotion, reviewed military school curricula and published text books, and provided radio and television programs for the troops. So-called strike groups worked with existing Islamic societies, basically IRP cells, in the military to indoctrinate, organize recreational and educational activities, hold daily prayers, and enforce Islamic behavior. Generally, they spied on the soldiers and served as snitches. Interference in military matters was quickly recognized as a problem, however, and over time the PID officials' authority was restricted to indoctrination and oversight.

Challenges to the New Order

Within a month of the revolution's triumph, Iran's ethnic minorities threatened the new government and its armed forces, but ultimately the Artesh's counter-insurgency operations helped restore confidence in and among the regular military. The unrest was fed by long-standing grievances, and the Kurds, Azeris, and Arabs were once again violently demanding autonomy. The regime looked first to the Artesh to take control, but indiscipline and the chaotic postrevolution environment undermined its performance. Pilots felt free to question commands and countermanded Bazargan's orders to deploy aircraft while junior army officers refused to order troops to fire on rioting Arabs in Khuzestan, fearing future prosecution. Later, twelve army officers were executed in September 1979 for refusing to fire at Kurdish dissidents. Turnover in the senior ranks was another harmful factor. General Qarani was replaced in March after his initial attempt to use the regular forces to quell Kurdish violence failed. His replacement, however, only lasted until late July, when a new general was ordered to take command. The air force lost its first two postrevolution commanders in a three-month period because of protests by air force personnel. Nearly six more months passed before Gen. Bahman Bagheri took charge of Iran's air arm. Admiral Madani was sent to govern the restive Khuzestan Province and was replaced as defense minister by Gen. Taqi Riahi, Mossadeq's chief of staff, who resigned a few months later in a dispute with Khomeini over control of the Gendarmerie.[18]

The Kurds, the first ethnic group to rebel, posed the most serious and longest lasting threat to the Islamic government's authority. Fighting in Kurdistan primarily involved Kurdish demands for autonomy. It later included conflicts between Kurds and Azeris and between Sunni Kurds and Kurdish and other Shia over the proposed constitution, which gave the Shia clergy a major role in government. Wanting to weaken the clerics in Tehran, Fedayeen leftists and Iraq aided the Kurdish tribal leaders, who cooperated under the banner of the Kurdish Democratic Party of Iran (KDPI). The Kurdish guerrillas, or Pesh Merga (those who face death), dressed in their distinctive baggy trousers and tightly wound turbans. They were lightly armed with bandoleers of ammunition and grenades. Weapons taken from army garrisons during the revolution or contributed by defectors provided recoilless rifles, mortars, 105-mm artillery, antiaircraft guns, and a limited number of tanks to the Kurds' arsenals. In putting down the rebellion, the Islamic government claimed that the Kurds wanted to secede, and captured Kurds were treated brutally. Roughly 1,200 Kurds were executed for instigating rebellion while up to 5,000 Kurds were killed in fighting that lasted well into 1981 and continued sporadically through the next seven years. More than three thousand government troops died trying to reestablish control over the region.

The rebellion began in mid-March 1979 when protesting Kurds in Sanandaj, after being dispersed by army troops, attacked and captured the local police station, army headquarters, and part of the army barracks. Unrest then spread to other Kurdish-dominated regions as the rebels took over towns and besieged army garrisons. In late April, hundreds died in large-scale sectarian fighting between Kurds and Azeris. The Pasdaran took the lead in government attempts to quash the rebellion after the Artesh's initial failures. Operating in rugged mountains rather than the urban areas that spawned them was arduous for the Guard, however. The *pasdars* had difficulty establishing control over roads and avoiding ambushes, suffering heavy casualties as a result. In mid-August 1979, after ignoring the army's advice, the Guard marched on the town of Paveh without adequate preparations and fire support and fell into another major ambush. The defeat prompted Khomeini to go over the heads of the government and military and directly order Iranian soldiers to win back Paveh. Although army officers had remained reluctant to combat internal unrest, the Supreme Leader's order encouraged the regular military to play a more effective role in supporting the Pasdaran against the rebels.

With the Imam's push for action and fresh supplies of ammunition, Pasdaran forces attacked Paveh from two sides and recaptured it in two days. Combined army, Gendarmerie, and Pasdaran forces, supported by helicopters and F-4 Phantoms, then started a three-week campaign to clear several thousand Kurdish rebels out of Saqqez, Mahabad, and other remaining strongholds. No match for Artesh firepower, the rebel defenders were overwhelmed by the heavy use of tanks, artillery, and aerial attacks, which left parts of the Kurdish cities in rubble. Fighting was brutal in each city, and army tank columns were twice repelled from Mahabad before Kurdish lines were broken. The severity of the combat spilled over into the treatment of prisoners, many of whom were summarily executed on both sides. Although the Pesh Merga took heavy casualties, the bulk of their fighters evaded capture and slipped into the mountains after their last stronghold fell.[19]

The Kurds resumed the offensive roughly six weeks later, returning to Mahabad and stopping army tanks with Molotov cocktails and rocket-propelled grenades in street-to-street fighting. A month later, at the end of November, the Kurds attacked Sanandaj, Saqqez, and other Kurdish cities and towns. The Kurds continued to hold the initiative as the American embassy takeover and hostage crisis distracted the provisional government and then the new administration of President Bani Sadr. In late January 1980, Guard units and progovernment Kurds battled unsuccessfully with the rebels throughout the Kurdish region, achieving little more than a stalemate until the spring. By May, Kurdish guerrillas controlled most of the region's roads and rural areas and had pinned down army and Guard forces in Kurdistan's four major cities. With Mahabad once again functioning as the Kurds' capital, the KDPI claimed the ability to muster more than seven thousand fighters. Because Iranian helicopters and fixed-wing aircraft were the most dangerous threat to the Pesh Merga, the Kurds did most of their fighting at night to avoid Iranian airpower. Kurdish ambushes and raids and the military's attendant casualties caused protests, desertions, and defections among some army units involved in counterinsurgency operations. The Pasdaran remained resolute, however, and, when the regime considered political approaches to end the fighting, Pasdaran commanders announced that they would continue fighting against the "unbelievers" even if a cease-fire were negotiated.[20]

Regardless of the Guard's determination, fighting diminished during the summer as tension with Iraq increased. At the end of August, Pasdaran forces backed by army artillery units tried to recapture Mahabad, which had been in Kurdish hands for ten months. The rebels, however, held the city for five more months, well after Iran's Kurdistan Province had become a theater of the Iran-Iraq War. Although President Bani Sadr ordered a cease-fire with the Kurds following the Iraqi invasion, the Pasdaran ignored his order and continued the counterinsurgency campaign. These units were not available to help stop Iraq's initial incursions into Iranian territory, but by late December reinforced Guard units were battling invading Iraqi troops and Iraqi-backed Kurdish fighters in the mountains along Iran's northwestern border.[21]

As the Pasdaran dealt with the Kurds in April and May 1979, they also were confronted by revolts by Arabs, Turkmans, and Baluchs. Revolutionary militias in Gonbad-e Qabus incited Turkman unrest in early April by firing on demonstrators who were calling for a boycott of the national referendum on making Iran an Islamic republic. Street fighting around barricades set up throughout the city lasted for eight days as the Turkmans, supported by leftists, battled with revolutionaries reinforced by air force personnel from Tehran. The Turkmans, who demanded cultural autonomy and attacked local Iranian landlords, eventually agreed to a cease-fire after more than fifty men on both sides were killed in the fighting. In late April and into May 1979, Sunni Arabs in Khuzestan protested against discrimination, and the regime responded by sending the newly formed Pasdaran units to work with navy and air force personnel already in Khorramshahr to squelch the violence. More than a dozen *pasdars* and one hundred Arabs died in the subsequent battles. Baluch tribes, like the Arabs, resented Tehran's disregard of their interests and sporadically challenged government authority in Sistan va Baluchistan Province in southeastern Iran. Protests came to a head after the Islamic Republic's constitution was approved in late 1979 because the Baluchs were unhappy with its provisions for minority rights. Tensions between the Sunni Baluchs, who were a majority in the province, and Shia Sistanis escalated into gun battles in the provincial capital of Zahedan in mid-December that left nearly one hundred dead and injured. Snipers targeted revolutionary militiamen and Pasdaran soldiers sent to protect the city while other Baluchs attacked patrolling army tanks and armored personnel carriers. Iran declared a state of emergency in the region and sent more troops into Baluchistan before calming the situation.[22]

The new constitution was the spark for the second most serious ethnic challenge to Khomeini's consolidation of his power. The Azeris, with a long history of resisting the concentration of power in Tehran, had staged the first massive protests against the shah in 1978. Most of the Turkic-speaking Azeris, however, were followers of Grand Ayatollah Shariat-Madari, who opposed the concept of *valiyat-e faqih* and its incorporation into the new constitution. In the view of Khomeini and his IRP followers, the Azeris, who were influential with the Tehran bazaar, were a much more serious if less active opponent than the Kurds because Shariat-Madari had the potential to delegitimize Khomeini's vision of an Islamic republic. After the vast majority of Azeris boycotted the constitutional referendum, the Imam's supporters in Qom attacked Shariat-Madari. Tabriz erupted at this outrage, and in early December 1979 protestors seized the local radio and television stations, the governor's office, and the Tabriz airbase to prevent government reinforcements from arriving by air. Local police and army soldiers backed the Azeri insurgents. As local radio stations broadcast patriotic Azeri music, the rebels rejected Tehran's rule and demanded the withdrawal of all non-Azeri Revolutionary Guards from the province. Shifting the blame for the violence to communists and leftists, the government tried to negotiate a settlement, but pro-Khomeini fighters armed with rifles and machine guns battled with the Azeris over government buildings and the broadcast facilities. The Pasdaran and units from the army's 64th Infantry Division clamped down on Tabriz, but clashes that left scores of people dead continued well into January 1980. Tehran eventually restored calm with a mix of promises of greater Azeri autonomy and repression that included the execution of some rebels, house arrest for Shariat-Madari, and the dissolution of the main Azeri political party.[23]

Defeating the Enemies of God

The final challengers to regime consolidation were removed between 1979 and 1983 as Khomeini and his followers violently eliminated the secular nationalist, liberal, and leftist parties; rival Islamic factions; and finally, the Tudeh Party, the last remaining political organization of any consequence. After the pro-Khomeini IRP was formed in 1979 by drawing on the MIR, smaller Islamic groups, and the nationwide mosque network of the Imam's clerical followers, it started to undermine the other antishah forces. The secular nationalists and liberals, who had no armed supporters, were the easiest to weaken. The Mujahedin-e Khalq and Fedayeen-e Khalq were more difficult opponents because of their guerrilla members. The MEK had settled on a strategy to support the military purges and the incorporation of Islamic values into government but resisted what members saw as dictatorship by the mullahs. The group was attractive to many secular Iranians, and Masud Rajavi, the MEK leader, emerged as the most popular revolutionary leader not associated with Khomeini. The Fedayeen, who had provided the main support to the air force mutineers in February, were torn between their secular ideals and submitting to the popular support for Khomeini. The Tudeh, meanwhile, initially helped the clerics in weakening the liberals in Bazargan's government while infiltrating the bureaucracy and the military with an eye toward the future.

From the provisional government's start in February 1979, the clerics of the IRP, backed by the Pasdaran, undercut Bazargan and other liberal politicians. They ensured that Khomeini became Supreme Leader and that the new constitution severely limited popular sovereignty. The mullahs also ensured that unelected and clerical-dominated government bodies could overrule the elected branches of government. Although Khomeini backed him, Bani Sadr was opposed by the IRP, which with a few allied radical parliamentarians controlled the new Majles elected in March 1980. The IRP used their new legislative powers to undermine Bani Sadr while the party's armed supporters kicked off a series of riots across the country that included attacks on the MEK and Fedayeen as well as on moderate secular groups deemed counterrevolutionary. Many groups were forced underground and became violent opponents of the clerical regime. The U.S. embassy hostage crisis, the Iraqi invasion, and an especially deadly MEK assassination campaign against government officials complicated the president's efforts to stem the clerics' influence. Bani Sadr's intention to merge the Guard into the regular military, his struggle with the clerics over control of the armed forces, and his differences with Pasdaran leaders over war strategy led to a falling out with Khomeini in 1981 and a subsequent impeachment effort by the Majles.

The armed forces suffered a new round of purges when this pressure caused Iran's first elected president, joined by MEK leader Rajavi, to flee the country in June 1981. The clerical regime suspected leftists and other disloyal elements in the military of helping Bani Sadr and Rajavi to escape and initiated new tribunals to cleanse the ranks. During these new purges the MEK stepped up its attacks on the government, bombing the IRP headquarters on June 28, 1981, and killing party founder Ayatollah Muhammad Beheshti and seventy other top party and government officials. The blast also injured future Supreme Leader Ali Khamenei, costing him the full use of his right hand. A similar explosion in late August killed the new president, Muhammad Rajai, and Prime Minister Muhammad Bahonar. The regime responded with a brutal campaign against MEK members and sympathizers in the military and government. It ruthlessly suppressed all dissent by real and imagined "enemies of God," executing more than 1,800 people between June and November. The MEK continued its fight, and Rajavi claimed in October 1982 that his group had killed more than two thousand pro-Khomeini political and religious leaders in Iran. His organization was beaten by then, however, and most members were in exile in Iraq or Europe. From late 1981 to 1983, the regime went after the Tudeh, outlawing the party; removing Capt. Bahram Afzali, the navy's commander, and about one hundred junior officers and NCOs from the military; and executing thirty-two Tudeh military members. Although MEK, Fedayeen, and Tudeh cells continued to harass the regime for many more years, they posed no serious threat after 1983.

Humiliating the Great Satan

The attacks on the Marxists and other regime opponents in April 1980 were started in part because a disastrous American hostage rescue attempt presented Khomeini with a pretext to seize absolute power and make Iran a full-blown theocracy. Although the United States tried to maintain ties to postrevolutionary Iran, radicals among the clerics and leftists torpedoed all attempts to improve relations. The American embassy in Tehran had been briefly taken over by the revolutionaries in February 1979. Still, the U.S. mission stayed in place to support the numerous Americans remaining in the country and to come to terms with the Bazargan government. As the first summer wore on, the American technicians working in Iran fled the turmoil in the Iranian military and defense industries. Because of Washington's concern about possible Soviet inroads to the region, arrangements were made to deliver nearly $300 million worth of military hardware and supplies previously paid for by the shah. These efforts fell apart on November 4, 1979, when a group of roughly three hundred Islamic militants, the Students Following the Line of the Imam, overran the embassy and took American diplomats and U.S. Marine Corps security guards hostage.

The fallout of the action was immediate for Iran and its armed forces. The prospect of U.S. military responses to the embassy takeover caused Khomeini to call for an expansion of the army to its former strength of 285,000 men, and the conscription period was increased to eighteen months. The Guard's standing was enhanced by its association with the students, who received Khomeini's and other government officials' approval after seizing the American embassy. The students claimed that, following the shah's admission into the United States in late October, they moved to prevent a replay of the 1953 coup by eliminating the embassy as a potential base. The ailing shah, however, had entered the United States from his exile in Panama for cancer treatments and soon left for Egypt where he died nine months later. Coup prevention was just one factor in the embassy seizure and taking of hostages. Primarily, it was "an act of vengeance for the 1953 coup, designed to humiliate the United States, to cause pain to the American people, and to assuage the angry psychological scars that the Iranian people still bore from that event."[24] The Guard's role in the incident remains unclear, but if the Pasdaran did not assist with the planning, the students had their quiet backing, because the Guard stood aside while the students stormed the American facility. Over time, *pasdars* replaced many of the students in guarding the hostages, and after the hostage rescue attempt some of the Americans were moved to Guard installations.[25]

On April 24, 1980, the United States launched Operation Eagle Claw, an exceptionally difficult plan to stage units in Iran to conduct a rescue of the American hostages. Eight U.S. Navy Sea Stallion helicopters from the carrier USS *Nimitz* followed by six C-130 transports entered Iranian airspace during the early evening carrying approximately ninety U.S. Army Delta Force soldiers, various support personnel and equipment, and fuel bladders to refill the helicopters for their subsequent flight to the Iranian capital. During the flight to Desert One, a remote desert site near Tabas two hundred miles from Tehran, two of the Sea Stallions developed problems. Vast clouds of suspended dust particles blown up from the Dasht-e Lut cut the pilots' visibility and clogged the engines. One helicopter returned to the *Nimitz* while the second had to be abandoned after its crew was picked up by another helicopter and taken to the landing site. The plan called for the Delta Force element to be carried by six of the refueled helicopters to Garmsar, east of Tehran, where CIA operatives would provide trucks to bring the special forces soldiers into the capital to assault the embassy and free the hostages. The American force would then move to an adjacent soccer stadium, meet the helicopters that would ferry the group to a nearby airfield, and then board C-141 cargo planes that would be escorted out of Iranian airspace by U.S. Navy fighters. The plan required six helicopters, however, and when the rescue force arrived at Desert One, a third helicopter developed mechanical problems and was unable to continue with the mission.

Left with only five operational helicopters, the leaders on the ground reluctantly recommended the mission's cancellation and President Carter agreed, ordering the forces to leave Iran. During the withdrawal, one helicopter accidentally collided with a fuel-laden C-130, sending a fireball roaring into the desert sky. Eight Americans died in the explosion, and several more were injured. Because of concerns about the compromise of the mission's operational security, the commander, Col. Charlie Beckwith of the U.S. Army, ordered the remaining helicopters abandoned and had all personnel board the remaining C-130s, which took off in the early morning hours of April 25 and left Iran without further incident. Across the country, most Iranians viewed the rescue mission as an attempted coup, and Khomeini credited God with throwing sand into the motors of the American helicopters to protect Iran. As for the fifty-two American hostages then held by Iran, they were not released until January 1981, 444 days after being taken captive. For the Iranian military, its failure to detect the American aircraft entering or leaving Iran put the armed forces once more on trial.

Military Rebellions

The failure of Operation Eagle Claw did not reassure the clerical regime, which feared that the country and the armed forces were penetrated with American agents who had helped the Delta Force bypass Iranian radars and had been ready to assist the rescue attempt. Iran's air force commander, General Bagheri, aggravated the radicals' suspicions when, in the only Iranian military reaction to the U.S. operation, he ordered the bombing of the abandoned American aircraft, allegedly out of concern that they had been booby-trapped to kill Iranian recovery teams looking for equipment and secret documents. In a subsequent purge, Bagheri was fired and then arrested while Gen. Hadi Shadmehr, the chief of the Joint Staff, was sacked for the military's failure to stop the American incursion. A general lawlessness in Iran in the spring of 1980 added to the climate of fear created by the regime's attacks on its political opponents following the rescue attempt. MEK and Fedayeen guerrillas, tribal dissidents, Islamic extremists, and common criminals regularly clashed with Iran's security forces and threatened everyone's peace and security with their assassinations, bombings, and robberies. In this environment, small groups of nationalist liberal politicians and military officers began plotting against the regime. An extensive and well-planned coup attempt, later called the Nuzhih plot, was potentially a significant threat to Khomeini's government, providing a hint of what might have been had Iran's military leaders shown similar initiative and determination in late 1978 or early 1979. By the summer of 1980, however, the governing clerics were well entrenched and fully on guard against threats from the distrusted regular military, which had "the Shah in their blood," according to Khomeini.[26]

The Iranians dealt with a number of other less serious and even feckless coup threats before the Nuzhih plot was uncovered in July 1980. Six plots, most of which involved exiles, allegedly were uncovered by the regime in the first half of the year. The former shah's nephew, Shahriar Shafiq, an expatriate Iranian naval officer, was planning an amphibious invasion of Iran when he was assassinated in December 1979. Gen. Bahram Aryana created an organization called Azadigan (Free Men) and launched small guerrilla attacks into Iran from a base in Turkey. In Iraq, General Oveissi had created a small network of exiled officers and tried to foment a nationwide uprising by broadcasting antiregime propaganda with Iraqi help. Mustafa Palizban, a former general with ties to Oveissi, concurrently formed a small group of Kurdish fighters to harass the Islamic Republic. In May and June 1980, the regime uncovered at least two coup plots linked to Oveissi. The latter attempt, centered on a military base in Piranshahr in Iranian Kurdistan, led to the execution and imprisonment of dozens of military personnel while another two hundred soldiers reportedly escaped with the help of the KDPI.[27]

Named after the airbase near Hamadan where the coup was to begin, the Nuzhih plot started in 1979 when Col. Muhammad Baqir Bani Amiri, a retired Gendarmerie officer, and Col. Ataullah Ahmadi, an army intelligence officer, assembled a small group of retired and active-duty officers to develop coup plans. The small group expanded into a network called the Patriotic Officers, who worked with former prime minister Shahpour Bakhtiar, then providing financial support from Paris. The network had a compartmentalized cell structure for operational security, and after recruiting two active-duty military intelligence officers with access to personnel files, ran background checks on all potential recruits. Bani Amiri even recruited two Pasdaran intelligence officers, who kept the network informed on government counterrevolutionary activities. With the money from Bakhtiar, safe houses, communications, light arms, and ammunition were acquired.[28]

The network continued to grow, and in the spring of 1980 the Patriotic Officers joined with a group of antiregime secular democratic nationalists called the Mask. Bani Amiri became a member of the Mask's central committee. Along with an air force officer, Lt. Nassir Rukni, and several other retired and active duty officers, Bani Amiri ran the military branch within the umbrella organization. The Mask also had civilian and financial branches that worked on contacts with tribal and bazaari leaders, prepared and distributed antiregime information, and provided the funds and material needed for the coup. By early summer Bani Amiri had assembled a group of 700 to 750 retired and active-duty officers, NCOs, and policemen while 100 civilian members in Tehran and another 300 to 400 outside the capital had joined the network. Careful approaches for support were made to Ayatollah Shariat-Madari, MEK leader Rajavi, and Admiral Madani, the former defense minister who had fled Iran in May, and only Rajavi declined. With all of the players and materiel lined up, the coup plotters decided to move on the night of July 9, 1980.

The plan to be executed was complex, and the large number of moving parts probably contributed to its ultimate failure. On the night of the coup, a force of three hundred paratroopers was to move in small groups to Hamadan and then assemble, attack, and capture the Nuzhih Air Base. At the same time, twenty air force pilots from Tehran led by Rukni and Gen. Ataullah Muhaqqiqi were to go to Nuzhih, join with thirty pilots stationed at the base, and commandeer the F-4 and F-5 fighters stationed there for attacks on the government. Three aircraft were to strike Khomeini's residence at daybreak in an effort to kill him while the other fighters bombed Pasdaran bases, Tehran's airfields, and government and IRP buildings. One of the attacking aircraft was to break the sound barrier as it flew over Tehran, signaling the ground forces gathered by the coup plotters to begin their part of the plan. Army members of the Patriotic Officers were to have a contingent of soldiers ready to go to Khomeini's house to ensure that the

Supreme Leader was dead while other groups attacked Pasdaran bases, seized media outlets, arrested regime leaders, and secured airfields. Tank units in Tehran and helicopter units at Esfahan were to be on call to support the coup.

Once the broadcast outlets were captured and martial law was declared, the penultimate phase of the coup would start outside the capital. Arrangements had been made for the armored division in Ahvaz and nearby units of Iranian marines to seize the oil fields and Dezful Air Base. The declaration of martial law also was to trigger army takeovers of Esfahan, Mashhad, and Zahedan. The coup plotters arranged for the rebellious army units in Khuzestan to be their backup should the Tehran operations fail. After securing Ahvaz and Dezful, these units were to attempt to capture as much key territory in the region as possible to use as a base for continued efforts to overthrow the clerical regime. The coup plot's final phase called for the civilian members to make radio and television broadcasts to stabilize the country.

With so many people involved in the plot, its discovery possibly was unavoidable. Although the method has never been revealed, the regime became aware of at least some of the plan's details. Guard units reached Nuzhih in time to arrest the paratroopers as they assembled for their attack. A security clamp-down on the airbase caused the pilots from Tehran to turn around and return to the capital. When the series of signals to initiate other parts of the coup were not made, the rest of the participants remained quiet and the civilian members of the Mask network went into hiding. Interrogations of the arrested paratroopers revealed details about the coup attempt, and the regime started to arrest other participants. Eventually, more than 280 network members were arrested along with hundreds of other uninvolved Iranians caught up in the regime dragnet. Most of those arrested came from the 92nd Armored Division at Ahvaz. The regime executed 144 coup participants over the course of several weeks, and Iranian assassins tried but failed to kill Bakhtiar in mid-July (he eventually was assassinated in 1991). The Pasdaran's haphazard initial response and failure to uncover many of the elements of the coup suggested that the regime was ignorant of the threat until as late as the day of the coup. Indeed, the regime may have learned of the plot only by chance, yet another intriguing "might have been" of the Nuzhih plot.

Bleeding Iran

Cumulatively, the purges preceding and following the Nuzhih plot seriously weakened Iran's regular armed forces, while the continued political terror left the country reeling. The tumult in the military was felt at the highest ranks. In addition to the removal of the air force commander and chief of the Joint Staff after Operation Eagle Claw, the navy commander was arrested and replaced, the

Gendarmerie commander was executed, and the chief of the national police was purged. More than ten thousand Iranians were executed by the various revolutionary tribunals, and thousands more died in the unrest, insurrections, and criminal violence between early 1979 and late 1980. More than a half-million Iranians, primarily from the middle and professional classes, emigrated from Iran. The clerical regime was clearly unpopular, and the Iraqi strongman in Baghdad was watching these developments closely. The arrest of the Nuzhih pilots and members of 92nd Armored Division, in particular, crippled Iran's ability to defend its southwestern border just as tensions with Iraq were increasingly pointing to war. Such turmoil, along with lies about Iran's vulnerability spread by Oveissi and other exiles, undoubtedly encouraged Saddam Hussein to put his plans for war in motion, creating the crucible in which Iran's postrevolutionary armed forces would be forged.

9

Horrible Sacrifice

The Iran-Iraq War

THE EIGHT YEARS OF WAR WITH IRAQ were instrumental in shaping the current structure and outlook of Iran's armed forces. Ironically, Iraq's invasion in September 1980 was a godsend for Khomeini and his allied hard-liners, who were facing waning popular enthusiasm for the new order. The Iraqi aggression ensured the clerical regime's survival by reviving the public's nationalism and diverting attention from the country's slide into tyranny. By bolstering the influence of religious militants on the shape of Iran's military, the conflict also made permanent the Artesh-Pasdaran divide. The interaction of religion and politics in military strategy and tactics grossly undercut the wartime sacrifice of Iran's fighting men, who again demonstrated their bravery, patriotism, doggedness, and ingenuity. Finally, the war forced unstable compromises on divisive interpretations of the relative values between religious zeal and technology and between military professionals and popular militias that still resonate in contemporary Iranian military doctrines. In the end, acting on its strong xenophobia and historical tendency to overreach, Iran squandered repeated opportunities to end the war on favorable terms. Instead, the Islamic Republic's unreasoning fanaticism led to a growing number of enemies aligning with Iraq, debilitating international isolation, and an undeclared war with the United States that virtually guaranteed Iran's ultimate defeat.

Iran's Provocative Path to War

Although Iraqi dictator Saddam Hussein deserves most of the blame, the Iranians' designation of the hostilities as the "Imposed War" ignores Iran's sizable role in provoking the conflagration and its even greater culpability in prolonging the conflict after 1983. In the revolution's first days Iraq tried to accommodate Khomeini, but the Iranians were eager to spread their ideals. They saw their country as a springboard for Islamic revolutions in other Muslim countries, especially those with large Shia populations, such as Iraq, where the Shia comprised as much as 60 percent of the inhabitants. Shortly after Khomeini's return, the provisional government began to support Iraq's senior Shia cleric, Ayatollah Muhammad Baqir al-Sadr, and soon publicly called for the overthrow of the Iraqi regime. In mid-July 1979, Saddam Hussein replaced Hassan Bakr as president of Iraq, and relations took a serious turn for the worse.

Saddam viewed Iran with a mix of opportunism and trepidation. The Iraqi dictator, who nursed numerous grievances against Iran, was tempted by his perceptions of Iranian weakness and disarray. Saddam had signed the 1975 Algiers Accord with Iran, which involved major Iraqi concessions on claims to Khuzestan and on control of the Shatt al-Arab waterway, its main trade outlet to the Persian Gulf. In addition, Iranian troops were still occupying territory that was supposed to be returned to Iraq under the accord. Iran's continuing turbulence presented the newly installed Iraqi president with the chance to recoup his earlier losses. Saddam could grab the leadership role in the Arab world he coveted as well as divert Iraqi Shia attention from their plight under his Sunni-dominated dictatorship. A quick war to humiliate a weakened Iran also would allow Iraq to achieve several strategic objectives. The two most important were the reassertion of control over the Shatt and favorable border adjustments. In a best case, however, Iraq might establish itself as the predominant regional power, gain control over large portions of oil-rich Khuzestan—ignoring declarations in support of local Arab autonomy there—and enhance its stature among the Arabs by forcing Iran to accept humiliating conditions to surrender Abu Musa and the Tunbs Islands. Iran seemed vulnerable to ethnic divisiveness, so Saddam gave additional support to the Kurds already rebelling against Tehran and to Arab nationalists in Iran's southwest. Of Iran's estimated forty-five million people in 1980, four million were Kurds and one million Arabs. The main Arab separatist group, the Arabistan Liberation Front, had not been a significant problem since its formation in the 1950s. With additional Iraqi money, arms, and training, the Khuzestan Arabs promised support to invading Iraqi soldiers, which added to Saddam's conviction that Iran was exposed to swift military action.[1]

A series of events in Iraq and London in the spring of 1980 signaled that both sides were ready to risk a war. When Shia militants associated with Ayatollah Sadr tried to assassinate Tariq Aziz, one of Saddam's key lieutenants, the Iraqi dictator arrested Sadr, crushed Shia rioters, and deported tens of thousands of Shia from Iraq to Iran. Saddam then tried to incite more unrest in Khuzestan to create the conditions for an Iraqi intervention, adding his own embassy takeover and hostage crisis to bolster the case. On the last day of April, a group of Iranian Arabs recruited by Iraq seized Iran's embassy in London to draw international attention to their cause. After one of the hostage takers violated his instructions and murdered an Iranian diplomat, British commandos stormed the embassy and captured the hostage takers. They had served Iraq's purpose, however, and created an additional pretext for hostilities. Diplomatic relations between Iran and Iraq were soon broken, and Saddam welcomed exiled oppositionists Shahpour Bakhtiar and General Oveissi to Baghdad. The former Iranian officials' assurances of Iran's weakness and of the Iranian people's unwillingness to rally to the regime, especially after the size of the Nuzhih coup was revealed, fed the Iraqi tyrant's confidence in his plans.

Large-scale conflict inched closer from June to early September as armed clashes along the border escalated with artillery and airpower thrown into the exchanges. Border towns were shelled by Iran and disputed territory "liberated" by Iraq. When Iranian Chief of Staff Gen. Valiollah Fallahi announced that Iran would no longer abide by the Algiers Accord, Saddam seized the opening and, citing Iranian violations, abrogated the treaty on September 17, 1980. Three days later, with a major Iraqi attack clearly in the offing, President Bani Sadr ordered Iran's reserves mobilized. Given the state of Iran's armed forces, the move was too little, too late to dissuade Saddam. The Iraqi dictator, however, had a flawed picture of the Iranian Arabs' likely greeting for the Iraqis and of the Iranians' willingness to fight.

The Artesh and Guard Go to War

On the eve of war the Artesh was a shell of its former self. Between 40 and 60 percent of the regular armed forces' manpower had been lost to desertions, purges, retirement, and reduced terms of conscription. The army fell from 285,000 men to no more than 150,000. The air force dropped from 100,000 to 65,000 personnel while the navy shrank from 28,000 to 23,000 men. Up to half of the majors and colonels in the army and air force had been removed and thousands of skilled technicians and junior officers had left the services. The loss of skilled manpower fell most heavily on the air force, which was left with few experienced senior commanders and a shortage of pilots. Many military professionals were leaving the services because the Islamic societies and unruly soldiers made command impossible. The fighting in Kurdistan and the increased fear of U.S. military action after the embassy seizure had caused Khomeini to call for a restoration of discipline, but reestablishing order was a slow and difficult process. Iran's reserve mobilization system, meanwhile, was broken. The navy had no reserves, and the shah's army and air force had ignored preparations for using the former conscripts who made up the reserves. After the revolution, mobilization issues received even less attention, and, when Iraq invaded, the regular military was pushed aside by the Pasdaran in organizing, training, and deploying the hundreds of thousands of volunteers that rallied to defend their country.[2]

Readiness and training suffered significant deterioration in the immediate postrevolutionary period. The clerics were content to allow logistical problems to fester while they focused on the military's political reliability. Iran's computerized logistic system was sabotaged by departing U.S. personnel, which paralyzed maintenance and repair work as procurement and inventory accountability were ruined. The loss of American and other foreign technicians, along with the cancellation of U.S. and British spare parts deliveries after the hostage crisis started, further crippled Artesh readiness. When the war began, around 30 percent of army equipment, 50 to 60 percent of air force equipment, and 60 percent of helicopters were nonoperational. Severe shortages of spare parts, ammunition, transportation, communications, and even food severely reduced the military's ability to train and deploy men to the front. Advanced training came to nearly a complete halt, and basic training devoted large amounts of time to indoctrination while training standards were reduced. A young Iranian armor lieutenant later reported that all training on tanks was in classrooms or on simulators with no live fire training.[3] Although the regular military kept most of its military schools open, teaching staffs suffered large turnover, and many qualified instructors were lost.

In such circumstances, greater demands were placed on the military's leadership at all levels, and Iranian officers were hard pressed to respond effectively. At the unit level, soldiers were unwilling to take direct orders well into the war with Iraq. One commander complained that army regulations were abandoned and that the troops had to be persuaded to follow directions rather than ordered to obey commands.[4] The purges had resulted in the promotion of inexperienced junior officers by several ranks to replace lost senior officers. Inexperience and promotions based on political reliability over competence led to a serious deterioration in the command and management of the armed forces. Many but not all of these problems were corrected over time, and the regular military's performance during the war indicates that some of their professional leadership and technical skills were maintained. Constant changes in senior commanders and the creation of politically oriented bodies such as the Political-Ideological Directorate and a revived Supreme Defense Council of civilian and military leaders undercut the Artesh's chain of command.

The Artesh's call to arms to meet the Iraqi invasion helped the regular armed forces restore their reputation as a genuine national institution. The public's anger and distrust were assuaged by the removal of officers associated with the shah, the military's sacrifices on the battlefield, and the changing face of the armed forces as younger, more overtly religious officers from the lower economic classes took leadership positions. As important, the regime curtailed the senior officers' authority, leaving them less power to abuse and fewer opportunities for corruption, which lowered popular resentment. Finally, the army, which had no role in internal security, began to be compared favorably to the Pasdaran, which adopted some of the privileges and lack of accountability of the shah's military. Over time, the regime's trust in the regular military grew, and its loyalty was rewarded with stronger ties and public recognition of its service. Also, after the Iraqi invasion, the Artesh was allowed to firm up its separate identity, starting with enforcement of the proper wear of uniforms and the observance of the daily flag ceremonies of reveille and retreat.[5]

The war initiated the rapid expansion of the Revolutionary Guard's size and capabilities, but in September 1980 the Pasdaran had only thirty thousand men in lightly armed units. Most *pasdars* had concentrated on internal security and policing duties and were not trained for heavy combat. Initially, new recruits and volunteers were sent to the front with virtually no training. By the summer of 1981 the Guard had organized basic military training centers with experienced Guard commanders and a select group of regular officers. Recruits were drawn primarily from the urban lower classes, and a family or other relationship with clerics was a major factor in acceptance and promotion. The average *pasdar* was between eighteen and twenty-six, unmarried, poor, and ethnic Persian. For several years the Guard had no problem attracting volunteers because of good pay and benefits. Many recruits also were attracted by the Guard's religious rhetoric and their desire to defend Iran. As the service expanded, more nonideological members were inducted for their skills and numbers. With only a few exceptions, however, the Guard refused to accept former officers of the shah's army. By early 1981, the Guard had fifty thousand members, and its strength would jump to one hundred thousand in 1983 and two hundred and fifty thousand in 1985.[6]

To meet all of its manpower needs on the war fronts, the Guard turned to its popular volunteer militia, the Basij. The mobilization of volunteers provided more troops than the Pasdaran could arm and fully use for many years. Although the Iranians claimed that the Basij organization had as many as three million members, at its height in 1985 it probably mobilized no more than six hundred thousand fighters. The average *basiji* came from Iran's rural areas, was poor and uneducated, and was between twenty and thirty years old, although boys as young as twelve and elderly men also served. Although a separate organization, the Basij was under Pasdaran control and integrated into its structure. Like most *pasdars*, *basijis* were lightly armed and motivated by religion and ideology. Military training for the Basij was only two weeks' worth of basic small arms training combined with nearly constant indoctrination. Once at the front, Basij leaders kept up efforts to imbue the volunteers with religious zeal with fiery speeches, Koranic readings, songs, and prayers. Because most of the *basijis* needed to be home for the planting and harvesting seasons, their mobilization was limited to the winter months, which was a serious constraint on Iranian operational planning and a weakness Iraq regularly tried to exploit. As the war dragged on and the Guard grew in size, the limits on Basij availability caused the Guard to rely more heavily on conscription to replace losses and fill new units.

The Guard's initial force structure was regional and based on internal security duties, which carried over into the Pasdaran's wartime organization. At the beginning of the war, local units were formed into companies, and over the course of the conflict these formations developed into a conventional-looking order of battle with battalions, brigades, and divisions. Guard commanders used the regional organizations to recruit men and mobilize the Basij augmentation, which caused Pasdaran units to vary widely in size, an unpredictable element that complicated operational planning. Most Guard units were infantry forces in which officers and enlisted men formed the base around which the *basijis* assembled for offensive operations. The more experienced and better trained *pasdars* manned the Guard's armored and artillery units, which were created in the early days of the war with captured Iraqi equipment. The Guard consulted with the Artesh through the Joint Staff, although cooperation with the regular forces was generally poor and grudging. Hostility toward the Artesh contributed to the Pasdaran later developing its own ministry, arms production and procurement capabilities, and separate air and naval services.

Because the Pasdaran often advanced its own interests over those of the regime, the Guard was not spared clerical supervision. The Imam's representatives and other mullah "commissars" were initially able to veto Guard military plans deemed outside regime guidelines. Still, the close links between Pasdaran leaders and the radical clerics gave the Guard significant autonomy. When the Guard defied President Bani Sadr's order for a cease-fire with the Kurds following the Iraqi invasion, it deprived the government of forces needed for more critical theaters. Although Pasdaran units became more conventional in appearance, the leadership remained thoroughly revolutionary in their outlook. Guard commanders at the highest level adopted Khomeini's ideological views, which emphasized sacrifice and used the concepts of jihad and martyrdom to mobilize public support. In turn, they counted on revolutionary zeal to prevail on the battlefield. Long after the Guard's tactics were shown to be unsound and costly, its leaders believed that their operations were revolutionizing warfare. For at least a few years, the *pasdars* maintained their commitment to martyrdom, enhanced by Iranian nationalism, in the service of the Islamic Republic. Many of the Guard's senior leaders also lived this commitment, and numerous senior Pasdaran commanders and Defense Minister Chamran were killed in combat. The Guard's zeal, steadfastness, and early battlefield success added to its prestige and contributed to its secure position in the regime. Being a path to become part of Iran's new elite also added to the Guard's appeal for some of Iran's most dedicated and ambitious young men.[7]

The Military Balance with Iraq

Iran's disadvantages in facing Iraq were significant. On paper, the balance of forces at the start of the war favored the Iraqis. In the preceding decade, Iraq had doubled the size of its army, increasing its divisional strength from six to twelve. The new formations included four armored and two mechanized divisions with roughly 1,600 new tanks and armored vehicles, including state-of-the-art Soviet T-72 main battle tanks and BMP-1 infantry fighting vehicles. It also improved the training, equipment, and quality of the Republican Guard, the elite regime security force and Baghdad's strategic reserve. Up to 200 new combat jets, including MiG-23 Floggers and older SU-22 Fitter fighter-bombers, had been added to the Iraqi air force. Overall, Iraq could muster 2,750 tanks, 4,000 other armored vehicles, 1,400 artillery pieces, and 340 combat aircraft. Iran, at best, had 500 operational Chieftain and Patton tanks, no more than 300 functioning artillery pieces, and fewer than 100 operational fixed-wing aircraft. With a quarter of the regular army involved in operations against the Kurds, Iran's forces along the Khuzestan border consisted of two divisions and two brigades, all of which were severely undermanned and short of equipment. Despite the months of tension, the Iranians made no effort to coordinate defensive preparations or move more tanks, artillery, and attack helicopters closer to the border. Only the existing Artesh units in the southwest, along with some lightly armed border security forces, gendarmes, and local Pasdaran groups, faced the nine fully manned and equipped Iraqi divisions staging for the invasion.[8]

Iran had some advantages, which included its strategic depth, large cash reserves, and continued oil revenues. Its large stockpile of weapons and supplies and the revolutionary and nationalistic fervor of the volunteers rallying to defend the homeland were equally important. Iraq was unpleasantly surprised when Iran poured tens of thousands of untrained fighters into Khuzestan to stem and then reverse the Iraqi assault. In fact, more Iranians volunteered to fight Iraq than could be absorbed by the Guard and army, and large numbers were sent instead to eastern Iran to battle drug smugglers. In many Guard infantry units during the war's first year and even later, some soldiers went into battle empty-handed, picking up weapons dropped by fallen comrades to continue the fight. Some armor units had twice as many officers and crews as needed for available tanks, a situation that resulted in a rotation of personnel that allowed men to spend only one week in four at the front. After the first year of the war, the Basij's winter mobilization schedule allowed Iran to muster its maximum manpower when weather and terrain advantages on the battlefront favored Iranian operations. Finally, Iran had the advantage of facing an Iraqi military that was led by incompetent and overly politicized senior officers. Similar to the shah's military in the 1970s, Iraq's armed forces had expanded too rapidly to absorb its new weapon systems properly and lacked adequately skilled junior officers, NCOs, and maintenance personnel. Although Iraq's military inventory possessed numerous modern weapon systems, the Iraqis were not prepared to use their capabilities fully. Despite parts of the army waging a long campaign against the Iraqi Kurds in the mid-1970s, the Iraqi armed forces had only limited combat experience to prepare them for the shock of Iran's passionate resistance.

Invasion

On September 22, 1980, Iraqi warplanes, in an attempt to copy Israel's devastating surprise attacks on Arab air forces in 1967, struck at Iranian air bases, garrisons, and cities as nine Iraqi divisions started rolling into Iran. Caught off guard by the air attacks, the Iranians still were able to withstand the bombings because the Iraqi air force overestimated its effectiveness and sent too few planes to do significant damage. The shah had built Iranian air bases to American standards with hardened and dispersed aircraft shelters and easily repaired runways. Iran's army bases also were large facilities with dispersed buildings and strong munition bunkers. Although every major air base in western Iran and Mehrabad Airbase in Tehran was attacked, many Iraqi bombs fell harmlessly on noncritical parts of the facilities. A second Iraqi wave hit smaller airfields and Iranian early warning radars closer to the southwestern border but was similarly unsuccessful. Subsequent Iraqi air raids over the next two days were no more effective, and Iran's air bases remained operational.[9]

On the ground, the Iraqi army crossed into Iran at several points between the Persian Gulf and the mountains of Kurdistan. In the south, Iraq sent three armored and two mechanized infantry divisions into Khuzestan to capture the major cities and roads and isolate the province and its oil facilities from the rest of Iran. Three Iraqi infantry divisions and another armored division attacked Iranian positions and cities in the central border region, targeting Mehran and Qasr-e Shirin. Iran initially offered only a few defensive stands by scattered regular army units, guerrilla-type operations by the Pasdaran and other revolutionary militias, and air attacks to meet the Iraqi onslaught. The Iranian air force, having lost only three aircraft to the Iraqi strikes, surged into battle first, flying between 100 and 160 sorties against Iraq on the second day of the war. Iranian warplanes bombed Iraqi military, industrial, and oil installations, which shocked the Iraqis, who did not think Iran was capable of such operations. Although the attacks were not especially effective, their psychological impact, combined with the Iranian pilots' victories in nearly all of the limited air-to-air combat, caused Baghdad to virtually ground its air force. The Iraqis did not return to the skies in force until Iran's maintenance problems reduced the number of Iranian sorties. Iranian army attack helicopters also entered the battle as early as the first day,

9.1 The September 1980 Iraqi Invasion and Iranian Counteroffensives, 1980–1982.

using pop-up tactics in the mountains around Mehran to fire antitank missiles, rockets, and machine guns at the onrushing Iraqi forces. Still, Iran's initial resistance was so slight that the invaders captured Mehran and Qasr-e Shirin and reached the outskirts of their other major objectives on the first day.

Iranian defenses stiffened in the south as the slow and overly cautious Iraqi forces closed on the major cities. Gendarmerie units, border police, local volunteers, and *pasdars* set up roadblocks and conducted ambushes. Army artillery units went into action as Iraqi troops came into range, causing the Iraqis to halt, bring up their own guns, and engage in artillery duels. The 92nd Armored Division at Ahvaz was in such bad shape, however, that it took several days to deploy its first company-sized elements to meet the Iraqi attack. With no central direction, the Iranians did not attempt any organized delaying operations but fought briefly and then withdrew to more defensible areas in the cities. About three thousand regular troops and thousands of *pasdars* defended Khorramshahr. Abadan, surrounded by rivers and marshes, was protected by roughly ten thousand army and navy personnel, including an armored brigade with fifty tanks. About five thousand Pasdaran fighters also defended Abadan. In these and other cities, Iranians with rifles, grenades, and Molotov cocktails took advantage of the built-up areas and the destruction caused by the Iraqi air and artillery bombardments to set up ambushes and tank traps. Because the oil storage tanks on Abadan Island were ablaze, the area was covered in a thick cloud of black smoke that hindered observation for Iraq's long-range weapon systems. Small groups of Iranian fighters tied down much larger Iraqi formations, and the Iraqis paid a heavy price for moving into urban terrain. Once again, the Iraqis slowed their attack while the tank and mechanized divisions waited for more infantrymen to be prepared for city fighting.

The Iranians needed every advantage provided by Iraqi delays and mistakes. Because the Iraqis failed to strike into Iran's rear areas or vigorously pursue retreating Iranian forces, the defenders repeatedly avoided being surrounded or overrun. Meanwhile, other Iranian units assembled unmolested, and defensive positions farther behind the front lines were quickly constructed and fortified. The Iraqis also failed to bypass Iranian cities to seal the Zagros Mountains' passes to block the unhindered flow of Iranian troops and supplies to the front. Iran's military shortcomings, however, kept it from fully exploiting the Iraqi deficiencies. With Iran's broken mobilization system performing poorly, Khomeini called for the creation of an "army of twenty million" in the form of Basij militias. Former Iranian army officers and air force pilots were ordered back to duty to fill critical leadership and skill gaps. But the chaotic handling of supplies and other support functions hampered the arming of the reservists as well as the delivery of men, war materiel, ammunition, and spare parts to the front. Overall, it took Iran until early November to complete the initial buildup of infantry, tanks, helicopter gunships, and artillery, reducing Iraq's advantage in troops from six to one to a more manageable two to one.

Khorramshahr was the only major city in Khuzestan lost to the Iraqis, but the Iranians held out for four weeks of bloody street-to-street fighting and caused the Iraqis to divert forces from Abadan that might have been the margin of victory for that besieged city. The Iraqi armored division assigned to capture Khorramshahr reached its outskirts a few days after the invasion's start, and fortunately for Iran the Iraqi commander delayed his attack to wait for artillery to arrive. After the Iranians inflicted heavy casualties while defeating the initial mechanized assaults, the Iraqis again stopped their attack to bring in special forces units and prepare their infantrymen for urban warfare. Amid the rubble created by Iraqi artillery, the Pasdaran and regular army units fought house-to-house and were rooted out only with great difficulty. The month-long battle cost Iraq eight thousand or more casualties and one hundred Iraqi tanks and armored vehicles while Iran lost roughly seven thousand dead and wounded. The Iranians then defeated a three-pronged Iraqi attack against the defensive lines around Susangerd to the north of Khorramshahr in mid-November. As the northern and center columns were repulsed, the Iranians opened sluice gates on the Kharkeh River to send a flood of water toward the southern Iraqi column. Approximately 150 Iraqi tanks and other armored vehicles sank into mud up to their turrets and had to be abandoned, still in battle formation, as Iranian tanks and antitank teams moved in for the kill. As November ended, the start of the rainy season made additional areas untrafficable for the more heavily mechanized Iraqi formations. The Iraqis had bogged down in the south and, seeking to salvage their faulty campaign, had voluntarily halted on the other fronts with an eye toward arranging a negotiated end to the hostilities.

Iran had stripped the initiative from the Iraqis in the air and sea theaters as well. The air force's early successes and high-profile attacks such as a late November raid on Iraq's Tuwaitha nuclear facility had given the Iraqis an exaggerated sense of Iranian capabilities. Baghdad was forced to redeploy its air defenses from the front to protect key installations. The Iraqi air force also sent its transports and bombers to Jordan for safety. Within weeks, however, maintenance problems and parts shortages caused a dramatic decline in Iranian air force operations. Weak early warning and command and control systems made intrusions into each combatant's airspace relatively easy. Interceptions were rare and dogfights few as a result. In addition, neither air force emphasized ground support or interdiction operations in the first phase of the war, nor did they do tactical reconnaissance well. To neutralize Iraq's advantage in air power, Iranian ground forces were careful to move at night and usually were supported by large numbers of antiaircraft artillery. Naval warfare ended after only a few Iranian attacks against Al Basrah, Umm Qasr, and Iraq's two oil export terminals in the northern Persian Gulf in late September. The small Iraqi navy stayed in port while Iran's naval forces withdrew from direct engagements and focused on blockade enforcement.[10]

The war settled into the first of many stalemates after Saddam announced on December 7, 1980, that Iraq was adopting a defensive strategy. Iraqi forces remained in Iran, however, and Baghdad clung to its war demands. Iran's leadership, with massive public support, took a hard line on cease-fire conditions and vowed to continue fighting. Both sides ignored a number of Arab, Muslim, and United Nations peace initiatives.

Over the next ten months Iran gradually developed new tactics to overcome some of its material shortcomings. Seeking to maximize Iran's firepower and mobility, the leadership tried to meld the Guard's ability to provide motivated but inexperienced manpower with the regular military's skills at planning, coordination, and logistics. Political differences over the two services' roles and institutional rivalries, however, impaired the desired collaboration. Despite this, Iran's combat leaders quickly learned to take advantage of Iraq's static defenses and overreliance on road-bound mechanized forces. The Iranians became proficient at reconnoitering enemy lines and identifying weak points defended by less stalwart Iraqi militiamen. Using diversionary attacks and constant pressure with probes and artillery exchanges to tie down Iraq's better units, Iran concentrated its assault force against vulnerable Iraqi positions. Massed formations of *pasdars* and *basijis* backed by army tanks and artillery were given the objective of breaking the Iraqi line to allow more mobile army mechanized forces to exploit the gaps. The Guard also became adept at infiltration tactics that allowed Iranian soldiers to create confusion and disrupt operations even within fortified Iraqi strongpoints. Still, the first operations were marked by hasty and inadequate preparations driven more by Iran's domestic politics than by sound military strategy. When the army stumbled, the Guard, backed by clerical supporters in Tehran, assumed the dominant role in the war.

As 1980 ended, President Bani Sadr was goaded by his clerical opponents into ordering the army to conduct a large counteroffensive before its units were ready. The plan called for secondary attacks to recapture key terrain around Qasr-e Shirin and Mehran in the central border region and to reduce an Iraqi salient near Ahvaz to push Iraqi artillery out of range of that city. The primary effort by two armored divisions aimed to relieve Abadan by breaking Iraqi lines farther north and then pushing south to link up with Iranian forces sallying out of the port city. By pressing for action in January, the clerical leadership forced the army to fight when winter flooding kept the tank and mechanized units confined to the roads. Their prospects for success were crippled further when sloppy communications security by Guard units enabled Iraqi intelligence to provide Iraqi commanders with a general concept of Iranian plans. The Iraqis responded to these warnings by concentrating several of their best tank regiments and the 10th Republican Guard Armored Brigade to meet the Iranian attacks.

Late on the night of January 4, 1981, the Iranians began their attack, and by day's end infiltrations of Iraqi lines and night attacks in the central region resulted in the capture of several ridges around Qasr-e Shirin and a few heights around Mehran. The supporting attack by Iran's 77th Infantry Division against the Iraqi salient near Ahvaz, however, made no progress. At Susangerd, the 16th Armored Division, backed by infantry from the 55th Airborne Brigade, assembled nearly three hundred tanks for a planned double envelopment. Because the Iranians had lost the element of surprise, the division rolled into an Iraqi trap instead. Hit on three sides, the lead brigade of Iranian tanks tried to maneuver out of the kill zone, but once off the road became mired in mud and was virtually destroyed. On the following day, the Iranians unwisely committed a second brigade, whose tanks tried to slug it out at close range with the Iraqi armor, but became sitting ducks in the churned-up battlefield muck. The division's third brigade also was ordered to attack, but with ammunition running low and no prospect of safely crossing the quagmire in front of the Iraqi positions, the commander withdrew. In general, Iranian tanks regularly outfought Iraqi units because of better gunners and tactics that emphasized maneuver to get flank shots against the Iraqi tanks' more vulnerable sides and rear engine compartment. Iranian tankers were brave and skillful at Susangerd and destroyed 100 of the 350 Iraqi tanks they confronted. Iran, however, lost two-thirds of its irreplaceable tanks, and the Sixteenth Division was nearly ruined. The offensive was stopped, and fortunately for Iran the Iraqis failed to pursue the Iranian units as they fell back to their lines.[11]

The Susangerd operation was presented in Tehran as an army failure, and the Revolutionary Guard was tapped to lead the next offensive against Qasr-e Shirin in late April. In one of the first uses of human wave tactics in the war, the Guard units, filled out with Basij volunteers, overran the panicked Iraqi defenders. The victory encouraged the Guard and its clerical supporters to tout this new way of "Islamic" warfare and increased their disregard of the professional military, which had advised against the bloody frontal infantry attacks. The regular military was criticized for abandoning offensive operations while the Pasdaran was credited with waging a comprehensive people's war against the invaders.[12] Khomeini initially played a mediating role, but when the issue was cast as a choice between military professionalism and revolutionary zeal in the spring of 1981, the Imam sided with the radicals. Once it became clear that the extremists' influence was rising, the Artesh's leadership again moved to the political sidelines. As internecine political warfare raged between President Bani Sadr and IRP hard-liners during the spring and summer of 1981, army and Pasdaran forces launched smaller attacks against the Iraqis that gained little territory but honed Iranian tactics and prepared the units for the larger battles to come.

Once Khomeini and his supporters consolidated control over all of Iran's armed forces, the Artesh and the Guard started to cooperate. Indeed, as the Guard gained more battlefield experience, Pasdaran commanders gained a better appreciation for conventional combined operations. While Iran's senior leadership deemed some competitiveness between the two forces as useful checks on each's power, they also wanted better battlefield performance and an end to the duplication of efforts and wasting of scarce resources. The regime began promoting army officers favored by the Guard to senior positions, which further improved the working relationship. Maj. Gen. Qasem Ali Zahir-Nejad, who played a large role in Kurdish operations and in organizing Iran's initial defense against Iraq, was named Chief of the Joint Staff. Brig. Gen. Ali Sayyid Shirazi was made army commander in 1981 after proving his loyalty battling the Kurds. Although differences between Guard commander Mohsen Rezai and Shirazi developed in later years, the two military leaders initially worked well together and set up a joint Army-Pasdaran field headquarters in northwestern Iran in 1982. Over time, the Pasdaran commanders even joined their army counterparts in complaining about the religious commissars, and Khomeini restricted the representatives' advisory roles and reduced their ability to meddle in command decisions.

As the summer of 1981 turned to fall, Iran prepared for another major attempt to lift the siege of Abadan. Aided by a deception campaign and diversionary attacks, Iran moved as many as twenty thousand men down the east side of the Karun River toward the city. These forces, when combined with the thirteen thousand to fifteen thousand soldiers and *pasdars* in Abadan, gave the Iranians a numerical advantage over the Iraqi forces in the salient across the Karun. Around midnight on September 26, 1981, the Iranians surprised the Iraqis with attacks from three sides. Guard units infiltrated Iraqi lines and helped turn the tactical withdrawal ordered by panicked Iraqi commanders into a rout. The mix of Iranian army heavy forces and Guard infantry inflicted severe casualties on Iraq's 10th Republican Guard Armored Brigade when it led to an unsuccessful counterattack. In all, Iraq lost several battalions in the salient and was forced back across the Karun. Iran might have accomplished more, but a C-130 transport carrying the minister of defense, army chief of staff, and regional Pasdaran commander crashed, killing the men most responsible for the victory at Abadan.

At the end of November, Iran launched the Tariq al-Qods (Path to Jerusalem) offensive with seven Guard brigades and three army brigades. The joint Army-Pasdaran plan called for a human wave assault against an Iraqi logistics base at Bostan in northern Khuzestan. The eager *pasdars* and *basijis* launched the attack before a scheduled army artillery barrage, which may have added to the shock as waves of lightly armed Iranians swarmed across the battlefield and engaged in hand-to-hand fighting with the Iraqis. Iranian mechanized forces then rolled into the Iraqi flanks and liberated Bostan, but could not prevent the Iraqis from slipping the noose.[13]

As 1981 ended, Saddam's troops still occupied Iranian territory, but Iran was winning battles, gaining ground, and faced no significant air or naval challenges. Iran was especially fortunate in the Iraqi air force's passivity, because the Iranian air force was in accelerating disarray. Following Bani Sadr's escape from Iran aboard an air force transport, the service was practically grounded for months as more than two hundred pilots and air crews were detained for questioning. Thereafter a committee of mullahs approved all flights, aircraft were given only enough fuel for their planned missions, and flying time to maintain piloting skills was restricted. Another bright spot for the Iranians was that their efforts to procure war materiel were seeing results as adherence to UN restrictions on selling arms to the combatants waned. North Korea, China, Libya, and Syria provided new Soviet-style weapons and ammunition to Iran while numerous Asian and European arms dealers sold munitions and spares for Iran's U.S.-made equipment. Even Israel, using third parties, transferred war materiel to Iran to help it bleed Saddam's army. The clerical regime's procurement system was seriously flawed, however. Iran regularly was defrauded by arms dealers, purchased obsolete arms and equipment, and had money stolen by corrupt regime officials.[14]

War until Victory

The war took a dramatic turn in 1982 as Iran turned the conflict from one of national defense to one extending the revolution and toward the Imam's seemingly preferred course, encapsulated in progovernment demonstrators' chant of "War! War until victory!" Khomeini ignored Iraqi offers to withdraw and negotiate an end to the hostilities. Instead, General Shirazi was put in command of a combined force of Army units, experienced Pasdaran fighters, and poorly trained Basij for a major push to liberate Khuzestan. The first offensive, Operation Undeniable Victory (Fath al-Mobin), targeted Iraqi forces around Dezful and Shush. In late March, Shirazi assembled four army divisions with 60,000 men and roughly 200 tanks and 150 artillery pieces, along with 80,000 Guard and Basij troops. Facing them were as many as 80,000 Iraqis and 600 tanks in 3 infantry, 2 armored, and 1 mechanized division with several infantry and militia brigades along the southern front.[15]

The offensive started shortly after midnight on March 22, 1982, when Iran's 21st and 84th Infantry divisions, led by Pasdaran spearheads, overran several Iraqi infantry and armored brigades on the northern portion of the Iraqi line. Human wave attacks exhausted the Iraqi militiamen defending the objectives.

After breakthroughs were achieved, the regular army units pushed into the gaps and turned against the exposed Iraqi flanks. Saddam had forbidden Iraqi units from ceding any ground, so the Iraqis were slow to redeploy and bring up reserves, which left their overall defensive scheme disjointed and weak. When Iranian units penetrated far into the Iraqi rear area and attacked the armored reserves there, the Iraqi corps commander panicked. He ordered frontal counterattacks by Iraq's 3rd and 10th Armored divisions and the 10th Republican Guard Armored Brigade, but the Iranians easily turned back these assaults. On the third night, Iran's southern wing, comprising the 88th and 92nd Armored divisions, 55th Airborne Brigade, and Pasdaran infantry, started a pincer movement to bag the Iraqi forces still in the salient. The Iranians broke through the Iraqi lines in several locations and rolled up Iraq's 5th Mechanized Division before completing a double envelopment. Both sides suffered heavy casualties, but Iran scored a major victory. In addition to pushing the Iraqis out of most of northern Khuzestan, Iran inflicted up to fifty thousand casualties, captured fifteen thousand to twenty-five thousand prisoners, and smashed an Iraqi mechanized division, armored division, and large numbers of smaller militia units. In addition to destroying two hundred Iraqi tanks, four hundred other armored vehicles, and several hundred artillery pieces, the Pasdaran captured enough Iraqi equipment and ammunition to start to organize and train its own armored units.

The Iranians next turned to the liberation of Khorramshahr and the elimination of the last Iraqi salient in Khuzestan. The operation involved a planned double envelopment with a three-pronged attack to tie down Iraqi forces and then collapse the shoulders of the pocket, trapping the Iraqis inside. The Iraqi defenses were formidable with seventy thousand to ninety thousand men in eight divisions deployed behind earthen barriers interspersed with bunkers and observation towers. In front of the Iraqis, the fields of fire had been cleared and criss-crossed with barbed wire and minefields. In the predawn darkness of April 30, 1982, as many as forty thousand *pasdars* and *basijis* along with the 16th Armored Division assaulted Iraq's hastily reorganized 5th Mechanized Division, 6th Armored Division, and their supporting militia on the northern side of the salient west of Susangerd. Although the Iranians suffered heavy losses, rows of *basijis* and *pasdars* fearlessly crossed the Iraqi obstacles and kill zones, piercing and then overrunning the Iraqi lines. On the following day, Pasdaran formations accompanied by Iran's 21st Infantry Division crossed the Karun River and overwhelmed a weak section of the southern Iraqi line held by reserve and militia units. At the same time, the 92nd Armored Division and supporting Guard units struck at the Iraqi center around Khorramshahr and punched through the first line of Iraqi defenses. After several days of merciless fighting in which Iranian attack helicopters played a critical role in disrupting Iraqi counterattacks, the northern wing advanced into position to close the trap on the Iraqi units in Khorramshahr.

Before delivering the final blow, Iran's forces had to overcome Iraq's armored reserves. In desperation, the Iraqi commander had ordered his 3rd and 9th Armored divisions to launch a major counterattack. Their objective was several key Karun River bridges to cut off the flow of Iranian reinforcements. Guard and Basij units were pushed back by the Iraqis but delayed the enemy heavy units long enough for the 92nd Division to get on the 3rd Armored Division's flank and shatter it. The rout of this Iraqi division exposed the 9th Armored Division's flank and forced it to retreat. The Iranian push to the Iraqi border isolated many Iraqi units, including up to two Iraqi divisions around Khorramshahr. After a brief pause to consolidate and reorganize, the Iranians renewed the attack, and a Pasdaran division cut the last major Iraqi supply route into Khorramshahr. Roughly eighty thousand Iranians attacked on May 22, and after suffering heavy losses breaking into the city, the Guard and Basij units recaptured Khorramshahr in less than two days of heavy street-to-street fighting. Fewer than half of the Iraqi forces escaped, and only then by abandoning their equipment and ferrying across the Shatt al-Arab. The Iranians bagged between twelve thousand and fifteen thousand Iraqi prisoners, up to two hundred tanks, and large amounts of equipment and supplies in ending the nearly nineteen-month occupation of Khorramshahr.

Many in Tehran viewed Iran's victories as confirmation of the revolution's virtue and a consecration of its most expansive goals. The radical clerics, Pasdaran, and General Shirazi, the architect of successful offensives, wanted to fight until Saddam fell. Propeace factions led by more pragmatic politicians, including future Supreme Leader Khamenei, and other military professionals argued against continuing the conflict, especially in light of the economic costs and the armed forces' problems and supply shortages. Saddam seized on the Israeli invasion of Lebanon in June 1982 as a pretext to order Iraqi forces out of the last bits of occupied Iranian territory, offering to end the fighting so Iraqi and Iranian troops could join together to oppose Israel. Khomeini wanted the war to continue, however, and his view was the deciding factor. The regime rejected Saddam's cease-fire offer, and its war goals evolved from ejecting the Iraqis from Iran to extending the revolution into Iraq, liberating the Shia holy cities of Karbala and Najaf, and overthrowing the Baathist regime.

The Iranian army got little credit for the battlefield successes, and after regular military officers were implicated in a plot to kill Khomeini in April and another coup attempt was uncovered in June, the regime shifted more resources and authority to the Revolutionary Guard. Still distrusted by the clerics, Artesh leaders made it easier for the hard-liners to disregard them by offering generally sound but unwelcome advice about not overreaching with offensive operations that were too costly and difficult to sustain. At this time the Pasdaran's support-ers created the cabinet-level Islamic Revolutionary Guards Corps Ministry. Because one of the primary disputes between the Artesh and the Pasdaran was the control of major weapon systems, the Guard accelerated efforts to build up its own tank and mechanized units using captured Iraqi equipment. During the next three years, the Guard continued to grow in size and came to resemble the regular military forces as air and naval wings were formed and more professional staffs were created to support the commanders and conduct operational plan-ning, administration, and logistics.[16]

As Iran embarked on the new phase of the war, it was slow to recognize that the transfer of battlefields from Iranian to Iraqi territory shifted the dynamics of the fighting to its disadvantage. Iran's main offensive arm, the Pasdaran infantry units, generally relied on the brute force of frontal assaults. Iraqi soldiers had been unwilling to fight the zealous *pasdars* and *basijis* to the death to hold Ira-nian territory that Saddam had repeatedly offered to return to end the war. Once in their homeland, however, the Iraqis' resistance stiffened. Saddam's army still outnumbered Iran in nearly all categories of combat power and, in the south, had the advantage of defending terrain marked by large waterways and marshes and better roads and support infrastructure for resupply and reinforcement. Iraq used the time between Iranian attacks to build extensive earthen berms, mine-fields, and other obstacles to enhance the southern region's natural defenses. The trench lines included firing positions for tanks, and antiaircraft guns were positioned on the front lines to fend off Iranian aircraft and drop into direct fire mode to blast Iranian infantry approaching the berms. To the rear of the Iraqi front lines, Saddam's army began constructing secondary fortifications, artil-lery complexes, supply depots, and hospitals. By mid-1982, the Iraqis also had started to use tear gas and experiment with chemical weapons to disrupt Iranian assaults.[17]

Operation Blessed Ramadan, Iran's first major offensive into Iraq, focused on Al Basrah, Iraq's second largest city and one dominated by Shia. The Irani-ans hoped that if they could capture the well-fortified city, Iraqi Shia would be prompted to revolt against the Baathist regime. In mid-July 1982, Pasdaran and Basij elements numbering ninety thousand men spearheaded an attack against seventy thousand to ninety thousand Iraqi troops in five reinforced infantry divisions with three armored divisions in reserve. The Iranian army provided six understrength divisions to support the offensive with tanks, artillery, attack helicopters, and a few diversionary attacks north of the Hawizeh Marshes. Dur-ing the bitter fighting, many *basijis* went into battle unarmed, urged on by mul-lahs to cross minefields to clear paths for the Pasdaran and army units. In the center, Pasdaran units were stopped by the formidable Iraqi defenses, but the 92nd Armored Division breached the Iraqi lines. Before the penetration could be reinforced, however, the Iraqi armored reserves surrounded the Iranian division and nearly destroyed it. To the south, the 21st Infantry Division and Guard units failed in their attempt to swing south of Fish Lake, a large water obstacle, and outflank the Iraqi defensive lines anchored there. Still relying on revolutionary zeal and the quest for martyrdom, the Iranians hurled more men at the Iraqi defenses until early August when the troops' exhaustion and supply shortages forced the leaders to call a halt.

The failed offensive against Al Basrah shone a spotlight on Iran's most significant military shortcomings. Iran's basic strategy was roughly equivalent to trying to use a hammer to destroy an anvil.[18] The Guard formations allowed the commanders to commit large numbers of infantry in repeated attacks, but the divisions were slow and plodding and lacked the training and mobility needed to counter Iraq's strong armored reserves. Because command and control capabilities were limited, lead Guard units were nearly autonomous, which, when coupled with the *basijis'* desire for martyrdom, sometimes made it difficult for commanders to redirect or recall their units. Coordination between the Guard units and their supporting army tank and artillery units also was weak, so the ability to shift fires or change attacks to take advantage of opportunities was seriously circumscribed. Iranian tankers were still better than their Iraqi counterparts in one-on-one engagements, but because of supply problems and the nature of the terrain, Iranian armor units were often caught at a disadvantage by antitank ambush teams and counterattacking Iraqi tank forces. Logistic shortcomings made the exploitation of breakthroughs difficult because the supply system was not able to keep up with advancing units. The Iranian army later judged that the Blessed Ramadan operation and Iran's other offensives after 1982 were generally doomed to failure because Iran's pride in its earlier victories caused the leadership to ignore the Iraqis' nationalistic will to fight in defense of their home soil. It also assessed that victory was an unlikely outcome because Iran overlooked its inadequate intelligence on the strength of Iraq's defenses and too rarely applied the principles of war to its operations.[19]

As 1983 progressed, the conflict devolved into a war of attrition. The development of trench works and no-man's-lands and the costly frontal attacks mimicked World War I battles in France. Still, Iran made enough gains to convince the clerical leadership that one more major offensive would be decisive. Operation Blessed Ramadan had shown that Iraq could use its superior firepower to offset Iran's manpower, killing as many as three to four Iranians for every Iraqi killed. The clerics, however, turned a blind eye toward this cost of the Pasdaran's "Islamic" way of war as resources were drained and the Guard eventually was bled of its experienced leaders and morale. The hard-liners in the government also ignored the growing problems with equipping their forces. In 1983, the Guard mobilized up to three hundred thousand men while the army had another three hundred thousand full-time, mostly conscript soldiers. Through heroic maintenance work and the cannibalization of parts from the rest of its inventory of weapon systems, Iran had about five hundred Western tanks in the army, between two hundred and three hundred Soviet tanks with the Guard, and up to one thousand other armored vehicles and one thousand artillery pieces available for battle. By some estimates, this represented about one-third of the equipment needed for a force of six hundred thousand men, and replacement equipment and spare parts still were difficult to acquire.[20] In such circumstances, a war of attrition, even the more defensive version advocated by the army, worked against the Islamic Republic.

Between February and November 1983, Iran conducted a series of five offensives that made very few gains while costing nearly three times as many casualties as Iraq suffered. These various Val Fajr (By the Dawn) offensives reflected a few modifications to Iranian tactics as the military planners tried to avoid attacking Iraqi strongpoints. Iran's first two offensives in February and April against the Baghdad–Al Basrah road in the region north of the Hawizeh Marshes were repulsed. The third and fifth attacks were in the mountains of Kurdistan in July and October, during which Iranian Kurds were ejected from Mahabad and other Iranian cities and a poorly defended Iraqi garrison at Hajj Umran was captured. Iranian and allied Iraqi Kurdish fighters also seized ridgelines east of As Sulaymaniyah, Iraq, that put them within striking distance of that major city. The fourth Val Fajr offensive was a July attack on Mehran in the central border region in which the Iranians carried a few strategic heights around the city. Iranian troops were hit by Iraqi chemical attacks during some of these battles, although the effect was limited because of Iraqi failures to account for wind and weather and to use their chemical weapons properly. By the end of 1983, Iran had made negligible gains, but its leadership was not yet dissuaded by the mounting costs of the war.

Marsh Madness

Iran's leaders failed to learn any lessons from the failures of the 1983 offensives. In a triumph of hope over experience, the radical clerics and the Pasdaran appear to have judged that slight changes in their battlefield fortunes could bring victory. They also appear to have consistently overestimated Iraqi casualties and the impact of Iranian attacks on Iraqi morale. The Guard made a few minor modifications to its tactics to reduce some wastage of their martyrs and to adjust for equipment losses and accompanying reductions in fire support. Although 1984 witnessed a switch from large attacks along broad fronts to more focused multiple attacks across terrain favorable to the attackers, the requirement to redeploy and concentrate Iranian forces slowed the tempo of operations. After

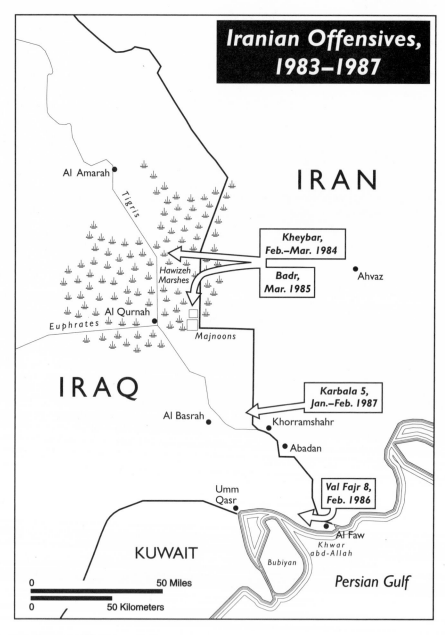

9.2 Iranian Offensives, 1983–1987.

Iran's main offensive in 1984, the Iranians slipped into a pattern of one major "annual offensive" followed by numerous smaller attacks and artillery exchanges during each of the war's remaining years. Iran's military leadership belatedly increased efforts to obtain new heavy combat equipment and organized its infantry and militia forces to conduct more controlled and cohesive mass attacks. In addition, more attention was given to logistics, depots, and roads, and limited improvements were made in training, especially for amphibious warfare.

The war forced Iran to make some institutional and procedural reforms in an attempt to centralize logistic and engineering efforts. Iran set up a joint supply command in March 1984, although the primary responsibility for supply matters rested with services, which had to coordinate with the Defense, Guard, and Interior ministries. Iran's defense-related factories were brought together and placed under a single organization called the Defense Industries Organization, or DIO. Production of items manufactured under the shah was resumed because the arms embargoes forced the Iranians to develop the means to produce spare parts and ammunition no longer available from overseas. Starting in 1983, the Pasdaran was allowed to create its own military factories, the first of which opened in early 1984 to produce 120-mm mortars. The Guard eventually opened factories for grenades, rocket-propelled grenades (RPGs), chemical defense equipment, and spare parts for Soviet tanks captured from Iraq. Raw material shortages, however, restricted production.

Even when the institutions and factories were working, Iran's logistic system faced other constraints that contributed to long lead times needed to prepare for offensives. The movement of supplies to the front was vulnerable to weather conditions, such as snow-blocked roads in the Zagros or flooded roadways in Khuzestan. Iran's railroad stock suffered from spare parts shortages, its ports were severely congested, and its aerial resupply capabilities were inadequate. Over time, the army and Guard adopted the Soviet practice of having subordinate units rely on higher echelons for transportation and the delivery of supplies. In some cases when supply breakdowns occurred Iranian units were forced to live off the land for days at a time. As in any country's armed forces, there was resentment among the various services over the distribution of resources, which fed the Artesh-Pasdaran rivalry.[21]

In early 1984, Iran prepared what it hoped would be the final blow against Iraq. The Iranians assembled between two hundred and fifty thousand and three hundred thousand men for a series of attacks along a 150-mile front from Mehran in the central border region south to the main objective, the main highway between Al Basrah and Baghdad to the west of the Hawizeh Marshes straddling the border. The initial phase of the plan involved two operations, Val Fajr 5 and 6, with one hundred thousand men. It began in mid-February and sought to tie down Iraqi forces north of the marshes and draw Iraqi reserves from the south to the Al Kut region of Iraq. In a week of heavy fighting, the Iranians seized some strategic high ground but were stopped about fifteen miles from the Tigris River and the Baghdad–Al Basrah road.

The main Iranian effort, called Operation Kheybar, aimed to set the stage for capturing Al Basrah by surprising Iraqi defenders between that city and Al Amarah. The initial objective was to interdict the narrow strip of land carrying the Baghdad–Al Basrah road by crossing the Hawizeh Marshes. Water levels in the marshes were three to nine feet deep, and thick clumps and islets of six-feet-tall reeds abounded in an area running forty miles from east to west and more than thirty miles from north to south. Saddam's generals did not think the Iranians would try to attack through such an impassable morass. As a result, the Iraqis had not strengthened the forty thousand troops opposite the marshes and had placed a boundary between two Iraqi corps there.

The Iranians launched a three-pronged attack covering the entire marsh on February 24, 1984. Between fifty thousand and one hundred and fifty thousand men pushed into the swamp using waves of barges, small boats, and rubber rafts. These forces were backed by another one hundred thousand reserves ready to enter the fray, while Iranian helicopters provided limited fire support and transport. The Iranians had prepared an innovative amphibious assault and assembled a strong engineering contingent to help facilitate movement in the swamps. They failed, however, to develop a means to bring heavy artillery and antitank guns forward quickly. The Iranian air force, meanwhile, was unable to provide air cover or offset Iraqi attack helicopters, which ranged over the marshes delivering deadly machine gun and rocket fire. In the north, the various Iranian watercraft in the initial attack surprised the Iraqis, and the Iranians seized Beida and other marsh villages. Guard units then moved quickly along a causeway to the western shore, where they established a bridgehead. The flotilla shuttled more Iranian troops to the slowly expanding toehold in Iraqi territory. Some Iranian troops may have reached the Baghdad–Al Basrah road before being stopped.

The central prong of the attack overran the Majnoon Islands, which were two manmade areas built above a capped oil field in the marshes. The Majnoons held a complex of buildings, were interspersed with dry and swampy areas, and were surrounded by causeways, dikes, and a canal. After seizing the two islands, roughly twenty thousand Iranians squeezed onto them and hastily built a lengthy pontoon bridge back to the eastern shore of the marshes for resupply. At the southwestern tip of the marshes, Guard and Basij units threw massed infantry across an exposed area of salt flats and sand, called the Ghuzail, against strongly entrenched Iraqis. Although the Iranians achieved surprise, the defenders held on for five days until the attackers lost their momentum and withdrew.[22]

In the Iranian bridgehead west of Beida, the Pasdaran units became trapped. The small craft moving Iranian troops and supplies across the marsh were interdicted by Iraqi attack helicopters and warplanes. Without reinforcements and lacking adequate fire support, the Guard forces were unable to expand their position. Iraq had time to redeploy its forces and use its superior firepower and chemical weapons, including the first use of nerve agents in any war. Other Iranian troops in the marshes were electrocuted when the Iraqis turned nearby power lines into weapons and diverted their currents into the swamp. Although the Guard bridgehead held out for three days against strong Iraqi counterattacks, the *pasdars* and *basijis* eventually fell back into the marshes, where many drowned. The Iranians on the Majnoons were forced to give some ground to counterattacking Iraqi forces, but the fighting was so fierce that the Iraqis eventually called off their attack and ceded all but a quarter of the southern island to Iran. The Iranians also maintained a hold on much of the rest of the Hawizeh Marshes, and Iranian engineers expanded the network of earthen causeways, mounds, and depots to improve mobility and sustainability for the frontline forces in the swamp. By the end of Operation Kheybar, over a half-million Iranian and Iraqi troops had been involved, making it one of the largest battles of the war. Between twelve thousand and twenty thousand Pasdaran and Basij personnel were killed between mid-February and mid-March while the army lost up to six thousand dead. The armed forces were too debilitated to conduct more than small attacks for the rest of the year.

Iran's annual offensive for 1985 was a more cautious replay of Operation Kheybar. Although the army ultimately supported the offensive, its senior commanders continued to advise that Iran's goal should be to win a war of attrition by attacking Iraqi weak points, overstretching Iraqi manpower, and provoking the Iraqis to make costly counterattacks into prepared Iranian positions. The radicals were not persuaded to abandon their goal of a final decisive battle and assembled one hundred thousand men for Operation Badr, as the 1985 offensive was called. The battle plan called for forty-five thousand to sixty-five thousand men to conduct the three phases of the attack. First, a spearhead of Guard and Basij units would cross the marshes to establish bridgeheads in Iraq. Iran then would conduct a rapid buildup of troops and supplies on the western shore. In the last phase, the Iranians would attack to cut the road and then send forces north and south to roll up the Iraqi defenses. Iranian troops on the Majnoon Islands also were to attack toward Al Basrah to interrupt the flow of reinforcements north. Benefiting from nearly a year's experience in operating in the marshes, the Iranians were better prepared for a renewed push to cut the Baghdad–Al Basrah road. In addition to the construction of causeways and pontoon bridges to move heavy weapon systems, Iran built large rafts to carry mortars and recoilless rifles. Guard and Basij members were armed with RPGs and large supplies of rockets to help hold off Iraqi armored counterattacks. More boats were assembled to reduce the number of trips needed to ferry men and supplies across the waterways. Finally, more Iranian soldiers had been equipped with chemical protective masks and clothing and nerve agent antidote.[23]

Opposite Iran's lines, the Iraqi defenders had not been idle in the face of Iranian forces in the marshes. Approximately ten divisions protected the western shore, with two divisions spread over the narrow strip of land along the Tigris River facing the marshes. The region had been covered by an extensive chain of earthen barriers, bunkers, minefields and other obstacles. The Iraqis had even set up pumps to move water and create additional flooded zones when needed.

Operation Badr began on the night of March 10, 1985, with a diversionary artillery barrage against Al Basrah. On the following night, Pasdaran and Basij units moved through the marshes to surprise the Iraqi defenders north of Al Qurnah. The offensive was executed much as it had been planned, and within three days a brigade's worth of Guard and Basij units reached the Tigris River. During the night, Iranian engineers put a few pontoon bridges across the Tigris, and by the next day about three thousand Guard personnel reached the Baghdad–Al Basrah road. The success was short-lived, however, and the bridgehead again became a trap. Iraqi reserves led by elite Republican Guard units counterattacked the Iranians from three sides. Iraqi air force sorties and fire from massed batteries of Iraqi artillery pounded the Iranian salient with high explosives and chemical agents. Iraqi helicopters again took a heavy toll of Iranian boats and support elements in the marshes. After two days of devastating Iraqi attacks, the Pasdaran forces retreated back into the marshes. The planned attack from the Majnoon Islands started while the Guards were withdrawing, and the assault quickly faltered in the face of strong Iraqi defenses. Iran's losses ranged from eleven thousand to seventeen thousand men, but the early success in reaching the road seemed to reassure the clerical leadership that Iran's strategy and tactics were working. Iran conducted other small attacks near Mehran, Sumar, and Qasr-e Shirin during the summer and around Rawanduz in Iraqi Kurdistan in September. The war remained deadlocked, however. Company- and battalion-sized operations along the entire front were used to keep the Iraqis on edge as the Iranians gathered their strength for the next round.

As 1985 ended, Khomeini and his supporters remained confident in their delusional views of Iraq's fragility, continued to ignore Iraqi and international efforts to broker a peace, and were even willing to expand the war to obtain their ends. Saddam's regime was the recipient of aid and loans from other Arab countries that allowed it to increase the Iraqi army's size and ensure that it was equipped with the most modern weapon systems and ample supplies of ammunition. Iraq also was getting intelligence support from the United States and other countries concerned about Iran's radicalism. Iraqi Arabs, whether Sunni or Shia, rallied to the regime when the Iranians invaded Iraq, making Tehran's hope for an Islamic revolution in Iraq a vain one. Iran was increasingly isolated and facing an imperfect but still painful arms embargo. It also was forced to rely on its cash reserves and oil revenues in the absence of international loans to fund the war while trying to keep its domestic economy afloat. The cleric's faulty strategy and the Guard's increasing aggressiveness worsened Iran's isolation and made victory less likely.

Exporting the Revolution

Despite the war's demands, the Guard expanded its missions by seizing on the export of the revolution to project Iran's power and influence. Iran's revolution had inspired Shia in Saudi Arabia, North Yemen, Turkey, and Pakistan, and Iran aided Muslim radicals as far away as Malaysia and the Philippines. The Guard also saw the revolution's export as a weapon to intimidate the oil-rich Persian Gulf Sunni Arab monarchies that were supporting Saddam. Iran armed and supported a group of Shia radicals who unsuccessfully tried to overthrow Bahrain's ruling family in 1981. During the annual Hajj pilgrimage in Mecca that year, Iranian pilgrims sponsored by the government conducted the first in a series of large yearly demonstrations that became increasingly violent in an effort to undermine the Saudi government. In November 1982 Iran formed the Supreme Council of the Islamic Revolution in Iraq (SCIRI), a group of Iraqi Shia that had political and military wings and shared the goal of overthrowing Saddam and establishing an Iranian-style government in Iraq. Within the Persian Gulf region, such intimidation failed to weaken support for Iraq and instead increased Gulf Arab efforts to counter Iran politically, economically, and militarily. By putting vital energy resources at risk by inciting instability, Iran's actions posed a threat to Western economies and increased international interest in insulating the world from Iran's revolutionary fervor.[24]

The Revolutionary Guard played the primary role in exporting the revolution, bringing its ideological and violent enthusiasm to the effort. The Guard established an Office of Liberation Movements, and throughout the region Iran looked to terrorist groups as the seedlings of larger revolutionary movements that would eventually attack the governments opposing the Islamic Republic. The Pasdaran seized on the situation in Lebanon, where civil war and the Israel invasion of 1982 offered enormous opportunities to extend Iranian influence and build an ally for opposing the West and Israel. Lebanon had one of the Middle East's largest Arab Shia communities, and Iranian-Lebanese ties predated the Islamic Revolution. When the Safavids seized Iran in the sixteenth century, they turned to Lebanese Shia communities for clerics to guide their subjects, initiating religious, communal, and personal ties that remained robust over the centuries. Between 1950 and 1979, the shah had kept Iranian intelligence officers in Lebanon to counter radical Arab nationalism and later to keep tabs on Iranian dissidents being trained by Palestinian militants there. In the spring of 1978, Iran sent troops to Lebanon as peacekeepers with the United Nations Interim Force in Lebanon (UNIFIL). Following the 1982 Israeli invasion, the clerical regime sent one thousand Guard personnel to Lebanon's Bekaa Valley, where the Iranians took a disorganized and rag-tag collection of Shia fighters and created Lebanese Hizballah, which quickly became a powerful guerrilla and terrorist group.[25]

Iran provided limited direct military assistance but considerable financial support to help Hizballah establish itself. With help from Syrian officials and Iranian diplomats and intelligence officers, the Guard worked with the nascent Hizballah organization to train and indoctrinate new members. The Pasdaran's commitment was relatively small, with the contingent peaking at roughly 1,500 men before leveling out at 300 to 500 trainers and advisors. Once the Guard created a cadre of well-trained Hizballah guerrillas and terrorists, these men then trained other Lebanese. The Pasdaran also increased the movement's appeal by developing social services and establishing fund-raising networks. The social welfare effort involved the building of schools, clinics, agricultural cooperatives, television and radio stations, hospitals, and mosques. Through these projects, the Iranians built popular support for Khomeini, Iran, and the revolution; stressed the value of martyrdom; and demonized Iran's enemies, especially the United States. Their reward was the creation of a devoted proxy that pledged its "absolute" loyalty to Khomeini in early 1985 in the first public declaration of its program and strategy.[26]

The Pasdaran provided both tactical and strategic direction to Hizballah, making it the vanguard for efforts to expel the Americans and Israelis from Lebanon and to crush pro-Iraqi groups there. Guard officials supervised attacks such as the suicide bombing of the U.S. embassy in April 1983, where sixty-three people, including seventeen Americans, died. The Guard also was behind the truck bombings of the American and French multinational forces in October 1983, in which 241 U.S. Marines and 58 French peacekeepers were killed. The Guard was involved in Hizballah's hostage operations during the rest of the decade when seventeen Americans and seventy other foreigners were kidnapped. Ten of these hostages died in captivity, including CIA Station Chief William Buckley, who was tortured and murdered. In 1985 and 1986, Hizballah conducted operations outside of Lebanon, carrying out several attacks in France on Iran's behalf because of French support for and military sales to Iraq. The Hizballah members in France worked closely with the Iranian embassy in Paris and the Guard officers stationed there. The kidnappings in Lebanon reduced Western influence in the country, but international anger at Iran continued to coalesce to the Islamic Republic's disadvantage.

The Tanker and Air Wars

With the ground war stalemated, Iran and Iraq increasingly looked to air and naval operations to undermine each other. The resulting escalation mostly worked against Iran. During the early phases of the war, Iran's navy easily blockaded virtually land-locked Iraq. The Iraqis turned to air power to go after Iran's oil infrastructure, coastal export facilities, and shipping to try to cut off the oil sales and revenues the clerical regime needed to continue the war. The Iranian air force was unable to stop the Iraqi raids, and Iran only retaliated occasionally for Iraqi attacks because of the general absence of Iraqi ships in the Persian Gulf.

Iran initially had no desire to escalate the maritime conflict because it was heavily dependent on merchant shipping and wanted to avoid inviting Western intervention. As a result, the regime generally refrained from going after merchant vessels that used Gulf Arab ports to move Iraqi imports and exports. Saddam, however, wanted to draw in the international community to increase pressure on Iran to stop the war, and by 1985 Iraq's air force had gained new capabilities that made its attacks on ships, oil facilities, and Iranian cities more effective. The Iraqis intensified their attacks in the Gulf, and when Iran responded, ship attacks moved from a sideshow to a key objective in the war. The so-called Tanker War became one of the most sustained assaults on merchant shipping since the Second World War. Although the Tanker War's impact on shipping in the region was relatively small, the repercussions for Iran were enormous because of Saddam's success in goading the Iranians to provoke the Western intervention they had sought to avoid.

Iran was frustrated because while Iranian naval patrols exercised their rights under international law and stopped ships suspected of carrying contraband to Iraqi ports, the Baathist regime got around the blockade. Iraq relied on overland transport and pipelines to export oil while nonbelligerent ships unloaded imports at neutral ports in the Gulf Arab states. Despite its problems, Iran's navy was still the largest in the Persian Gulf and was able to dominate this relatively small body of water. Only 615 miles long and 210 miles across at its widest point, the Gulf is shallow with an average depth of just 100 feet with coral reefs lining the coasts. At its mouth, the Strait of Hormuz is only 20 to 25 miles wide, and the main shipping channels are within easy striking distance of Iranian ships, aircraft, and other weapon systems. To the west of the strait, numerous islands belonging to Iran or under its control provided bases for coastal radars, artillery, and small boat operations against merchant shipping. Iran's options to affect Iraqi exports and imports, however, were limited to attacks on neutral ships carrying war materiel to Kuwaiti ports or tankers carrying oil from the Gulf Arab states supporting Saddam.[27]

Over the first years of the war, Iran was able to ignore the minor losses caused by Iraqi attacks against its oil export capacity, although the perceived injustice of the situation was infuriating. After a lull in attacks from late 1980 until mid-1981, the Iraqis began targeting Bandar Khomeini and ships using the port. The loss of access to Khorramshahr and reduced port operations at Bandar Khomeini created major demands on Iran's southern ports that overwhelmed their capacity, increased waiting times and costs, and delayed deliveries of essential goods and war materiel. The Iraqis also attacked the Khark Island export terminal, and while redundant capacity at the terminal kept it operating, disruptions to Iran's oil exports reduced much needed revenues. For the initial attacks on merchant shipping, the Iraqis used French-made Super Frelon helicopters firing Exocet antiship missiles. In mid-1983, Saddam's regime leased five Super Etendard strike aircraft from the French Navy while awaiting the delivery of Mirage F-1 fighters ordered before the war. Iran responded with threats to close the strait and cut off the flow of oil to the West if France delivered the aircraft to Iraq. Iranian officials also repeated warnings about targeting neutral tankers, and to back up the threats the Iranians began strengthening artillery positions and naval bases on their various Gulf islands.

The crux of Iran's warning was that if it could not ship oil, then no other Gulf country could export oil, which was exactly the response Saddam wanted. Days after the Super Etendards arrived, Iraq declared a naval exclusion zone in the northern Persian Gulf and warned ships to stay away. The clerics in Tehran, still wary of Western intervention, debated but hesitated to fulfill their threats. After a slow start, the Iraqis intensified air operations against Iranian shipping in February 1984 and soon dominated the air over Bandar Khomeini and Khark Island. Iran tried to rely on passive air defenses and set up a convoy system in which Iranian tankers moved oil from Khark Island to safer anchorages in the southern Gulf for transfer to foreign vessels. The convoys still were vulnerable to air attack, but the system reduced the risk to non-Iranian shippers. Iranian navy destroyers were the only ships with significant air defense capabilities, but these were seldom available for convoy escort duties because of maintenance problems. Not surprisingly, the undefended convoys became targets themselves. In an attack on a five-ship convoy, Iraqi Super Frelon helicopters damaged one vessel beyond repair with a missile strike, two ships collided while trying to evade the Iraqi helicopters, and the entangled vessels then ran into two other merchant ships, running one aground.

Iran reluctantly began retaliatory attacks on the nominally neutral shipping using Gulf Arab ports in May 1984. The Iranian navy focused on merchant shipping because it was too small to enforce a blockade of the strait, and closing the two main channels was impractical. The channels were too deep to block by sinking vessels in them as the Egyptians had done in the Suez Canal in 1956 and

1967, and the strait's swift currents limited the utility of minefields. Instead, Iran turned to its remaining F-4 Phantoms firing Maverick television-guided bombs to target tankers carrying Gulf Arab oil. Between September 1980 and February 1984, Iran had struck only five merchant ships in retaliation for twenty-three successful Iraqi ship attacks. Iran would continue to lag behind Iraq in antiship operations, but in 1984 Iran started to close the gap as its attacks jumped to seventeen in response to thirty-seven Iraqi strikes on Iranian shipping.

As the Tanker War began in earnest, the air war escalated with renewed efforts by Iraq to terrorize Iran's populace and undermine the regime. Iran retaliated as best it could with little effect on the Iraqis. Iraq had attacked civilians at the start of the war when it bombed Ahvaz and fired Soviet-produced FROG (Free Rocket Over Ground) rockets into Dezful. The FROG, with a one-thousand-pound warhead and a range of up to forty miles, had no guidance system and often missed even large targets such as cities and oil installations. Saddam renewed attacks on cities in 1983 in response to Iran's efforts to invade Iraq. By the end of that year the Baathists were conducting attacks on cities with Soviet-made SCUD B surface-to-surface missiles (SSMs), an inaccurate system based on the Nazi V-2 rocket from World War II, with a nearly two-thousand-pound warhead and a 186-mile range. Iran responded to these Iraqi attacks with occasional air strikes involving two to four warplanes to show that it could penetrate Iraqi air defenses. Neither side inflicted significant damage, but the campaign was harder on Iran because the air force was unable to replace its occasional losses to Iraqi air defenses.[28]

The Iraqis initiated an intense series of air raids and missile attacks against Iran in February 1984 that, after Iran retaliated with strikes on Iraq, became known as the "war of the cities." Iraq's goals were to dissuade Iran from launching its looming Fajr and Kheybar offensives and weaken Iranian morale. Because its air force was unable to surge aircraft for the strategic bombing role, Iran's retaliation was limited. Although Iran had no direct answer to the fifty-eight Iraqi SCUDs launched between late 1983 and the end of 1984, it subjected Al Basrah and other important Iraqi cities close to the front lines to regular rocket and artillery attacks. The impact of the war of the cities on both sides' determination to persist in the conflict was negligible, however. A cease-fire for attacks on civilians was arranged in June 1984 with the United Nations serving as a mediator. Sporadic air and missile attacks continued, and, in March 1985, the Revolutionary Guard fired Libyan-supplied SCUD missiles at Iraqi cities. The Pasdaran later acquired more SCUDs from North Korea but was not able to match the Iraqis, who fired eighty-two SCUDs in 1985 against Iran's thirteen to fifteen SCUD missile attacks.[29]

Iran's ability to defend its air space was severely limited by the air force's incapacity to generate sufficient sorties to maintain regular combat air patrols. Air force pilots were scrambled only after Iraqi aircraft were identified on radar and only infrequently got airborne in time to intercept the Iraqi fighters on the return leg of their attack. Dogfights were rare as a result, especially after Iran's air-to-air missile (AAM) inventory, including the long-range Phoenix missile, became unreliable. In desperation, Iran started Project Sky Hawk in 1985 to adapt the I-HAWK SAM for use by F-14 Tomcats, successfully testing the modified missile in 1986 and reportedly firing one or two in combat before abandoning the effort because of guidance problems.

When Iraq began to send its warplanes farther south in the Gulf in 1984, the Iranians had a greater opportunity to engage the Iraqis and tried to take advantage of it. Saddam's pilots, however, used Kuwaiti and Saudi airspace for part of their journey, which caused the Iranians to violate Saudi airspace in their efforts to intercept the Iraqis. Iran's leaders may have believed that the Saudis would not risk a confrontation, but their assumption was wrong. In early June 1984 two patrolling Saudi F-15 Eagles responded to an Iranian violation of Saudi air space. The American-trained Saudi pilots were backed by a U.S. Air Force Boeing E-3A Sentry AWACS (Airborne Warning and Air Control System) aircraft, which was part of a detachment of four U.S. AWACS and two tankers under the ELF-1 mission dispatched by President Carter to Saudi Arabia in October 1980. The Sentry directed the Saudi F-15s toward the Iranian aircraft, and outclassed by the fully operational Eagles, at least one and possibly two Iranian Phantoms were shot down. Iran's air force immediately ceased using Saudi airspace in its attempts to stop the Iraqi attacks.

With few other options, Iran relied on passive defenses and countermeasures against Iraqi ship attacks. The shuttle service reduced some of the Iraqi pressure because it relieved foreign shippers from the costs and dangers of transiting the exclusion zone. The Iranian tankers, however, were vulnerable because none of the escorting Iranian warships had SAMs or early warning radars while Iran's air force was unable to provide air cover for the movements. Instead, Iran stationed empty tankers on the seaward side of the convoys to absorb missile hits. Later, the Iranian convoys towed radar reflectors on buoys behind them. The reflectors generated a much larger radar return signal to deceive and draw the Iraqi Exocet missiles away from the tankers. During the summer of 1985 Iraq received the more capable Mirage F-1 aircraft, and the contingent of Iraqi pilots trained in France returned to bring the Exocet-carrying fighter into the war. Starting in August, the Iraqi air force began an intense campaign against the Khark Island oil terminal, where nearly 90 percent of Iran's oil was loaded for export. The facility was well defended by American-made I-HAWK and Swedish RBS-70 SAMs and Oerlikon 35-mm antiaircraft artillery directed by Skyguard fire control radars. The terminal also was a difficult target to destroy because of its redundant systems and multiple dispersed and buried pipelines. Iranian engineers also arranged a system of flexible underwater pipelines supported by buoys to load tankers away from the island's platforms. In addition, radar reflector decoys were placed all around the island. Between August and December 1985, Iraq conducted approximately sixty raids against Khark Island as part of a campaign to hurt Iran and focus international attention on the war.

Increase the Calamity

As 1986 began, Iran was making a major push to overcome the many problems that hindered its earlier offensives. More effort was put into the annual mobilization, and more *basijis* and reserves were called up for duty. Iran even began using women for the first time in rear area operations to free men for the front line. Local citizens were used to support the combat forces by running kitchens to feed the troops and small facilities that made shoes and clothing. The regular army and the Pasdaran each had around three hundred and fifty thousand men under arms. New weapon acquisitions offset some combat and maintenance losses. Iranian purchasing agents were finding parts for U.S. and Western weapon systems, which kept readiness rates and inventories from dropping faster. More new weapon systems were procured in 1985, and Iran took delivery of more than $4.5 billion dollars' worth of North Korean and Chinese weapons, including SCUD missiles, SA-2 high-altitude SAMs, Silkworm antiship cruise missiles, and tanks. Iran even acquired the first of two thousand much needed TOW antitank missiles, eighteen I-HAWK SAMs, and hundreds of I-HAWK spare parts through a covert arms-for-hostages deal with the Reagan administration. Chemical protective gear also was purchased in large amounts to try to counter Iraq's increasing use of blister and nerve agents on the battlefield.[30]

At the start of 1986, however, Iran's operational inventory had no more than 1,000 tanks, 1,400 other armored vehicles, and 600 to 800 artillery pieces. The Iranian air force had, at best, 60 to 80 aircraft kept operational by cannibalizing some aircraft and reverse-engineering parts. In contrast, Iraq had 700,000 to 800,000 men in forty divisions backed by nearly a quarter-million reservists. Although Iran had forty million citizens to Iraq's thirteen and a half million people, Iraq kept more men on active duty. The Iraqi army also had 4,000 tanks, 3,800 other armored vehicles, and nearly 600 combat aircraft, which gave it a quantitative and qualitative advantage over Iran in all categories of arms.

The Pasdaran again took the lead in planning and preparing for Iran's next major offensive. The objective for 1986 was to cross the Shatt al-Arab at the southern tip of Iraq, advance into the lightly defended Al Faw Peninsula, and attempt to outflank Iraq's Al Basrah defense, creating opportunities to rout the Iraqis or seize part of Iraq's second-largest city. At a minimum, once established on the peninsula, Iran could disrupt the production of Iraq's southern oil fields, block Iraqi access to Kuwaiti ports, and try again to incite the Iraqi Shia to revolt. The Guard followed its earlier pattern of relying on surprise, local numerical superiority, human wave attacks, and the will of God to achieve victory. Because of their earlier experience with amphibious operations in the Hawizeh Marshes, the Pasdaran recognized that crossing the Shatt at virtually its widest point required additional planning and preparations. The Guard started five to six months before the attack to provide specialized training for SCUBA and amphibious operations. More than three thousand *pasdars* were trained as combat divers to conduct extensive reconnaissance of the Iraqi shore and form special commando units to spearhead the coming attack. The Guard also prepared and quietly staged the small craft, pontoon bridges, and other material needed for an amphibious assault.

The Guard built up a force of roughly two hundred thousand men in the south with three Pasdaran divisions and its Special Martyrs Brigade positioned to lead the attack. The army's 30th and 77th Infantry and 81st Armored divisions and various aviation units were deployed to support the operation. The Guard, aware that Iraq was receiving American and Russian satellite reconnaissance information, conducted deception operations by erecting phony tent camps with boats and air defenses in the region east of the Hawizeh Marshes. Daytime troop movements were conducted to give the impression of a buildup far to the north of Al Faw. The Guard also used an Iraqi spy in Ahvaz to feed false information to Baghdad. The deception effort apparently worked, because in early January 1986 the Iraqis launched a spoiling attack against the southern Majnoon Island while the militia forces on the Faw peninsula remained under-strength and unprepared.[31]

During a heavy rainstorm on the night of February 10, 1986, Guard soldiers started the attack on Faw by reciting a prayer and crying, "Oh God, increase the calamity!" The stormy weather made for a difficult swim, but the Iranian frogmen, many trained in demolitions, crossed the Shatt under the cover of darkness and cleared paths through the Iraqi shore obstacles. After receiving a signal from the Iraqi side of the waterway, the amphibious assault began, and nearly a division's worth of infantrymen, aided by a massive artillery barrage on the main Iraqi lines, quickly gained control of the first line of Iraqi defenses. The attackers were lightly armed but were trained to use captured Iraqi tanks and ammunition, which they put to immediate use in mopping up the last few positions on the Iraqi front lines before advancing against Iraqi strongpoints and rear area facilities. Intercepts of Iraqi communications revealed to the Iranians that the Iraqi defense was disorganized and disintegrating. Farther north a second prong of the amphibious assault landed on Umm al-Rasas, a group of islands in the Shatt between Faw and Al Basrah, but was defeated. This action and a diversionary attack started a day earlier from the Hawizeh Marshes against the city of Al

Qurnah confused the Iraqis about the location of the main Iranian effort and slowed their initial response to the fighting at Faw. The Iraqi commanders apparently viewed the isolated peninsula, which was surrounded by salt flats and marshes, as unimportant and only slowly recognized the danger an Iranian lodgment posed to the oil fields, Iraqi ports, and links to Kuwait.[32]

By the end of the first day, Iran had made significant gains as continued bad weather prevented the Iraqi air force from providing close air support to the defenders. As the second night began, Iran brought more engineering units across the waterway to build up the embankments to support resupply operations and build fortifications and obstacles to help stop Iraqi counterattacks. The Iranians poured up to twenty thousand troops into the Faw salient and continued attacking through the night across multiple layers of wire, mines, and entrenchments, pushing north and west toward Al Basrah and the port of Umm Qasr. When the weather cleared on the second day Iraqi aircraft entered the battle, but Iranian air defenses, bolstered by I-HAWK batteries on the eastern short of the Shatt, caused the Iraqi pilots to drop their bombs from high altitude with an attendant decrease in accuracy. The improved weather also allowed Iranian Cobra gunships to take to the skies, and with Iraqi armored vehicles road-bound because of the soft terrain, these helicopters and ambushes created by infantry tank-killer teams armed with TOWs and RPGs inflicted heavy losses on Iraq's hasty counterattacks. After only a few hours, the Iraqis were in retreat, and Iranian forces captured a coastal missile base opposite Kuwait and threatened to break out to attack Umm Qasr.

Although the Iranians defeated repeated counterattacks during the following days, the constant pressure caused their assault to lose steam. Despite the absence of a coherent plan for stopping the Iranians, the steady stream of Iraqi reinforcements and heavy use of chemical weapons took their toll on Iranian forces. Iranian sustainment problems also began to undermine the Guard's zeal. Resupply was limited to the hours of darkness, and each evening the Pasdaran threw pontoon bridges across the Shatt only to partially disassemble them at dawn. The nearby HAWK batteries, sporadic bad weather, and darkness helped to prevent the Iraqi air force from interdicting the flow of supplies across the waterway. Still, river-crossing operations of all types had to stop at low tide each day because the water receded far from the bank and the exposed mudflats could not bear the weight of heavy equipment, supply vehicles, or even soldiers. The resulting shortage of heavy equipment hampered the pursuit of retreating Iraqi forces, and when Iraq belatedly committed the Republican Guard and additional armored and mechanized units to the battle, the Iranians had to stop their advance and prepare to meet this major Iraqi counterattack.

The Iranian forces had enough strength on the peninsula to defeat several multidivision Iraqi counterattacks and hold on to most of their gains, but the cost was heavy. The Iraqis desperately tried to evict the Iranians, although they relied on firepower over skill and maneuver. Iraqi armor units wore out two hundred main gun barrels during the fighting, and so much artillery ammunition was expended that Baghdad had to make emergency deals with arms dealers all over the world to rebuild their stockpiles. The Iranians made the Iraqis pay high costs for small amounts of recovered territory and for pressing home their air attacks, causing eight thousand to ten thousand Iraqi casualties and shooting down twenty to twenty-five Iraqi aircraft during the campaign. Although the Iranians were chewing up counterattacking Iraqi units and capturing more equipment, including advanced T-72 tanks, Iran suffered an estimated twenty-seven thousand to thirty thousand casualties in the fighting. Many of Iran's losses came from Iraq's heavy use of chemical weapons. Despite the greater availability of masks and protective gear, the *basijis* were poorly trained in using their equipment. In particular, as good Muslims the *basijis* did not shave their beards, which prevented their gas masks from sealing properly. Both sides were exhausted by the end of February, but fighting continued into late March before the Iraqis relented and ended their counterattacks. The war returned to a bloody stalemate with sporadic fighting in Kurdistan and the central border region around Mehran later in the year.

Iran's victory at Faw was a turning point in the war, but not in the way the clerical regime initially believed. The shock of the loss roused deep fears in Baghdad and among the Gulf monarchies, especially Kuwait, which now faced Iranian troops across the narrow Khawr Abd-Allah channel. Iranian confidence and assertiveness reached a high point, and Khomeini issued a fatwa demanding that the war end by the next Iranian new year in March 1987. The clerical regime arrogantly rejected renewed offers by Saddam for a cease-fire. When it became clear that Iran was spent for the year and that Iraq's fall, while a possibility, was not imminent, the panic subsided and the negative consequences for Iran began to pile up. First, Saddam and the Iraqi military leadership made much needed reforms to improve the Iraqi armed forces' effectiveness. The Iraqi dictator limited his micromanagement of operations, allowed Iraq's increasingly competent and professional commanders more control, and expanded the Republican Guard into six divisions of the best men and equipment in Iraq, making it more than a match for Iran's most determined units. The Iraqis also stepped up the air and tanker wars, aided by recently added aerial refueling capabilities that allowed Iraq's Mirage F-1 fighters to strike critical infrastructure targets deep in Iran and oil tankers in the southern Gulf. In early May, Tehran suffered its first major air raid in which Iran's main oil refinery and the Parchin arms production complex were hit. The always cautious Gulf Arabs, fearful of losing Iraq as a barrier to Iranian hegemony, continued to aid Saddam with billions in loans. The major Western powers, led by the United States, increased efforts at the United

Nations to strengthen the arms embargo on Iran and, with the passage of Security Council Resolution 598, to end the war by demanding a cease-fire and joint withdrawals from occupied territory.[33]

Even beyond the Iraqi and international efforts to stop Iran, the Islamic Republic's confidence was unwarranted. In the aftermath of Faw, the clerical regime was more divided over military strategy, and the Artesh-Pasdaran rivalry was flaring up again. The hard-line clerics and Pasdaran leaders, in line with Khomeini's fatwa, wanted to attack Al Basrah, believing that one more push there would be decisive. Experienced army commanders and even some senior Guard officers argued that attempting to break through the six rings of fortifications and obstacles surrounding Al Basrah was suicidal. Offering instead only their long-standing proposal to wage a war of attrition to wear down the Iraqis, the army lost the argument, although not before Army Chief of Staff General Shirazi came to blows with Pasdaran commander Rezai and was relieved of his position. For the coming "final offensive" Iran would rely again on faith in its revolutionary mission and its soldiers' patriotism and religious fervor with the perceived added psychological advantage from the Faw victory. Signs that faith was not enough were increasing, however. In particular, in order to mobilize the men needed for the new offensive, Iran had to change its conscription laws because the number of volunteers was insufficient. For the first time, the Basij drafted men, and the Guard and Basij were allowed to recall reservists who had already met their service commitments. As summer turned to fall in 1986, Iran even closed its universities to make more students and teachers available for the war.[34]

Iran's Last Great Offensive

After assembling up to two hundred thousand men on the southern front, Iran tried to emulate its success at Faw in Operation Karbala 4, which started on the night of December 23, 1986. The plan involved using frogmen, commandos, and amphibious units to seize Umm al-Rasas and then jump across to the Iraqi mainland and cut off the Faw peninsula. The Iranians again carefully reconnoitered Iraqi positions and struck at the boundaries of the two corps defending Basra and Faw. Although the Pasdaran had some well-trained troops in the vanguard, they relied heavily on inexperienced volunteers who faltered badly when confronted by Iraq's superior firepower and defensive barriers. Supported by artillery from the eastern bank of the Shatt, the Guard seized the island during the night and continued the attack after daybreak against Iraqi strongpoints on the western shore. Up to sixty thousand men in human wave assaults broke against the Iraqi front lines as *pasdars* and *basijis* became entangled in barbed wire and minefields and were mowed down while crossing well-prepared kill zones. Iran lost between nine thousand and twelve thousand dead and wounded, and the survivors retreated back across the Shatt, taking the forces on Umm al-Rasas with them. The failed frontal assault was later rationalized as a diversionary attack after Iran renewed the offensive on Al Basrah in early January.[35]

As pointed out by Iran's army commanders, Al Basrah was a frightfully difficult objective. The manmade Fish Lake, which was filled with sensors, obstacles, and power sources that could electrify some of its areas, was joined by numerous other water barriers and small canals between the border and the Shatt. The region also was covered by earthen berms and fighting positions that had to be crossed before getting to the main defensive lines. Six rings of earthworks, each dotted by observation posts, hardened bunkers, and dug-in firing positions for tanks surrounded Al Basrah. In addition, the network of roads, headquarters, artillery complexes, and supply depots that Iraq used to support the front lines and facilitate multidivision counterattacks had expanded and improved during the preceding years.

Nonetheless, the Guard leaders had been considering ways to capture the city for years and during 1986 held exercises around Anzali to practice combined arms operations and new methods to cross the water barriers. Their plan for the offensive, called Karbala 5, was hardly inventive, however. Iranian forces in the Faw salient, where Baghdad seemed to expect an attack, were to tie down as many Iraqi forces as possible with demonstrations. The main attack would be a two-pronged effort to the north and south of Fish Lake. The northern force of sixty thousand men was to attack through the town of Salamcheh, less than twenty miles from Al Basrah, toward the city. A second contingent of roughly similar size was to breach the fortified gap between the southern tip of Fish Lake and the Shatt and then advance along the eastern bank of the waterway into Al Basrah.

Despite the buildup of Iranian forces and the late December attack, Iran caught the Iraqis off guard when they launched Karbala 5 just after midnight on January 9, 1987. With the advantage of surprise and the willingness to sacrifice large numbers of *basijis*, the Guards captured Salamcheh and broke through the first two defensive lines northeast of Al Basrah. Iran's southern forces also penetrated Iraq's front lines and reached the outer suburbs of the city. The Pasdaran's performance in these early assaults had been improved by two major adjustments based on their experiences at Faw. First, the Pasdaran were well armed and equipped at the start for the anticipated difficult fighting. Second, in response to command and control breakdowns from insufficient tactical radios that resulted in missed opportunities and disorganization, the Pasdaran's leaders tried to improve battle management by ensuring that its small unit leaders were experienced officers and NCOs and by assigning well-defined tactical objectives to each unit. Heartened by their initial gains, the Iranians poured more troops into the fighting. Iraq, however, was able to respond with its reserves, including most of the Republican Guard divisions. By mid-January, Iran's assault had lost momentum and its troops inched forward under heavy Iraqi air, artillery, and chemical attacks, before digging in to stop the repeated Iraqi counterattacks. Although the two prongs failed to link up as planned, the northern Guard units advanced within nine miles of the city and began pounding Al Basrah with artillery and rockets.

Iran continued its attacks, but its ultimate objective remained out of reach. Iran penetrated the third ring of Al Basrah defenses with a night attack on January 29, and Pasdaran troops reached the west bank of the Jasmin River, a tributary of the Shatt. Iran's losses were so heavy in the assault that the Guard surrendered most of its gains two days later to Iraqi counterattacks. By the start of February, Iran had committed more than one hundred thousand men to the offensive, and the fighting continued at a brutal pace as Khomeini demanded a victory. The southern Guard contingent remained bottled up in the narrow strip of land between Fish Lake and the Shatt, and the rest of Iran's forces were unable to break through the last defensive rings. At the end of the month, Iranian army units launched a final push along the Salamcheh-Basrah road but were stopped with heavy losses after only minor gains.

Although Iran was able to hold on to the territory it captured, Karbala 5 was a failure. The hard-liners in the government were forced to accept that Iran was unlikely to defeat Iraq by throwing men against well-prepared defenses backed by massive firepower. With a decisive "final offensive" more unfeasible than ever, the clerical regime finally heeded the army's advice and settled for a war of attrition. Iran launched a few more small attacks along the border during the rest of 1987 but could not muster the forces or the will for more significant efforts. For the remainder of the war, Iran was reduced to hoping that the bleeding of the Iraqi military and internal dissent by Kurds and Iraqi Shia would bring about the demise of the Baathist regime. Indeed, Iran's moment to win the ground war had passed. The Iranian people were increasingly war-weary, and the *pasdars* and *basijis,* having lost so many of their battle-hardened veterans and experienced troop leaders, were no longer willing to sacrifice themselves in wasteful attacks. Arms embargoes, lower oil revenues, and waning cash reserves crippled Iran's capacity to build up the war materiel needed for a major offensive surge. Finally, Khomeini and his supporters made the fateful decision to respond to the defeat at Al Basrah by ignoring the risks of Western intervention and expanding the war in the Gulf. Having been stymied by Iraq, the mullahs appeared bent on confronting a new enemy.

Iran's Naval War with the United States

In the months preceding Karbala 5, Iran had stepped up attacks on Saudi and Kuwaiti shipping in response to Iraq's raids on Khark Island and long-range

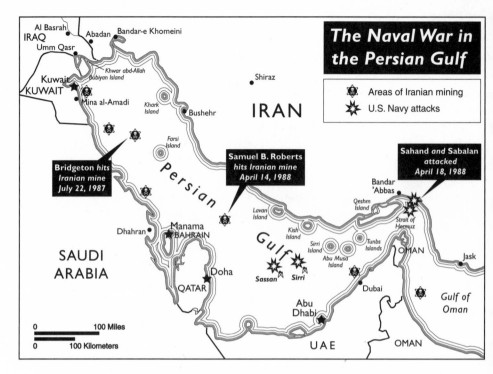

9.3 The Naval War in the Persian Gulf.

attacks against shipping near Iranian oil-loading terminals in the southern Gulf. Kuwait was fearful of Iran's aggressive posture, and the international community, still in the grip of Cold War concerns, took more notice of the Tanker War and its potential implications in the East-West competition. In September 1986, Iranian warships fired on, stopped, and searched a Kuwaiti-bound Soviet merchant ship, which caused Moscow to send the first Red Navy warship into the Gulf since 1978. For the next two years, a Soviet frigate, destroyer, or minesweeper accompanied all Soviet arms carriers transiting the strait. In December, in its bid to get Kuwait to stop aiding Iraq, Iran sent terrorists to conduct a series of car bombings against the U.S. embassy and other targets in Kuwait. Once again Iran's actions backfired, and the intimidated Kuwaitis turned to the United States and the Soviets for protection, setting off a chain of events that brought a multinational armada of approximately fifty warships to protect Gulf shipping by the end of 1987.

In shifting its efforts to the Gulf, Iran was hardly playing to its strength. Iran's aviation assets, which had played the lead role in the Tanker War through early 1986, were dwindling by the day. Iran had relied on F-4 Phantoms and Italian-made Augusta-Bell utility helicopters and American Sea Cobra attack helicopters for most ship attacks, but none of these aircraft had dedicated anti-ship weapons. The Augusta-Bell fired a French antitank missile, and the Sea Cobras used rockets and a 20-mm chain-gun. The Phantoms relied on the Maverick antitank missile, but the pilots apparently did not know naval architecture and did not exploit the television-guided Maverick's accuracy for targeting the vulnerable parts of ships. Iran had an estimated twenty-five to thirty Phantoms, thirty to forty-five F-5 Tigers, and seven to twelve F-14 Tomcats available in 1986, but most lacked fully functional avionics. From the start of the war, Iranian antishipping operations were hindered by problems with finding suitable targets because of the large volume of ship traffic, the Gulf's heat haze, and inadequate radars. By late 1986, the radar and computers on the Iranian navy's P-3 Orions no longer worked, which made target detection more difficult. Iran rarely had more than two Orions in service, and its maritime patrols wasted countless flying hours with no results. Unable to increase the effectiveness of its aviation assets and wanting to preserve air force capabilities for ground support operations, Iran turned to the regular navy's warships to pick up the mission.[36]

The regular navy was in poor shape because of a lack of maintenance, but naval units were able to operate day and night, remain on station for long periods, and approach civilian shipping to identify targets correctly. Iran's two U.S.-built destroyers, *Babr* and *Palang,* were largely inoperable, and only two of four British-built frigates, the *Sahand* and *Sabalan,* were fully seaworthy. Four French-made Combattante II patrol boats and four landing ships also were available for patrols and other duties. The operational warships' radars, electronic systems, and weapon systems, however, were unreliable or not working properly. The frigates and Combattante II patrol boats had Sea Killer antiship missiles, but these were beyond their reliable shelf life. Operating inside the strait to the south of Bandar Abbas, the frigates briefly took the lead for Iran against merchant shipping in late 1986. The *Sabalan* acquired a notorious reputation among shippers because its commander, nicknamed Captain Nasty, had a penchant for targeting the bridge and crew quarters of his victims. Because hard-liners in Tehran were not satisfied with the navy's performance, the new Pasdaran naval forces were encouraged to assert themselves in the Tanker War.[37]

The Revolutionary Guard's naval element had its origins in patrol boats purchased for "customs duty" as early as 1983 and was formally organized in 1985. By late 1986, the Guard navy had established a major naval headquarters on Farsi Island in the central Gulf and had twenty thousand men, making it larger than the regular navy. The Pasdaran had a large number of small craft, including the Swedish-built Boghammer fast interceptor craft, fiberglass-hull Boston Whalers with outboard motors, Zodiac rubber boats, and even jet skis. The Guard also had fishing dhows that could mix with the Gulf's civilian traders and fishermen for clandestine operations. After training on the Boghammers in the Caspian Sea in 1985, the Pasdaran deployed the Swedish boats to the Gulf, because they were the only Guard vessel capable of carrying heavy infantry weapons. The Boghammers were armed with heavy machine guns supplemented by RPGs and grenade and rocket launchers. The Pasdaran navy also controlled Iran's Chinese-built Silkworm coastal defense missiles and had a miniature submarine from North Korea that did not see action during the war. Pasdaran sailors were trained in all types of small boat and SCUBA operations, and although they never used the tactic, some Guard naval personnel were trained to conduct suicide attacks with explosives-laden boats.

In line with its equipment and revolutionary heritage, the Pasdaran navy focused on a type of guerrilla war at sea. Its hit-and-run attacks seldom did much damage but aimed at terrorizing merchant shipping and the Gulf Arabs while avoiding, at least initially, direct conflict with Western and Soviet warships. The Guard set up small naval bases with about one thousand men each on Hormuz, Sirri, Larak, Abu Musa, and a few other small islands. Smaller Guard detachments were posted on the many oil platforms in Iran's oil fields in the Gulf, from which they directed Pasdaran speedboats against their targets. The islands were excellent locations for launching patrols or attacks with three to four Boghammers. These small boats were difficult to detect by radar and could hide behind the large number of dhows and other civilian vessels that sailed the southern Gulf. A swarm of Pasdaran speedboats could appear quickly and conduct a high-speed rocket or machine gun attack against unprepared ships. Taking a page from Captain Nasty's tactics, the Guard attack craft targeted crew quarters to increase casualties and dissuade shippers from carrying Kuwaiti and Saudi cargoes. The clusters of Guard personnel and boats on the islands and along Iran's coast also posed a potential threat to Saudi and other Gulf Arab oil facilities in the Gulf. By early 1987 the Pasdaran was conducting the majority of Iranian ship attacks. Taking advantage of the Guard's reputation for zealotry, the clerical regime tried to escape responsibility for some of the Pasdaran's guerrilla actions, denying Iranian involvement or claiming the attacks were rogue operations or the result of revolutionary exuberance.[38]

Introducing the concept of rogue elements and "hidden hands" served other Iranian interests as the Pasdaran and the regular navy considered introducing naval mines. The Iranians had been thinking about "guerrilla" mining in the Gulf for many years. Following a joint Iranian-U.S. exercise, MIDLINK 73, in the early 1970s, the Iranian commander remarked to a senior American officer that such tactics could play havoc with merchant ships and the flow of oil in the Gulf.[39] In mid-1984, the Islamic Jihad, a Palestinian terrorist group with close ties to the Guard, claimed responsibility for naval mines laid by Libya in the Red Sea. Although no ships were sunk in this incident, eighteen hit mines and the cost to Egypt in disrupted trade was high. Iran denied having a role but almost certainly was pleased with the attack, which caused the West to set up a multinational force to sweep the mines and harmed Egypt, which was sending "volunteers" to fight with the Iraqis. Iran had some U.S.-made contact mines from the shah's era and had acquired Soviet air-laid contact mines and some ship-laid magnetic influence mines, which exploded in response to the metal of a vessel's hull. Its mines of choice, however, were the M-08, a spherical contact mine with horns based on a 1908 Russian model, and the smaller Iranian-manufacture Myam contact mine of North Korean design. The navy installed mine-laying rails on a few of its Ajr-class landing ships while the Pasdaran converted dhows into minelayers by adding a mechanical crane that could handle the half-ton mines. Although the strait was unsuitable, other areas in the Gulf provided good environments for mines, especially those where deep draft tankers had to follow specific lanes through the relatively shallow waterway.[40]

In early January 1987, the government of Kuwait approached Washington about protecting its tankers against Iranian attacks. The U.S. Navy had started to escort American merchant vessels in 1986, and the Kuwaitis hoped to make similar arrangements for their ships. The United States initially turned down the Kuwaiti request, but after the emirate contacted Moscow and leased three Soviet oil tankers to gain a degree of Russian protection, Washington reconsidered. The Kuwaiti-Soviet deal and loud concerns about American commitment and credibility from regional allies in the aftermath of America's 1986 arms-for-hostages deal with Iran combined to increase pressure on the Reagan administration to take a strong stand against the clerical regime. In early May, the United States agreed to reregister eleven Kuwaiti tankers under the American flag and to use U.S. forces to protect these ships.

Not surprisingly, Iran saw the reflagging as an unfair attempt to bolster Iraq and as American interference in a life-and-death matter. The mullahs in Tehran warned Kuwait against the proposed reflagging and threatened serious consequences for any neighbor that allowed the United States to use its bases or ports. Pro-Iranian Kuwaiti Shia demonstrated in the Kuwaiti capital in April, and Iran openly set up a Silkworm battery on the Faw peninsula in range of Kuwait City to underscore its unhappiness. The Pasdaran emplaced twelve Silkworm launchers around the Strait of Hormuz and on Qeshm Island in a bid to signal Iranian defiance and raise doubts in Washington about the reflagging effort.

Iran upped the ante in mid-May when mines it laid in the Mina al-Ahmadi channel, the main deepwater entrance to Kuwait's harbor, damaged the first leased Soviet tanker to arrive there. Pasdaran naval forces probably laid the mines using dhows that hid among the large number of fishermen, traders, and smugglers who plied the northern Gulf. Over the next few weeks, three more ships hit mines in the channel. Iran denied responsibility, and claims were made that the mines had broken free from Iraqi fields around Umm Qasr and floated into the

Gulf. Adding to the confusion, a day after the Soviet tanker was struck, an Iraqi F-1 fighter accidentally attacked a U.S. Navy frigate, the USS *Stark*. Two Exocet missiles struck the *Stark*, which was seriously damaged and lost thirty-seven sailors to blast and fires. The subsequent political debate in Washington about the mission in the Gulf may have encouraged Iran, already emboldened by the seeming precedent set by the 1983 U.S. withdrawal from Lebanon, to go after American interests and allies.

As Iran set out to increase regional insecurity, the U.S. Navy was preparing Operation Earnest Will, its first convoy operation to protect merchant shipping since World War II. American naval forces in the Indian Ocean had been increased to a full carrier group to support the U.S. Navy's Middle East Task Force, which had been stationed in the Gulf for years. Iran's Silkworm deployment was responsible, in part, for the size of the U.S. effort. Although the Silkworm was an old system, the radar-guided missiles were effective, and each 1,100-pound warhead could cause significant damage. Iran's threatened guerrilla warfare and suicide attacks also caused the U.S. Navy to deploy a larger mix of forces to counter them. Staging from the Gulf islands or nearby ports and airfields, Iranian warships and aircraft could quickly reach their targets, which put a premium on having a robust American presence.

The U.S. convoy force consisted of four frigates, three cruisers, and a destroyer. One of the first escorts, the USS *Kidd*, was from a group of four frigates that had been built for, but not delivered to, Iran and was jokingly referred to as an "Ayatollah-class" frigate. The plan called for three to four warships to escort two tankers while the cruisers and combat air patrols from an American carrier in the Arabian Sea provided air defense. The United States hoped that this show of force would deter the Iranians. The clerical regime was left a perfect opening, however, when the U.S. Navy failed to include mine warfare defenses with the convoy force.

The United States misjudged Iran's willingness to fight and inexplicably downplayed the mine threat. Initially, the U.S. Central Command (CENTCOM), the unified command in charge of American military operations in southwest Asia, considered mining a likely Iranian response to Earnest Will. Yet CENTCOM and the U.S. Navy were more concerned with the Silkworm threat, even though Iran was judged less likely to use its Chinese-made cruise missiles. A small Mine Countermeasures Assistance Team sent to Kuwait to help clear mines in the Mina al-Ahmadi channel determined that the recovered mines were Iranian. The specialists also noted that the Iranian minefields were getting larger and more carefully laid, which suggested that Iran was using larger craft, such as trawlers or landing ships, as minelayers. CENTCOM and the U.S. Navy accepted that the mining threat was becoming more serious but apparently did not consider that Iran might shift its efforts from the northern to the southern Gulf.[41]

When the first U.S. convoy began on July 22, 1987, the Iranians anticipated the route and sowed three fields with some sixty mines. On the morning of July 24, the reflagged Kuwaiti tanker *Bridgeton* struck a mine, which blasted a hole in the ship's hull and flooded four of its thirty-one compartments. Despite this damage, the *Bridgeton* was able to continue its voyage to Kuwait at reduced speed. The tanker, even in its injured condition, was the only ship in the convoy sturdy enough to survive another mine hit, and with no minesweepers to clear the way, the U.S. warships fell behind the *Bridgeton*. The escorts from the world's most formidable naval power were reduced to posting lookouts and sharpshooters to spot and fire on any floating mines. Iran credited "invisible hands" for the attack but enjoyed the propaganda victory gained from the spectacle of sophisticated American warships being forced by pre–World War I technology to hide behind the *Bridgeton*. Because the United States did not uncover evidence of Iranian responsibility for the attack until much later, the clerical regime escaped an immediate reprisal while convoy operations were delayed until minesweepers were brought into the Gulf.

The emboldened Iranians increased their mining operations and political pressure on the Gulf Arabs. Days after the *Bridgeton* mining, Iran turned up tensions by having its pilgrims at the Hajj in Mecca conduct a major demonstration. Many of the Iranians advanced on Saudi security forces with sticks, knives, and stones, causing the Saudis to respond with tear gas and batons. In the ensuing fighting and flight by panicked non-Iranian pilgrims, more than 600 people were injured and approximately 400, including 275 Iranians and 85 Saudi security personnel, were killed. As the United States increased its efforts to stop the mining, Iran, in a serious misstep, shifted these operations into the Gulf of Oman. After a tanker hit a mine off the Omani coast and several other mines were found nearby in mid-August, the Europeans, who had been ignoring American requests for help, agreed to send naval forces to assist with mine clearing and mine countermeasures. With Washington's NATO allies now involved, the frightened and cautious Gulf Arabs became more willing to support efforts to restrain Iranian naval actions. After more Western forces assembled to protect shipping in the Gulf, Iran avoided the convoys, and the *Bridgeton* was the only escorted ship out of approximately 125 convoys to be attacked.

Iran's minelayers became the focus of intense search efforts. The Gulf Arabs were unwilling to let their small mine-countermeasure forces operate outside their territorial waters and remained reluctant to allow U.S. forces to base in their territory. Instead, the U.S. Navy set up offshore floating bases to support the hunt for Iranian minelayers. Reviving an old Vietnam War–era concept called Sea Float, the Americans set up two mobile sea bases using oil construction barges rented by Kuwait for this purpose. The barges were manned by SEAL teams equipped with patrol boats and a reinforced Marine rifle platoon. Later, the U.S. Army sent a task force of its aviators flying helicopters with specialized equipment for night surveillance. Both barges were filled with high-tech sensors and electronic warfare equipment and were defended by Stinger MANPADS (man-portable air defense systems) and Phalanx antimissile systems. The largest barge, named *Hercules,* was moved just twenty miles north of Farsi Island to keep constant watch on Pasdaran activities there. Fixed- and rotary-wing aircraft from U.S. warships in the Gulf and Arabian Sea patrolled areas subject to mine laying. The CIA also sent two turbo-prop planes designed specifically for nighttime surveillance to join U.S. Navy helicopters and Marine Corps Radio Recon units with sophisticated signals interception equipment to track the Iranians.

In mid-September, an Iranian troop landing ship, the *Iran Ajr,* came to American attention and was kept under close observation for several days. The *Ajr* was caught red-handed laying mines in Bahrain's main shipping channel on September 21, 1987, by a U.S. Army helicopter flying from the USS *Jarrett.* After an attack with rockets and machine guns, the disabled *Ajr* was boarded by U.S. Navy SEALs, who captured crewmen, mines, and documents. The seized material showed that mining was a deliberate policy involving regular navy and Guard naval units and was not conducted by "rogue" forces. Satisfied with exposing the Iranians and benefiting from increased foreign support for its actions, the United States limited its retaliation to scuttling the ship.

The Iranians, who possibly saw this restraint as a sign of faint-heartedness, refused to back down. In late September, American intelligence monitored the massing of roughly sixty Iranian small boats around Bushehr. Other intelligence information indicated that the Guard was planning to attack Saudi and Kuwaiti offshore oil facilities. On the night of October 3, the Pasdaran flotilla assembled around Khark Island and appeared ready to begin its attack. After U.S. and Saudi air and naval forces moved to intercept the Iranians, the attack failed to materialize and apparently was aborted. A few days later, three Guard speedboats reacted to patrolling U.S. Army helicopters by launching a shoulder-fired SAM at them. The Americans retaliated, sinking two Boston Whalers, damaging a Boghammer, and killing eight Iranian crewmen. When American patrol boats recovered six surviving Iranians, they found a battery case for a Stinger shoulder-fired MANPADS, the first evidence that Iran had acquired these sophisticated U.S. weapon systems. (Iran apparently had taken or bought them from anti-Soviet Afghan mujahedin armed by the United States.) At roughly the same time as this incident, twenty to forty Iranian small craft moved toward a U.S. mobile sea base. The Iranians turned away when an American frigate, patrol boats, and helicopters moved to intercept them, leading some U.S. Navy officers to believe they had disrupted an attack.[42]

Iran struck back by launching Silkworm missiles at Kuwaiti ports in mid-October, hitting two tankers, including the U.S.-flagged *Sea Isle City.* The ship's

American captain was blinded and eighteen crewmen were injured in the attack. In response, the United States conducted Operation Nimble Archer, an attack on the Rashadat and Resalat oil platforms in the southern Gulf that the Pasdaran was using for targeting ships. Washington chose the platforms because the Silkworm batteries at Faw were mobile and had been dispersed after the attacks. With American naval aviators providing air cover, four U.S. destroyers approached the platforms and, after allowing the Iranians to evacuate, fired more than 1,000 five-inch rounds at them. SEAL teams set demolition charges to complete the platforms' destruction. Iran was still undeterred and on October 22 fired another Silkworm at the Mina al-Ahmadi oil complex, damaging Kuwait's main oil-loading terminal. Two days later, the Pan American Airways office in Kuwait was bombed by terrorists, and Iranian-backed dissidents tried to bomb Kuwait's Interior Ministry in November. In demonstrating that the U.S. presence and reprisals would not deter them, the Iranians seemed oblivious to the faulty strategy they were following. As Iran's ground commanders were struggling to mobilize resources to weaken the Iraqi enemy, Iranian naval forces were provoking the intervention of new foes.

After Nimble Archer, Iran exercised more caution for several months, possibly because it was concentrating on the next phase of the land war. The Pasdaran continued to attack merchant shipping but was careful to avoid U.S. forces, which now included twenty-nine warships in the Gulf and eight as part of a carrier battle group in the Arabian Sea. On April 13, 1988, however, Guard naval forces laid a new minefield approximately fifty-five miles northeast of Qatar. The next day the U.S. frigate *Samuel B. Roberts* sailed into the field. The warship tried to back away from the danger after lookouts spotted the mines. The *Roberts* was not fated to escape, however, and it struck a mine that blew a twenty-one foot hole into its port side and lifted the stern into the air. The blast snapped the frigate's keel and the ship was held together only by its deck plate. Because the *Roberts* was at battle stations when it struck the mine, the crew was ready and valiant damage control efforts saved the ship and ensured that no Americans died in the incident. Mines recovered from the field were from the same production series as those captured on the *Iran Ajr* and more mines were found a few days later in areas used by U.S. Navy ships and tankers. This time Washington decided to conduct a stronger but still proportional retaliation, and because Iran had deliberately attacked an American warship it was agreed that the U.S. Navy would destroy an Iranian frigate along with several armed Iranian oil platforms. Strategically and operationally, the Guard's insistence on continuing its mining operations made little sense other than it showed yet again the hard-liners' reliance on the mere hope that their actions would provide favorable results. Instead, their purposeless attack made Iran the target of the largest surface action by the U.S. Navy since the end of World War II.

On the morning of April 18, many of the Pasdaran personnel on Iran's Sassan and Sirri oil platforms were panic-stricken when three U.S. Navy warships approached their position as part of Operation Praying Mantis. At the scene of the first encounter at Sassan, the Iranians were given five minutes to evacuate the platform. Most immediately departed, but a few remained and manned ZSU-23 antiaircraft guns. Two U.S. destroyers, the *Merrill* and *Lynde McCormack,* quickly silenced these guns, and the surviving *pasdars* reconsidered their situation and left aboard an Iranian tugboat. After the U.S. destroyers shelled the platform, U.S. Marines from the amphibious transport *Trenton* secured it, seized material for intelligence exploitation, and placed explosives to complete the facility's destruction. The scene at the Sirri platform was a virtual replay of the earlier attack. A few Iranians made a brief stand against the cruiser *Wainwright* and two U.S. frigates, the *Simpson* and *Bagley,* before the survivors departed. While these attacks were occurring, a third group of U.S. warships waited for the *Sabalan,* the Iranian frigate chosen for attack because of its bad reputation, or any other Iranian vessel that might sortie out.[43]

Initially, the Iranians stayed in port, but around midday three Pasdaran speedboats boldly sailed into the southern Gulf and attacked merchant vessels, a nearby U.S.-operated oil platform, and an American-flagged supply ship, the *Willi Tide.* Two A-6E Intruders from the U.S. carrier *Enterprise* spotted the Iranians and attacked the lead Boghammer, sinking it and causing the other two speedboats to run aground on Abu Musa Island. Undeterred, the Iranian navy Combattante II fast attack craft *Joshan,* which was armed with a 76-mm gun and Harpoon and Sea Cat missiles, sortied out of Bandar Abbas and closed to within ten miles of the *Wainwright.* The Iranian captain declared no hostile intent but ignored American orders to stop and abandon the ship. Instead, the *Joshan* fired its single Harpoon missile at the *Wainwright* but missed. The *Wainwright* and *Simpson* returned fire with Standard and Harpoon missiles, sinking the Iranian attack boat. Two Iranian F-4 Phantoms from Bandar Abbas were inbound toward the *Wainwright* during the engagement with the *Joshan.* After failing to heed calls to turn away, one Phantom was damaged by a SAM from the *Wainwright,* and both retreated back to base.

The Iranian navy's determination to retaliate was brave but foolish given the unequal nature of the battle. Iran could have cut its losses had it ceased operations after losing the *Joshan,* because the U.S. Navy had been authorized to sink only one Iranian warship. Additional U.S. attacks had to be in self-defense or specifically approved by Washington. Unaware of this constraint, Iran's leaders still wanted to punish their Gulf Arab neighbors, and the frigate *Sahand* was ordered to attack oil platforms belonging to the United Arab Emirates. Because of poor operational security, Iran's plans were quickly discovered by the Americans, and the *Enterprise* launched a strike group to go after the *Sahand.* A-6 Intruders found the Iranian frigate, which fired SAMs and antiaircraft guns at the American warplanes. The Intruders responded with several missiles and bombs while the nearby U.S. frigate *Joseph Strauss* launched a Harpoon at the *Sahand*. The Iranian frigate was devastated by the missile strikes and burned furiously. When fire hit the ship's magazines, a violent explosion ruptured the hull, sending the *Sahand* rapidly beneath the waves. As the day ended, the *Sabalan* was discovered by U.S. air patrols shortly after leaving port. The frigate fired a missile at the U.S. frigate *Jack Williams* and attacked the U.S. jets overhead. The *Sabalan*, in turn, was struck by a 500-pound laser-guided bomb from an Intruder that went straight down the ship's smokestack. The *Sabalan* lost power and was taking on water when it was saved by Washington's decision to call off the attack. The frigate was eventually towed back to Bandar Abbas, but its role in the war was over. After Operation Praying Mantis, Iran did not stop its ship attacks, but the Tanker War was winding down as the Islamic Republic faced greater dangers along its land borders with Iraq.

Collapse

At the start of 1988 Iran was preparing for another new offensive, but the leadership seemed uncertain about how to deal with the country's overall weakness. The years of massive losses of men and equipment and the disastrous effect of the war on Iran's economy had sapped most Iranians' desire to continue to sacrifice for the sake of removing Saddam. Military and civilian morale had nose-dived in 1987, and discontent among the poor, the bedrock of the regime, was high. The pool of volunteers for the Basij virtually dried up, and draft dodging was rampant. Iran was forced to extend the conscription period from twenty-four to twenty-eight months in early 1988, but mustered less than half the manpower mobilized for its 1987 offensive. Iranian civilians had started antiwar and antigovernment protests, and even some Pasdaran units demonstrated in favor of ending the war. Distracted by the Tanker War and increased tensions with the West and the Gulf Arabs, the ruling clerics and the military commanders seemed unaware of Iraq's improved military capabilities and the ever larger imbalance in military power between Iraq and war-weary Iran. A few brave senior Iranian officials were quietly urging Khomeini to end the war, but the Imam refused to yield until the fortunes of war turned irreversibly against Iran.

Iran's "major" offensive of 1988, Val Fajr 10, was a small affair in Iraqi Kurdistan around the town of Halabjah. Regular army and Pasdaran commanders had abandoned the idea of attacking into the heart of strong Iraqi defenses and chose the Kurdish region to achieve surprise and gain assistance from Iraqi Kurdish insurgents. Because of winter weather and its mobilization problems, Iran did not start its offensive until mid-March, when Guard and Basij forces attacked to

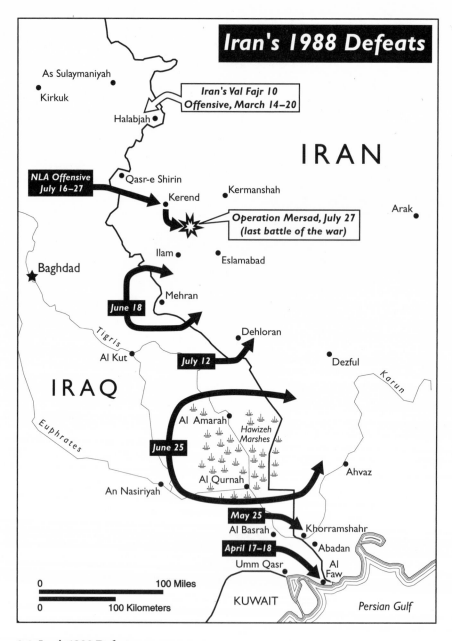

9.4 Iran's 1988 Defeats.

seize the hydroelectric dam at Darbandikhan and move into artillery and rocket range of Iraq's northern oil fields and pipelines. The Iranians surprised the Iraqis, destroying most of an Iraqi infantry division in the initial assault. With fewer men in the field, Iran apparently had enough arms and ammunition for its forces and with help from purchases from China, North Korea, and Austria had even doubled its artillery strength. The Iranians made slow progress in the rugged mountain terrain, however, and were unable to break through Iraq's defenses. Iran's commanders had hoped that the mountains would limit Iraq's ability to conduct armored counterattacks, but Baghdad compensated with attack helicopters, artillery barrages, and chemical warfare. Iran's troops were better protected against chemical attacks in 1988 but still lacked the training, detectors, and decontamination equipment to handle Iraq's heavy use of nerve agents. Fighting was particularly barbarous around Halabjah, where Kurdish villagers were caught in the crossfire. Iran held the town long enough to film the Kurdish civilian casualties killed by Iraqi chemical use and gained a brief propaganda victory. The offensive stalled soon thereafter, and the Iranians were gradually pushed back, leaving them with nothing to show for their last offensive.

As Iran struggled to maintain the initiative in the ground war, Iraq had been preparing to go on the offensive. Taking advantage of the Iraqi army's increased size, better equipment, and improved effectiveness, Baghdad was able to hold the front lines against Iran's sporadic attacks with only a portion of its army. Starting in late 1987, the remaining units concentrated on training in combined arms operations. The Republican Guard, which now had one hundred thousand men, conducted large corps-level exercises that focused on mobile defensive and offensive operations. As 1988 began, Republican Guard and Iraqi armored and mechanized formations were training on full-size mockups of key Iranian defensive positions. Other elements of the Iraqi armed forces also were improving. The chemical corps was more competent in using chemical agents, including advanced persistent and nonpersistent nerve agents, and in protecting Iraqi soldiers operating in contaminated environments. Air force operations and planning had improved markedly, and the Iraqis had built up a large stockpile of conventional and chemical bombs and artillery shells with the help of Gulf Arab loans. Baghdad also had acquired large numbers of SCUD missiles from the Soviet Union. After modifying most to reach targets more than three hundred miles distant, Iraq was ready to resume the "war of the cities" to increase Iran's suffering.

Iran was feeling a pinch from Iraq's air campaign against its oil infrastructure by late 1987. After one Iraqi attack, Iran's Rey oil refinery was so badly damaged that the clerical regime had to start rationing gas and heating oil. In an effort to deter the Iraqis, Iran attacked Baghdad with SCUD missiles, although these struck mostly unpopulated areas and did little damage. Iraq retaliated with five of its modified SCUDs, called the Al Hussein, on February 29, 1988, striking Tehran and Qom. To extend the missile's range, Iraq had reduced the warhead's weight. Still, the blast was frighteningly loud, the warhead and the mass of the rocket debris caused moderate damage on impact and blew out the windows of nearby buildings. Iran responded with SCUD attacks on Baghdad, Mosul, Kirkuk, and Saddam's hometown of Tikrit but lacked the inventory to match the Iraqis. Unlike past "wars of the cities," Iraq was prepared to sustain its campaign, and the Iranians were surprised when the SCUDs continued to rain on Tehran. The capital's citizens began to flee the city, spurred by the constant pounding and by fears that Iraq might use chemical warheads, a dread self-defeatingly spread by Iranian authorities in propaganda to increase international pressure to stop Iraq. By mid-March nearly a million people had left Tehran, and these were joined by several million more by the time the last SCUD struck at the end of April. During the fifty-two days of the last "war of the cities" Iran fired approximately 50 SCUDs at Iraq, but was hit by just over 200 Al Husseins and SCUDs, including roughly 140 Al Husseins that struck Tehran. Still, the missile campaign did not fundamentally alter Khomeini's position on the war. Iran clung to its demands and rejected international attempts to broker a cease-fire.

By coincidence, on the same day that the United States launched Operation Praying Mantis in 1988, Iran's ground forces at Al Faw were subjected to the first of a series of large Iraqi offensives designed to restore the border and destroy Iranian army and Guard units. In the months before this attack, Iran's military manpower had dropped to six hundred thousand while Iraq had more than a million men in its armed forces. In every category of combat power, Iran was inferior to Iraq, and in 1988 Iranian army and Pasdaran units were often outnumbered in men and weapons by ratios of ten or more to one. The Iraqis had exhaustively planned and scripted their offensives, and aided by massive amounts of chemical agents, they fought with an effectiveness previously unseen on the war's battlefields.

In the battle at Al Faw, eight thousand to fifteen thousand Iranian troops were hit by a massive air and artillery bombardment of chemical and high explosive munitions and then struck by roughly one hundred thousand Iraqi troops spearheaded by Republican Guard armored units. The Iranians were caught while rotating troops during celebrations of the last day of the Muslim holy month of Ramadan, so many positions were undermanned. Despite some effective fire support from Iranian batteries on the eastern side of the Shatt, the surprised defenders were flanked by amphibious assaults from the Khwar Abd-Allah and overrun in thirty-five hours after suffering heavy casualties and losing most of their equipment. The hard-line clerics in Tehran blamed the regular military for the defeat, fired the army chief of staff, and belatedly began to urge the services to work together.[44]

Although Iran had a monthlong breather before Iraq's next offensive against Salamcheh and Iranian positions east of Al Basrah, the armed forces were unable to improve their situation. Iran's defensive lines were a strong mix of trenches, berms, minefields, tank traps, and other obstacles that would make an Iraqi assault costly. Some of Iran's forces were out of position, however, after an Iraqi deception campaign succeeded in causing Iranian reserves to be deployed farther north around the Hawizeh Marshes. On the morning of May 25, 1988, the Iranians were hit by tons of nonpersistent nerve agents in one of the largest artillery barrages in history. Iran's flanks were then struck and enveloped by Iraqi armor and mechanized forces. Despite managing to conduct one counterattack, the Iranian defenders retreated in disorder to escape the Iraqi pincers. As their predecessors had done in World War II, the Iranian officers and men on the Al Basrah front commandeered cars and buses to speed their flight to the rear areas, and in less than ten hours the Iranians had surrendered all their gains from 1987. Most of the engaged Iranian units' irreplaceable heavy equipment was left behind, and more than 100 of Iran's remaining tanks and 150 artillery pieces were captured by the Iraqis.

After the defeat east of Al Basrah, the fight went out of Iran's soldiers and civilians. Appeals by Khomeini for new volunteers to continue resistance were poorly received. A few Iranian politicians criticized the Imam for Iran's failing fortunes as antiwar protests became more frequent. In early June, probably to distance himself from developments in the war, the Supreme Leader officially named Majles speaker Ali Akbar Hashemi Rafsanjani the commander in chief of Iran's armed forces, a role he had been performing for several months. Shifting leaders and commanders and urging greater cooperation, however, was no solution to Iran's problems. In mid-June Pasdaran units in the Mehran area were overwhelmed by an Iraqi double envelopment, which destroyed nearly two Guard divisions as the Iraqis advanced almost twenty miles inside Iran. To add insult to injury, Saddam used the Mujahedin-e Khalq's National Liberation Army (NLA) in the attack. The NLA, which was organized, armed, and supported by Iraq, was created in mid-1987, and the roughly twenty thousand Iranian dissidents in its ranks had previously conducted only small raids, sabotage, and subversion against the clerical regime.

At the end of June six to eight Pasdaran and army divisions were mauled in another double envelopment by Iraqi forces in a fourth offensive, which ejected the Iranians from the Majnoon Islands and Hawizeh Marshes. In this battle, Iran had fewer than sixty tanks to stand against nearly two thousand Iraqi tanks, which, at the time, was the largest concentration of tanks on a battlefield since

World War II. The Iranian air force committed up to thirty-five of its remaining aircraft to try to stop the Iraqis but failed even to slow their advance.

Khomeini and his closest followers stubbornly refused to countenance any weakening of resolve through June. Despite the decline in public support for the war, the regime had arranged for prowar hard-liners to gain more seats in the Majles during elections in April. In the following months, government spokes-men and media denied Iran's losses, called retreats "planned withdrawals," and inflated Iraqi casualty figures while making false claims about Iranian victories in unimportant sectors. The Pasdaran navy continued to attack merchant ships in the Gulf and, in a possible effort to compensate for Iran's defeats, became more aggressive around U.S. warships as July began. On July 3, 1988, a group of Guard speedboats swarmed against merchant ships near the strait, setting the stage for a new tragedy.

The Guard attacks occurred near the U.S. frigate *Elmer Montgomery,* and the nearby American cruiser *Vincennes* launched a reconnaissance helicopter to ob-serve the speedboats. The U.S. Navy only reluctantly had deployed the highly advanced Aegis-class cruiser to the Gulf to help guard against the Silkworm threat. The ship's state-of-the-art sensors and weapons were not designed to operate in an enclosed environment like the Persian Gulf, where peacetime air and surface traffic were active. Because of the 1987 *Stark* incident and the U.S. Navy's concerns about losing such a high-value ship, the *Vincennes'* rules of en-gagement were less strict than usual. At the time, the *Vincennes* was tensely alert because it had intelligence and operational reports that Iranian attacks were pos-sible after suspected hostile Iranian aircraft had been warned away from other U.S. warships the day before. After the Pasdaran speedboats fired on the *Vin-cennes'* helicopter, the cruiser and the *Montgomery* began maneuvers to engage the fast moving Iranian craft. At roughly the same time, a civilian airline flight, Iran Air 655, departed Bandar Abbas airfield, which also was used by Iran's air force. Slightly behind schedule on its twice-weekly flight to the United Arab Emirates, the airliner flew directly at the U.S. warships. Because of a series of errors and bad assumptions, the *Vincennes* mistakenly identified Iran Air 655, a European-built Airbus, as an F-14 fighter. After the Iranian pilots failed to re-spond to or failed to receive repeated warnings and requests for identification, the *Vincennes* fired two SAMs and destroyed the plane in midair, killing all 290 passengers and crew.[45]

The Iranians viewed the accident as a deliberate attack, ignoring their own role in the airliner's misfortune. Even though President Reagan apologized for the accident and offered compensation to the victims' families, the downing of Iran Air 655 just months after Operation Praying Mantis seemed a clear signal to the mullahs that Washington was prepared to use any means to defeat the Islamic Republic. In addition, the lack of international outrage over the incident made clear to many Iranians the extent of their isolation. Still, Khomeini was un-moved and tried to use the accident to revive the Iranians' flagging patriotism. Most of Iran's other political and military leaders, however, saw the accident as a suitable pretext for ending the war. Rafsanjani called a commanders' confer-ence to assess Iran's strategic situation, and Army and Guard leaders reached the unanimous conclusion that Iran lacked the resources to defend the country against Iraq and the United States. The majority of the participants agreed that Iran had to bring the war to an end. Backed by nearly all of Iran's senior clerical, political, military, and economic leadership, Rafsanjani took this recommenda-tion to the Supreme Leader.

Iran's troubles continued to mount as Khomeini pondered his options. On July 12, the Iraqis launched another offensive in the central border region, meet-ing little resistance from the demoralized Iranian ground units. The Iraqis ad-vanced more than twenty-five miles into Iran and captured the city of Dehloran. With both sides discussing the possibility of a cease-fire by mid-July, the Iraqis withdrew from Iranian territory, taking back captured Iranian arms but leaving the NLA behind to control a small "liberated" area. Iran was now practically na-ked before the Iraqis, having lost most of its ground forces while its remaining units were disheartened. The Iraqis set up a large propaganda display to show the Iranian people and the world how much equipment had been stripped from the Iranian army and Pasdaran. In addition to tens of thousands of rifles, the Iraqis flaunted nearly 600 tanks, more than 400 other armored vehicles, and 320 artillery pieces, claiming that they also had taken hundreds more tanks and pieces of heavy engineering equipment and nearly 2,000 trucks and jeeps.[46]

Khomeini was still reluctant to concede. Most of Iran's leaders viewed with trepidation Iraq's apparent ability to destroy Iran's armed forces at will, the mis-sile attacks and air campaign, and the costly clashes with U.S. forces. The hard-liners, looking at Iran's near bankruptcy, its devastated economy, and growing antiregime sentiment, were becoming more concerned about saving the revolu-tion. On July 13, while Iranian forces around Dehloran were being trounced, Saddam threatened to invade Khuzestan again if Iran did not evacuate territory in Iraqi Kurdistan. Rafsanjani quickly announced the next day that Iran would withdraw its forces. A few days later, the Iraqi dictator called for peace negotia-tions, but warned that Iraq would continue its air attacks and would prevent Iran from rebuilding its forces. At this point, Iran's leaders prevailed upon Khomeini to agree to a cease-fire. In a letter sent to Pasdaran commanders and Friday prayer leaders, the Imam explained that military and political officials had advised him that the war could not be continued because Iran could not obtain the weapons needed to match even a tenth of what Saddam was receiving. Khomeini quoted at length from a letter written by Guard commander Rezai that suggested Iran needed five years to rebuild and expand the armed forces and needed the ability to make "laser and atomic weapons" to win the war. He closed his letter by urging the addressees to direct all their efforts at justifying the cease-fire.[47]

After Khomeini's decision, President Khamenei informed Baghdad that Iran was ready to negotiate and sent a letter to the U.N. Secretary General that unconditionally accepted U.N. Resolution 598 on July 17, 1988. Saddam, however, was not satisfied and demanded a public acceptance by Khomeini. On July 20, the Supreme Leader reluctantly went on Iranian radio and agreed to the cease-fire, saying, "Taking this decision was more deadly than taking poison. I submitted myself to God's will and drank this drink for his satisfaction." Like many political leaders in wartime, he pointed an accusatory finger at his military officials for advising him to accept the cease-fire. Not totally contrite, the aged ayatollah also used the statement to warn Western forces to leave the Gulf before they were "drowned in the quagmires of death."[48]

A few weeks of disputatious negotiations between the Iranians and Iraqis passed before the cease-fire began on August 20, 1988. During this time Iraq allowed the NLA to strike some sixty miles into Iran toward Kermanshah. The Iraqis may have been trying to use the NLA to spark a popular uprising in Iran and provided tank and artillery support to the dissidents. In the mountains between Kerend and Eslamabad, however, the NLA force became trapped and was decisively defeated in Operation Mersad by Pasdaran and army forces aching to restore their reputation. The Iranians inflicted several thousand casualties on the Mujahedin-e Khalq fighters, and the survivors retreated back to Iraq. The group had no popular support in Iran because of its collaboration with Saddam, but the Guard, after killing its NLA prisoners, followed up the battle by launching a campaign of arrests and executions throughout Iran to stamp out the remnants of the MEK and its sympathizers.

The Imposed War's Balance Sheet

After eight years of fighting, the end result of the conflict was a return to the status quo antebellum. Many issues, such as the status of the Shatt al-Arab and the return of prisoners of war (POWs), were left unresolved until many years later when Iran was able to take advantage of Iraq's problems with the United States. Iran recovered the territory occupied by Iraq in the 1988 offensives and got Iraqi acceptance of the 1975 Algiers Accord as the price for its neutrality following the Iraqi invasion of Kuwait in 1990. After the cease-fire the International Red Cross estimated that Iraq held nearly 13,000 Iranian POWs and the clerical regime detained almost 50,000 Iraqis. Although Iraq claimed that it returned all Iranian POWs by early 1993, Iran continued to hold thousands of Iraqi soldiers over disputes about the prisoner exchange process and the status of Iranian combatants missing in action or whose remains were in Iraqi territory. The Islamic Republic agreed to release the last 1,200 Iraqi POWs in return for nearly 350 Iranians imprisoned by Iraq for various reasons only when Baghdad succumbed to Iranian demands hours before the start of Operation Iraqi Freedom in March 2003.

The war was an unmitigated disaster for Iran and its armed forces. The CIA estimated the financial cost of war for Iran at $160 billion and the total cost of repairing damage from the war and revolution at $450 billion. Iraqi bombing and shelling destroyed 65 percent of Iran's refinery capacity and left Khorramshahr, its port, and parts of Abadan, Susangerd, and Dezful in ruins. The conflict created more than two million Iranian refugees from the war zone, increasing the burden on Iran's economy. Western estimates of Iranian casualties—some running as high as one million total dead and wounded—were inflated and based on incomplete information. Iran's actual losses were much lower, but they still represented a terrible sacrifice by the country. Immediately after the war, Iran claimed that it suffered just over 170,000 military deaths. Later, Iranian officials, some of whom were responsible for taking care of Iran's veterans, made statements that suggested Iran's total losses were between 200,000 and 220,000 battlefield deaths, 350,000 to 400,000 wounded, and approximately 16,000 civilian deaths. Not surprisingly, the Basij suffered the most deaths, representing nearly 43 percent of Iran's wartime "martyrs," according to Iranian officials. Army and Pasdaran personnel killed in battle accounted, respectively, for 23 percent and 19 percent of Iran's total deaths.[49]

The Iranian military was in ruins but retained a framework for future growth with a cadre of veteran combat commanders and junior leaders. These men could take some pride in their wartime performance in the field, in garrison, and in maintenance and production facilities. The Artesh and Guard had responded well to Iraq's initial invasion and kept the larger and better-equipped Iraqi army on the defensive for most of the war. Both military services demonstrated the skill and intelligence of the Iranian people, which helped them to overcome Iraq's significant material advantages for many years. Although not able to maintain the most sophisticated equipment, the Iranians kept some of their weapons at least partially operational much longer than most Western specialists thought possible. The Iranians also produced a wide range of weapons and ammunition, reconditioned artillery and armored vehicles, and modified or produced equipment to suit the unique conditions of the war's battlefields. The major failing of the armed forces was the antagonism between the regular forces and the Pasdaran. The lack of cooperation crippled tactical planning, fire support, and logistics. The foolish splitting of resources between the Guard and the Artesh kept them from marshaling the means for effective and sustained combined arms operations. In turn, the lack of firepower, mobility, and cooperation brought to naught Iran's repeated penetrations of Iraqi defenses and denied the clerics the breakthrough they too long believed would result from their new "Islamic" way of war.[50]

The lengthy war demonstrated without a doubt that the Iranian military's greatest asset was the individual soldier's willingness to fight and die to defend his beliefs. The Iranian soldiers, sailors, and airmen maintained their morale for most of the war despite horrendous conditions and horrible sacrifices. Many of the volunteers accepted Khomeini's call to treat the "Imposed War" as jihad and consciously made the decision to forfeit their lives as needed in Iran's cause. In the end, the clerics' overreaching and lack of strategic foresight wasted these Iranian lives and guaranteed a longer recovery for their armed forces following the devastating and humiliating losses of 1988.[51]

10

Despise Not Your Enemy

Iran's Armed Forces in the Twenty-first Century

TWO DECADES AFTER THE END OF THE IRAN-IRAQ WAR the Iranian armed forces have been slowly rising from the ashes to help their country reclaim what the government sees as its rightful place in the world. Iran still has significant shortcomings in most categories of combat power and military effectiveness. Still, the Iranian military had improved its strengths enough by 2005 to be called a significant threat to U.S. interests and allies in the Persian Gulf by senior U.S. intelligence officials.[1] Of course, as mentioned in the introduction, Iran's armed forces have not formed a continuous identifiable group from the time of Cyrus to today and are not truly immortal. But there are many interesting parallels in Iran's development and use of its military power over the ages that highlight still extant historical influences and can help explain the current and future course of the Revolutionary Guard and regular military. If there is one lesson for Iran and its potential opponents to draw from the preceding narrative of its military accomplishments and failures, however, it may best be captured, appropriately enough, in the Greek tragedy *The Persians*. Written by Aeschylus, who had witnessed the defeat of Xerxes' fleet at Salamis, the play's message for both victors and vanquished was that hubris—particularly the Great King's disdain for his Greek adversaries—was behind the Persian defeat. A more recent and succinct version of this warning can be taken from an 1879 cartoon from the British humor magazine *Punch*. Titled "A lesson from the Zulu War," the cartoon was published roughly a month after forces of the British superpower were defeated by tribal warriors at the Battle of Isandlwana. It showed a Zulu chief instructing a chastened John Bull by writing on a blackboard the admonition "Despise Not Your Enemy."[2]

Iran's military power today should not be underestimated or disdained because, as opponents ranging from Crassus through Suleiman the Magnificent to Saddam Hussein learned to their sorrow, the fighting men of Iran can deliver unexpected tactics and unpleasant surprises to overconfident enemies. By the same token, Iran's armed forces should not be perceived with exaggerated appraisals of strength, malevolence, and fanaticism. Iranian military personnel have shown themselves capable of the highest levels of self-sacrifice and bravery. They also have demonstrated that, while as susceptible to the tocsins of patriotism and religion as any other people, they are not automatons in the thrall of even the most unworthy ruler.

Aeschylus took Xerxes to task for his overweening ambition as another calamitous aspect of Iranian hubris. Similarly, many of the Parthians' misfortunes were a result of their unwillingness to stop meddling in Mesopotamia and Armenia, which heightened Roman concerns about frontier security. The first Safavid shah's provocative anti-Sunni repression invited responses from the Ottomans. Ignoring their own weakness and in some cases pushed by their mullahs, the Qajars initiated losing wars with Russia and Great Britain. In Muhammad Reza Shah's case, his pretentious pursuit of great power status put him on a collision course with his own people. Some of the current regime's unpopularity stems from Iranians' misgivings about the revolutionaries' continuation of the Iran-Iraq War. Many now see the fighting after 1983 as an abuse of Iranian nationalism and idealism by the clerical leadership to consolidate their power rather than to spread the revolution.[3] Iranian attempts to advance the Islamic Republic's interests and influence throughout the region in recent years have contributed to growing Sunni-Shia tension and provoked neighboring Sunni states to seek countermeasures to keep Iranian hegemony at bay.[4]

Factors Shaping Iran's Military

Iran presents a complex picture in its approach to building and using military might. Over the centuries Iran's leaders repeatedly wrestled with many of the same problems as they sought to create a national military that could defend Iran's interests and territory and avoid the erosion of power that contributed to the fall of earlier dynasties. The Iranians, like so many other peoples, have at various times created militaries with superior leadership, high morale, and a mastery of logistics, training, and contemporary weaponry that made their soldiers appear invincible. Yet, time and time again, military excellence gave way to ineptitude and dissolution as the Iranians lost the struggle to maintain their hard-won proficiency. In almost all of these cases, it has been the Iranian military's relationship to its government that has contributed to each dynasty's eventual demise.

Not surprisingly, many of the influences that formed Iran's fighting forces in the past continue to resonate today and can help provide a clearer view of Iran's future military power. The largest factors shaping Iran's military remain the continuation of its dual militaries, inconsistent and sometimes antagonistic views toward military professionalism, and persistent problems with politicization.

Iran's ultimate success in developing an effective military will likely rest on how it overcomes a historically uneven appreciation of new technologies and the weapons best suited for its armed forces. Along these same lines, Iran's military has achieved its greatest success when its rulers paid close attention to maximizing the perseverance, resourcefulness, and patriotism of their military personnel. More often than not, however, Iran's rulers have failed to support their fighting men, and the current level of care bears close observation. Beyond the militaries' capabilities and effectiveness, Iran's intentions for the use of military force will continue to flow from the clerical regime's vision of its role in the world, which springs from a strong Iranian identity based on nationalism, feelings of insecurity, and Shia Islam.

Dueling Militaries

The split in the Iranian armed forces between the Artesh and the Pasdaran is just the latest in a long line of dual militaries and will likely shape Iran's military performance for the foreseeable future. Since Ardeshir attempted to create a loyal standing army independent of the provincial levies during the Sassanian Empire, Iran's political elites have resorted to competitive militaries to prevent challenges to central authority regardless of the cost to military effectiveness. Similar divides were seen in the Gendarmerie-Cossack rivalry, the mutual suspicion and antagonism between the Qajar Nezam-e Jadid and tribal levies, and even the Qizilbash horsemen's detachment from the Persianized *ghulam* formations of the Safavids. Just as the last shah's political control mechanisms hobbled the Artesh, the clerical regime's continued use of a dual military structure is likely to interfere in the transformation of the basic strengths of Iranian military personnel and their arms into effective fighting power.

For the Islamic Republic, the Iran-Iraq War, the international arms embargo, and the political divisions that splintered the clerical regime during its early years postponed efforts to craft a new Iranian military. Following the 1988 cease-fire, the clerical regime wanted to strengthen the armed forces and restrict the autonomy of the Revolutionary Guard. Change was possible, in large part, because the Pasdaran suffered a temporary decline in its political standing following the humiliating defeats at Iraqi hands. Guard commander Mohsen Rezai was publicly disgraced that year when he was forced to admit to the misappropriation of public funds and take responsibility for the defeat at Faw. Majles politicians criticized the Guard's war strategy for the first time in closed debates and accused Guard members of mass desertions and corruption. The Pasdaran, however, fought back with an emphasis on protecting their status as "guardians of the revolution." As early as September 1988, the high command assembled the Guard's national and local commanders in Tehran to display their remaining strength and implicitly threaten the political leadership against attempts to weaken the Pasdaran's position and ideology. Khomeini sealed this rapid revival by publicly supporting the Guard. In the end, Rezai kept his position, while a more hard-line officer, Ali Shamkhani, replaced Mohsen Rafiq-Dust as Guard Minister. Determined to maintain its independent identity and still distrustful of the regular military, the Pasdaran ensured that, despite proposals to merge the services and reduce redundant organizations, Iran maintained its dual military structure.[5]

Perhaps the most important postwar development was the formalization of the Revolutionary Guard's role as the preeminent service. In many respects, the Pasdaran are the true heirs of Reza Shah's military. Going back to the Constitutional Revolution, the traditionalist clergy and their supporters have sought to assert their conception of a conservative and idealized Islamic past without Western influences. In contrast, Iranian nationalists, personified by the pre-Pahlavi Gendarmerie, have wanted to restore Iran's greatness by incorporating the observable benefits of Western science, technology, and political liberalism. Today, the clerics use the Revolutionary Guard and Basij much like the Persian Cossacks and Reza Shah's Artesh to fight against Western-style political reforms and culture. The Guards even mimic the Pahlavi military in its role as the regime's protector, devoted to supporting Iran's ruler, influential in politics, bathed in privileges, and an economic force in its own right because of its involvement in defense production and public works.

The Artesh seems to have accepted its lower status as it works to become capable of deterring, defending against, and defeating foreign aggressors. The regular military's popular standing, recovered during the war with Iraq, appears relatively high, although it benefits from favorable comparisons with the Guard and Basij. The Artesh is part and parcel of the regime, however, and the clerical leaders have continued efforts to mold the regular military by indoctrination and the promotion of officers on the basis of loyalty and political reliability.

The postwar principles guiding Iran's dual military structure were established and codified in the regulations of the Iranian armed forces in 1992 when the residual strength of Khomeini's legacy ensured that ideology would be a keystone for Iran's conception of war and military doctrine.[6] In addition to stressing Islamic ideology as a basic precept for organizing and equipping the armed forces, the principles demanded loyalty to the Supreme Leader, sought self-sufficiency, and held defense—deterring, defending against, and ultimately punishing an aggressor against Iran—as the armed forces' primary orientation. They also included in Iran's security goals the protection of other Muslim and "oppressed" nations.[7] The principles, which mirrored the Guard's ideological preferences, strengthened its role in Iran. In particular, the demand for loyalty to the concept of *valiyat-e faqih* seemed to fix the bond between hard-line Guard commanders and Khomeini's successor as Supreme Leader, Ayatollah Ali Khamenei. Defining

Iran's security to include the protection of the oppressed created an opening for the Guard to pursue its desire to export the revolution at a time when the clerical regime was being more cautious. After the United States liberated Kuwait from Iraq in 1991 by easily defeating the Iraqi army that only a few years earlier had crushed Iran's ground forces, the regime grew more deliberate and calculating to avoid unnecessary risks, but the Pasdaran's leadership remained militant.

The Guard used its new authorities to expand its capabilities to conduct clandestine overseas operations in support of other Muslims and against Iran's perceived enemies. Through the 1980s and early 1990s, the Guard already had forged its own military-to-military ties with other countries, including Syria, Pakistan, and Sudan. The Guard also took existing elements involved in exporting the revolution and formed the Qods (Jerusalem) Force in 1990. The Qods Force became an elite unit that conducts clandestine operations outside Iran; provides training, financial, and other support to Islamic militant groups; and collects strategic and military intelligence against Iran's enemies, especially the United States. While Iran remained neutral during the 1991 Gulf War, the Guard supported Iraqi Shia groups and fomented rebellion there. Later that year, three Iranians connected to the Pasdaran assassinated Shahpour Bakhtiar, the shah's last prime minister, in France. Other Iranian dissidents were murdered in Europe during the early 1990s at the hands of Guard or Iranian intelligence operatives.[8]

Over the course of the next fifteen years, the Guard and the Qods Forces became increasingly professional and expert in their overseas operations. The Qods Force established paramilitary training camps for militants in Iran, Lebanon, and Sudan. The Guard expanded the support given to Lebanese Hizballah and Islamic Jihad and began aiding the Palestinian terrorist group Hamas and other Muslim militants throughout the world, including groups in Iraq, Bosnia, Egypt, Turkey, and Kashmir. During the mid-1990s, the Guard, along with Iranian intelligence officers, mounted a comprehensive surveillance campaign against Americans and U.S. facilities in the Persian Gulf and Central Asia. The Iranians' activities clearly had the goal of identifying targets of opportunity for terrorist operations, supported contingency planning for future attacks in the event of a conflict with the United States, and may have been done relatively openly to send a deterrent message to Washington. Although terrorism is historically a weapon of the weak and dispossessed, the Guard devoted considerable resources to make such unconventional operations an important element of Iran's overall national military strategy.

The New Professionals

Another historical influence on Iran's force structure and administration that has been given concrete form in the division between the Artesh and the Pasdaran is the mixed views on professionalism and modernization. Going back to the Qizilbash's disdain for the Persian administrators and *ghulam* artillerymen and musketeers of the Safavid army, various Iranian groups have been antagonistic toward change that challenged traditional methods and relationships. Even as some Iranians recognized the need to learn from and emulate more advanced foreign military forces, others were more concerned with maintaining their place in Iranian society. The Qajar-era tribal khans and mullahs opposed Abbas Mirza's and Mirza Taqi Khan's reforms because they feared a strengthening of central authority and foreign influences that would undermine their power. The two Pahlavi shahs only partially embraced the creation of a professional military. Their political controls ensured that senior Iranian commanders paid less attention to mastering the military art and the requirements for administering a modern military than to the politics of royal favor.

Most of the leaders of the Islamic Republic initially were overtly hostile to the concept of a professional military, favoring revolutionary ardor over military skills and modern weapon systems. Only the Iraqi invasion and the subsequent failure of the regime to translate its ideological fervor into victory saved the Artesh and undermined the idea that professional military forces were unnecessary. Following the cease-fire with Iraq, the clerical regime could not focus on the military because of economic needs and internal political problems following Khomeini's death less than a year later in June 1989. Short of money and facing strong competition for government funds, Iran's military leaders looked instead to improving discipline and training. The Artesh escaped this period with no major changes to its organization and order of battle. The regular military worked to prevent the dilution of its professionalism and technical skills and was willing to accept some reductions in size to maintain its combined arms capabilities to distinguish it from the Pasdaran. In turn, as the Guard demobilized in the fall of 1988, its leadership adopted a more conventional force structure and accepted the imposition of more hierarchy and discipline in its organization and administration. The Guard was to remain a predominantly light infantry force and was reorganized into understrength divisions and independent brigades with supporting armor, artillery, air defense, engineering, and chemical defense units. By late 1991 Guard personnel were given new uniforms and standardized military ranks to go along with the increased emphasis on discipline.

After he was named Supreme Leader Ayatollah Khamenei became the head of the armed forces, but changes were made to give significant day-to-day authority over military policy to the popularly elected president. When Rafsanjani gained this post in July 1989, his administration had the political strength to undertake changes to rationalize the military establishment and correct administrative problems. Economic difficulties made efforts to reduce wasteful military spending essential, and many politicians wanted to use efforts to improve the

military establishment's proficiency to curtail the Guard's resurgent independence. In a victory of more pragmatic leaders over the hard-liners, the Revolutionary Guard Ministry and its subordinate defense procurement and production organizations were merged into the Ministry of Defense to create a new
Ministry of Defense and Armed Forces Logistics. The impact of this change on
day-to-day operations was slight for many years but may have helped regularize
financial operations and procurement efforts, reducing opportunities for corruption and fraud.[9]

Despite the loss of its ministry, the Guard was able to maintain its influence
by aligning itself closely with Supreme Leader Khamenei. Also it continued to
be well represented on the Supreme Defense Council, and Hassan Firouzabadi, a
prominent Pasdaran leader, was put in charge of the Armed Forces General Staff
Headquarters, the primary joint staff that evolved from the various wartime joint
commands and councils.[10] Perhaps the most significant organizational change
was the merger of the Gendarmerie, national police, and remaining *komitehs*
into the Law Enforcement Forces (LEF) in 1991. Although the Guard remained
the ultimate guarantor of the regime's survival, the new LEF was to take the lead
in handling sporadic internal dissent and violent unrest, reducing the Guard's
internal security role and freeing it to focus on other missions.[11]

Supreme Leader Khamenei continued to deal directly with the Artesh and
the Pasdaran and maintained representatives with the services to guide their
daily activities. "Commissars" are still deployed at all levels of the armed forces
to ensure loyalty and conduct indoctrination. The General Staff and other joint
organizations, meanwhile, brought Artesh and Pasdaran officers into regular
contact and occasional close working relationships despite the persistent rivalry
between the two militaries. In the early 1990s the competition for resources,
missions, and prestige occasionally led to clashes that resulted in bloodshed, but
this level of discord has diminished. Since the revolution the regime's careful
selection of officers for senior posts has fostered the development of Iran's traditional informal networks of family and religious affiliations within the military. These links facilitate institutional politics and shape cooperation among
the services and between the armed forces and the politicians. The networks
also provide venues for other, sometimes opposing, viewpoints, such as those
expressed in the early 1990s by senior army officers who argued for greater
professionalization of the Guard and closer integration of logistic and support
systems. Although their recommendations were never fully accepted, many of
the Artesh's senior war veterans remained among the regime's advisors in the
postwar period.[12]

In another effort to increase military expertise and competency, Iran expanded its military education system for officers. Building on the tradition of
the Dar al-Fonun and the Pahlavi military schools, all of the services under the

Islamic Republic have command and staff colleges, and a Supreme National Defense University was established for doctoral-level work in applied defense sciences and management. The Iranian armed forces also appear to have benefited from the relatively low turnover in the senior military ranks, which has ensured consistent development plans and leadership by experienced war veterans. The only major shake-up in the high command in the first decade after the end of the Iran-Iraq War occurred following the 1997 presidential election. Khamenei used the change of administration to replace officials close to Rafsanjani with men aligned with or acceptable to him. As commander in chief, Khamenei appointed new service commanders and influenced newly elected president Muhammad Khatami's choices for Iran's defense, intelligence, and interior ministers. Ali Shamkhani, the hard-line Pasdaran officer who had become the commander of Iran's regular and Guard naval forces earlier in the decade and who was strongly aligned with Khamenei, was made defense minister, a position he held until 2005.[13]

Politicization and Praetorianism

Iran has experienced the intervention of its military in political affairs since ancient times, and the prospect of Revolutionary Guard officers becoming predominant political actors by virtue of their actual or threatened use of force appears to be growing. The Sassanians suffered numerous military coups, most notably the overthrow of Hormizd IV by an ambitious Persian general that led to years of civil war until Hormizd's son, Chosroes II, reclaimed the throne with Byzantine help. Persian troops from Khorasan helped the Abbasids seize the caliphate in 750, and, over time, the caliphs became puppets to their army commanders, some of whom were Persian. In fact, one of the first generals to carve out his own independent state from Abbasid provinces in the early ninth century was a Persian named Tahir ibn al-Hussein. Military disorder, such as the repeated Qizilbash tribal challenges to the Safavid shahs, has been a reliable sign of imperial decline. The presence of weak shahs also has increased the likelihood of intervention, as seen in the military coups led by Nader Shah against the Safavids and Reza Shah against the Qajars. The divide-and-rule policies of the Islamic Republic and the clerics' other methods to maintain the military's loyalty have decreased the threat of coups, but have not reduced the armed forces' occasional inclination to become involved in politics.[14]

The Guard's power and role in politics has grown steadily since the end of the Iran-Iraq War, and its politicization in favor of the current order is likely to cast the shadow of militarism over Iran well into the future. Anti-regime politicization has been limited despite continued dissatisfaction with conditions in Iran and the military. Some war veterans from the Artesh and Guard protested against the government in the early 1990s while a regular army officer, Gen. Amir Rahimi, issued public condemnations of the regime in 1994 and 1996. During antiregime riots in Qazvin in 1994, Guard units refused to carry out commands to use force to reestablish order. After these disturbances, some Guard officers expressed public concerns that were seen as critical of the ruling clerics. For the most part, however, the regular military services have remained apolitical while threats to suppress dissidence from their leaders have quieted opposition among the *pasdars*.[15]

The Guard's leadership has become closely intertwined with more hard-line elements of the regime since the revolution and has viewed it as their duty to intervene in politics when needed. For much of the past twenty years the ruling clerics' concern has been not that the Guard might move against them so much as that Pasdaran would be too slow or reluctant, as the Imperial Armed Forces had been in 1978, to respond to threats to the regime. Indeed, for much of the late 1990s, the senior commanders could not be certain of the rank and file's loyalty. Most *pasdars*, sharing the views of their families and peers, seemed to have supported President Khatami, a moderate cleric who sought to reform Iran's government, and voted in the 1997 election in percentages similar to the rest of the country. In response, the regime developed special Basij paramilitary units, the Ashura Battalions and the all-female Al-Zahra Battalions, to handle violent unrest. To man these new units the clerics relied on poor Iranians, who were still beholden to the regime for subsidies, work, and religious guidance. These *basijis* have been equipped for riot control and containing internal unrest and conduct regular urban defense exercises.[16]

The major postwar test for the Guard came in July 1999 when an assault by conservative vigilantes and security forces on a Tehran University student dormitory precipitated some of the largest antigovernment protests since the Islamic Revolution two decades earlier. The Khatami administration's moderate approach to handling the unrest did not satisfy Iranian hard-liners. A conservative Iranian newspaper "leaked" a letter sent by twenty-four senior Revolutionary Guard officers to Supreme Leader Khamenei that effectively threatened a military coup. Unlike the 1979 declaration of neutrality by the shah's most senior commanders, the Guard officers' message showed their confidence in their power and their fervent belief in the revolution that they swore to protect. In short order, dissent was squelched, undermining the Khatami government and the efforts to reform the Islamic Republic's authoritarian nature. Artesh officers weakly proclaimed that the defense establishment should not have views on political matters, and the Guard leaders, having made their point and accomplished their goal, retracted their comments.[17]

The Guard has continued to embrace its role as Iran's praetorians since 1999 and stands ready to intervene whenever regime actions or inaction threaten the Pasdaran's corporate interests. Between the summers of 2004 and 2006 the Revolutionary Guard took on a more overt role in Iranian politics, involving itself in the 2004 Majles elections and arranging for more than one hundred former Guard officers to gain seats in the legislature. The following year, the Guard and its Basij militia were denounced for interfering in the presidential polls by massive vote buying and vote rigging on president-elect Mahmud Ahmadi-Nejad's behalf. A year later, one Guard commander claimed that the election of the former Tehran mayor and political firebrand was the result of two years of a multilayered and sophisticated strategy executed by the Pasdaran. The Guard's reward was to have current and former members made governors, ministers, undersecretaries, and diplomats. This added to the Guard's existing clout, which flowed from its internal security mission, intelligence service, prisons, and economic interests. The prospect of the Guard's growing influence over the Islamic Republic today calls to mind the Qizilbash, Cossack Brigade, and Iran's militarization between the end of World War II and the Islamic Revolution.[18]

Arming Iran's Soldiers

Since the Islamic Revolution Iran has faced numerous obstacles in equipping its fighting men, while its procurement efforts have shown a historical tendency for inappropriate purchases. Few Iranian states since the Sassanians have done well in creating forces that incorporated and sustained state-of-the-art technology in inventories well suited to the government's strategic goals. The Safavids' slow embrace of muskets and artillery was a result of the Qizilbash's cultural aversion to "unmanly" weapons but also of the tribal khans' concern about power shifting to the throne. Even Nader Shah, who otherwise embraced available weapon systems and emphasized training to improve his soldiers' technical skills, adopted the use of siege engines with some difficulty and little success. Given their poverty of means, the Qajars deserve at least some credit for their sporadic attempts to modernize their inventories with European help. Reza Shah tried to arm his military with modern if not quite state-of-the-art equipment. But he followed in the steps of the Qajars and failed to lay the needed groundwork to provide skilled crews, maintenance personnel, and logisticians to make the most of his inventory of armored vehicles, aircraft, and warships.

Financial constraints have played an important role in Iran's approach to new technologies, but the Iranians have been no more immune than other countries to buying prestige weapons systems or pursuing costly and ineffective indigenous production programs that have not served the country's best interests. Perhaps the most notable example of the latter was Nader Shah's murderous attempt to build a navy by forcing laborers to drag timber hundreds of miles over rough terrain. Muhammad Reza Shah's quest for advanced weapon systems that he could not afford to sustain may be the most conspicuous example of the former. Even the Islamic Republic has not been able to resist some prestige purchases, including the acquisition of three Russian Kilo-class diesel submarines in the early 1990s that have faced serious problems with readiness and operations in the warm waters around Iran. The Islamic Republic, however, has moved from the Revolutionary Guard's initial disdain for heavy weapons and combined arms operations to their ready acceptance of ballistic missiles and other more sophisticated systems and technology. Still, Iran's procurement efforts over the past twenty years have left the bulk of its armed forces reliant on aging or outmoded weapon systems.

In the immediate aftermath of the war with Iraq, Iran received some of the weapons it had ordered earlier, but it lacked the money and access to loans to fund the major rearmament and modernization program the armed forces' needed. Iran was able to spend nearly $6 billion on existing contracts in the first full year after the war, but defense expenditures in subsequent years dropped markedly. Plans announced in 1989 to spend up to $10 billion over five years on weapons alone were not realized. (All figures on Iran's defense budget are rough estimates because the regime does not reveal its actual defense spending figures.) Part of Iran's problems was caused by continued Western restrictions on arms sales and the collapse of the Soviet Union and the Warsaw Pact, which removed potential sources of military aid and favorable weapons deals. Iran had to be tightfisted and relied on less expensive North Korean and Chinese arms. Through the 1990s defense spending fluctuated because of lower oil revenues and the growing pressure from demographic changes; Iran's population nearly doubled between 1980 and 2000, increasing the need for social spending. At the turn of the century, a recovery in Iranian defense spending began as budgets grew from an estimated $2.3 billion in 2000 to $6.2 billion in 2006, a 170 percent increase for the period. Still, the military's share of government revenues has remained low relative to the shah's era. By some estimates, the Islamic Republic has been spending as little as 25 percent of what is needed to modernize and recapitalize the armed forces to the level of Muhammad Reza's 410,000-man military with current generation armor, artillery, aircraft, and warships.[19]

Faced with such problems, Iran tried a three-pronged strategy to rearm. Its first action after the war was to reduce the armed forces' size, which fell from just over 600,000 men in 1990 to a low of 513,000 in 1992 before rebounding to its current end strength of roughly 545,000 in 1997. Next, Iranian leaders made the key decision to focus on the acquisition of the deterrent and retaliatory capabilities provided by long-range ballistic missiles and antiship and air defense systems. The Iranians also looked to less expensive repairs and rebuilds to maintain their existing equipment. In 1993, then Iranian defense minister Akbar Torkan described Iran's procurement priorities by saying, "The first priority is spare parts, the second priority is spare parts, and the third priority is spare parts."[20] Finally, the clerical regime put a great effort into increasing its self-sufficiency by developing indigenous defense industries to reduce Iran's reliance on undependable or expensive foreign supplies. Since the revolution, Iran's Defense Industries Organization has slowly increased spending on operations, maintenance, research, and design while managing roughly 250 sites with 50,000 workers.[21]

Although true self-sufficiency in the production of arms is still limited to light weapons and ammunition, the Iranians have been making progress in many other areas such as missiles, rockets, electronic and mechanical engineering, and more advanced fields of research and design. Nearly all of the major weapon systems that Iran claims to produce, however, are assembled under license from kits or are put together using foreign components. The quality of Iranian upgrades and indigenously produced arms is uncertain. Notwithstanding its problems, Iran has surprised many observers by its ability to maintain obsolescent and worn-out weapon systems. The Iranians have been adept at reverse engineering to replace foreign spare parts and at black market acquisitions since the 1980s. Because of its difficulties in procuring adequate and appropriate weapons, however, Iran's military capabilities are likely to improve only at the margins in accuracy, effectiveness, and lethality in the foreseeable future. In turn, the shortcomings of the Iranian arsenal make the performance of Iran's soldiers, sailors, and airmen key to the country's overall military effectiveness.

Supporting Iran's Military Personnel

Iran's history has shown repeatedly how poor leadership, stingy support, and outright maltreatment have regularly undercut Iran's fighting men. Outside observers repeatedly credited the Iranians with all of the best qualities of soldiers anywhere in the world. Herodotus praised the Persians as not inferior to the Greeks in boldness and warlike spirit. A millennium later, the Emperor Maurice held the Sassanians as the Byzantines' most dangerous foe. The British admired the courage and hardiness of the otherwise pitiable Qajar fighting men. During World War I the National Gendarmerie and other volunteers withstood terrible winter weather in the Zagros Mountains to slow the larger and better equipped Russian forces. More recently, Artesh soldiers and the *pasdars* distinguished themselves by fighting in the climatic extremes of mountains, swamps, and desert that marked the lengthy front lines of the Iran-Iraq War. Their deep reconnaissance missions, amphibious operations, and other tactics regularly resulted in surprise over and defeat of the Iraqis. In addition, the dedication and self-sacrifice seen in the Iranian soldiers who threw themselves across minefields against entrenched Iraqi defenders were unquestionable. With this history, there has been little gainsaying of Iranian military personnel's bravery and will to fight.

In the modern era, in particular, Iran's successes on the battlefield owed much more to its soldiers than its military systems or generalship.

Iran's shame is that its rulers repeatedly have taken its soldiers for granted or taken a cavalier attitude toward their sacrifices. In his war against the Greeks, Xerxes set up thrones overseeing the battlefields, convinced that his soldiers would fight more forcefully under his eye. His impatience at Thermopylae and Salamis, however, put his troops and fleet at a serious disadvantage that resulted in bloody defeats. Similarly, Yazdegird's pushing for a fight at Qadisiyah revealed a too casual disregard for putting his army at a serious disadvantage by placing its back against a river. The Qajars were undoubtedly the worst at taking care of their soldiers and generally ignored the military's needs throughout their dynasty. The Pahlavis did little better in caring for their mostly conscript armies. Reza Shah was repaid with the humiliating collapse of his army in 1941 while Muhammad Reza Shah's Artesh was never put to the test of a major conflict. The Islamic Republic's waste of the bravery and spirit of sacrifice of Iran's fighting men, especially the boy soldiers, is perhaps the darkest mark against Iran's rulers. By ignoring the professional military's advice, the hard-line clerics and Pasdaran took advantage of the *basijis'* patriotism and devotion, condemning tens of thousands to needless death.

Iran is still shortchanging its soldiers, sailors, and airmen, and a shift in this treatment might be one of the best future indicators of improvements in Iran's military effectiveness. For now, it does not appear that Iran's rank and file have become significantly more disciplined, have higher morale, or have been less affected by ethnic and cultural differences among the conscripts than in the past. Nearly half of Iran's manpower are eighteen-month conscripts who receive limited training and have marginal military effectiveness. Most Iranian units are understrength and not fully equipped, which compromises the commanders' ability to conduct training. In general, units also appear to lack the resources and the widespread expertise needed for effective training, which cause the armed forces to keep training standards low. Much of the instruction for soldiers appears to rely on rote memorization while unit training and major exercises are scripted. Because Iran's communication capabilities are inadequate, combined arms operations and the integration of its air, sea, and land components have only been developed slowly. The Guard's naval, missile, and special operations forces apparently have been the exception to this problem, and Iran has been diligent about training these assets, building up their skills to a reasonably high level.[22]

The latent qualities of Iran's fighting men, especially their ingenuity and tenacity, should not be discounted. Except for occasional internal security duties, sporadic border clashes with Iraq during the 1990s, and antismuggling and fishery protection operations at sea, Iran's military personnel have not seen any significant combat operations since the end of the Iran-Iraq War. Some sense of Iran's capabilities, however, can be gleaned from the Revolutionary Guard's support to Lebanese Hizballah. Like the Pasdaran, Hizballah has a small core of full-time highly trained and highly motivated fighters, backed by part-time reserves. The Iranian-trained and -armed group survived Israel's 1996 Grapes of Wrath campaign into southern Lebanon and eventually drove the Israelis out with terrorist attacks and guerrilla operations. During the summer of 2006, Hizballah stymied Israel's largest military operation in Lebanon since 1982. Using elaborate bunker systems, rockets, antitank weapons, and well-designed explosive mines capable of crippling Israeli tanks, Hizballah put up strong resistance. The Lebanese fighters also were able to use passive air defenses and the mobility of their Iranian-supplied rockets to frustrate Israeli air attacks and maintain heavy rocket barrages of northern Israel for the course of the monthlong conflict. Although Iran has given less attention to its ground forces than its other services, the Islamic Republic is trying to keep alive the threat, embodied in the Hizballah example, of inflicting consequential casualties on invaders by its patriotic and religiously inspired warriors.[23]

Nationalism, Insecurity, and Religion

Perhaps foremost among the influences that have contributed to the shape and quality of the armed forces have been those emerging from the interplay of Iran's national pride, religious beliefs, and insecurity. The Great Kings of Achaemenid Persia ruled by the favor of the god Ahuramazda, who conferred power to and directed these monarchs to promote justice by extending their domains. The Persians took war to heart, making conquest a matter of royal and national honor.[24] The Zoroastrian Sassanian shahanshahs were devoted to similar concepts. Following the Safavids' adoption of the Shia creed of Islam, Iran's rulers advocated a revised conception of a just and moral order that also centered on their country and a type of Iranian "exceptionalism." The Pahlavi shahs consciously tried to promote Iranian pride and nationalism by recalling Iran's imperial greatness. Ayatollah Khomeini and his successors, in turn, encouraged reflection on Islam's golden age and on the historical persecution of the Shia to heighten sentiments for a national duty to fight against injustice, defend the oppressed, and view martyrdom as a virtue. These factors still drive Iran's defensiveness and occasional adventurism in its military policies.

During each era following the Achaemenids, the Iranians evoked images of greatness to offset the nagging insecurity and fears of a larger world that had repeatedly proven to be hostile, dangerous, and domineering. Since at least Alexander's conquest, Iranian rulers have sought to secure their country's freedom from foreign influence and domination. Qajar efforts to offset the imperialist policies of Russia and Great Britain by appealing to France, Germany, and the United States have been echoed today in Iran's relations with Russia and China. What the Qajars called a policy of "equilibrium" was incorporated by Ayatollah Khomeini into the slogan "Neither East nor West" to show Iran's rejection of the unwanted influence of outside powers. The legacy of foreign conquest and domination will continue to contribute to Iran's prickliness over real and imagined challenges to its security and reinforce its desire to build military forces capable of deterring a superpower and attacking its enemies' weakpoints through unconventional or asymmetric warfare.

Sir Percy Sykes's suggestion that the Sassanians followed the counsel to "consider the altar and the throne as inseparable" applies as easily to many subsequent dynasties and the Islamic Republic. This merger of church and state influenced the rulers' relationships with their armed forces, especially when the military's role in centralizing authority has put it at odds with Iran's clerics. Much of the Qajar failure to modernize its armed forces can be laid at the feet of clerical opponents while the Pahlavis' success can similarly be attributed, in part, to their ability to overcome religious opposition. Since Iran became a theocracy, the regime has repeatedly stumbled over contradictions between its faith and the requirements of modern warfare, especially as seen in the Revolutionary Guard's bloody battles during the Iran-Iraq War. Since 2005, Iranian hard-liners, including the Supreme Leader, have reemphasized the Islamic Republic's connection to the Hidden Imam and his coming return for the final battle between good and evil. They appear to be trying to reinvigorate Iran's revolutionary spirit and restore its reliance on religious zeal and martyrdom as a basis for success in military operations. The combination of Iran's contemporary Islamic fervor with its imperial tradition is a major factor that, if left unbalanced by more cautious forces in Iran, inflates the Iranians' willingness to take risks and increases the threat of conflict with the United States and the West.

The Iranian Threat Today

Despite its military shortcomings, in the twenty years between 1988 and 2008, Iran has become more threatening to Western interests in the Middle East and to world energy security. In January 2005, the heads of the CIA, Defense Intelligence Agency, and Department of State Bureau of Intelligence and Research reported to the U.S. Congress that Iran had the air and naval capability to close the oil export route through the Strait of Hormuz and threaten key U.S. allies and Persian Gulf oil production facilities with its short- and medium-ballistic missiles. Tehran continues to be designated by the United States as the foremost state sponsor of terror, and its history of conducting terrorist attacks makes it a significant threat to regional peace and stability. As of mid-2008, the United

States and key European allies remained concerned that Iran is determined to use its nuclear energy program to develop a nuclear weapons capability. Ironically, the still hobbled Iranian phoenix has been aided greatly in improving its regional position by the United States, the country the clerical regime regards as its most dangerous enemy. The U.S. military's rapid defeat of the Taliban in 2001 and Saddam Hussein in 2003 removed Tehran's two closest foes. Initially, the demonstrated excellence and presence of U.S. ground forces near its borders raised concerns in Tehran about being surrounded by U.S. military power. By 2005, however, the Iranians had started to see the United States as bogged down in Iraq. In turn, the clerical regime saw U.S. forces in the region as potentially vulnerable to Iranian unconventional warfare and more susceptible to the deterrent strategy that had been developed during the preceding decade. Iran's military strategy and doctrine are primarily defensive, however, and its ability to project power and threaten its neighbors with anything but unconventional capabilities is limited.[25]

Iran's deterrence-based strategy rests on a strategic triad of the threat to close the Persian Gulf oil export routes, missile or air attacks against high-value targets in the region, and worldwide terrorism. Iran wants to avoid a conventional military conflict, especially with the United States, and instead seeks to rely on irregular warfare and the implicit threat of weapons of mass destruction (WMD) and terrorism to deter its enemies and inhibit any opponent's actions. Building on lessons learned from the conflict with Iraq, Iran seeks to reduce its costs in war by maximizing its passive defenses and taking advantage of its strategic depth and manpower mobilization capabilities. At the same time, the Artesh and Guard will try to increase the costs to Iran's enemies through attrition at home and unconventional warfare against an opponent's interests anywhere in the world. Finally, Iran's military strategy appears to call on using its threat to regional oil exports to internationalize the conflict and bring diplomatic pressure to end the fighting on terms less costly to Tehran. As it has in the past, Iran will emphasize its ability to withstand losses while avoiding decisive defeats to prolong the war and prevail in a contest of wills.[26]

Because of the potentially catastrophic global impact of disruptions to Persian Gulf oil exports and production facilities, the naval leg of Iran's strategic triad is the most threatening. Because of Iran's dominant position over the Gulf and the Strait of Hormuz and because of the relative ease and reliability with which its naval power can be brought to bear, the naval threat is perhaps the most daunting. Even after losing the *Joshan* and *Sahand* in 1988, Iran still had the largest navy among the regional states, and Pasdaran speedboats and mining vessels had proven their ability to create problems with merchant shipping. Iran's surface forces, however, were mostly obsolete and not fully seaworthy, while naval aviation was increasingly decrepit. Lacking the resources for a major naval rearmament, Iran had little choice but to develop the Pasdaran's naval "guerrilla warfare" capabilities and mobile coastal antiship missile force. Because of the importance of this leg of the strategic triad, Iran's naval forces became much better integrated than the other regular and Guard services and have conducted periodic naval exercises to improve coordination among the various surface, submarine, naval aviation, and marine elements.[27]

Iran's naval procurement since the early 1990s has emphasized its two navies' sea-denial mission to prevent the deployment of enemy forces to the Gulf, if possible, and to close the Strait of Hormuz. The purchases of three Russian Kilo-class submarines and Chinese coastal defense missiles and fast missile boats point to intentions to create a naval force structure capable of backing up deterrence, intimidating U.S. allies, and threatening vital Persian Gulf oil shipping lanes. Throughout the past decade, Iran's Revolutionary Guard naval forces have continued to emphasize unconventional warfare training using small boat attacks, mini-submarines, and mines. More recent efforts include the acquisition of modern wake-homing and wire-guided torpedoes from Russia and various antiship cruise missiles for its Chinese and North Korean fast attack boats. Iran's older Silkworm and other antiship missiles are being phased out as the inventory of new Chinese cruise missiles with upgraded guidance and extended ranges grows. The increasing number of antiship missile systems helps to compensate for Iran's weak air power while the greater numbers of launch platforms and the use of dummy sites to complicate detection and targeting add to the threat posed to Gulf shipping and opposing navies. The regular navy has maintained its focus on traditional "blue water" capabilities but still relies on its remaining shah-era inventory. The regular navy's warships have received only a few upgrades to missile and fire-control systems while the amphibious forces are barely sufficient to move a marine brigade. Regardless of its orientation, the regular navy lacks the support ships to sustain ocean operations or support an amphibious task force.[28]

Iran's current concept of war at sea emphasizes the avoidance of direct or lengthy confrontations with other naval forces and relies on layered defenses, surprise attacks, and psychological victories. Senior Iranian naval officers have written that Iran seeks, first and foremost, to take advantage of the Persian Gulf's geography, which limits enemy navies' ability to maneuver and eases Iranian naval and amphibious operations. First among Iran's wartime objectives would be the use of its difficult to detect mobile antiship cruise missiles and mines to blockade oil export routes and terminals. The effectiveness of mines was demonstrated in 1987–88, while the missile threat was demonstrated in the 2006 war in Lebanon when Hizballah fired Iranian-supplied C-802 antiship missiles, damaging an Israeli missile corvette and allegedly sinking a merchant ship. Iran has indicated that it will take advantage of the region's many coastal inlets to stage its speedboats for hit-and-run and swarming attacks to harass the enemy. Iran also has prepared commando forces to target oil installations on the Arabian Peninsula. Other offensive operations, including punitive attacks, would be staged from the many Iranian islands in the Gulf. In both October 1994 and February 1995, Iran fortified Abu Musa in reaction to American naval buildups in the Gulf, reportedly moving SAMs, chemical artillery shells (possibly just tear gas), and 4,500 troops to the island. Finally, Iran intends to use the Gulf of Oman as its first defensive perimeter, making it an operational area for the Kilo submarines and, as occurred in 1987, a location for Iranian minefields. The strategic effect of higher oil prices and economic disruptions could be greatly out of proportion to any damage Iranian naval forces are actually able to inflict.[29]

Iran's ballistic missiles are the strategic arm of Iranian air power and the heart of its deterrent doctrine, especially because they have been tied to an implicit threat to use WMD. Iran has one of the largest missile inventories in the Middle East and has developed the infrastructure to build a wide array of ballistic missiles and unguided rockets. The Iranians' perceptions of missiles apparently were shaped by Iraqi use during the wars of the cities and the 1991 Gulf War. As early as 1985 the regime decided to pursue indigenous missile development and later received technology from North Korea and China to produce artillery rockets and build SCUD production facilities. In early 1990, Iran received one hundred to two hundred SCUD B missiles from North Korea along with training for production, testing, and deployment. Over the next few years, Iran and North Korea cooperated on the manufacture of the long-range No Dong-1 ballistic missile, which became the Shahab-3 in Iran.

The Islamic Republic's current inventory consists of perhaps 250 to 300 SCUD B and longer-range SCUD C missiles with ranges from 190 to 310 miles and an undetermined number of Shahab-3 missiles with an 800-mile range and powerful warhead. Following tests of modified Shahab-3 missiles in late 2004, Iranian officials claimed to have extended the missile's range to 1,200 miles. The Revolutionary Guard controls Iran's missile and rocket forces, nearly all of which can be armed with chemical and possibly biological warheads. In mid-2000 the Pasdaran announced that it had formed five missile units and was constructing facilities and launch pads for the Shahab-3. The Guard has operational experience with its missiles and fired more than sixty missiles and rockets against Iranian dissident bases in Iraq in April 2001. In a major military exercise in November 2006, Iran simultaneously launched twenty missiles and rockets. Iranian officials typically threaten missile attacks against large military bases and critical infrastructure but repeatedly have linked missiles to threats of preemptive and retaliatory attacks that would cause massive casualties. The limited number and lack of accuracy of Iran's longer-range ballistic missiles suggest Tehran will have few options but to target strategic locations, such as capitals and other population centers, rather than tactical ones. Still, the clerical regime's past actions suggest that they would be cautious in initiating attacks on population centers against an opponent that can retaliate in kind.[30]

Iran's air and air defense forces also have a role in deterrence, but their missions appear to be more defensive to protect Iran's airspace. By 1986 the Islamic Republic had decided to revive its air power, which could provide a rapid deterrent response and intimidate weaker neighbors with its retaliatory potential. In addition to efforts to improve indigenous production and maintenance, Iran planned to acquire new warplanes and set up an aeronautical university to produce the needed pilots, warrant officers, technicians, ground crew, and engineers. Iran purchased some antiquated Chinese aircraft during the war and after the cease-fire turned to the Soviet Union for MiG-29 Fulcrum interceptors and Su-24 Fencer fighter-bombers. In January 1991 the clerical regime got an unexpected gift from Saddam when Iraqi pilots flew ninety-one Soviet- and French-built aircraft, including twenty-four Fencers, to Iran at the height of the U.S.-led coalition's air campaign. The Iranians later went back to China and purchased F-7M Airguard fighters, an updated version of the venerable MiG-21 Fishbed. The Guard's air arm consists primarily of Russian transports and helicopters to support rapid deployment and airborne operations for internal security missions. Iran's air defenses, which were inadequate under the shah, still rely on the aging I-HAWK system and have been only marginally improved with the acquisition of Russian SA-5 Gammon long-range and SA-15 Gauntlet mobile short-range SAMs. Although it was later denied by Moscow and other parts of the Iranian government, Iran's defense minister publicly claimed in late 2007 that Iran had reached an agreement with Russia for the eventual delivery of a long-range SAM system from the S-300 family, designated by NATO as the SA-10 or, if the more advanced version, as the SA-20. In early 2008 the director of the Defense Intelligence Agency reported to Congress that Iran was close to acquiring the SA-20. If it is delivered, this more modern air defense system will provide greater area coverage around sensitive Iranian facilities and, depending on the variant, limited ballistic missile defense.[31]

For the most part, few of the air and air defense forces' major shortcomings, such as land-based air defense integration or beyond-visual-range air-to-air combat capabilities, have been corrected. Of Iran's three hundred combat aircraft, the majority are obsolescent and face serious problems with readiness and sustainment. Iran is the only country in the region that does not receive ongoing support from the original manufacturers of its aircraft and related systems. The air force continues to rely on illegally sold surplus parts to keep its American-made aircraft flying, and in early 2007 a U.S. government investigation and congressional pressure prompted the Pentagon to suspend sales of surplus F-14 components to prevent them from being transferred illegally to Iran. One sign of

Iran's desperation is its repeated claims over the years to have mounted HAWK missiles to F-14 Tomcats to replace the inoperable Phoenix AAM and increase the fighter's capabilities for long-range engagements.

Iran's slow development of air defenses through the 1990s possibly was influenced by the limited threat posed by its immediate enemies, Iraq and Afghanistan, while any preparations in subsequent years to stop U.S. air power required more systems than the country could afford. Iran also may have taken lessons from the NATO campaign in Kosovo in 1999. Serbian medium- and high-altitude systems were ineffective against Western aircraft, but mobile SAM systems and relatively inexpensive shoulder-fired SAMs successfully inhibited NATO low altitude air operations and degraded their effectiveness. Still, inhibiting enemy air operations and avoiding destruction is of little value if, as occurred with Serbia, the enemy presses its attacks and inflicts sufficient damage to force capitulation.[32]

Iran's apparent air doctrine flows from its experience during the war with Iraq and the confrontation with U.S. naval forces in the Persian Gulf. With its current force structure, Iran apparently seeks to maximize passive defenses by dispersion, hardened shelters, and hidden facilities. The 2006 war in Lebanon gave another example of Iran's likely strategy and its effectiveness. Hizballah's passive defensive practices enabled the group to maintain a high tempo of rocket barrages on northern Israel despite more than four thousand Israeli air strikes. Iran also appears to be planning to use its limited number of air defense systems to protect high-value point targets around its capital city and to serve as one layer of the defenses of its main ports and southern coast. Iran's Su-24 Fencers provide the ability to threaten limited deep strikes against the Arabian Peninsula. Such a psychological approach might help undercut the Gulf Arabs' willingness to provide access to U.S. forces and be more effective than actual attacks on allied bases that are likely to fail. Over Iran and the Gulf, the Fulcrums, Airguards, and aged F-4s and F-5s, which have upgraded weapons packages, can perform standard air defense and attack missions within their shorter ranges. Aerial bombs in Iran's inventory are capable of holding chemical and biological agent payloads, which adds the air forces to the WMD threat.[33]

The implicit yet ambiguous WMD threat is an important element of Iranian deterrence. The Iran-Iraq War was the first conflict to witness the large-scale use of both chemical weapons and ballistic missiles. Following Iraq's heavy use of chemicals during the 1988 offensives and the public reaction to the threat of chemical attacks during the last war of the cities, Iran probably recognized the value of a terror weapon for deterrence or as a diplomatic bargaining chip. As early as December 1986, Prime Minister Hussein Musavi announced that Iran had developed its own chemical warfare technology and a year later proclaimed that the Iranian military had produced sophisticated chemical weapons.[34] In

1987 Majles Speaker and future president Rafsanjani publicly described WMD as decisive and stated, "Chemical and biological weapons are a poor man's atomic bombs and can easily be produced. We should at least consider them for our defense."[35] Iran's chemical arsenal at the time was comprised of mustard gas, chlorine and phosgene gas, and the blood agent hydrogen cyanide, but Khomeini reportedly controlled and opposed their use.[36] The one major alleged use of chemical warfare by Iran was during the fighting around Halabjah in 1988 when some of the Kurdish victims were reported to have died from exposure to blood agents. No conclusive evidence, however, is available to confirm that these cyanide-based agents were used during that battle.[37]

Because of the international community's general inaction in response to Iraqi use of chemical weapons, the Iranians regularly denigrated international arms control treaties. Iran, however, has consistently claimed that it is against such weapons on religious grounds. The regime is a signatory of the Chemical Weapons Convention and Biological Weapons Convention, which call for the prohibition of developing, producing, or stockpiling these weapons and commit Iran to short-notice inspections. Suspicions about Iran's intentions and capabilities remain, however, and the CIA assessed in 2004 that Iran was stockpiling chemical weapons, including blister, blood, choking, and probably nerve agents. Iran's production capacity and the size and readiness of its inventory, however, are unknown. The status of Iran's biological warfare effort has been more difficult to ascertain, but the Iranians reportedly have conducted research on lethal agents, diseases, and toxins; sought technology and equipment needed for biological weapons research; and allegedly received help from Cuba's weapons program.[38]

Iran is suspected by the United States and other countries of having the ambition to add nuclear weapons to its military inventory, or at least gain the capability to develop nuclear arms quickly. The regime has devoted significant resources and diplomatic political capital to develop an overt civilian nuclear program that gives it the potential to produce the fissile material needed to build nuclear arms. The lack of accuracy and relatively small payloads of Iran's longer-range ballistic missiles seemingly would cause the Iranians to consider the need for WMD warheads more powerful than chemical agents to make the systems an effective deterrent in a high-stakes scenario.

Suspicions of Iran's nuclear intentions predate the Islamic Republic. Iran signed a civil nuclear cooperation program with the United States as part of the Atoms for Peace program in 1957. The shah established Iran's civilian nuclear program under the Atomic Energy Organization of Iran (AEOI) a few years later and after several more years quietly started a nuclear weapons research program at the Tehran Nuclear Research Center. At the time his government fell, the shah had Iranians working on various technologies to create or acquire fissile material and had established a small nuclear weapons design team. Iran signed the Nuclear Non-Proliferation Treaty (NPT) in 1970 and advocated a WMD-free zone in the Middle East, but the shah made clear that Iran would acquire bombs if other regional states got them. This nuclear program collapsed between 1979 and 1984 as nuclear engineers and other experts fled the revolution. The program was further hampered after Iraq bombed and severely damaged the unfinished Bushehr nuclear power plants three times during the war. Khomeini reportedly opposed nuclear development on theological grounds, but low-level research was allowed to continue in the 1980s. It was during this period that Iran had its first contacts with A. Q. Khan, the father of the Pakistani nuclear bomb, who admitted in 2004 to providing extensive support to the clerical regime's nuclear program.[39]

After Khomeini's death, the Islamic Republic revived the civil nuclear program and expanded its overt and clandestine research activities on dual-use nuclear technologies. Iran's renewed interest in pursuing nuclear capabilities may have been spurred by the 1991 revelations of Iraq's massive secret nuclear program and its potential resurrection. Increased U.S. efforts to isolate Iran and persuade Russia and China to halt nuclear cooperation with the Islamic Republic in the mid-1990s also may have contributed to Iran's attempts to invigorate the program. In 1997, shortly after the election of the reformist president Khatami, Iran replaced the AEOI head with Gholamreza Aghazadeh, Iran's oil minister between 1982 and 1997 and a highly respected manager, to reenergize the nuclear effort. Later, following Pakistan's and India's nuclear weapons tests in 1998, the desire to match the Sunni Pakistanis and gain the prestige and regional power status afforded India may have played a role in Iran's growing interest in nuclear technology.[40]

In early 2003, after an Iranian opposition group publicized charges that Iran had built two undisclosed nuclear facilities, the International Atomic Energy Agency (IAEA) inspected an underground uranium enrichment facility at Natanz and a heavy-water plant at Arak. After the inspection, the IAEA declared that Iran had failed to comply with its NPT obligations. Defense Minister Ali Shamkhani acknowledged in 2004 that the Iranian military had been involved in the production of centrifuges to enrich uranium. By April 2006 Iran was claiming that it had successfully enriched uranium to a level suitable for use in a nuclear reactor. A year later, in April 2007, the regime announced that it was ready to start industrial-scale enrichment. Although Iran claims its production of fissile material is intended to fuel reactors for generating electricity, if the effort is successful in producing highly enriched uranium, Iran would have the material for a nuclear bomb. In early 2007, the Director of National Intelligence (DNI) testified before Congress that Iran was determined to develop nuclear weapons and could do so as soon as early next decade.[41]

In December 2007, the issue of Iran's nuclear ambitions became more clouded when the DNI released unclassified judgments from a National Intelligence Estimate (NIE) that reversed one of the U.S. Intelligence Community's earlier assessments. The NIE judged with high confidence that Iran had halted its nuclear weapons program in late 2003 and, with moderate confidence, assessed that Tehran had not restarted the program as of mid-2007. In the controversy surrounding the NIE and its effect on U.S. and international policies toward Iran, however, some of the Intelligence Community's more salient judgments about Iran's nuclear program were overshadowed. The NIE confirmed the assessment that Iran had a secret nuclear weapons program (defined as weapon design, weaponization work, and covert attempts to produce bomb-grade fissile material) in violation of its NPT commitments. It also pointed out that Iran, against United Nations Security Council and IAEA obligations, was continuing to develop uranium enrichment, reprocessing, and heavy-water capabilities for creating fissile material that was unnecessary for Iran's civil nuclear program but was essential for nuclear weapons development. The NIE also assessed that Iran will be capable of producing highly enriched uranium for nuclear weapons sometime between 2010 and 2015 and possibly as early as late 2009. According to the NIE, Iran has the scientific, technical, and industrial capacity to produce nuclear weapons and could easily restart its weaponization efforts at its discretion. Although the NIE suggested that Iran had responded to international pressure in stopping its weaponization effort, it also highlighted that Iran's intentions were unknown. In sum, Iran's continued efforts to produce fissile material and long-range ballistic missiles suggest that the Islamic Republic is keeping its options open.[42]

Because the Pasdaran is responsible for Iran's missile program, it presumably would be the service in charge of Iran's nuclear weapons, should these be produced. Maintaining nuclear missile warheads and bombs probably would be, first and foremost, a deterrent against attacks on Iran and a means to threaten retaliation in kind. Given Iran's harsh rhetoric about the elimination of Israel, an Iranian willingness to use or threaten to use nuclear weapons offensively cannot be ruled out. It seems less likely, however, that Iran would use nuclear weapons as a shield to protect it from the consequences of its covert warfare. Iran has not needed such a deterrent to protect it from its past use of terrorism and unconventional operations, and adding nuclear weapons to the mix would unnecessarily raise the risk of escalation.

The third leg of Iran's strategic deterrent triad is unconventional warfare and the use of proxies, which also represent some of the clerical regime's most active peacetime ventures to advance Iranian national interests. Iranian-sponsored attacks against Kuwait and the smaller Gulf Arab states during the Iran-Iraq War contributed to their refusal to allow U.S. forces to use their territory, waters, and air space while the clerical regime still touts the 1983 American withdrawal from Lebanon as evidence of Iran's superior will to win. Carrying on the tradition of the "hidden hand" attacks in the Gulf and the use of sympathetic militant groups to export the revolution during the 1980s, the Guard and its Qods Force have kept Iran actively involved in terrorism. In March 1992, Hizballah, working with the Iranian embassy, detonated a bomb outside the Israeli embassy in Buenos Aires, Argentina, killing twenty-nine and injuring dozens more. Later that year, the Guard worked through Hizballah and local neo-Nazis to attack a Jewish community center in the Argentine capital. In mid-1995, a plot to overthrow the government of Bahrain by Bahraini Hizballah, a group of Shia militants connected to the Guard, was thwarted by local security forces. Iran's support to the extremist Palestinian groups Hamas and Islamic Jihad in the 1990s was a way of undermining the Middle East peace process and striking at Israel. Iran's demonstrated capabilities to use proxy groups to attack its enemies make its unconventional and terrorist operations a significant deterrent threat.[43]

Iran has occasionally curtailed its use of unconventional warfare when risks of wider conflict increased, but the clerical leadership and the Guard remain opportunistic. After an Iranian-supported Saudi Shia group attacked U.S. military personnel at the Khobar Towers complex in Saudi Arabia, killing 19 and wounding 372 Americans, the clerical regime withdrew its support from Gulf Arab Shia because it feared an increase in political, economic, and military pressure. The Iranians also became more cautious after their relations with Europe were harmed when a German court in April 1997 found Iranian agents guilty of murdering Iranian Kurdish leaders in Berlin in 1992 and declared that the assassinations had been ordered by Khamenei, Rafsanjani, and other top officials. Since late 2001, however, Iran has been active in numerous areas, such as Afghanistan, to advance Tehran's interests at American expense. Iran continues to support Hizballah in Lebanon and was caught by Israel in 2002 moving arms, ammunition, and explosives to the Palestinians aboard the ship *Karine-A*. The Guard and Qods Force also have been active in Iraq, building up relations with the Iraqi Shia, supporting political factions, and providing weapons and military training to armed groups opposing coalition forces there.[44]

Finally, another aspect of Iran's overall deterrent posture is its goal of protecting the homeland by increasing the costs in blood and treasure to invading enemy ground forces. As Iran applies the lessons of Afghanistan, Iraq, and Lebanon, it appears to be aligning the regular army and Pasdaran ground forces' limited capabilities with a defensive, attrition-oriented doctrine that relies heavily on guerrilla warfare and special forces operations. One of the primary reasons for emphasizing the defense is that Iranian ground forces lack mobility. Twenty years after the end of the Iran-Iraq War, the regular army and Guard ground forces still consist primarily of infantry units relying on towed artillery.

Moreover, the Pasdaran, which represents more than 50 percent of Iran's ground forces, depends heavily on the mobilization of poorly trained reserves to bring its units up to full strength. Although it claims the capacity to mobilize as many as a million men in wartime, the Basij has ninety thousand men on active duty for internal security and probably only three hundred thousand reservists on its rolls. To rebuild its armored inventory and improve the ground forces' mobility, Iran has purchased more ex-Warsaw Pact and Chinese tanks. These have been supplemented by the indigenous assembly of Russian vehicles and constant attempts to upgrade the surviving Western tanks and armored vehicles. Yet Iran still lacks sufficient armor and infantry fighting vehicles to fully equip its divisions, would likely have difficulty sustaining them in combat, and depends on its large inventory of artillery pieces to provide the ground force's firepower.[45]

In the late 1990s, hostility between Shia Iran and the Sunni Taliban government in Afghanistan peaked over the Taliban's anti-Shia violence, the two million Afghan refugees in Iran, Afghan drug trafficking into Iran, and Iranian support to the Taliban's opponents. When Taliban forces overran Mazar-e Sharif, Afghanistan, in August 1998, they killed eleven Iranian diplomats working with the Afghan opposition there. Iran quickly and effectively deployed roughly two hundred thousand troops to the eastern border while the regime's leadership debated ordering a full-scale invasion. The Pasdaran wanted to attack the Taliban, but the regular army advised against hostilities because of the risks of getting sucked into Afghanistan's civil war. Khamenei and other leaders agreed with the army and soon thereafter created a new position of Artesh commander, which ended the practice of having the regular services report separately to Khamenei. The abandonment of the approach used by Muhammad Reza Shah to limit collaboration that might foster a coup suggested that the leadership's suspicion of the military had declined. By giving the Artesh one strong voice in senior decision-making councils, the regime probably increased the regular military's clout.[46]

Following the fall of Baghdad in March 2003, Iran's regular army announced that guerrilla operations had been introduced into all of its training. The army claimed in 2004 that it was increasing training on the use of irregular and partisan warfare to wear down enemy invaders. This echoed statements by Muhammad Reza Shah in the mid-1970s that, in confronting the superior might of the Soviet Union, Iran might have to implement a total partisan war and scorched-earth tactics.[47] Among some of the training scenarios featured in post-2003 Iranian maneuvers were ambushes, guerrilla attacks, the massing of shoulder-fired weapons against enemy helicopters, and the mobilization of local forces. The Guard also announced that it had changed its doctrine to a "mosaic defense." This purportedly relies on unconventional warfare and the mobilization of Iran's reserve militia and the Iranian populace to defend in depth to ensure that there would be "no safe zone" for an invading army advancing toward the center of Iran. In late July 2006, during the conflict between Israel and Hizballah in Lebanon, Guard commander Safavi claimed that Hizballah's tactics were based on the "mosaic defense."[48]

As a result of these tactics and continuing material shortcomings, Iranian ground forces probably will try to exploit their strength in manpower, accepting high losses in return for maximizing enemy casualties. Iran's military forces are not foolhardy, however, and they will try to avoid or dislocate enemy strengths. In an echo of Safavid warfare, the Iranians probably will employ scorched-earth tactics to slow enemy advances and rely on stay-behind commando and irregular forces to disrupt an invader's rear area operations similar to Jangali activities in World War I. To avoid enemy airpower and slow mechanized formations, Artesh and Guard formations are likely to fight in the built-up areas in and around the cities along the main lines of communication into Iran. In addition to taking advantage of Iran's difficult terrain and strategic depth, Iranian ground forces will constantly seek tactical surprise, as they were able to do repeatedly against Iraq, in an effort to break their opponent's will. Like the Hizballah forces that faced Israel in 2006, Iran will defend its homeland with well-armed and highly motivated fighters combining guerrilla and conventional tactics. Unlike Hizballah, however, Iran has numerous strategic facilities and infrastructure that will be vulnerable to long-range precision air and missile attack, and the costs of its defensive plans could be very high for the country before the first ground troops are ever engaged.

Looking Back, Looking Ahead

Until Iran's conventional forces improve some time in the distant future, the Iranians must depend on missile and WMD deterrence and unconventional warfare, the least reliable and most risky elements of their military power. Deterrence, in Iran's case, is problematic because, in situations where the stakes are high, the relatively small size and uncertain capabilities of its missile and WMD inventory may be insufficient to deter a determined opponent or could invite preemptive attacks. Unconventional warfare will continue to be attractive to Iranian leaders because of its plausible deniability and past successes in Lebanon and elsewhere. Yet such operations are seldom decisive and always run the risk of provoking an uncontrolled escalation. The terrorism and missile threats also antagonize neighbors and Western trading partners, undermining diplomatic efforts to increase Iranian influence in southwest Asia. Another major shortcoming of Iran's deterrence policy is its poor communications with its most likely opponents, which increases the chances of misunderstandings and unabated hostility. For deterrence to work, Iran has to demonstrate its resolve to act, and the clerical regime's resort to harsh rhetoric and occasional saber rattling often appears provocative and threatening. This characteristic, and Iran's record of misreading U.S. intentions and actions, do not bode well for effective communications and signaling in support of a deterrence policy.[49]

In addition to its somewhat flawed deterrence policy, Iran's leaders often deal with the strategic imbalance between its ambitious ends and restricted means with political warfare that keeps distrust among other countries high. In this, they are following in the footsteps of earlier Iranian states. The Achaemenids during the Peloponnesian War funneled resources to Sparta to fight the Athenians and, after Sparta gained supremacy, provided funds to Athens and Thebes to defeat the Spartans. Later, Darius III tried to save his empire by funding sedition against Alexander the Great. The Parthians and Sassanians were regularly caught up in the political machinations of Armenia, which caused repeated conflicts with Rome and Byzantium. Today, the Iranians have been active in Lebanon, Iraq, Afghanistan, and other locations and show no signs of reducing these efforts despite protests from the United States and other regional countries.

The misgivings engendered by the Islamic Republic's political warfare have been aggravated by Iran's repeated violation of diplomatic norms to advance its interests. This history has unveiled repeated examples of Iranian bad faith, from the capture of Crassus and Valerian during negotiations by the Parthians and Sassanians to the murder of U.S. vice-consul Robert Imbrie during Reza Shah's reign. Although Iran's seizure of the American embassy in 1979 is perhaps the most well-known transgression, it was not the first attack on an embassy by Iranians. In January 1829, the Qajars stood by while mobs incited by mullahs attacked the Russian legation in Tehran for refusing to surrender three Armenian Christians who had sought sanctuary with the Russians after fleeing the royal harem. Several thousand Iranians stormed the Russian legation and tore the Russians and Armenians to pieces. In more recent times, the Revolutionary Guard, through Hizballah, has targeted American and Israeli embassies, and, in early 2007, Pasdaran naval forces captured British military personnel operating between the coasts of Iraq and Iran. Claiming trespass into Iranian waters, the Guard held the Britons hostage for two weeks.[50]

In all, Iranian officials can be prideful, stubborn, and aggressive, and compelling or persuading the Iranians to change course has been difficult throughout their modern history. During the first Qajar war with Russia, the Iranians turned aside repeated offers by Czar Alexander to end the conflict. In 1837 and 1858 British military expeditions were required to turn aside Iran's appetite for reasserting control over Herat in Afghanistan. In early 1982, the Soviets were similarly disappointed when they tried to persuade Iran to accept a negotiated settlement with Baghdad. Although they warned that stalled Soviet arms deliveries to Iraq would resume if Iran extended operations into Iraqi territory, the clerical regime proceeded to do just that.[51] In each of these cases, Iran's tenacity in the face of difficult odds led to consequential, if not foreseeable, defeats. Despite its rhetoric and obstinacy, Iran does respect strength and shows caution when it must. During Operation Earnest Will, the Iranians made repeated threats of horrible outcomes for the West because of the American intervention. Instead, Iran became more careful in its operations, relying on the "hidden hand" of mines but refusing to use its antiship cruise missiles or its small boats in direct assaults against U.S. warships. Still, the American presence failed to deter mine attacks, and the Iranians bravely, if foolishly, sortied out to fight the U.S. Navy during Operation Praying Mantis.

As the Islamic Republic enters its fourth decade, its armed forces continue to play a significant role in their country's future and fortunes. Iran's conservative elite has become increasingly composed of "second generation" hard-liners, whose formative experience was service in the Revolutionary Guard during the Iran-Iraq War. Iranian president Ahmadi-Nejad, who was elected to a four-year term in 2005, is a former Guard officer while his defense minister, Mostafa Mohammad Najjar, is another Guard veteran who helped establish the Hizballah movement in Lebanon. These new leaders appear to be taking the country in a more nationalist and possibly militaristic direction. At a minimum, because the new leaders are closer to the revolutionary form of Shia Islam preached by Grand Ayatollah Khomeini, they are likely to pursue an Iranian foreign policy inimical to the West and the United States.[52]

While the West should not underestimate Iran, the Iranians, given the state of their armed forces for the foreseeable future, hopefully are aware of the risks of provoking the West's military might. In ancient times, the Achaemenids' pride had made it axiomatic that Persian arms must prevail until the myth of Persian invincibility was shattered by Xerxes' defeat at the Battle of Salamis.[53] Looking at Iran over the coming years, it is fair to wonder if the Iranians might once again be getting caught up in their national pride and the conviction that their revolutionary Islamic movement must prevail. If so, the likelihood will be much greater that Iran will be more assertive, if not aggressive, and its leaders much more likely to succumb to the temptation to risk war by overreaching in their strategic goals. One can only hope that Iran's military leaders reflect on the words, as imagined by Aeschylus in *The Persians,* of the ghost of Xerxes' father, Darius the Great:

> *But you, whose age demands more temperate thoughts,*
> *With words of well-placed counsel teach his youth*
> *To curb that pride, which from the gods calls down*
> *Destruction on his head.*[54]

Notes

Introduction

1. The comparison of Middle Eastern military orders of battle in 1978 was taken from the International Institute for Strategic Studies, *Military Balance, 1978–1979,* 91.

2. Powell, *My American Journey,* 240–42.

3. Ibid., 242.

4. This assessment of Iranian military power was derived from Cordesman, *Iran's Evolving Military Forces,* 9–24. Population ranking developed by the U.S. Census Bureau, www.census.gov (December 2006).

5. On Iran's reputed aversion to the sea and problems with shipbuilding, see Savory, "Ancient Period," 5–6; and Cook, *Persians,* 95. For the British Indian officer's report and quote, see Hopkirk, *Great Game,* 66–67, 70–71.

6. On these pre-1979 naval developments, see Bavand, "Territorial Challenges"; Fuller, *"Center of the Universe,"* 60–63; Savory, "Ancient Period," 5–6; and Cook, *Persians,* 95.

7. On Iran's lack of ferrous metals, see Jones, *Art of War in the Western World,* 14. On Cyrus's early unmounted forces, see Cook, *Persians,* 59–62, 93.

8. On Iran's terrain in this and subsequent paragraphs, see Cordesman and Wagner, *Lessons of Modern War,* vol. 2, *Iran-Iraq War,* 72–74.

9. Daniel, *History of Iran,* 5; and Cordesman and Wagner, *Lessons of Modern War,* 74.

1. Heritage of Greatness, Legacy of Loss

1. Dupuy and Dupuy, *Encyclopedia of Military History,* 21.

2. Green, *Greco-Persian Wars,* 6.

3. Herodotus, *Persian Wars,* 687.

4. Cook, *Persians,* 138.

5. Green, *Greco-Persian Wars,* 44.

6. Information on fleet sizes from Strauss, *Battle of Salamis,* xviii, xix–xxi, 17; Green, *Greco-Persian Wars,* 60–62; and Cook, *Persians,* 156–58, 176.

7. Cook, *Persians,* 178.

8. Hanson, *Carnage and Culture,* 29.

9. Xenophon's view from May and Stadler, *Ancient and Medieval Warfare*, 36–37.

10. Cook, *Persians*, 339; and Jones, *Art of War in the Western World*, 21–23, 26.

11. On Persian intentions for the battle, see Mixter, "Alexander's First Great Victory," 50–53.

12. Cook, *Persians*, 340–41; Jones, *Art of War in the Western World*, 34; and May and Stadler, *Ancient and Medieval Warfare*, 40–42.

13. Filson, "Battle of Gaugamela," 70–73; Cook, *Persians*, 342–43; and Dupuy and Dupuy, *Encyclopedia of Military History*, 50.

14. Filson, "Battle of Gaugamela," 67; and Jones, *Art of War in the Western World*, 57–58.

15. Sykes, *History of Persia*, 392.

16. Shahbazi, "Army I. Pre-Islamic Iran," 495; and Sykes, *History of Persia*, 348–49.

17. Jones, *Art of War in the Western World*, 36.

18. On General Surena, see Suren-Pahlav, "General Surena, The Hero of Carrhae."

19. Luttwak, *Grand Strategy of the Roman Empire*, 105; and Strauss, "Rome's Persian Mirage," 20–21.

20. Sykes, *History of Persia*, 398.

21. Frye, *Golden Age of Persia*, 14–15; Cornuelle, "Overview of the Sassanian Military"; and Luttwak, *Grand Strategy of the Roman Empire*, 135.

22. Cornuelle, "Overview of the Sassanian Military"; Luttwak, *Grand Strategy of the Roman Empire*, 151; and Shahbazi, "Army I. Pre-Islamic Iran," 496–98.

23. Mackey, *Iranians*, 62–63.

24. Bosworth, "Army II. Islamic, to the Mongol Period," 501; and Pollack, *Persian Puzzle*, 10.

25. Heral, "Yasotay and the Mangoday of Genghis Khan," 38–69; Tanner, *Afghanistan*, 78, 87–88; and Weatherford, *Genghis Khan and the Making of the Modern World*, 108–10.

26. Durand-Guedy, "Iranians at War under Turkish Domination," 591–94, 599–601; and Nyrop, *Iran*, 39.

2. Powerful Predecessors: The Safavids and Nader Shah

1. Cole and Keddie, *Shi'ism and Social Protest*, 1–2.

2. Savory, *Iran under the Safavids*, 1–2, 19–20, 24–29, 35–36; and Babaie et al., *Slaves of the Shah*, 6.

3. Discussion of the Safavid military in this and subsequent paragraphs derived from Haneda, "Army III. Safavid," 503–4; Arjomand, *Turban for the Crown*, 16–17; and Savory, *Iran under the Safavids*, 43–44.

4. The discussion of Chaldiran in this and subsequent paragraphs derived from Ghasemi, *Safavid Empire, 1502–1736*; Savory, *Iran under the Safavids*, 39–48; and Haneda, "Army III. Safavid," 504.

5. Discussion of Tahmasp's military in this and subsequent paragraphs derived from Babaie et al., *Slaves of the Shah*, 4–6, 28; and Savory, *Iran under the Safavids*, 51–75.

6. Savory, *Iran under the Safavids*, 91.

7. Details on Abbas's reign from Babaie et al., *Slaves of the Shah*, 6, 49–51; Ghasemi, *Safavid Empire, 1502–1736*; and Savory, *Iran under the Safavids*, 83, 91. Also see Newman, *Safavid Iran*, 50–72.

8. Details on Safavid military derived from Chegnizadeh, "Persian Military Modernization, 1921–1979," 62; Babaie et al., *Slaves of the Shah*, 7, 23; and Haneda, "Army III. Safavid," 504–5.

9. More complete discussions of the new scholarship on the Safavid decline can be found in Axworthy, *Sword of Persia*, 27–44; and Newman, *Safavid Iran*, 1–12, 82–90, 94–100, 106–24.

10. Axworthy, *Sword of Persia*, 45–50; Savory, *Iran under the Safavids*, 226, 231, 248, 150, 253–54; and Tanner, *Afghanistan*, 114–16.

11. Olson, *Siege of Mosul and Ottoman–Persian Relations, 1718–1743*, 93, 101–2; and Axworthy, *Sword of Persia*, 161–67.

12. Perry, "Army IV. Afsar and Zand," 505–7; Olson, *Siege of Mosul and Ottoman–Persian Relations, 1718–1743*, 93, 101–2; and Axworthy, *Sword of Persia*, 249–50.

13. The discussion of Nader's army in this and subsequent paragraphs derived from Axworthy, *Sword of Persia*, 1, 83–84, 95, 147, 197, 260; and Perry, "Army IV. Afsar and Zand," 505–7.

14. "The Shah's Northern Navy"; Perry, "Army IV. Afsar and Zand," 505–7; and Olson, *Siege of Mosul and Ottoman–Persian Relations, 1718–1743*, 121, 136.

15. The discussion of Persian naval operations in this and the next paragraph is taken from Kelley, *Britain and the Persian Gulf, 1795–1880*, 9; and Axworthy, *Sword of Persia*, 229, 263.

16. Details on Nader Shah's campaigns in this and subsequent paragraphs derived from Axworthy, *Sword of Persia*, 128–41, 151–52, 181–85, and 194–208.

17. Details on the Mosul campaign from Olson, *Siege of Mosul and Ottoman–Persian Relations, 1718–1743*, 120–24, 133, 153, 165, 170–75, 185–87; and Axworthy, *Sword of Persia*, 241–53.

18. Axworthy, *Sword of Persia*, xv, 284–85.

3. Laughingstock: The Qajar Military

1. Details on the early Qajar dynasty and its security situation in this and subsequent paragraphs from Goldschmidt, *Concise History of the Middle East*, 155; Yarshater, "Observations on Nasir al-Din Shah," 10–11; Bakhtiari, *Peaks and Troughs*, 47–48; Abrahamian, *Iran between Two Revolutions*, 28; and Mackey, *Iranians*, 128–29.

2. Ghods, *Iran in the Twentieth Century*, 15.

3. Mackey, *Iranians*, 129.

4. On Russian and British goals, see Kelley, *Britain and the Persian Gulf, 1795–1880*, 62–63, 262.

5. Statements by British officials from Abrahamian, *Iran between Two Revolutions*, 28–29.

6. The discussion in this and subsequent paragraphs on the Qajar military drawn from Tousi, "Persian Army, 1880–1907," 206–29; Atkin, *Russia and Iran, 1780–1828,* 108–10; Keddie, *Modern Iran,* 27–28, 40–41, 53; Ringer, "Education and Reform in Qajar Iran, 1800–1906," 26–31; and Upton, *Armies of Asia and Europe,* 88–95.

7. Arjomand, *Turban for the Crown,* 23–24.

8. Andreeva, *Russia and Iran in the Great Game,* 59–62; Ekhtiar, "Dar Al-Funun," 17–19; Keddie, *Qajar Iran and the Rise of Reza Khan,* 21–22; Atkin, *Russia and Iran, 1780–1828,* 126, 135; Ghods, *Iran in the Twentieth Century,* 18–19; and Ringer, "Education and Reform in Qajar Iran, 1800–1906," 17–22, 97–98.

9. Atkin, *Russia and Iran, 1780–1828,* 126, Ekhtiar, "Dar Al-Funun," 17–19; Ghods, *Iran in the Twentieth Century,* 18–19; Keddie, *Qajar Iran and the Rise of Reza Khan,* 21–22; 135; and Ringer, "Education and Reform in Qajar Iran, 1800–1906," 17–22, 97–98.

10. Mirfakhraei, "Imperial Iranian Armed Forces and the Revolution of 1978–1979," 84; Abrahamian, *Iran between Two Revolutions,* 29, 52–53; Ekhtiar, "Dar Al-Funun," 19; and Ringer, "Education and Reform in Qajar Iran, 1800–1906," 17–22, 97–98, 312–14.

11. Ekhtiar, "Dar Al-Funun," 25, 85–86, 139–42, 211, 215, 217, 311–19; and Ringer, "Education and Reform in Qajar Iran, 1800–1906," 125, 131, 133, 146.

12. Yarshater, "Observations on Nasir al-Din Shah," 4–5.

13. Cronin, *Army and the Creation of the Pahlavi State in Iran, 1910–1921,* 4.

14. Keddie, *Qajar Iran and the Rise of Reza Khan,* 27–28, 53; Tousi, "Persian Army, 1880–1907," 208–9, 228; and Yarshater, "Observations on Nasir al-Din Shah," 4, 9.

15. Andreeva, *Russia and Iran in the Great Game,* 112.

16. Ibid., 113; and Tousi, "Persian Army, 1880–1907," 211–12, 215.

17. Tousi, "Persian Army, 1880–1907," 211–12, 215.

18. Ibid., 217–18; Cronin, *Army,* 5–6; and Upton, *Armies of Asia and Europe,* 90–91.

19. Andreeva, *Russia and Iran in the Great Game,* 112; and Tousi, "Persian Army, 1880–1907," 218–19.

20. Bakhtiari, *Peaks and Troughs,* 71. Other details from Tousi, "Persian Army, 1880–1907," 218–19, 227; and Kelley, *Britain and the Persian Gulf, 1795–1880,* 468–69.

21. Description of the war with Russia in this and subsequent paragraphs derived from Atkin, *Russia and Iran, 1780–1828,* 99–101, 104–11; Sykes, *History of Persia,* 312–13; Bakhtiari, *Peaks and Troughs,* 54–56, 70–71; and Hopkirk, *Great Game,* 61–66.

22. Sykes, *History of Persia,* 312.

23. Bakhtiari, *Peaks and Troughs,* 55.

24. Ibid., 54.

25. Andreeva, *Russia and Iran in the Great Game,* 18.

26. Ibid., 50.

27. Details on the siege can be found in Hopkirk, *Great Game,* 178–80.

28. On British actions, see Yapp, "British Policy in the Persian Gulf," 77–78. Information on the war in this and subsequent paragraphs derived from Kelley, *Britain and the Persian Gulf, 1795–1880,* 466–99.

29. Upton, *Armies of Asia and Europe,* 95. On Upton's unhappiness with the generally poor state and need of reform of the U.S. Army, see White, "Civilian Management of the Military," 43–59.

30. Curzon, *Persia and the Persian Question,* 607.

31. Ringer, "Education and Reform in Qajar Iran, 1800–1906," 312–14; and Ekhtiar, "Dar Al-Funun," 212.

32. Mirfakhraei, "Imperial Iranian Armed Forces and the Revolution of 1978–1979," 40. On the early days of the Cossack brigade, see Chegnizadeh, "Persian Military Modernization, 1921–1979," 116–17; and Mirfakhraei, "Imperial Iranian Armed Forces and the Revolution of 1978–1979," 39–41.

33. Discussion of the Cossack brigade in this and subsequent paragraphs taken from Chegnizadeh, "Persian Military Modernization, 1921–1979," 116–17; Cronin, *Army,* 56–57; and Tousi, "Persian Army, 1880–1907," 208–9, 219–26.

34. Browne, *Persian Revolution of 1905–1909,* 37.

35. Ibid., xv–xvi.

36. Andreeva, *Russia and Iran in the Great Game,* 114.

37. Tousi, "Persian Army, 1880–1907," 208, 216–18; and Chegnizadeh, "Persian Military Modernization, 1921–1979," 95–96.

38. Bakhash, "Failure of Reform, 1897–8," 16–28; Chegnizadeh, "Persian Military Modernization, 1921–1979," 92–97, 115–20; Mirfakhraei, "Imperial Iranian Armed Forces and the Revolution of 1978–1979," 41–42; and Cronin, *Army,* 18.

39. Curzon, *Persia and the Persian Question,* 3–4.

40. Discussion of Qajar rule at the turn of the century derived from Lenczowski, "Foreign Powers," 76; Yapp, "1900–1921," 1–10; Bakhash, "Failure of Reform, 1897–8," 20–21; Chegnizadeh, "Persian Military Modernization, 1921–1979," 109–14; Keddie, *Qajar Iran and the Rise of Reza Khan,* 44–45, 53; and Mackey, *Iranians,* 139.

41. Curzon, *Persia and the Persian Question,* 480.

4. Nationalism Unleashed: From Revolution to the Great War

1. Much of the following discussion of the mujahedin and their role was developed from Afary, *Iranian Constitutional Revolution, 1906–1911.*

2. Afary, *Iranian Constitutional Revolution, 1906–1911,* 174.

3. Quotations from Kasravi, *History of the Iranian Constitutional Revolution,* 105.

4. For details of the development of the constitution, see Afary, *Iranian Constitutional Revolution, 1906–1911,* 4, 55–58; Ghods, *Iran in the Twentieth Century,* 36; Mackey, *Iranians,* 144–49; and Pollack, *Persian Puzzle,* 21.

5. Mackey, *Iranians,* 149.

6. Afary, *Iranian Constitutional Revolution, 1906–1911,* 132; Cronin, *Army,* 59–60; and Mackey, *Iranians,* 149–52, 161–62.

7. The following discussion of the Constitutional Revolution derived from Shuster, *Strangling of Persia,* xxxiii–xlii; Browne, *Persian Revolution of 1905–1909,* 165–67,

206-8, 249-58, 265-75; Afary, *Iranian Constitutional Revolution, 1906-1911*, 132, 140-41, 212-26; Cronin, *Army*, 58-61; and Mackey, *Iranians*, 149-52.

8. Kasravi, *History of the Iranian Constitutional Revolution*, 268-70.

9. Afary, *Iranian Constitutional Revolution, 1906-1911*, 218.

10. Browne, *Persian Revolution of 1905-1909*, 257.

11. Curzon, *Persia and the Persian Question*, 388.

12. Hone, *Persia in Revolution*, 28.

13. Ibid., 48.

14. On the aftermath, see Afary, *Iranian Constitutional Revolution, 1906-1911*, 261, 286, 298-305; Cronin, *Army*, 62; and Shuster, *Strangling of Persia*, 60-61, 87, 93-94.

15. Shuster, *Strangling of Persia*, 55.

16. The description of Shuster's mission derived from *Strangling of Persia*. Also see Chegnizadeh, "Persian Military Modernization, 1921-1979," 122, 126-27; and Mackey, *Iranians*, 164-65.

17. Shuster, *Strangling of Persia*, 190.

18. On the events and battles surrounding Muhammad Ali's return, see Afary, *Iranian Constitutional Revolution, 1906-1911*, 321-23; and Shuster, *Strangling of Persia*, 79, 83-87, 116-35.

19. Arjomand, *Turban for the Crown*, 55-56; Abrahamian, *Iran between Two Revolutions*, 107-10; Afary, *Iranian Constitutional Revolution, 1906-1911*, 336; and Mackey, *Iranians*, 154-55.

20. The discussion of the National Gendarmerie in this and the next few paragraphs derived from Lustig, "Muhajarat and the Provisional Government in Kirmanshah, 1915-1917," 92-99, 131; Majd, *Persia in World War I*, 23-25; Cronin, *Army*, 1, 3-8, 17-33; and Chegnizadeh, "Persian Military Modernization, 1921-1979," 118-24.

21. Majd, *Persia in World War I*, 12.

22. On the situation in Iran between early 1914 and the start of the war, see Arjomand, *Turban for the Crown*, 58-59; Keddie, *Qajar Iran and the Rise of Reza Khan*, 67-68; Lenczowski, "Foreign Powers," 76-78; and Majd, *Persia in World War I*, 12-13, 16-22, 31-33, 46-47.

23. Details on British and Turkish operations in Iran derived from Wilson, *Loyalties*; Moberly, *Operations in Persia, 1914-1919*; Moberly, *Campaign in Mesopotamia, Vol. 1*; and Moberly, *Campaign in Mesopotamia, Vol. 4*.

24. Ghods, *Iran in the Twentieth Century*, 46; Keddie, *Qajar Iran and the Rise of Reza Khan*, 68; Lenczowski, "Foreign Powers," 78-79; Majd, *Persia in World War I*, 37, 40; and Moberly, *Campaign in Mesopotamia, Vol. 1*, 173.

25. On the plans, interactions, and clandestine activities between Iran and the Europeans during 1915, see Lenczowski, *Russia and the West in Iran*, 149; Cronin, *Army*, 35-37; Ghods, *Iran in the Twentieth Century*, 48-50; Keddie, *Qajar Iran and the Rise of Reza Khan*, 70-72; Lenczowski, "Foreign Powers," 80-82; Lustig, "Muhajarat and the Provisional Government in Kirmanshah, 1915-1917," 131-33, 156-59, 162-71, 175-77; and Majd, *Persia in World War I*, 55-66, 69-73, 219-21.

26. On Allied efforts to control Iran's government and the Gendarmerie and their

views of the Swedish officers, see Lustig, "Muhajarat and the Provisional Government in Kirmanshah, 1915–1917," 131–33; and Majd, *Persia in World War I*, 55–59.

27. Cronin, *Army*, 38. The discussion of Iranian activities against the Russians in this and subsequent paragraphs derived primarily from Lustig, "Muhajarat and the Provisional Government in Kirmanshah, 1915–1917," 178, 201–13, 216–17; Majd, *Persia in World War I*, 79–80, 219–21; and Moberly, *Operations in Persia*, 161–62.

28. For Goltz's complete assessment, see Moberly, *Operations in Persia*, 472–73.

29. Discussion of events in southern Iran developed from Lenczowski, "Foreign Powers," 86–87; Majd, *Persia in World War I*, 101, 106, 108–11, 114–18; and Moberly, *Operations in Persia*, 151–52, 154, 158–59 176–77, 181–82; 200–202; 205–7; 210–11, 217–23, 226, 245–47.

30. Lenczowski, "Foreign Powers," 84–85; Lustig, "Muhajarat and the Provisional Government in Kirmanshah, 1915–1917," 260–67, 275–81; Majd, *Persia in World War I*, 80–83, 93–96; and Moberly, *Operations in Persia*, 161–62, 173, 180–81, 194.

31. On Iranian actions against the South Persia Rifles, see Majd, *Persia in World War I*, 121–29, 132–34. The American assessment of the Qashqai from Majd, *Great Britain and Reza Shah*, 23.

32. Majd, *Persia in World War I*, 225.

33. For details on the Jangalis and Norperforce operations, see Lenczowski, "Foreign Powers," 87–88; Moberly, *Campaign in Mesopotamia, Vol. 4*, 200–201; and Majd, *Persia in World War I*, 191, 225–34.

5. Two Paths: The Birth of the Modern Iranian Armed Forces

1. Cronin, *Army*, 44.

2. On the development of the Gendarmerie, see Cronin, *Army*, 42–44, 50–51; Chegnizadeh, "Persian Military Modernization, 1921–1979," 128–29; and Mirfakhraei, "Imperial Iranian Armed Forces and the Revolution of 1978–1979," 46–47. On the role of the provincial fighters, see Forbes-Leith, *Checkmate*, 51–53, 117, 121.

3. On the Cossacks' activities, see Cronin, *Army*, 68–77; and Mirfakhraei, "Imperial Iranian Armed Forces and the Revolution of 1978–1979," 43–47.

4. Discussion of the Cossacks in this and the next paragraph derived from Arfa, *Under Five Shahs*, 91; Cronin, *Army*, 78–82; and Mirfakhraei, "Imperial Iranian Armed Forces and the Revolution of 1978–1979," 46–47.

5. Ghods, *Iran in the Twentieth Century*, 94.

6. On the so-called Paysan Mutiny, see Arfa, *Under Five Shahs*, 112–13, 125–31; and Cronin, *Army*, 11–12, 95–103.

7. Cronin, *Army*, 107.

8. This section's discussion of Reza's unification and consolidation of control over the military derived from Sheikh-ol-Islami, "Army V. Pahlavi Period," 508; Abrahamian, *Iran between Two Revolutions*, 119–20; Arfa, *Under Five Shahs*, 112, 126–27; Chegnizadeh, "Persian Military Modernization, 1921–1979," 139–40, 148–49; and Cronin, *Army*, 90–95, 106–10, 137–39.

9. Information on Reza's rise to power taken from Elwell-Sutton, "Reza Shah the Great," 28; Abrahamian, *Iran between Two Revolutions*, 120, 132–34; and Arjomand, *Turban for the Crown*, 61–62.

10. Imbrie murder reports are found in Majd, "Great Britain and Reza Shah," 167–68.

11. Bakhtiari, *Peaks and Troughs*, 210.

12. On Reza's plans for the nomads, see Trapper, "Introduction," 27.

13. Ansari, *Modern Iran since 1921*, 60. Descriptions of the army's behavior also are found in Millspaugh, *Americans in Persia*, 25; and Majd, *Great Britain and Reza Shah*, 111.

14. Trapper, *Frontier Nomads of Iran*, 267–68.

15. Cronin, *Army*, 124.

16. McDowall, *Modern History of the Kurds*, 223; Arfa, *Under Five Shahs*, 127; and Cronin, *Army*, 121–25.

17. On Simko's fight with Iran, see van Bruinessen, "Kurdish Tribes and the State of Iran," 379, 383–92. Also see McDowall, *Modern History of the Kurds*, 215–21.

18. The discussion of Khuzestan's subjugation from Arfa, *Under Five Shahs*, 169–70; Bakhtiari, *Peaks and Troughs*, 202–6; Cronin, *Army*, 111–12, 141; and Ghods, *Iran in the Twentieth Century*, 98–99.

19. On the fate of the tribes, see Beck, *Qashqai of Iran*, 131–37; Cronin, *Army*, 140, 162, 210; and Mackey, *Iranians*, 174.

20. Majd, "Great Britain and Reza Shah," 217–18.

21. On the military from 1930 to 1941, see Majd, "Great Britain and Reza Shah," 285–92.

22. Cronin, *Army*, 135; and Majd, "Great Britain and Reza Shah," 296–97, 301.

23. Majd, "Great Britain and Reza Shah," 288–89, 299–302.

24. On *Persepolis* and *Muzafferi* problems and the American report on the German ship, see Majd, "Great Britain and Reza Shah," 292–93.

25. Cronin, "Conscription and Popular Resistance," 166.

26. Details on conscription in this and subsequent paragraphs drawn primarily from ibid., 145–66.

27. For information on soldiers' disaffection and the Puladin incident, see Cronin, *Army*, 152–57 and 176–77. On the coup plotting and defection, see Majd, "Great Britain and Reza Shah," 290.

28. Gasiorowski, *U.S. Foreign Policy and the Shah*, 39.

6. Sidelined: The World at War in Iran

1. Except as noted otherwise, many of the details in this and subsequent paragraphs on the war were derived from Stewart, *Sunrise at Abadan*.

2. On Allied concerns about the German presence, see Motter, *Persian Corridor and Aid to Russia*, 160–61; and War Office Central Office of Information, *PAIFORCE: The Official Story of the Persia and Iraq Command, 1941–46*, 62 (hereafter cited as *PAIFORCE*).

Allied worries about German subversion are explained in Buckley, *Five Ventures*, 136; Miller, "How the Soviets Invaded Iran," 30; and Palmer, *Guardians of the Gulf*, 20–21.

3. For information on the shah's address at the military academy, see Buckley, *Five Ventures*, 144; Ghods, *Iran in the Twentieth Century*, 119–20.

4. On the armed forces' deployments and actions prior to the invasion discussed in this and subsequent paragraphs, see Pal, *Official History*, 290–95; Chegnizadeh, "Persian Military Modernization, 1921–1979," 162, 208–9; and Stewart, *Sunrise at Abadan*, 66, 80–85, 91, 97–98, 108.

5. Pal, *Official History*, 297.

6. Stewart, *Sunrise at Abadan*, 98, 104.

7. Discussion of fighting in the south developed from Buckley, *Five Ventures*, 151–52; Stewart, *Sunrise at Abadan*, 100–105, 107–28; and Pal, *Official History*, 317–21, 325–29.

8. *PAIFORCE*, 65.

9. For more details on the second day's fighting, see Stewart, *Sunrise at Abadan*, 155, 160–61, 169, 171–77; and Pal, *Official History*, 336.

10. Buckley, *Five Ventures*, 152–53.

11. The discussion of the fighting in the west in this and subsequent paragraphs derived from Buckley, *Five Ventures*, 147, 154–56; *PAIFORCE*, 69; Pal, *Official History*, 340–44; and Stewart, *Sunrise at Abadan*, 129–31, 155–57, 160–65, 172–83.

12. Stewart, *Sunrise at Abadan*, 176.

13. The following discussion of fighting in the north from ibid., 100, 132–52, 166–70. Also see Miller, "How the Soviets Invaded Iran," 30.

14. Arfa, *Under Five Shahs*, 298–99. Other details on activities in Tehran from Stewart, *Sunrise at Abadan*, 138–40, 142–46, 150, 166–70, 178–80.

15. Stewart, *Sunrise at Abadan*, 181–84, 196.

16. Developments after the cease-fire announcement from Arfa, *Under Five Shahs*, 299–300; and Stewart, *Sunrise at Abadan*, 184–97, 201, 209–11.

17. Stewart, *Sunrise at Abadan*, 195.

18. Motter, *Persian Corridor and Aid to Russia*, 435.

19. Details on Iran's dealings with the Allies derived from Bill, *Eagle and the Lion*, 20–21, 31; Ramazani, *Iran's Foreign Policy*, 74–75; Sheehan, *Iran*, 13, 16; Abrahamian, *Iran between Two Revolutions*, 177–78; Lenczowski, *Russia and the West in Iran*, 175, 194–95, 271–72; and Motter, *Persian Corridor and Aid to Russia*, 169–70.

20. On the American missions, see Ricks, "U.S. Military Missions to Iran," 168–72; and Motter, *Persian Corridor and Aid to Russia*, 464–65, 470.

21. Motter, *Persian Corridor and Aid to Russia*, 465.

22. Ansari, *Modern Iran since 1921*, 84–85.

23. Motter, *Persian Corridor and Aid to Russia*, 467.

24. See recommendations in declassified secret letter from Major General Ridley to Chief of Operations and Plans Division, U.S. War Department in U.S. Military Mission with Iranian Army, "Subject: Supplies for the Iranian Army, dated March 17, 1943," RG 334, National Archives. Also see Motter, *Persian Corridor and Aid to Russia*, 469, for details on the arrangements to produce trucks for the army.

25. On conscript language problems, see Abrahamian, *Iran between Two Revolutions,* 206; and on Shah's response to Millspaugh, see Millspaugh, *Americans in Persia,* 77.

26. Allred, "Persian Corridor," 14, 18.

27. The sixty combat divisions estimate is from Sheehan, *Iran,* 7. Also see Jones, *Roads to Russia,* 84; Allred, "Persian Corridor," 18, 20–22; Lenczowski, *Russia and the West in Iran,* 273–74; and Ricks, "U.S. Military Missions to Iran," 165.

28. Motter, *Persian Corridor and Aid to Russia,* 435.

29. For Iranian views toward the Americans, see Bill, *Eagle and the Lion,* 46–47; and Lenczowski, *Russia and the West in Iran,* 275–76. On the activities of the bandits and military police, see Jones, *Roads to Russia,* 203; and Motter, *Persian Corridor and Aid to Russia,* 435. On Iranian officer views, see Arfa, *Under Five Shahs,* 306.

30. Beck, *Qashqai of Iran,* 143–44, 148; and Lenczowski, *Russia and the West in Iran,* 248.

31. Details on the Kurdish rebellion from Ray Brock, "Soviet, Iran Quash Kurdish Pillaging," *New York Times,* May 22, 1942, 11; Eagleton, *Kurdish Republic of 1946,* 15; "Guerrillas Fight Iranian Patrols," *New York Times,* September 28, 1941, 1, 8; "Iran Uprising Reported," *New York Times,* April 6, 1942, 2; "Tehran Reports Fight on Rebels," *New York Times,* April 24, 1942, 2; Arfa, *Under Five Shahs,* 308–11, 333; McDowall, *Modern History of the Kurds,* 231–33; *PAIFORCE,* 72; and Stewart, *Sunrise at Abadan,* 201.

32. For Tudeh Party activities, see Ghods, *Iran in the Twentieth Century,* 124–33; Lenczowski, *Russia and the West in Iran,* 223–35, 238; and Mackey, *Iranians,* 192.

33. Arfa, *Under Five Shahs,* 343–44; Bakhtiari, *Peaks and Troughs,* 295–97; Ghods, *Iran in the Twentieth Century,* 137; Lenczowski, *Russia and the West in Iran,* 238–39; and Ramazani, *Iran's Foreign Policy,* 115.

7. Cold War Pillar: The Rise of the Imperial Armed Forces

1. Information on the People's Army taken from Kuniholm, *Origins of the Cold War in the Near East,* 286, Ghods, *Iran in the Twentieth Century,* 166; and Lenczowski, *Russia and the West in Iran,* 289–90. On police state tactics, see Miller, "How the Soviets Invaded Iran," 32; and Kuniholm, *Origins of the Cold War in the Near East,* 309.

2. The discussion of the autonomous republics in this and subsequent paragraphs derived from Gene Currivan, "Rebels Take Over New Area in Iran," *New York Times,* March 9, 1946, 1; Gene Currivan, "Russians at Karaj," *New York Times,* March 14, 1946, 1–2; "Fighting in Progress in North Iran; Rebels Clash with Teheran Army," *New York Times,* February 22, 1946, 1; "Underground Army in Azerbaijan Fights New Autonomous Regime, Official Says," *New York Times,* January 9, 1946, 14; Arfa, *Under Five Shahs,* 352–56, 364; Bill, *Eagle and the Lion,* 33–34; Eagleton, *Kurdish Republic of 1946,* 74–83; Ghods, *Iran in the Twentieth Century,* 155, 163–69; Kuniholm, *Origins of the Cold War in the Near East,* 286, 309–19, 384–90; Lenczowski, *Russia and the West in Iran,* 291, 297–306; McDowall, *Modern History of the Kurds,* 240–42; and Miller, "How the Soviets Invaded Iran," 34.

3. Arfa, *Under Five Shahs*, 352–56.

4. On the Joint Chiefs of Staff's warning, see Cohen, *Fighting World War Three from the Middle East*, 1–2. Truman quotation from Feis, *From Trust to Terror*, 83.

5. The discussion of the Iranian military's defeat of the autonomous republics in this and the following paragraphs derived from Arfa, *Under Five Shahs*, 377–78; Eagleton, *Kurdish Republic of 1946*, 86, 90–99, 108–18, 128–29; McDowall, *Modern History of the Kurds*, 224–46; Kuniholm, *Origins of the Cold War in the Near East*, 394–95; Lenczowski, *Russia and the West in Iran*, 308–9; and Ramazani, *Iran's Foreign Policy*, 151–52.

6. Much of the following discussion of the events surrounding the 1953 coups derived from Kinzer, *All the Shah's Men*. Also see Abrahamian, *Iran between Two Revolutions*, 263–78; and Ghods, *Iran in the Twentieth Century*, 177, 180–82.

7. Kinzer, *All the Shah's Men*, 171.

8. New York Times assessment from Kenneth Love, "Iran's Army Now Holds the Balance of Power," *New York Times*, August 23, 1953, E5. Roosevelt quotation from Roosevelt, *Countercoup*, 210.

9. On the Soviet intelligence presence, see Andrew and Mitrokhin, *World Was Going Our Way*, 169. On the Tudeh Party's pre-1953 activities, see Abrahamian, *Iran between Two Revolutions*, 337–38. The summary of postcoup Tudeh actions was taken from Gasiorowski, *U.S. Foreign Policy and the Shah*, 86–87; and, for more details on the Qashqai threats to the regime in support of Mosaddeq, see Beck, *Qashqai of Iran*, 154.

10. Pahlavi, *Mission for My Country*, 105.

11. On the NSC and JCS studies, see Alexander and Nanes, *United States and Iran*, 265–66, 268, 273. The shift of responsibilities from army to Gendarmerie and national police summarized in Gasiorowski, *U.S. Foreign Policy and the Shah*, 110–13. For U.S. plans regarding the defense of the Middle East, see Cohen, *Fighting World War Three from the Middle East*, 319.

12. Singh, *Quest for Security*, 62.

13. Ramazani, *Iran's Foreign Policy*, 360.

14. On shah's concerns about the 1965 war and CENTO, see Cottrell, "Iran's Armed Forces under the Pahlavi Dynasty," 399; and Singh, *Quest for Security*, 73–76. Iranian justifications for a forward-based defense taken from Chegnizadeh, "Persian Military Modernization, 1921–1979," 248–49n.

15. On oil revenues, see Pollack, *Persian Puzzle*, 108; and Chegnizadeh, "Persian Military Modernization, 1921–1979," 321–22. On the Nixon Doctrine and the shah's reaction, see Palmer, *Guardians of the Gulf*, 87–88, 90; and Ghods, *Iran in the Twentieth Century*, 201. For details on arms spending and defense budgets, see Chegnizadeh, "Persian Military Modernization, 1921–1979," 303; and Mirfakhraei, "Imperial Iranian Armed Forces and the Revolution of 1978–1979," 187.

16. Pollack, *Persian Puzzle*, 104.

17. Schlesinger quotation from Irani, *Arms Transfer and National Security*, 7. On the Twin Pillars policy, see Palmer, *Guardians of the Gulf*, 87–89.

18. On Iranian security concerns, see Ramazani, *Iran's Foreign Policy*, 348–51. Description of Soviet activities from Andrew and Mitrokhin, *World Was Going Our Way*, 173–74.

19. Palmer, *Guardians of the Gulf*, 90–91.

20. On the U.S. Senate report, see Alexander and Nanes, *United States and Iran*, 408–14. The comment on popular Iranian views of the shah's servile posture was taken from Pollack, *Persian Puzzle*, 104.

21. Iranian military figures in this section derived from the International Institute for Strategic Studies, *Military Balance*, various editions.

22. Ramazani, *Iran's Foreign Policy*, 427–28.

23. Singh, *Quest for Security*, 280.

24. On Project Flower, see Muslim Students Following the Line of the Imam, *Documents from the U.S. Espionage Den*, vol. 16, 345–68; and Elaine Sciolino, "Documents Detail Israeli Missile Deal with the Shah," *New York Times*, April 1, 1986, A17.

25. Reports found in U.S. Military Mission with Iranian Army, RG 334, National Archives at College Park, Maryland. Also, various reports and personal papers of former ARMISH officers available at Army Military History Institute in Carlisle, Pennsylvania, as noted in bibliography, were reviewed.

26. Specific examples taken from U.S. Military Mission with Iranian Army, "ARMISH Memo, C/S 611, Subject: Report of Inspection, 3rd Division, Tabriz, Iran, dated March 3, 1951," RG 334, National Archives; U.S. Military Mission with Iranian Army, "ARMISH Memo, C/S 653, Subject: Field Inspection of 7th Division (Kerman), dated April 28, 1951," RG 334, National Archives; U.S. Military Mission with Iranian Army, "ARMISH Memo, C/S 659, Subject: Report of Advisory Department Representative Visit to 8th Division, Meshed, dated May 5, 1951," RG 334, National Archives; U.S. Military Mission with Iranian Army, "ARMISH Memo, C/S 675, Subject: Inspection of 3d Division, Tabriz and 4th Division, Rezaiyeh, dated May 20, 1951," RG 334, National Archives; and U.S. Military Mission with Iranian Army, "ARMISH-MAAG, Effectiveness of Forces Report for Iran, December 31, 1956," RG 334, National Archives. Assessment of outstanding Iranian officers in 1953 and later found in U.S. Military Mission with Iranian Army, "ARMISH Memo, C/S 90, Subject: Outstanding Iranian Officers, dated 18 March 1953," RG 334, National Archives, and U.S. Military Mission with Iranian Army, "Subject: Debriefing of Senior and Designated Key Officers Returning from Field Assignments, dated August 26, 1965," RG 334, National Archives. The American colonel's recollections are from Meyer, *Proud to Be*, 220–21, available at the Army Military History Institute.

27. Assessments of the Iranian Army found in U.S. Military Mission with Iranian Army, "U.S. Army Attaché, Tehran, Report Number 2846041463, Subject: Status of the First Imperial Iranian Army, dated May 20, 1963," RG 334, National Archives; U.S. Military Mission with Iranian Army, "Subject: Debriefing of Senior and Designated Key Officers Returning from Field Assignments, dated August 26, 1965," RG 334, National Archives; and U.S. Department of State, Office of the Inspector General, "Inspection Report: The Conduct of Relations with Iran" in Muslim Students Following the Line of

the Imam, 101; on scope of the 1963 unrest, see Graham, *Iran,* 69; Bakhtiari, *Peaks and Troughs,* 477–82; and Pollack, *Persian Puzzle,* 89.

28. On Iran-Iraq relations, see Abdulghani, *Iraq and Iran,* 121, 140–41; and Ramazani, *Iran's Foreign Policy,* 417–18, 434. For the ARMISH assessment, see U.S. Department of the Army, Office of the Adjutant General Memo, "Subject: Senior Officer Debriefing Report," 11. The American assessment found in Director of Central Intelligence, "Iran's International Position."

29. On the disputed islands, see Mobley, "Deterring Iran," 115–16. On Iranian military pressure on Iraq in late 1974, see Jim Hoagland, "Iran Downs 2 Iraqi Planes, Baghdad Says," *Washington Post,* December 17, 1974, 1, A7. Other details derived from Abdulghani, *Iraq and Iran,* 141–42; McDowall, *Modern History of the Kurds,* 338; and Ramazani, *Iran's Foreign Policy,* 436–37.

30. Peterson, *Oman in the Twentieth Century,* 187–92; Allen and Rigsbee, *Oman under Qaboos,* 27–29; and Cottrell, "Iran's Armed Forces," 408–9.

31. Anthony, "Insurrection and Intervention," 297–99; Joseph Fitchett, "Oman Rebels on Run in Mountain War," *Washington Post,* March 10, 1974, A21; Allen and Rigsbee, *Oman under Qaboos,* 70–73; Bakhtiari, *Peaks and Troughs,* 728–29; Cottrell, "Iran's Armed Forces," 410–11; and Peterson, *Oman in the Twentieth Century,* 96, 154.

32. Jeapes, *SAS,* 161, 167, 193–94, 203, 224; Eric Pace, "Iran Said to Vow Defense of Oman," *New York Times,* February 3, 1975, 53; Eric Pace, "Iranian Troops Helping Oman to Quell Rebels," *New York Times,* February 7, 1975, 4; Ray Vickers, "The Mideast's Forgotten War," *Wall Street Journal,* April 18, 1974, 18; Jim Hoagland, "Shah's Force Jolted in Oman," *Washington Post,* December 16, 1974, A1, A16; Allen and Rigsbee, *Oman under Qaboos,* 70–73; Bakhtiari, *Peaks and Troughs,* 728–29; Cottrell, "Iran's Armed Forces," 411–412; and Peterson, *Oman in the Twentieth Century,* 189–91.

33. Perkins, "Death of an Army," 21–23; Cottrell, "Iran's Armed Forces," 409–11; Hoagland, "Shah's Force Jolted in Oman," A1, A16; and Mirfakhraei, "Imperial Iranian Armed Forces and the Revolution of 1978–1979," 180–81.

34. Ricks, "U.S. Military Missions to Iran," 186.

35. On congressional assessments, see Alexander and Nanes, *United States and Iran,* 407–8.

36. On the Cobra pilots, see U.S. Military Mission with Iranian Army, "ARAA-AVN Memorandum for Record, Subject: Briefing on IAA Progress to Top Level GOI Officials, 13 April 1975, Presented by Brigadier General Partain, Chief, Army Section, ARMISH/MAAG," RG 334, National Archives. On the twenty years of negotiations, see Curtis J. Herrick, "Experiences in the Imperial Iranian Army Aviation FMS Program, 1970–1976," 31. On the estimates for ten thousand personnel, see Neuman, "Arms Transfers, Indigenous Defense Production and Dependency," 137, 146n.

37. On the problems with the F-14, see Daugherty, *In the Shadow of the Ayatollah,* 51; and Cooper and Bishop, *Iranian F-14 Tomcat Units in Combat,* 14–15.

38. Zabih, *Iranian Military in Revolution and War,* 5–6, 8; Chegnizadeh, "Persian Military Modernization, 1921–1979," 253; and Mirfakhraei, "Imperial Iranian Armed Forces and the Revolution of 1978–1979," 235–42.

39. Huyser, *Mission to Tehran*, 27; Mirfakhraei, "Imperial Iranian Armed Forces and the Revolution of 1978–1979," 238; and Zabih, *Iranian Military in Revolution and War*, 5.

40. On shah and Zahedi disagreements, see Central Intelligence Agency, "Iran." Other details derived from Gasiorowski, *U.S. Foreign Policy and the Shah*, 174–75; and Mirfakhraei, "Imperial Iranian Armed Forces and the Revolution of 1978–1979," 239–40, 249–50, 258–59.

41. Huyser, *Mission to Tehran*, 7–8.

8. Old Guard, New Guard: Iran's Armed Forces in the Islamic Revolution

1. Description of capabilities and Shah's declaration of new Persian Empire from Mackey, *Iranians*, 244.

2. Bakhash, *Reign of the Ayatollahs*, 9; Stempel, *Inside the Iranian Revolution*, 25–27; and Abrahamian, *Iran between Two Revolutions*, 480–82, 489–95.

3. Schahgaldian, *Iranian Military under the Islamic Republic*, 16–17; Arjomand, *Turban for the Crown*, 111–15; Keddie, *Modern Iran*, 255–56; Mirfakhraei, "Imperial Iranian Armed Forces and the Revolution of 1978–1979," 399; Stempel, *Inside the Iranian Revolution*, 133–36; and Zabih, *Iranian Military in Revolution and War*, 42.

4. Sullivan, *Mission to Iran*, 74–76.

5. Hickman, *Ravaged and Reborn*, 7.

6. Cann and Danopoulous, "Military and Politics in a Theocratic State," 274.

7. Sullivan, *Mission to Iran*, 212.

8. Cottam, *Iran and the United States*, 186; Roberts, *Khomeini's Incorporation of the Iranian Military*, 18, 21; Mirfakhraei, "Imperial Iranian Armed Forces and the Revolution of 1978–1979," 338; Pollack, *Persian Puzzle*, 134–35; Stempel, *Inside the Iranian Revolution*, 50–51, 158–59; and Zabih, *Iranian Military in Revolution and War*, 39–40.

9. Huyser, *Mission to Tehran*, 17–18, 48, 59, 60–62.

10. Ibid., 130.

11. Cottam, *Iran and the United States*, 185; and Zabih, *Iranian Military in Revolution and War*, 98–101.

12. Zabih, *Iranian Military in Revolution and War*, 71–72, 78.

13. The discussion of the military's switch to neutrality and the collapse of the Bakhtiar government in this and subsequent paragraphs derived from Arjomand, *Turban for the Crown*, 127–28; Cottam, *Iran and the United States*, 189; Huyser, *Mission to Tehran*, 282–83; Mirfakhraei, "Imperial Iranian Armed Forces and the Revolution of 1978–1979," 343–45; Roberts, *Khomeini's Incorporation of the Iranian Military*, 30–31; and Zabih, *Iranian Military in Revolution and War*, 36–37, 73–80, 96, 102–10.

14. O'Ballance, *Gulf War*, 20.

15. On the Guard's origins, see Katzman, *Warriors of Islam*, 8–9, 32–33. The following discussion of the Guard's early evolution derived from Katzman, *Warriors of Islam*, 1, 14–17, 31–34, 82–83; Schahgaldian, *Iranian Military under the Islamic Republic*, 64–75, 90–91; and Zabih, *Iranian Military in Revolution and War*, 210–11.

16. On the revolutionaries' plans and tribunals, see Roberts, *Khomeini's Incorporation of the Iranian Military*, 42–43; Schahgaldian, *Iranian Military under the Islamic Republic*, 18–27; and Zabih, *Iranian Military in Revolution and War*, 115–23.

17. Data on results of purges from Schahgaldian, *Iranian Military under the Islamic Republic*, 21, 26–27; and Zabih, *Iranian Military in Revolution and War*, 123.

18. Jonathan Kandell, "Many in Iran Seek the Revival of an Effective Army," *New York Times*, June 26, 1979, A2; Bakhash, *Reign of the Ayatollahs*, 87; Ghods, *Iran in the Twentieth Century*, 221; O'Ballance, *Gulf War*, 21–22; Roberts, *Khomeini's Incorporation of the Iranian Military*, 46; and Stempel, *Inside the Iranian Revolution*, 209.

19. John Kifner, "Kurdish Tribesmen Battle Iran," *New York Times*, March 20, 1979, A3; "Kurds Press Attacks on Iranian Troops," *New York Times*, March 21, 1979, A12; "Kurdish Rebels Are Said to Kill 20 Iranian Soldiers," *New York Times*, July 29, 1979, A12; "Iran Is Said to Crush Kurd Revolt: Khomeini Bypasses Army Leaders," *New York Times*, August 19, 1979, A1; "Khomeini Offers Money to Kurds in Apparent Effort to End Uprising," *New York Times*, August 23, 1979, A1; "Kurdish Rebels in Fierce Battle with Iran Force," *New York Times*, August 24, 1979, A1; "Kurd Stronghold Reported Seized by Iran's Forces," *New York Times*, August 25, 1979, A1; "Iran Relief Force Reaches Garrison Besieged by Kurds," *New York Times*, August 26, 1979, A1; "Iran's Troops Crush Kurdish Rebel Siege: New Fight Expected," *New York Times*, August 27, 1979, A1; "Kurds Said to Repel 400 Iranian Troops from Rebel Center," *New York Times*, September 3, 1979, A1; "Kurdish Rebels Flee Stronghold as Iranians Drive through Lines," *New York Times*, September 4, 1979, A1; "Iran's Troops Take Control of Kurdish Rebel Center," *New York Times*, September 5, 1979, A4; and "Teheran Says Its Forces Capture Kurdish Rebels' Last Stronghold," *New York Times*, September 7, 1979, A10.

20. "Kurds Said to Control City in Northwest Iran after Heavy Fighting," *New York Times*, October 21, 1979, A8; "Kurds Attack Several Iran Towns," *New York Times*, November 13, 1979, A10; "Kurds Declare a Truce in Iran and Offer Aid in a Fight with U.S.," *New York Times*, November 26, 1979, A14; "Heavy Toll Reported in Fighting by Kurds and Iran Guard Units," *New York Times*, February 1, 1980, A8; and John Kifner, "Uprising by Kurds Strains Iranian Regime," *New York Times*, May 31, 1980, A1, A6.

21. "Kurds and Iran's Troops Reported in Major Battle," *New York Times*, August 31, 1980, A16; "Iraq Invades Iran's Kurdistan Province, Extending Front Full Length of Border," *New York Times*, December 27, 1980, A8; and "Heavy Fighting by Iran and Iraqi-Backed Kurds Reported," *New York Times*, December 31, 1980, A6.

22. John Kifner, "Iran Reports Cease-Fire with Turkoman Rebels after 8 Days of Fighting," *New York Times*, April 3, 1979, A3; John Kifner, "Turkomans Battle Iranian Forces in New Outbreak of Tribal Separatism," *New York Times*, March 28, 1979, A3; Pranay B. Gupte, "Iran Declares State of Emergency in Baluchistan as Fight Continues," *New York Times*, December 23, 1979, A1, A14; and Pranay B. Gupte, "For Now, the Baluchis Hold Their Fire," *New York Times*, December 25, 1979, A4.

23. Pranay B. Gupte, "Rebels in Azerbaijan Bar Governor from Gaining Access to Statehouse," *New York Times*, December 9, 1979, A12; and Pranay B. Gupte, "Fighting

Breaks Out for Tabriz Station: 3 Reported Killed," *New York Times*, December 10, 1979, A1, A16.

24. Pollack, *Persian Puzzle*, 155.

25. Bowden, *Guests of the Ayatollah*, 13, 202; O'Ballance, *Gulf War*, 22; and Katzman, *Warriors of Islam*, 36.

26. Bakhash, *Reign of the Ayatollahs*, 119.

27. Gasiorowski, "Nuzhih Plot and Iranian Politics," 649–50; Bakhash, *Reign of the Ayatollahs*, 118; and Zabih, *Iranian Military in Revolution and War*, 124.

28. The following discussion of this failed coup attempt developed from Gasiorowski, "Nuzhih Plot and Iranian Politics," 650–60.

9. Horrible Sacrifice: The Iran-Iraq War

1. Ansari, *Modern Iran since 1921*, 229–30; and Cordesman and Wagner, *Lessons of Modern War*, 13, 23, 36n.

2. On the status of Iran's regular military before the war, see Gerard, "Impact of Ideology," 169–70, 197; Cordesman and Wagner, *Lessons of Modern War*, 34–35, 64–67; Roberts, *Khomeini's Incorporation of the Iranian Military*, 51, 53; Schahgaldian, *Iranian Military under the Islamic Republic*, 42–45, 51–52, 57; and Zabih, *Iranian Military in Revolution and War*, 142–43.

3. McCaul, "Iranian Tank Commander," 44–49.

4. Ibid., 46.

5. Schahgaldian, *Iranian Military under the Islamic Republic*, 36–38, 43.

6. The discussion of the Guard's growth in this and subsequent paragraphs developed from Cordesman and Wagner, *Lessons of Modern War*, 35; Gerard, "Impact of Ideology," 250–54; Katzman, *Warriors of Islam*, 8–9, 67–68, 86–89; Schahgaldian, *Iranian Military under the Islamic Republic*, 78–79; and Zabih, *Iranian Military in Revolution and War*, 156, 212, 217–18.

7. On the Guard's adoption of Khomeini's views, see Gerard, "Impact of Ideology," 30–35, 43. Other details derived from Katzman, *Warriors of Islam*, 13, 19, 55, 62 and Zabih, *Iranian Military in Revolution and War*, 216–17.

8. Military balance between Iran and Iraq derived from Pollack, *Arabs at War*, 182–87; and Cordesman and Wagner, *Lessons of Modern War*, 35, 40–41.

9. The discussion of the Iraqi invasion and the Iranian response developed from Cordesman and Wagner, *Lessons of Modern War*, 81–89; O'Ballance, *Gulf War*, 37–40; Pollack, *Arabs at War*, 186–90, 193; and Zabih, *Iranian Military in Revolution and War*, 173.

10. Cordesman and Wagner, *Lessons of Modern War*, 99–102; O'Ballance, *Gulf War*, 43; and Schahgaldian, *Iranian Military under the Islamic Republic*, 52.

11. Cordesman and Wagner, *Lessons of Modern War*, 112–14; O'Ballance, *Gulf War*, 62; and Pollack, *Arabs at War*, 194–95.

12. The Guard's assessment of Artesh and Pasdaran approaches to the war from Rashid, "Study of the Formation of the Policy to Liberate the Occupied Territories," 23–34.

13. Ground Forces of the Islamic Republic of Iran, Assistant Chief of Staff for Operations, *Atlas of Unforgettable Battles*, 67 (hereafter cited as *Unforgettable Battles*); Cordesman and Wagner, *Lessons of Modern War*, 123–26; Pollack, *Arabs at War*, 195–96; and Zabih, *Iranian Military in Revolution and War*, 176.

14. Cordesman and Wagner, *Lessons of Modern War*, 120–21; and O'Ballance, *Gulf War*, 71.

15. The discussion of the 1982 offensives in this and subsequent paragraphs derived from Cordesman and Wagner, *Lessons of Modern War*, 129–43; Pollack, *Arabs at War*, 198–99; *Unforgettable Battles*, 70–79; and Zabih, *Iranian Military in Revolution and War*, 177–79.

16. Katzman, *Warriors of Islam*, 104–5, 129.

17. On Iran's 1982–83 offensives, see Cordesman and Wagner, *Lessons of Modern War*, 147–53, 168–69, 175–78; Gerard, "Impact of Ideology," 218–19, 232; Pollack, *Arabs at War*, 203–5; and Zabih, *Iranian Military in Revolution and War*, 185–86.

18. Cordesman and Wagner, *Lessons of Modern War*, 152.

19. *Unforgettable Battles*, 62, 79, and 87.

20. Cordesman and Wagner, *Lessons of Modern War*, 168–69.

21. Schahgaldian, *Iranian Military under the Islamic Republic*, 53–56, 60–62.

22. On the 1984 offensive, see Cordesman and Wagner, *Lessons of Modern War*, 179–83; and O'Ballance, *Gulf War*, 143–47.

23. On the 1985 offensives, see Cordesman and Wagner, *Lessons of Modern War*, 201–5; O'Ballance, *Gulf War*, 160–63; and *Unforgettable Battles*, 105–12.

24. Byman, *Deadly Connections*, 37–39; and Cordesman and Wagner, *Lessons of Modern War*, 127.

25. Muhammad Reza's interest in Lebanon from Samii, "Shah's Lebanon Policy," 66, 84. Iran's view of terrorist groups as seedlings from Byman, *Deadly Connections*, 17, with other details on Iran-Hizballah relations on 5, 80–81, 89.

26. Byman, *Deadly Connections*, 81–83, 87–88, 90.

27. The discussion of the early naval war derived from El-Shazly, *Gulf Tanker War*, 113–22, 343–44; Gamlen and Rogers, "U.S. Reflagging of Kuwaiti Tankers," 123–24; Navias and Hooton, *Tanker Wars*, 43–82; and Palmer, *Guardians of the Gulf*, 121.

28. The discussion on the air war developed from Shemirani, "War of the Cities," 36–37; Cordesman and Wagner, *Lessons of Modern War*, 157–58, 195, 205–11; El-Shazly, *Gulf Tanker War*, 269; and Navias and Hooton, *Tanker Wars*, 78, 87, 93, 103. For detailed but unconfirmed accounts of Iranian air operations based on interviews with Iranian pilots, see Bishop and Cooper, *Iranian F-4 Phantom II Units in Combat*, 17–96; and Cooper and Bishop, *Iranian F-14 Tomcat Units in Combat*, 22–84.

29. Cordesman and Wagner, *Lessons of Modern War*, 157–58, 205–8; and Shemirani, "War of the Cities," 36–37.

30. On Iranian mobilization activities and procurement, see U.S. Government, Foreign Broadcast Information Service, *Iran: Battle of Faw*, 8 (hereafter cited as "Battle of Faw"). Also see Cordesman and Wagner, *Lessons of Modern War*, 217, 232–33, 241; Shemirani, "War of the Cities," 33.

31. Hoseyn Zakariani, "Safavi: If the Enemy Acts Foolishly, Our Response Will Be Very Strong and Crushing," *Jomhuri-ye Islami*, September 22, 2004, translated by FBIS (IAP20040922000119).

32. On the battle in this and subsequent paragraphs, see "Battle of Faw," 17–21, 25–35, 37, 42–44; Cordesman and Wagner, *Lessons of Modern War*, 220–221; Pollack, *Arabs at War*, 217; and Pollack, *Persian Puzzle*, 219–20.

33. Karsh, *Iran-Iraq War*, 48–50; Cordesman and Wagner, *Lessons of Modern War*, 221, 227; and Pollack, *Persian Puzzle*, 221.

34. Cordesman and Wagner, *Lessons of Modern War*, 232; and Pollack, *Persian Puzzle*, 221.

35. Details on Iran's last large offensive from Cordesman and Wagner, *Lessons of Modern War*, 246–60; Gerard, "Impact of Ideology," 259–60, 276–77; and Pollack, *Arabs at War*, 221–24.

36. Cordesman and Wagner, *Lessons of Modern War*, 271–73; and Navias and Hooton, *Tanker Wars*, 85–87, 108, 121–22.

37. Cordesman and Wagner, *Lessons of Modern War*, 271–73, 283–84; and Navias and Hooton, *Tanker Wars*, 121–22, 138.

38. On Iran's claims of rogue operations, see Navias and Hooton, *Tanker Wars*, 152.

39. Palmer, *Guardians of the Gulf*, 130.

40. Red Sea mining details from Navias and Hooton, *Tanker Wars*, 90–91; and Palmer, *Guardians of the Gulf*, 130–31. Also see Navias and Hooton, *Tanker Wars*, 142–43.

41. On CENTCOM actions, see Crist, "Operation Earnest Will," 109–10, 123–26.

42. Cordesman and Wagner, *Lessons of Modern War*, 323–26; and Crist, "Operation Earnest Will," 186–88, 190–92.

43. The discussion of Operation Praying Mantis was derived from Cordesman and Wagner, *Lessons of Modern War*, 375–78; Crist, "Operation Earnest Will," 218–24; and Palmer, *Guardians of the Gulf*, 140–44.

44. Details on Iraq's offensives and the Iranian military's collapse derived from Cordesman and Wagner, *Lessons of Modern War*, 320, 373–75, 381–90; Pollack, *Arabs at War*, 224–28, 232; and Pollack, *Persian Puzzle*, 229–31.

45. Cordesman and Wagner, *Lessons of Modern War*, 390–94; Crist, "Operation Earnest Will," 108, 233–37; and Palmer, *Guardians of the Gulf*, 145–47.

46. Cordesman and Wagner, *Lessons of Modern War*, 320, 387–90, 395–96; Pollack, *Arabs at War*, 227–28; and Pollack, *Persian Puzzle*, 231.

47. "Rafsanjani Publishes Letter by Khomeyni to Iran-Iraq War Cease-Fire Claim," *Iranian Labor News Agency*, September 29, 2006, translated by U.S. Government Open Source Center (IAP20060929950049); and "Rafsanjani's Office Issues Statement Saying Khomeyni's Letter 'Not Classified,'" *Islamic Republic News Agency* internet version in English, October 2, 2006, transcribed by U.S. Government Open Source Center (IAP20061002950047).

48. Khomeini quotations from Cordesman and Wagner, *Lessons of Modern War*, 397. Also see Karsh, *Iran-Iraq War*, 79; and Pollack, *Persian Puzzle*, 229.

49. Iranian casualty claims from presentations by academic experts on Iran and from "Statistics Official Reveals 188,015 Martyrs during War with Iraq," *Islamic Republic News Agency,* September 23, 2000, translated by FBIS (IAP20000923000075). CIA estimates and other details on economic losses from Bakhash, *Reign of the Ayatollahs,* 128; Cordesman and Wagner, *Lessons of Modern War,* 398–99; Karsh, *Iran-Iraq War,* 83; Palmer, *Guardians of the Gulf,* 169; and Pollack, *Persian Puzzle,* 238.

50. Comment on Iranian skill and intelligence from Bill, "Morale vs. Technology," 203. Other aspects of Iran's performance from Cordesman and Wagner, *Lessons of Modern War,* 424–27.

51. Discussion of Iranian morale and willingness to sacrifice derived from Bill, "Morale vs. Technology," 204–6.

10. Despise Not Your Enemy: Iran's Armed Forces in the Twenty-first Century

1. David S. Cloud, "US Cites Iran Threat in Key Strait," *Wall Street Journal,* February 17, 2005, A4.

2. *Punch* cartoon found in Pakenham, *The Scramble for Africa,* 56.

3. Molavi, *Soul of Iran,* 270–71.

4. Nasr, *Shia Revival,* 211–54.

5. Hashim, *Crisis of the Iranian State,* 55–56; and Katzman, *Warriors of Islam,* 59.

6. U.S. government, "Iran: Complete Regulations of the Islamic Republic of Iran Armed Forces," *Near East and South Asia Supplement,* FBIS-NES-94-208-S, U.S. Foreign Broadcast Information Service, October 27, 1994.

7. Ward, "Continuing Evolution of Iran's Military Doctrine," 560.

8. Details on Pasdaran and Qods Force activities in this and the next paragraph derived from Buchta, *Who Rules Iran?* 68; Central Intelligence Agency, "Iranian Surveillance of U.S. Persons and Facilities in 1995," 3–5; Cordesman and Kleiber, *Iran's Military Forces,* 78–81; Eisenstadt, *Iranian Military Power,* 70; Levitt, "Iranian State Sponsorship of Terror"; Katzman, *Warriors of Islam,* 174; and Pollack, *Persian Puzzle,* 248, 256–57, 267, 281.

9. Sayigh, "Arms Production in Iran and Pakistan," 192.

10. Byman et al., *Iran's Security Policy,* 37.

11. Dasgupta, "Internal Security and Military Reorganization," 271; and Central Intelligence Agency, "Iran," 1–7.

12. Eisenstadt, "Military Dimension," 72, 92n; Pollack, "Regional Military Balance," 75; and Byman et al., *Iran's Security Policy,* 24–26, 34–35.

13. On Iranian military education, see Ward, "Continuing Evolution of Iran's Military Doctrine," 563.

14. Historical conditions surrounding military intervention from Haddad, *Revolutions and Military Rule,* 19–21, 27.

15. Byman et al., *Iran's Security Policy,* 45; and Cann and Danopoulous, "Military and Politics in a Theocratic State," 280–81.

16. Samii, "Iran: Paramilitary Force Prepares for Urban Unrest"; and Byman et al., *Iran's Security Policy*, 49–51.

17. Details on the events of July 1999 are from "Iran's Military Leaders Threaten President—Hard-liners Hint at Coup if Unrest Continues," *Seattle Times*, July 21, 1999; Marc Carnegie, "Iran's Revolutionary Guards Denounce Khatami," *Agence France Presse*, July 20, 1999; "Suspicions Grow Iran Hardliners Are Trying to Unseat Khatami," *Mideast Mirror*, July 22, 1999; and Byman et al., *Iran's Security Policy*, 50.

18. On the Pasdaran's growing political role, see Siavosh Ghazi and Stefan Smith, "Hardliner and Rafsanjani to Battle in Iran Vote Run-Off," *Agence France Presse*, June 18. 2005; Abbas Milani and Michael McFaul, "Inside Iran's Fractured Regime," *Washington Post*, June 25, 2006, B05; Stuart Williams, "Iranian Hardliners Dismiss Vote Fraud Complaints," *Agence France Presse*, June 20, 2005; "The Revolutionary Guard Are Back," *Economist* (June 19, 2004), 69; and Robin Wright, "Elite Revolutionary Guard Broadens Its Influence in Iran," *Washington Post*, April 1, 2007, A21.

19. *Jane's Sentinel Security Assessment*, 63, 107; Byman et al., *Iran's Security Policy*, 42; Cordesman, *Iran's Evolving Military Forces*, 25; Cordesman and Kleiber, *Iran's Military Forces*, 30–31; Cordesman and Wagner, *Lessons of Modern War*, 402; and Pollack, "Regional Military Balance," 72.

20. Eisenstadt, *Iranian Military Power*, 35n.

21. Details in this and the next paragraph taken from Knights, *Troubled Waters*, 62; Byman et al., *Iran's Security Policy*, 42; Cordesman and Wagner, *Lessons of Modern War*, 402; Hashim, *Crisis of the Iranian State*, 50–51, 56, 57; *Jane's Sentinel Security Assessment*, 126; and Pollack, "Regional Military Balance," 72.

22. Pollack, "Regional Military Balance," 72; and Cordesman, *Iran's Evolving Military Forces*, 14; Eisenstadt, *Iranian Military Power*, 44.

23. Steven Erlanger and Thom Shanker, "Israel Finding a Difficult Foe in Hezbollah," *New York Times*, July 26, 2006, 1; and Scott Wilson and Edward Cody, "Hezbollah Proves a Formidable Foe," *Washington Post*, July 27, 2006, 1.

24. Cook, *Persians*, 184.

25. Cordesman, *Iran's Evolving Military Forces*, 9–24. The U.S. assessment of the Iranian threat was reported in Cloud, "US Cites Iran Threat in Key Strait," A4. A summary of Iran's role as a state sponsor of terrorism is found in Levitt, "Iranian State Sponsorship of Terror." Iran's views on U.S. vulnerability in the region were taken from Ward, "Continuing Evolution of Iran's Military Doctrine," 564–65.

26. Knights, *Troubled Waters*, 56; and Ward, "Continuing Evolution of Iran's Military Doctrine," 567.

27. Byman et al., *Iran's Security Policy*, 37–38; and Hashim, *Crisis of the Iranian State*, 53–54.

28. For detailed information on the development of Iran's forces and its weapons procurement efforts, see Katzman, *Arms and Technology Acquisitions*; and Cordesman and Kleiber, *Iran's Military Forces*. Other information about Iran's naval forces from Cordesman, *Iran's Evolving Military Forces*, 16–20; Cordesman and Kleiber, *Iran's Military Forces*,

18; Eisenstadt, *Iranian Military Power,* 48–51; Hashim, *Crisis of the Iranian State,* 54–55; and Knights, *Troubled Waters,* 70–73.

29. Fulghum and Barrie, "Iranian Connection," 20; Eisenstadt, *Iranian Military Power,* 48–50; Knights, *Troubled Waters,* 67; and Ward, "Continuing Evolution of Iran's Military Doctrine," 568–69.

30. Cordesman, *Iran's Evolving Military Forces,* 13; Cordesman and Kleiber, *Iran's Military Forces,* 17, 134–56; Eisenstadt, *Iranian Military Power,* 27–32; Hashim, *Crisis of the Iranian State,* 58–59; *Jane's Sentinel Security Assessment,* 111; Knights, *Troubled Waters,* 75; and Ward, "Continuing Evolution of Iran's Military Doctrine," 570–71.

31. "Defense Minister Najar: Russia to Deliver S-300 SAM System to Iran," *Voice of the Islamic Republic of Iran Radio Network 1,* Open Source Center, December 26, 2007 (IAP20071226950068); Doug Richardson, "Iran May Have Lined Up S-300 SAM Systems," *Jane's Missiles and Rockets,* January 7, 2008, www.janes.com (January 2008); Tony Capaccio, "Iran Gets 'Quantum' Boost from Russian Missiles, General Says," *Bloomberg News,* February 28, 2008, www.bloomberg.com (March 2008); Director of the Defense Intelligence Agency, "Oral Statement"; Cordesman, *Iran's Evolving Military Forces,* 21–23; Cordesman and Kleiber, *Iran's Military Forces,* 84–107; Eisenstadt, *Iranian Military Power,* 45–47; and Hashim, *Crisis of the Iranian State,* 51–53.

32. Haghshenass, "Iran's Air Forces"; Maxon, "Iran Receives Smuggled Surplus F-14 Parts," 37; "Iran: Air Force Announces Successes of the Air Segment of 'Zarbat-e Zulfaqer' Exercise," Open Source Center, September 6, 2006 (IAP20060906427001); Cordesman, *Iran's Evolving Military Forces,* 21–23; and Eisenstadt, *Iranian Military Power,* 45–47.

33. Cordesman, *Iran's Evolving Military Forces,* 21; Fulghum and Barrie, "Iranian Connection," 20; and Ward, "Continuing Evolution of Iran's Military Doctrine," 570–71.

34. Hiro, *Longest War,* 201.

35. Knights, *Troubled Waters,* 78.

36. Ali, "Chemical Weapons and the Iran-Iraq War," 51–52; and Hiro, *Longest War,* 201.

37. On Iran's use of chemicals during the fighting at Halabjah, see Cordesman and Wagner, *Lessons of Modern War,* 371. Information suggesting that blood agents were not used by Iran or that information about their use is unavailable or suspect can be found in Defense Intelligence Agency, "Study of IZ Abilities to Conduct Chemical Warfare"; Defense Intelligence Agency, "Responses to Newsweek Questions, Task OICC 4006"; and "Subject: Task Force V Lessons Learned," 2. Also any cyanide compound, if present, may have been the residue of Iraq's impure Tabun nerve agent. See "Testimony of Dr. Christine M. Gosden."

38. Samore, *Iran's Strategic Weapons Programmes,* 69–76; Cordesman and Kleiber, *Iran's Military Forces,* 158–64; Hashim, *Crisis of the Iranian State,* 58; *Jane's Sentinel Security Assessment,* 113; and Knights, *Troubled Waters,* 78.

39. Kibaroglu, "Good for the Shah," 213–14; Chubin, *Iran's Nuclear Ambitions,* 7; Cordesman and Wagner, *Lessons of Modern War,* 519–21; Hashim, *Crisis of the Iranian*

State, 60–61; Pollack, *Persian Puzzle,* 363; and Samore, *Iran's Strategic Weapons Programmes,* 12.

40. *Jane's Sentinel Security Assessment,* 110. On Iranian motivations, see Hashim, *Crisis of the Iranian State,* 61–63; Kibaroglu, "Good for the Shah," 216–20; and Samore, *Iran's Strategic Weapons Programmes,* 12–13.

41. Director of National Intelligence, "Annual Threat Assessment," January 11, 2007; "DNI Testimony to Senate Armed Services Committee on Global Threats," Federal News Service, February 27, 2997, n.p.; and David E. Sanger, "Inspectors Cite Big Gains by Iran on Nuclear Fuel," *New York Times,* May 15, 2007, A1.

42. Director of National Intelligence, *Nuclear Intentions and Capabilities.*

43. Byman, *Deadly Connections,* 26–32, 80–86.

44. On the Khobar Towers attacks, see Byman, *Deadly Connections,* 50–51; and Pollack, *Persian Puzzle,* 282–83. On the German trail results, see Byman, *Deadly Connections,* 50; and Pollack, *Persian Puzzle,* 290. Information on Iran's activities since 2001 can be found in Milani, "Iran's Policy towards Afghanistan," 246–56; Michale Ware, "Inside Iran's Secret War for Iraq," *Time* (August 22, 2005), 26–31; Deputy Director of National Intelligence for Analysis, "Global Security Assessment," 10–11; Byman, *Deadly Connections,* 86–88; Levitt, "Iranian State Sponsorship of Terror"; Pollack, *Persian Puzzle,* 350–51; and Ward, "Continuing Evolution of Iran's Military Doctrine," 574.

45. Details on Iran's ground forces taken from Cordesman, *Iran's Evolving Military Forces,* 9–16; Cordesman and Kleiber, *Iran's Military Forces,* 40–83; Byman et al., *Iran's Security Policy,* 38–39; and Eisenstadt, *Iranian Military Power,* 43–45.

46. Byman et al., *Iran's Security Policy,* 37; Milani, "Iran's Policy towards Afghanistan," 244–45; and Pollack, *Persian Puzzle,* 329.

47. Irani, *Arms Transfer and National Security,* 10.

48. "Commander-in-Chief of the IRGC: Hezbollah's Resistance Has Been Designed Based on an Uneven and Mosaic Defense," *Hemayat,* Open Source Center, July 25, 2006 (IAP20060728011005); and Ward, "Continuing Evolution of Iran's Military Doctrine," 572–73. For a more detailed discussion of Hizballah's tactics and Iran's support, see Matthews, "We Were Caught Unprepared," 17–22.

49. Ward, "Continuing Evolution of Iran's Military Doctrine," 573–74.

50. On Russian legation attack, see Hopkirk, *Great Game,* 112–13. Details on incident with British personnel derived from John Ward Anderson, "Freed Britons Return Home as Calls for Probe Intensify," *Washington Post,* April 6, 2007, A12; and Mary Jordan and Robin Wright, "Iran Seizes 15 British Seaman," *Washington Post,* March 24, 2007, A11.

51. Sick, "Iran's Quest for Superpower Status," 709.

52. On the Guard's involvement in politics, see Blanche, "Pasdaran Power," 22–25; Thomas Erdbrink, "Iran's Clerical Old Guard Being Pushed Aside," *Washington Post,* February 11, 2008, A1; and "The Revolutionary Guard Are Back," *Economist* (June 19, 2004), 69.

53. Cook, *Persians,* 184.

54. Aeschylus, *Persians,* 31.

Bibliography

Abdulghani, Jasim M. *Iraq and Iran: The Years of Crisis.* Baltimore: John Hopkins University Press, 1984.

Abrahamian, Ervand. *Iran between Two Revolutions.* Princeton, NJ: Princeton University Press, 1982.

Aeschylus. *The Persians.* N.p.: Kessinger Publishing, n.d.

Afary, Janet. *The Iranian Constitutional Revolution, 1906–1911: Grassroots Democracy, Social Democracy, and the Origins of Feminism.* New York: Columbia University Press, 1996.

Alexander, Yonah, and Allan Nanes, eds. *The United States and Iran: A Documentary History.* Frederick, MD: University Publications of America, 1980.

Ali, Javed. "Chemical Weapons and the Iran-Iraq War: A Case Study in Noncompliance." *Nonproliferation Review* (Spring 2001): 43–58.

Allen, Calvin H., Jr., and W. Lynn Rigsbee II. *Oman under Qaboos: From Coup to Constitution, 1970–1996.* London: Frank Cass, 2000.

Allred, Kenny. "The Persian Corridor: Aid to the Soviets." *Military Review* 65 (April 1985): 13–25.

Andreeva, Elena. *Russia and Iran in the Great Game: Travelogues and Orientalism.* New York: Routledge, 2007.

Andrew, Christopher, and Vasili Mitrokhin. *The World Was Going Our Way: The KGB and the Battle for the Third World.* New York: Basic Books, 2005.

Ansari, Ali M. *Modern Iran since 1921: The Pahlavis and After.* London: Longman, 2003.

Anthony, John Duke. "Insurrection and Intervention: The War in Dhofar." In *The Persian Gulf and Indian Ocean in International Politics,* ed. Abbas Amirie, 287–320. Tehran: Institute for International Political and Economic Studies, 1975.

Arfa, Hassan. *Under Five Shahs.* New York: William Morrow and Company, 1965.

Arjomand, Said Amir. *The Turban for the Crown.* Oxford: Oxford University Press, 1988.

Atkin, Muriel. *Russia and Iran, 1780–1828.* Minneapolis: University of Minnesota, 1980.

Axworthy, Michael. *The Sword of Persia: Nader Shah, from Tribal Warrior to Conquering Tyrant.* London: I. B. Tauris, 2006.

Babaie, Sussan, Kathryn Babayan, Ina Baghdiantz-McCabe, and Massumeh Farhad. *Slaves of the Shah: New Elites of Safavid Iran.* London: I. B. Tauris, 2004.

Bakhash, Shaul. "The Failure of Reform: The Prime Ministership of Amin al-Dawla, 1897–8." In *Qajar Iran: Political, Social and Cultural Change, 1800–1925,* ed. Edmund Bosworth and Carole Hillenbrand, 14–33. Edinburgh: Edinburgh University Press, 1983.

————. *The Reign of the Ayatollahs: Iran and the Islamic Revolution.* London: I. B. Tauris, 1985.

Bakhtiari, Ali Murtaza Samsam. *Peaks and Troughs: A Tentative Interpretation of Iran's Modern History.* London: Minerva Press, 1996.

Bavand, Davood Hermidas. "Territorial Challenges and Iranian Identity in the Course of History." The Circle of Ancient Iranian Studies at the School of Oriental and African Studies (SOAS), University of London. www.cais-soas.com/CAIS/Iran/ identity.htm (accessed December 1, 2005).

Beck, Lois. *The Qashqai of Iran.* New Haven, CT: Yale University Press, 1986.

Bill, James A. *The Eagle and the Lion: The Tragedy of American-Iranian Relations.* New Haven, CT: Yale University Press, 1988.

————. "Morale vs. Technology: The Power of Iran in the Persian Gulf War." In *The Iran-Iraq War: The Politics of Aggression,* ed. Farhang Rajaee, 198–209. Gainesville: University Press of Florida, 1993.

Bishop, Farzad, and Tom Cooper. *Iranian F-4 Phantom II Units in Combat.* Oxford: Osprey, 2003.

Blanche, Ed. "Pasdaran Power." *Middle East* 360 (October 2005): 22–25.

Bosworth, C. Edmund. "Army II. Islamic, to the Mongol Period." In *Encyclopedia-Iranica,* vol. 2, ed. Ehsan Yarshater, 499–503. London: Routledge, 1985.

Bowden, Mark. *Guests of the Ayatollah.* New York: Atlantic Monthly Press, 2006.

"Brief History of the Persian Empire." The Circle of Ancient Iranian Studies at the School of Oriental and African Studies (SOAS), University of London. www.cais-soas .com/CAIS/History/brief_history_of_persian_empire.htm (accessed September 20, 2008).

Browne, Edward G. *The Persian Revolution of 1905–1909.* Washington, DC: Mage, 1995.

Buchta, Wilfried. *Who Rules Iran? The Structure of Power in the Islamic Republic.* Washington, DC: Washington Institute for Near East Policy, 2000.

Buckley, Christopher. *Five Ventures: Iraq-Syria-Persia-Madagascar-Dodecanese.* London: Her Majesty's Stationery Office, 1954.

Byman, Daniel. *Deadly Connections: States That Sponsor Terrorism.* Cambridge: Cambridge University Press, 2005.

Byman, Daniel, Shahram Chubin, Anoushiravan Ehteshami, and Jerrold Green. *Iran's Security Policy in the Post-Revolutionary Era.* N.p.: RAND, 2001. www.rand.org/ publications (accessed March 1, 2007).

Cann, Rebecca, and Constantine Danopoulous. "The Military and Politics in a Theocratic State: Iran as Case Study." *Armed Forces and Society* 24 (Winter 1997): 269–88.

Central Intelligence Agency. "Iran: A Changing of the Guard," November 3, 1989, declassified July 7, 1999, www.foia.cia.gov (accessed March 1, 2007).

———. "Iranian Reaction to Recent Military Setbacks," April 21, 1988, declassified September 14, 1999, www.foia.cia.gov (accessed March 1, 2007).

———. "Iranian Surveillance of US Persons and Facilities in 1995," January 1996, declassified November 13, 2001, www.foia.cia.gov (accessed March 1, 2007).

Chegnizadeh, Gholamali. "Persian Military Modernization, 1921–1979." PhD diss., University of Bradford, 1997.

Chubin, Shahram. *Iran's Nuclear Ambitions*. Washington, DC: Carnegie Endowment for International Peace, 2006.

Cohen, Michael J. *Fighting World War Three from the Middle East: Allied Contingency Plans, 1945–1954*. Portland, OR: Frank Cass, 1997.

Cole, Juan R. I., and Nikki R. Keddie, eds. *Shi'ism and Social Protest*. New Haven, CT: Yale University Press, 1986.

Cook, J. M. *The Persians*. London: Folio Society, 1999.

Cooper, Tom, and Farzad Bishop. *Iranian F-14 Tomcat Units in Combat*. Oxford: Osprey, 2004.

Cordesman, Anthony H. *Iran and Iraq: The Threat from the Northern Gulf*. Boulder, CO: Westview Press, 1994.

———. *Iran's Developing Military Capabilities*. Washington, DC: CSIS Press, 2005.

———. *Iran's Evolving Military Forces*. Washington, DC: Center for Strategic and International Studies, 2004. www.csis.org (accessed December 10, 2006).

Cordesman, Anthony H., and Martin Kleiber. *Iran's Military Forces and Warfighting Capabilities: The Threat in the Northern Gulf*. Westport, CT: Praeger Security International, 2007.

Cordesman, Anthony H., and Abraham Wagner. *The Lessons of Modern War*. Vol. 2, *The Iran-Iraq War*. Boulder, CO: Westview, 1990.

Cornuelle, Chris. "An Overview of the Sassanian Military." The Circle of Ancient Iranian Studies at the School of Oriental and African Studies (SOAS), University of London. www.cais-soas.com/CAIS/Military/sasanian_military.htm (accessed December 12, 2006).

Cottam, Richard W. *Iran and the United States: A Cold War Case Study*. Pittsburgh, PA: University of Pittsburgh Press, 1988.

Cottrell, Alvin J. "Iran's Armed Forces under the Pahlavi Dynasty." In *Iran under the Pahlavis*, ed. George Lenczowski, 389–432. Stanford, CA: Hoover Institution Press, 1978.

Crist, David B. "Operation Earnest Will: The United States in the Persian Gulf, 1986–1989." PhD diss., Florida State University, 1998.

Cronin, Stephanie. *The Army and the Creation of the Pahlavi State in Iran, 1910–1921*. London: Tauris Academic Studies, 1997.

———. "Conscription and Popular Resistance in Iran (1925–1941)." In *Arming the State: Military Conscription in the Middle East and Central Asia, 1775–1925*, ed. Erik J. Zurcher, 145–68. London, I. B. Tauris, 1999.

Curzon, George N. *Persia and the Persian Question*. Vol. 1. London: Cass, 1966.

Daniel, Elton L. *The History of Iran*. Westport, CT: Greenwood Press, 2001.

Dasgupta, Sunil. "Internal Security and Military Reorganization: The Rise of Paramilitaries in Developing Societies." PhD diss., University of Illinois at Urbana-Champaign, 2003.

Daugherty, William J. *In the Shadow of the Ayatollah: A CIA Hostage in Iran.* Annapolis, MD: Naval Institute Press, 2001.

Defense Intelligence Agency. "Study of IZ *(Iraqi)* Abilities to Conduct Chemical Warfare," February 8, 1991, File 961031_950825_0150pgv_91d.txt, p. 91d, www.gulflink .osd.mil/declassdocs/dia/19961031/961031_950825_150pgv_91d.html (accessed September 20, 2008).

———. "Responses to Newsweek Questions, Task OICC 4006," February 1, 1991, File 950811_0174pgv_91d.txt, p. 91d, www.gulflink.osd.mil/declassdocs/dia/ 19950811/950811_0174pgv_91d.html (accessed September 20, 2008).

Dennis, George T., ed. and trans. *Maurice's Strategikon: Handbook of Byzantine Military Strategy.* Philadelphia: University of Pennsylvania Press, 1984.

Deputy Director of National Intelligence for Analysis. "Global Security Assessment for the House Armed Services Committee," July 11, 2007, www.odni.gov/testimonies/ 20700711_testimony.pdf (accessed September 20, 2008).

Director of Central Intelligence. "Iran's International Position," Special National Intelligence Estimate 34–70, September 3, 1970, declassified June 10, 1999, www.foia .cia.gov (accessed December 10, 2006).

Director of the Defense Intelligence Agency. "Oral Statement by the Director of the Defense Intelligence Agency, Lieutenant General Michael D. Maples to the Senate Select Committee on Intelligence Annual Threat Assessment Hearing," February 5, 2008, www.dia.mil/publicaffairs/Testimonies/statement29.html (accessed September 20, 2008).

Director of National Intelligence. "Annual Threat Assessment," January 11, 2007, http://intelligence.senate.gov/070111/negroponte.pdf (accessed May 1, 2007).

———. *Iran: Nuclear Intentions and Capabilities,* National Intelligence Estimate, November 2007, www.dni.ic.gov/DNI/documents/20071203_release.pdf (accessed December 7, 2007).

Dupuy, R. Ernest, and Trevor N. Dupuy. *The Encyclopedia of Military History: From 3500 B.C. to the Present,* 2nd rev. ed. New York: Harper and Row, 1986.

Durand-Guedy, David. "Iranians at War under Turkish Domination: The Example of Pre-Mongol Isfahan." In *Iranian Studies* 38 (December 2005): 587–606.

Eagleton, William, Jr. *The Kurdish Republic of 1946.* London: Oxford University Press. 1963.

Eisenstadt, Michael. *Iranian Military Power: Capabilities and Intentions.* Washington, DC: Washington Institute for Near East Policy, 1996.

———. "The Military Dimension." In *Iran under Khatami: A Political, Economic, and Military Assessment,* ed. Patrick Clawson, Michael Eisenstadt, Eliyahu Kanovsky, and David Menashri, 71–98. Washington, DC: Washington Institute for Near East Policy, 1998.

Ekhtiar, Maryam D. "The Dar Al-Funun: Educational Reform and Cultural Development in Qajar Iran." PhD diss., New York University, 1994.

El-Shazly, Nadir El-Sayed. *The Gulf Tanker War: Iran and Iraq's Maritime Swordplay.* New York: St Martin's Press, 1998.

Elwell-Sutton, L. P. "Reza Shah the Great: Founder of the Pahlavi Dynasty." In *Iran under the Pahlavis,* ed. George Lenczowski, 1–50. Stanford, CA: Hoover Institution Press, 1978.

Fatemi, Khosrow. "Leadership by Distrust: The Shah's *Modus Operandi.*" *Middle East Journal* 36 (Winter 1982): 48–62.

Feis, Herbert. *From Trust to Terror: The Onset of the Cold War, 1945–1950.* New York: W. W. Norton, 1970.

Filson, Stormie. "Battle of Gaugamela: Conquest of a Continent." *Military History* (October 2000): 66–73.

Forbes-Leith, F. A. C. *Checkmate: Fighting Tradition in Central Persia.* New York: Robert M. McBride and Company, 1927.

Frye, Richard N. *The Golden Age of Persia: The Arabs in the East.* London: Weidenfeld, 1993.

Fulghum, David, and Douglas Barrie. "The Iranian Connection." *Aviation Week and Space Technology,* August 14, 2006, 20.

Fuller, Graham E. *The "Center of the Universe": The Geopolitics of Iran.* Boulder, CO: Westview Press, 1991.

Gamlen, Elizabeth, and Paul Rogers. "U.S. Reflagging of Kuwaiti Tankers." In *The Iran-Iraq War: The Politics of Aggression,* ed. Farhang Rajaee, 123–51. Gainesville: University Press of Florida, 1993.

Gasiorowski, Mark J. "The Nuzhih Plot and Iranian Politics." *International Journal of Middle East Studies* 34 (2002): 645–66.

———. "The Qarani Affair and Iranian Politics." *International Journal of Middle East Studies* 25 (1993): 625–43.

———. *U.S. Foreign Policy and the Shah: Building a Client State in Iran.* Ithaca, NY: Cornell University Press, 1991.

Gerard, Joseph T. "The Impact of Ideology on the Iranian Military in the Iran-Iraq War (1980–1988)." PhD diss., Catholic University of America, 2002.

Ghasemi, Shapour. *Safavid Empire, 1502–1736.* Iran Chamber Society. www.iranchamber.com/history/safavids/safavids.php (accessed March 20, 2006).

Ghods, M. Reza. *Iran in the Twentieth Century: A Political History.* Boulder, CO: Lynne Rienner, 1989.

Goldschmidt, Arthur, Jr. *A Concise History of the Middle East.* 2nd ed. Boulder, CO: Westview Press, 1983.

Graham, Robert. *Iran: The Illusion of Power.* New York: St. Martin's Press, 1979.

Green, Peter. *The Greco-Persian Wars.* Berkeley: University of California Press, 1996.

Ground Forces of the Islamic Republic of Iran, Assistant Chief of Staff for Operations. *Atlas of Unforgettable Battles: Ground Forces Operations in Eight Years of Holy Defense, September 1980–August 1988.* Tehran: Holy Defense Research Center, 2005.

Haddad, George M. *Revolutions and Military Rule: The Northern Tier.* New York: Robert Speller and Sons, 1965.

Haghshenass, Fariburz. "Iran's Air Forces: Struggling to Maintain Readiness." *Policy-watch* 1066 (December 28, 2005): n.p.

Haneda, Mashashi. "Army III. Safavid." In *Encyclopedia-Iranica,* vol. 2, ed. Ehsan Yar-shater, 503–6. London: Routledge, 1985.

Hanson, Victor Davis. *Carnage and Culture: Landmarks Battles in the Rise of Western Power.* New York: Anchor Books, 2002.

Hashim, Ahmed. *The Crisis of the Iranian State.* Adelphi Paper 296, International Institute for Strategic Studies. London: Oxford University Press, 1995.

Heral, Ethan. "Yasotay and the Mangoday of Genghis Khan." *Armed Forces Journal* (January 1985): 38–69.

Herodotus. *The Persian Wars,* trans. George Rawlinson. New York: Modern Library, 1942.

Herrick, Curtis J. "Experiences in the Imperial Iranian Army Aviation FMS Program, 1970–1976." Unpublished report. Army Military History Institute (accessed November 12, 2006).

Hickman, William F. *Ravaged and Reborn: The Iranian Army, 1982.* Washington, DC: Brookings Institution, 1982.

Hiro, Dilip. *The Longest War: The Iran-Iraq Military Conflict.* New York: Routledge, 1991.

Hone, Joseph M. *Persia in Revolution.* London: T. F. Unwin, 1910.

Hopkirk, Peter. *The Great Game: The Struggle for Empire in Central Asia.* New York: Kodansha International, 1992.

Huyser, Robert E. *Mission to Tehran.* New York: Harper and Row, 1986.

International Institute for Strategic Studies. *The Military Balance,* various years. Dorking: Adlard and Son, Ltd.

Irani, Robert G. *Arms Transfer and National Security: An Interpretation of Iran's Perspective.* Carlisle Barracks, PA: U.S. Army War College Strategic Studies Institute, 1978.

Jane's Sentinel Security Assessment: The Gulf States, no. 18. Alexandria, VA: Jane's Information Group, 2006.

Jeapes, Tony. *SAS: Operation Oman.* London: William Kimber, 1980.

Jones, Archer. *The Art of War in the Western World.* Urbana: University of Illinois Press, 1987.

Jones, Robert H. *The Roads to Russia: United States Lend-Lease to the Soviet Union.* Norman: University of Oklahoma Press, 1969.

Karsh, Efraim. *The Iran-Iraq War, 1980–1988.* Oxford: Osprey, 2002.

Kasravi, Ahmad. *History of the Iranian Constitutional Revolution,* vol. 1, trans. Evan Siegel. Costa Mesa, CA: Mazda, 2006.

Katzman, Kenneth. *Iran: Arms and Technology Acquisitions.* Washington, DC: Congressional Research Service, 2001.

———. *The Warriors of Islam: Iran's Revolutionary Guard.* Boulder, CO: Westview Press, 1993.

Keddie, Nikki R. *Modern Iran: Roots and Results of Revolution.* New Haven, CT: Yale University Press, 2003.

———. *Qajar Iran and the Rise of Reza Khan, 1796–1925*. Costa Mesa, CA: Mazda, 1999.

Kelley, J. B. *Britain and the Persian Gulf, 1795–1880*. London: Oxford University Press, 1968.

Kibaroglu, Mustafa. "Good for the Shah, Banned for the Mullahs: The West and Iran's Quest for Nuclear Power." *Middle East Journal* 60 (Spring 2006): 207–34.

Kinzer, Stephen. *All the Shah's Men: An American Coup and the Roots of Middle East Terror*. Hoboken, NJ: John Wiley and Sons, 2003.

Knights, Michael. *Troubled Waters: Future U.S. Security Assistance in the Persian Gulf*. Washington, DC: Washington Institute for Near East Policy, 2006.

Kuniholm, Bruce R. *The Origins of the Cold War in the Near East: Great Power Conflict and Diplomacy in Iran, Turkey, and Greece*. Princeton, NJ: Princeton University Press, 1980.

Lackey, Earl E. *Iran: Environmental Conditions Affecting Logistics*. Washington, DC: U.S. Department of the Army, U.S. Quartermaster Corps, Research and Development Division, July 1951.

Lenczowski, George. "Foreign Powers' Intervention in Iran during World War I." In *Qajar Iran: Political, Social and Cultural Change, 1800–1925*, ed. Edmund Bosworth and Carole Hillenbrand, 76–92. Edinburgh: Edinburgh University Press, 1983.

———. *Russia and the West in Iran, 1918–1948: A Study in Big-Power Rivalry*. Ithaca, NY: Cornell University Press, 1949.

Levitt, Matthew. "Iranian State Sponsorship of Terror: Threatening U.S. Security, Global Stability, and Regional Peace." *Policywatch* 964 (February 23, 2005): n.p.

Lustig, Michael J. "The Muhajarat and the Provisional Government in Kirmanshah, 1915–1917: Conflict and Cooperation between the First Political Parties in Iran and Their Participation in the National Liberation Movement during the First World War." PhD diss., New York University, 1987.

Luttwak, Edward N. *The Grand Strategy of the Roman Empire: From the First Century A.D. to the Third*. Baltimore: Johns Hopkins University Press, 1976.

Mackey, Sandra. *The Iranians: Persia, Islam, and the Soul of a Nation*. New York: Plume, 1998.

Majd, Muhammad Gholi. *Great Britain and Reza Shah: The Plunder of Iran, 1921–1941*. Gainesville: University Press of Florida, 2001.

———. *Persia in World War I and Its Conquest by Great Britain*. Lanham, MD: University Press of America, 2003.

Matthews, Matt M. "We Were Caught Unprepared: The 2006 Hizbollah-Israeli War," *The Long War Series, Occasional Paper 26*. Fort Leavenworth, KS: U.S. Army Combined Arms Center Combat Studies Institute Press, 2008.

Maxon, Philip. "Iran Receives Smuggled Surplus F-14 Parts." *Arms Control Today* (March 2007): 37.

May, Elmer C., and Gerald P. Stadler. *Ancient and Medieval Warfare*. West Point, NY: United States Military Academy Department of History, 1973.

McCaul, Ed. "Iranian Tank Commander." *Military History* 21 (April 2004): 44–49.

McDowall, David. *A Modern History of the Kurds*. London: I. B. Tauris and Company, 1996.

Meyer, James J. *Proud to Be: Memoir of Colonel James J. Meyer*. Unpublished memoir, 2001. Army Military History Institute (accessed November 12, 2006).

Milani, Mohsen M. "Iran's Policy towards Afghanistan." *Middle East Journal* 60 (Spring 2006): 235–56.

Miller, Marshall L. "How the Soviets Invaded Iran." *Armed Forces Journal International* 124 (February 1987): 30–34.

Millspaugh, Arthur. *Americans in Persia*. Washington, DC: Brookings Institution, 1946.

Mirfakhraei, Hooshmand. "The Imperial Iranian Armed Forces and the Revolution of 1978–1979." PhD diss., State University of New York at Buffalo, 1984.

Mixter, John R. "Alexander's First Great Victory." *Military History* (December 1997): 50–56.

Moberly, Frederick J. *The Campaign in Mesopotamia, 1914–1918*. Vol. 1. London: His Majesty's Stationary Office, 1923.

———. *The Campaign in Mesopotamia, 1914–1918*. Vol. 4. London: His Majesty's Stationary Office, 1927.

———. *Operations in Persia, 1914–1919*. Facsimile ed. London: Her Majesty's Stationary Office, 1987.

Mobley, Richard A. "Deterring Iran, 1968–71: The Royal Navy, Iran, and the Disputed Persian Gulf Islands." *Naval War College Review* 56 (Autumn 2003): 107–19.

Molavi, Afshin. *The Soul of Iran: A Nation's Journey to Freedom*. New York: W. W. Norton, 2002.

Motter, T. H. Vail. *The Persian Corridor and Aid to Russia*. U.S. Army in World War II Series. Washington, DC: Center of Military History, 1952.

Muslim Students Following the Line of the Imam. *Documents from the U.S. Espionage Den: America; Supporter of Usurpers of the Qods*. Vol. 16. Tehran: Center for the Publication of the U.S. Espionage Den's Documents, n.d.

Nasr, Vali. *The Shia Revival: How Conflicts within Islam Will Shape the Future*. New York: W. W. Norton, 2006.

Navias, Martin S., and E. R. Hooton. *Tanker Wars: The Assault on Merchant Shipping during the Iran-Iraq Conflict, 1980–1988*. London: I. B. Tauris, 1996.

Neuman, Stephanie G. "Arms Transfers, Indigenous Defense Production and Dependency: The Case of Iran." In *The Security of the Persian Gulf*, ed. Hossein Amersadeghi, 131–50. London: Croom Helm, 1981.

Newman, Andrew J. *Safavid Iran: Rebirth of a Persian Empire*. London: I. B. Tauris, 2006.

Norwich, John Julius. *A Short History of Byzantium*. New York: Vintage, 1997.

Nyrop, Richard F., ed. *Iran: A Country Study*. Washington, DC: American University, 1978.

O'Ballance, Edgar. *The Gulf War*. London: Brassey's, 1988.

Olson, Robert W. *The Siege of Mosul and Ottoman-Persian Relations, 1718–1743*. Bloomington: Indiana University, 1975.

Pahlavi, Muhammad Reza Shah. *Mission for My Country.* New York: McGraw-Hill, 1961.

Pakenham, Thomas. *The Scramble for Africa: The White Man's Conquest of the Dark Continent from 1876 to 1912.* New York: Avon Books, 1991.

Pal, Dharm. *Official History of the Indian Armed Forces in the Second World War, 1939–1945: Campaign in Western Asia.* Calcutta: Sree Saraswaty Press, 1957.

Palmer, Michael A. *Guardians of the Gulf: A History of America's Expanding Role in the Persian Gulf, 1833–1992.* New York: Free Press, 1992.

Perkins, Ken. "The Death of an Army: A Short Analysis of the Imperial Iranian Armed Force." *Royal United Services Institute for Defense Studies* 125 (June 1980): 21–23.

Perry, John R. "Army IV. Afsar and Zand." In *Encyclopedia-Iranica,* vol. 2, ed. Ehsan Yarshater, 506–8. London: Routledge, 1985.

Peterson, J. E. *Oman in the Twentieth Century: Political Foundations of an Emerging State.* London: Croom Helm, 1978.

Pollack, Kenneth M. *Arabs at War: Military Effectiveness, 1948–1991.* Lincoln: University of Nebraska Press, 2002.

———. *The Persian Puzzle: The Conflict between Iran and America.* New York: Random House, 2004.

———. "The Regional Military Balance." In *The United States and the Persian Gulf: Reshaping Security Strategy for the Post-Containment Era,* ed. Richard D. Sokolosky, 61–87. Washington, DC: National Defense University Press, 2003.

Powell, Colin, with Joseph E. Persico. *My American Journey.* New York: Random House, 1995.

Ramazani, Ruhollah K. *Iran's Foreign Policy, 1941–1973: A Study of Foreign Policy in Modernizing Nations.* Charlottesville: University Press of Virginia, 1975.

Rashid, Gholam Ali. "Study of the Formation of the Policy to Liberate the Occupied Territories." *Journal of Defense Policy* (Summer–Fall 1996): 23–34, translated by FBIS (97N10060).

Ricks, Thomas M. "U.S. Military Missions to Iran, 1943–1978: The Political Economy of Military Assistance." *Iranian Studies* 12 (Summer–Autumn 1979): 163–93.

Ringer, Monica M. "Education and Reform in Qajar Iran, 1800–1906." PhD diss., University of California, Los Angeles, 1998.

Roberts, Mark J. *Khomeini's Incorporation of the Iranian Military.* McNair Paper 48. Washington, DC: National Defense University, 1996.

Roosevelt, Kermit. *Countercoup: The Struggle for the Control of Iran.* New York: McGraw-Hill, 1979.

Rose, Gregory F. "The Post-Revolutionary Purge of Iran's Armed Forces: A Revisionist Assessment." *Iranian Studies* 27 (Spring–Summer 1984): 153–194.

Samii, Abbas W. "Iran: Paramilitary Force Prepares for Urban Unrest." *Radio Free Europe/Radio Liberty,* September 30, 2005. www.rferl.org (accessed October 20, 2005).

———. "The Shah's Lebanon Policy: The Role of SAVAK." *Middle Eastern Studies* 33 (January 1997): 66–91.

Samore, Gary, ed. *Iran's Strategic Weapons Programmes: A Net Assessment*. New York: Routledge, 2005.

Savory, Roger M. "The Ancient Period." In *The Persian Gulf States: A General Survey*, ed. Alvin J. Cottrell, 3–13. Baltimore: Johns Hopkins University Press, 1980.

————. *Iran under the Safavids*. Cambridge: Cambridge University Press, 1980.

Sayigh, Yezid. "Arms Production in Iran and Pakistan: The Limits of Self-Reliance." In *Military Capacity and the Risk of War: China, India, Pakistan, and Iran*, ed. Eric Arnett, 161–94. New York: Oxford University Press, 1997.

Schahgaldian, Nikola B. *The Iranian Military under the Islamic Republic*. R-3473-USDP. Santa Monica, CA: RAND, 1987.

Shahbazi, A. Shapur. "Army I. Pre-Islamic Iran." In *Encyclopedia-Iranica*, vol. 2, ed. Ehsan Yarshater, 489–99. London: Routledge, 1985.

"The Shah's Northern Navy." *The Persian*, July 31, 2001. www.Persian.com/Books/2001/July/Caspian/index5.html (accessed November 1, 2004).

Sheehan, Michael K. *Iran: The Impact of United States Interests and Policies, 1941–1954*. Brooklyn, NY: Theo. Gaus' Sons, 1968.

Sheikh-ol-Islami, Muhammad Javad. "Army V. Pahlavi Period." In *Encyclopedia-Iranica*, vol. 2, ed. Ehsan Yarshater, 508–14. London: Routledge, 1985.

Shemirani, S. Taheri. "The War of the Cities." In *The Iran-Iraq War: The Politics of Aggression*, ed. Farhang Rajaee, 32–40. Gainesville: University Press of Florida, 1993.

Shuster, W. Morgan. *The Strangling of Persia*. Washington, DC: Mage, 1987.

Sick, Gary. "Iran's Quest for Superpower Status." *Foreign Affairs* 65 (Spring 1987): 697–715.

Singh, Kajendra R. *Iran: Quest for Security*. New Delhi: Vikas, 1980.

Stempel, John D. *Inside the Iranian Revolution*. Bloomington: Indiana University Press, 1981.

Stewart, Richard A. *Sunrise at Abadan: The British and Soviet Invasion of Iran, 1941*. New York: Praeger, 1988.

Strauss, Barry. *The Battle of Salamis: The Naval Encounter That Saved Greece—and Western Civilization*. New York: Simon and Schuster, 2004.

————. "Rome's Persian Mirage." *Military History Quarterly* 12 (August 1999): 18–27.

"Subject: Task Force V Lessons Learned: The Iran-Iraq War, Appendix B Chemicals," n.d., File 120596_aaday_02.txt, p. 2, www.gulflink.osd.mil/declassdocs/af/19961205/120596_aaday_02.html (accessed April 6, 2007).

Sullivan, William H. *Mission to Iran*. New York: W. W. Norton, 1981.

Suren-Pahlav, Shapur. "General Surena, The Hero of Carrhae." The Circle of Ancient Iranian Studies at the School of Oriental and African Studies (SOAS), University of London. www.cais-soas.com/CAIS/History/ashkanian/surena.htm (accessed December 7, 2006).

Sykes, Percy M. *A History of Persia*. 3rd ed. London: MacMillan and Co., 1930.

Tanner, Stephen. *Afghanistan: A Military History from Alexander the Great to the Fall of the Taliban*. New York: Da Capo Press, 2002.

"Testimony of Dr. Christine M. Gosden before the Senate Judiciary Subcommittee on Technology, Terrorism and Government and the Senate Select Committee on Intelligence on Chemical and Biological Weapon Threats to America: Are We Prepared?" April 22, 1998, www.fas.org/irp/congress/1998_hr/s980422-cg.htm (accessed April 1, 2007).

Tousi, R. Ra'iss. "The Persian Army, 1880–1907." *Middle Eastern Studies* 24 (April 1988): 206–29.

Trapper, Richard. "Introduction." In *The Conflict of Tribe and State in Iran and Afghanistan*, ed. Richard Trapper, 1–84. New York: St. Martin's Press, 1983.

———. *Frontier Nomads of Iran: A Political and Social History of the Shahsevan*. Cambridge: Cambridge University Press, 1997.

Upton, Emory. *Armies of Asia and Europe: Embracing Official Reports on the Armies of Japan, China, India, Persia, Italy, Russia, Austria, Germany, France, and England*. New York: Greenwood Press, 1968.

U.S. Army, Commander in Chief, Supreme Allied Command, Exercise DELAWAR. "After Action Report, May 19, 1964." Army Military History Institute (accessed November 2006).

U.S. Army, National Ground Intelligence Center. Translation of "From Khorramshahr to Al Fao, Military and Political Analysis from a Four-Year Excursion in War (July 1982 until August 1986)." General Headquarters of Political Assistance, War Research and Studies, Islamic Revolutionary Guard Corps, 1988. Translation Number: NGIC-HT-0142-98. Charlottesville, VA: U.S. Army National Ground Intelligence Center, 2000.

———. Translation of "The Passing of Two Years of War." Political Office of the Islamic Revolutionary Guard Corps, 1982. Translation Number: NGIC-HT-0143-98. Charlottesville, VA: U.S. Army National Ground Intelligence Center, 2002.

———. Translation of "The Victory of Victories of the Sacred Defense," Supplement to *Saff* 223, 1999, n.p. Translation Number: NGIC-2000-00105HT. Charlottesville, VA: U.S. Army National Ground Intelligence Center, 2001.

U.S. Congress, Senate, Committee on Foreign Relations, Subcommittee on Foreign Assistance. *U.S. Military Assistance to Iran: A Staff Report on the Subcommittee on Foreign Assistance of the Committee of Foreign Relations, United States Senate*. Washington, DC: U.S. Government Printing Office, 1976.

U.S. Congress, Senate, Committee on Foreign Relations. *U.S. Arms Sales Policy: Hearings before the Committee on Foreign Relations and the Subcommittee on Foreign Assistance of the Committee of Foreign Relations, United States Senate, 94th Congress, 2nd session, on proposed sale of arms to Iran and Saudi Arabia, September 16, 21, and 24, 1976*. Washington, DC: U.S. Government Printing Office, 1976.

U.S. Department of the Army. Office of the Adjutant General Memo. "Subject: Senior Officer Debriefing Report: BG Theo. C. Mataxis, Chief, Army Section, ARMISH/MAAG, April 1968 to May 1970, dated June 26, 1970." Available at the Army Military History Institute.

U.S. Department of State, Office of the Inspector General. "Inspection Report: The Conduct of Relations with Iran." In Muslim Students Following the Line of the Imam. *Documents from the U.S. Espionage Den: U.S. Interventions in Iran.* Vol. 8. Tehran: Center for the Publication of the U.S. Espionage Den's Documents, n.d.

U.S. Government. Foreign Broadcast Information Service. "A Confrontation of Strategies, the Iran-Iraq War: The Effect of the Changes on the Battlefield in the Iran-Iraq War on the Policies of the Great Powers." IAP20010518000001, May 18, 2001. This report is a translation of Hoseyn Ardestani, *A Confrontation of Strategies, the Iran-Iraq War: The Effect of the Changes on the Battlefield in the Iran-Iraq War on the Policies of the Great Powers.* Tehran: Revolutionary Guards Command and Staff College, Advanced War Course, Center for Publication, 1378 (March 21, 1999–March 20, 2000).

———. "Iran: Battle of Faw," *Near East and South Asia Supplement,* FBIS-NES-94-076-S, April 20, 1994. This report is a translation of *Battle of Faw.* Tehran: Islamic Revolutionary Guard Corps, Political Deputy of the General Command Post, War Studies and Research, 1988.

———. "Iran: Complete Regulations of the Islamic Republic of Iran Armed Forces," *Near East and South Asia Supplement,* FBIS-NES-94-208-S, October 27, 1994.

U.S. Military Mission with Iranian Army, 1942–53. RG 334. National Archives, College Park, MD.

van Bruinessen, Martin. "Kurdish Tribes and the State of Iran: The Case of Simko's Revolt." In *The Conflict of Tribe and State in Iran and Afghanistan,* ed. Richard Trapper, 364–400. New York: St. Martin's Press, 1983.

Ward, Steven. "The Continuing Evolution of Iran's Military Doctrine." *The Middle East Journal* 59 (Autumn 2005): 559–76.

War Office Central Office of Information. *PAIFORCE: The Official Story of the Persia and Iraq Command, 1941–46,* London: His Majesty's Stationary Office, 1948.

Weatherford, Jack. *Genghis Khan and the Making of the Modern World.* New York: Crown, 2004.

White, Richard D. "Civilian Management of the Military: Elihu Root and the 1903 Reorganization of the Army General Staff." *Journal of Management History* 4 (Winter 1998): 43–59.

Wilson, Arnold T. *Loyalties: Mesopotamia, 1914–1917.* London: Oxford University Press, 1930.

Yapp, Malcom E. "1900–1921: The Last Years of the Qajar Dynasty." In *Twentieth Century Iran,* ed. Amirsadeghi Hossein, 1–22. London: Morrison and Gibb, 1977.

———. "British Policy in the Persian Gulf." In *The Persian Gulf States: A General Survey,* ed. Alvin J. Cottrell, 70–100. Baltimore: Johns Hopkins University Press, 1980.

Yarshater, Ehsan. "Observations on Nasir al-Din Shah." In *Qajar Iran: Political, Social and Cultural Change, 1800–1925,* ed. Edmund Bosworth and Carole Hillenbrand, 3–13. Edinburgh: Edinburgh University Press, 1983.

Zabih, Sepehr. *The Iranian Military in Revolution and War.* London: Routledge, 1988.

English-Language News Media

The Economist
Jane's
New York Times
Time
Wall Street Journal
Washington Post

Non-English-Language News Media

Agence France Presse
Farhang-e Ashti
Hemayat
Iranian Labor News Agency
Iranian Students News Agency
Islamic Republic News Agency
Jomhuri-ye Islami
Siyasat-e Ruz
Voice of the Islamic Republic Radio

Index

Note: Page numbers in italics represent figures (maps) in the text.